*New Cloak, Old Dagger*

# New Cloak, Old Dagger

How Britain's Spies Came in from the Cold

## MICHAEL SMITH

VICTOR GOLLANCZ

LONDON

*This book is dedicated to my parents*
*Joseph and Joyce Smith*

First published in Great Britain 1996
by Victor Gollancz
An imprint of the Cassell Group
Wellington House, 125 Strand, London WC2R 0BB

© Michael Smith 1996

A catalogue record for this book is
available from the British Library.

ISBN 0 575 06150 2

Typeset by Rowland Phototypesetting Ltd
Bury St Edmunds, Suffolk
Printed and bound in Great Britain by
Mackays of Chatham plc, Chatham, Kent

96 97 98  5 4 3 2 1

# Contents

**New Threats**

# Preface

The British obsession with secrecy has led to a dearth of accurate literature on the intelligence services. Most of the current authoritative material takes the form of autobiographies by insiders, covering only the particular field in which they worked, academic research published in specialist journals, or examinations by outsiders of one single agency. Sadly, the intelligence services' reluctance either to confirm or deny allegations made about them has also led to the publication of a number of other books which bear only a passing resemblance to reality.

But in the past fifteen years the veil that covered the activities of Britain's spies has begun to lift. Although Mrs Thatcher was an ardent advocate of keeping secret everything the intelligence services did, it was during her period as prime minister that the first small steps towards more openness began. She commissioned the Franks Report which examined the role of the intelligence services in the run-up to and during the 1982 Falklands Conflict and, despite some initial doubts, allowed the publication of the official history of British Intelligence in the Second World War.

She was also responsible for the 1989 Security Service Act which regularized MI5's activities and, inadvertently, to a much wider public knowledge of the existence of GCHQ, the British signals intelligence organization, through the 1984 decision to ban workers there from joining trade unions. But she remained adamant that the existence of MI6 could not be revealed, a position which led to Britain's spies being held up to ridicule during the *Spycatcher* affair. During the government's 1987 civil action in the New South Wales Supreme Court, which tried to prevent the book's publication, Sir Robert Armstrong, the cabinet secretary, refused to confirm the existence of MI6. When it was pointed out that he had already agreed that Sir Dick White was the head of MI6 from 1956 to 1968, he replied that, this being the case, he could not confirm that the organization had existed before 1956 or after 1968.

Thankfully times have changed. Since 1992, when John Major officially confirmed that MI6 did indeed exist, there have been a number of moves towards more candour about what our spies do. The 1994 Intelligence

Services Act put both MI6 and GCHQ on a legal footing and created a new parliamentary Intelligence and Security Committee to provide a limited form of oversight. The government has published official booklets outlining how the various agencies work, and both MI5 and MI6 have become more open about such matters, most notably in a number of lectures by Stella Rimington, the former MI5 Director-General. In addition, as part of the so-called Open Government initiative, a large number of new files relating to the intelligence services have been released into the Public Records Office at Kew.

The aim of this book is to pull together all the information that is now in the public domain and, using a number of interviews with both serving and former intelligence officers, to provide a comprehensive picture of Britain's intelligence community and how it works, not just MI5, MI6 and GCHQ, but also the Joint Intelligence Committee, which co-ordinates Britain's intelligence operations, the Defence Intelligence organizations and the police.

I am grateful to all those serving and former intelligence officers who agreed to be interviewed for this book, many of whom were far more candid than I might have hoped. But I must also thank a number of other people who generously helped me, in particular: Ken Robertson and Philip H. J. Davies at the University of Reading; Shlomo Shpiro at Birmingham; Sheila Kerr at Salford; Richard J. Aldrich at Nottingham; and Christopher Andrew at Cambridge. Thanks also go to the staff at the PRO; the House of Lords Records Office; Berkshire County Library and the *Daily Telegraph* Library, who were always polite and helpful. I am also grateful to Simon Trewin, my agent, and Sean Magee at Victor Gollancz for their constant encouragement; to Bob Davenport, the most meticulous of copy editors; and to my wife Hayley, who for more than two years put her own life on the back burner for the sake of her husband's obsession.

# *Prologue*

If the 'watchers' from Urzad Ochrony Panstwa, the Polish equivalent of MI5, had any doubts about the mysterious man seeking to buy a large consignment of arms, these were dispelled after the third change of taxi. He was clearly determined to shake off anyone who was following him across Warsaw to the southern commercial district of Mokotow and the offices of the newly established Eloks import-export business. 'We knew then that it could not be legal,' Gromoslaw Czempinski, the head of the UOP, said later.

Not that there had ever been any doubt in the first place. Eloks was a fake company set up by the Poles in mid-1993, part of a joint operation with the British aimed at preventing huge amounts of former Warsaw Pact weapons from being spirited out of the country to Northern Ireland. An MI5 agent inside the Ulster Volunteer Force, a small Loyalist terrorist group of around 200 trained men, had reported that two of its members had been given £250,000 in cash with which to buy Polish arms and explosives. The Protestant paramilitaries were looking for the sort of firepower that would enable them to destabilize the fragile moves towards peace that were already underway.

Using the anti-terrorist links set up among Europe's security services during the Gulf War, T Branch, the MI5 department that handles Irish terrorism, had asked the UOP for its help. The Polish officer handling the Warsaw end of the operation was now about to meet the terrorists' intermediary – the man with the penchant for changing taxis – who would hand her their shopping list. For their £250,000, his UVF clients were to receive two tons of plastic explosive; a large number of detonators; 320 Kalashnikov assault rifles together with 60,000 rounds of ammunition; 500 hand grenades; and 53 Russian Makarov 9mm pistols with 14,000 rounds of ammunition.

The weapons – all supplied from the Polish authorities' own armouries – were loaded into a steel container and customs documents were discreetly arranged listing it as container number 2030255, a consignment of ceramic tiles destined for Frackleton and Sons, a Belfast company that had previously imported tiles from Europe but which knew nothing at all of this particular transaction. Another reputable company, the Szczecin-based hauliers Fast Baltic, was paid 40 million zlotys, about £1400, to transport the container to the Baltic port of Gdynia where it was loaded on to the MV *Inowroclaw*.

The 6300-ton Polish freighter set sail for Britain on 19 November 1993, stopping off at Tilbury to unload a number of its 230 containers, before heading north for Teesport where customs officers were lying in wait. T Branch had decided to seize the arms there before they could be unloaded and smuggled across the Irish Sea to Belfast. In the early hours of 24 November, the customs officers moved in, ordering container 2030255 to be removed from the ship.

Both sides held press conferences to announce their arms 'find'. Evidence that MI5 was operating just as much against Protestant paramilitaries as against their Republican counterparts was no doubt helpful in persuading both the IRA and Dublin that London was serious in its search for peace in Northern Ireland. The Poles, anxious to show that they were responsible members of the new Europe, were more open about what had occurred. But even they were cagey about giving precise details of the operation. 'If these were to be revealed, it could cost eight lives on the British side alone,' Czempinski said. 'The UVF do not mess around.'

# CHAPTER 1

# *The Art of Espionage*

Intelligence is a very imprecise art as a matter of fact.
David Gore-Booth, in evidence to the Scott Inquiry

The popular fascination with the world of espionage has spawned a wealth of fiction ranging from Ian Fleming's highly romanticized version of Britain's MI6, in which James Bond's 007 designation gave him a licence to kill, to the more realistic style epitomized by John le Carré's George Smiley. As a result most people have a reasonable, if limited, perception of how spies work. They will understand terms like 'double agent', 'safe house' and 'tradecraft'. Pressed, they will even admit to being aware that there is much more to intelligence than the popular Cold War image of a secret agent nervously waiting in an east-European café for the 'drop' that may never come. But very few will know the total scale of international espionage, an industry that costs the United States alone $28 billion a year.[1]

Information is power, and governments are prepared to pay a heavy price to obtain it. The demise of the Warsaw Pact, which many saw as signalling the end for the spy, and indeed the spywriter, has only increased the need for intelligence as fragile new democracies threaten to plunge back into totalitarianism, weapons-grade nuclear materials are traded on the black market, and Third World countries that were previously kept in check by their superpower mentors turn into dangerous mavericks.

Throughout history, war has followed peace as night follows day. Neither the League of Nations, set up at the end of the First World War amid a determination that such a conflict would never happen again, nor its successor, the United Nations, has been able to prevent states from using aggression to gain an advantage at their neighbour's expense or from redressing perceived grievances by force of arms. International relations may be governed by diplomatic etiquette, but there are few real rules. Those that do exist are observed only by countries which fear the consequences of others ignoring them, and when that happens the only truly effective sanction is war.

In such circumstances, intelligence becomes indispensable and so for centuries spies have found useful employment with the state, according espionage a dubious reputation as 'the second oldest profession'. Governments and military commanders can make sensible judgements as to their future actions only if they know the other side's true position and intentions. In such a situation, diplomacy becomes like a game of poker, with each side protecting the details of its hand. It is the job of the spy to find out what cards the other side is holding. But, as well as gathering information on the enemy's secrets, the intelligence services must also protect their own from enemy attempts to uncover them.

The art of espionage can be divided into three separate categories. The first – strategic intelligence – is the collection of information which keeps political leaders and their advisers, be they civil servants or diplomats, well-informed on the situation in target countries and allows them a better chance of predicting how those countries will react in the future. It will include assessments of the political situation, the leaders and their potential successors, and economic and sociological factors that might influence policy, together with details of the target's economic activities and scientific and technological capabilities.

The main British agency for gathering strategic intelligence, taking the vast bulk of the £800 million annual intelligence budget, known as the Single Intelligence Vote, is the Government Communications Headquarters, based at Cheltenham in Gloucestershire. GCHQ monitors the communications of Britain's enemies and friends from a number of remote sites around the world, providing the British government with intelligence that will help it to formulate its security, foreign, defence and economic policies.[2] The other main collection agency for strategic intelligence is the Secret Intelligence Service, or MI6. According to the Foreign and Commonwealth Office, under whose control both agencies come, MI6 collects exactly the same type of information as GCHQ, acquiring it 'through a variety of sources, human and technical, and by liaison with a wide range of foreign intelligence and security services'.[3]

The second type of intelligence is tactical: simply put, that information which would be useful to military commanders in the field. It includes working out the precise order of battle of the enemy's armed forces, tracking the deployments of individual units, and monitoring and examining their peacetime training exercises in order to determine the type of tactics they will employ in war and how those tactics can best be countered. Not unnaturally, this information is collected in the main by the military intelligence agencies, whose activities under the British system are co-ordinated by the Defence Intelligence Staff.

It is acquired by a wide variety of means, from the information collected by small infantry patrols probing the forward edge of the battle area, through the cocktail-party chat of the military attachés based in Britain's embassies abroad, to the most advanced technology that money can buy, including spy satellites like the American Keyhole system, which is able to produce highly detailed pictures of what is going on far behind the enemy lines. Satellites are not just deployed to gather what is known as imagery intelligence (IMINT); they can also be highly effective as 'ferrets', remote platforms for the interception of signals intelligence, which provides a vital part of tactical intelligence.[4] Sir John Adye, Director of GCHQ, told a news conference, called in 1993 as part of the Conservative government's drive for more openness, that there were 3000 members of the armed forces working for his organization.[5]

The last type of intelligence is counter-intelligence, famously defined in the post-war directive of Britain's domestic Security Service, MI5, as 'the defence of the realm'.[6] Counter-intelligence is not purely confined to ensuring that a nation's secrets are secure against the machinations of foreign spies – an activity that is perhaps better described as counter-espionage or security. Counter-intelligence operations can in themselves yield a great deal of information about the enemy's intentions, the depth of his knowledge and the operations of his intelligence services.

The expulsion of a foreign spy, and the inevitable tit-for-tat gesture by his employers, will attract great interest in the media, but only infrequently will the full story behind the expulsion emerge. Before a spy is unmasked, his activities will have been monitored by the domestic security services. His contacts, quite possibly involving a network of agents, will have been noted, and the aims and successes of their operations will have been analysed. Some of these agents may even have been turned against him to feed him false information and provide more details of the enemy intelligence operations, thereby becoming double agents. This may have been going on for some time – in occasional cases for years – and the expulsion is unlikely to have come without a decision that the spy's presence is no longer useful for the collection of counter-intelligence. Once he is expelled, his masters must assume, unless they have very good information to the contrary, that the network he ran is also compromised and has been closed down – or, in the jargon of the spy, folded.[7]

MI5's role in domestic counter-intelligence was laid down in a 1952 directive issued by Sir David Maxwell Fyfe, the then Home Secretary, as being 'the Defence of the Realm as a whole, from external and internal dangers arising from attempts at espionage and sabotage, or from actions of persons and organizations, whether directed from within or without the country, which may be judged to be subversive to the State'.[8]

The 1989 Security Service Act updated the Maxwell Fyfe directive, defining MI5's function as 'the protection of national security and, in particular, its protection against threats from espionage, terrorism or sabotage, from the activities of agents of foreign powers and from actions intended to overthrow or undermine parliamentary democracy by political, industrial or violent means'.[9]

The rivalry between the domestic and foreign services over who controls counter-intelligence derives not from the traditional security role but from the potential for gathering exceptionally valuable intelligence. The information provided by well-placed double agents can justify budgets and earn knighthoods. It may even lead eventually to high-profile defections – the ultimate intelligence success. No agency would like to see its main rival gain the credit for an intelligence scoop that could have been its own.

Although all spies fight shy of publicity – not unnaturally, since secrecy is the lifeblood of their profession – the plaudits that follow the acquisition of a defector and the information he can supply are valuable as a means of warding off the criticism that results from what at best is the public suspicion – at worst, opprobrium – which secrecy inspires. In part, the suspicion derives from a belief that the spies would not need to be so secretive if they were not doing anything wrong. The assumption is made – not always incorrectly – that behind their cloak of secrecy the spies must be wielding the dagger in an unnecessary and arbitrary way.

There has always been a moral streak in society that has considered espionage to be somehow unethical. It was perhaps best epitomized by the words of Henry Stimson, the pre-war American Secretary of State, in 1929 when he closed down the Black Chamber, the predecessor of the National Security Agency, America's equivalent of GCHQ: 'Gentlemen do not read each other's mail.'[10]

The main ethical worry on foreign intelligence, however, concerns not the monitoring of enemy communications but covert action: special operations behind enemy lines, and in particular that type of operation which the KGB used to describe as *mokrie dela* – wet affairs – a graphic reference to the spilling of blood.[11]

Britain's 1994 Intelligence Services Act prohibits MI6 agents, or anyone else who might act on behalf of MI6 (the SAS, for example), from taking part in any criminal activity for which they would normally still be liable in the United Kingdom even if it occurs abroad.[12] They are thereby prevented from committing genocide, murder, kidnapping or indeed bigamy – unless the Foreign Secretary deems it necessary for the proper discharge of one of the service's statutory functions, in which case the agents will be absolved of all liability under British criminal law.

This appears to provide an easy opt-out solution, although Sir Gerry

Warner, who as Intelligence Co-ordinator in the mid-1990s had responsibility for determining how Britain's intelligence requirements were met, said it would be 'unthinkable' for MI6 officers to be authorized to use violence in peacetime and that they do not carry weapons. However, given the nature of their work, which now includes not just espionage operations abroad but also 'the prevention or detection of serious crime', it is simply not credible that MI6 agents involved in that type of operation could be left unarmed in the face of what would inevitably be a serious risk of violence.[13]

But the deep suspicion in which most secret services are held has little to do with their behaviour abroad, when to the vast majority of people they become 'our brave boys', but rather more with their potential use at home against their own citizens. The all-pervading domination of east-European society maintained by the KGB, Stasi, Securitate et al. was far more effective than the sub-legal activities in this field of MI5 and the police Special Branch in Britain. But in its way the latter were infinitely more shocking and damaging to the public perception of the intelligence community. The KGB was expected to behave in that way; Britain's security forces were supposed to be the upholders of right and truth.[14]

The reputation of MI5 was badly damaged by the seemingly indiscriminate surveillance of a rag-bag collection of largely ineffective left-wing 'subversives' – including members of trade unions and groups like the Campaign for Nuclear Disarmament.[15] While few people believed some of the more bizarre claims made by the former senior MI5 official Peter Wright in his book *Spycatcher*, the boast that 'for five years, we bugged and burgled our way across London at the state's behest, while pompous bowler-hatted civil servants in Whitehall pretended to look the other way' was entirely credible.[16]

An expansion of such surveillance operations against British citizens – begun in the 1970s under the Heath government, largely as a reaction to the power of the unions, who were seen by politicians of both right and left as having become 'too mighty' – continued through both the Wilson and Callaghan Labour administrations before reaching its peak under the Thatcher government in the early 1980s, when, according to Cathy Massiter, an MI5 officer who left the service because she disagreed with what was going on, the Ministry of Defence was routinely asking MI5 to set up surveillance operations against CND members whose activities could not possibly have been regarded as posing a serious threat to the state.

But following the demise of the Soviet Union and the search for new intelligence targets, the major criticism of the spies has concerned the ever-increasing cost of the technology that long ago took over from the human agent as the main means of intelligence collection.

Until the invention of radio and the realization of its potential for military communications, information collected from and by human spies – known in the jargon of the intelligence community as HUMINT – was by far the most important to the spymaster, whether obtained by using the secret agent as immortalized in spy fiction, traitors within the enemy camp, or information collected by diplomats and travellers. Tourists and businessmen were a common source of information before the information explosion dramatically increased the amount of data readily accessible in open sources like books, periodicals, newspapers and radio and television broadcasts, and they remain useful in closed societies or remote areas where their genuine reasons for being in the country provide good cover for intelligence work, as Paul Henderson, the managing director of Matrix-Churchill, found to his cost when MI6 recruited him to spy on Iraq. Britons abroad – expatriates and businessmen – are still seen by MI6 as its most reliable source of intelligence.[17]

But HUMINT is more readily identified with the James Bond-style secret agent, who was previously thought to have been made redundant by the increasing use of technology to acquire intelligence. By the end of the First World War technical means had taken over from the man on the ground as the main source of information on enemy intentions, activities and capabilities, providing, according to some reports, as much as 90 per cent of the usable intelligence available to military commanders.[18]

The part played in the Second World War by the Ultra 'special intelligence', collected by the Government Code and Cypher School (GC&CS) at Bletchley Park, is now universally known. There are those who, quite wrongly, have attempted to play down both its role in Hitler's defeat and the continued influence of intelligence collected from the interception of radio signals.[19] But signals intelligence, or SIGINT – which includes information derived from the interception of numerous types of radio signal, not just straightforward voice communications – remains to this day one of the most important forms of intelligence, if not the most important. Signals intelligence divides into two main forms: communications intelligence, or COMINT, and intelligence derived from the interception of electronic emissions, ELINT.

In recent years the interpretation of imagery intelligence – whether from straightforward photography or other methods such as infra-red thermal imaging – has assumed far greater importance with the introduction of the surveillance satellite. High-altitude reconnaissance aircraft, like the American U-2 and the SR-71 Blackbird, proved themselves particularly useful in the garnering of intelligence on developments in Soviet military missile technology during the Cold War. But their capabilities were as nothing compared to those of the modern surveillance satellite, which has proved indispensable for arms-control verification and as an early-warning system. Paradoxically, it is the very ability of the apparently all-seeing eye that has led to the spy satellites being held responsible by many in America for virtually any perceived failure of intelligence.

# CHAPTER 2

# A New Order for the Spies

Next to the acquisition of information, its distribution to those
who may be able to use it is the most important duty of the
Intelligence branch.
Lieutenant-Colonel David Henderson, *Field Intelligence,
Its Principles, Its Practices*, 1904

The immense cost of technical intelligence – $25 billion in the 1995
US intelligence budget, compared to a mere $3 billion for human
intelligence – and the failure of its expensive systems to detect the Iraqi
invasion of Kuwait has led many both inside and outside the intelligence
community to call for a return to the old world of James Bond, a revival
of human espionage.[1]

Brent Scowcroft, National Security Adviser in both the Ford and the
Bush administrations, described the present intelligence community's
emphasis on technical means of collection as 'way overblown'. Following
the demise of the Warsaw Pact and the end of the Cold War, 'we need
a new kind of intelligence, a different kind of intelligence that is less
directed at technical collection, where we are good,' he said. There is a
need to go back to basics, 'back to human intelligence, where we don't
do as well'.[2]

But Admiral Stansfield Turner, Director of Central Intelligence from
1977 to 1981, dismissed this as just 'what one inevitably hears when there
has been an intelligence failure', such as not predicting Iraq's invasion
of Kuwait. 'The litany is familiar,' he said. 'We should throw more and
more human agents against such problems, because the only way to get
inside the minds of adversaries and discern intentions is with human
agents. As a general proposition that simply is not true. Not only do
agents have biases and human fallibilities, there is always a risk that
an agent is, after all, working for someone else.'[3]

To a certain degree, both arguments are true. The Gulf War allies
were caught cold by the invasion of Kuwait precisely because they had
no human agents close to Saddam Hussein who could warn them of his
plans. But, once the invasion had taken place, their spy satellites provided
them with far more intelligence on what was going on in Iraq and Kuwait,

much of it crucial to the outcome of the war, than could ever have been acquired by human spies.[4]

The real lesson to be learned from the failure to predict the Iraqi invasion of Kuwait was that both technical and human intelligence have their own roles to play. While the bulk of intelligence can now be acquired through technical means, there will always be a role for the human spy, pointing up the fine detail and confirming or rebutting intelligence analyses. 'The new world order will yield technical systems that will serve as the sword, the broad cutting edge of intelligence collection, and human spying operations that will serve as the rapier, to be applied judiciously to very specific requirements,' said Stansfield Turner. 'Each system has its strengths and weaknesses. We must make them play to each other.'[5]

The arguments for and against the different types of system have more to do with a feeling that with the end of the Cold War there should be a financial 'peace dividend'. Western politicians have demanded major restructuring of the intelligence agencies, and drastic budget cuts, to take into account the reduced need to watch eastern Europe.[6]

The fight to maintain the intelligence budgets has not been helped by large amounts of the information the agencies previously collected now being freely available in the open media. This has led to suggestions that this material should no longer be a matter for the spies and that their role, and by extension their budget, can therefore be reduced. In a world where a surveillance satellite costs an estimated $400 million to $700 million to build and a further $60 million to $200 million to launch, it is difficult to argue that such increasingly expensive means of collection should be used to acquire information that could be found for the cost of a newspaper.[7]

But spy satellites are primarily directed at closed societies where information is not as readily available as it is in the West, while the information now available in open sources will still have to be incorporated into the intelligence agencies' reports to governments or military commanders if those reports are to have any value. Indeed, one of the main criticisms in the Franks report into the Falklands War, which led to a major restructuring of the way Britain's spies are controlled, was that information freely available in the newspapers in Buenos Aires during late 1981 and early 1982 was not taken into account by the analysts who provided the Foreign Office and the Ministry of Defence with intelligence reports on Argentinian intentions.[8]

Lord Franks, whose committee of six privy counsellors was able to see all the intelligence available during the Falklands conflict, reported that 'the changes in the Argentinian position were, we believe, more evident on the diplomatic front and in the associated press campaign than in the intelligence reports'. Any reorganization should aim 'to ensure that the assessments are able to take fully into account both relevant diplomatic and political developments and foreign press treatment of sensitive foreign policy issues'.

While there is indeed a wealth of open source information available in the West, the same cannot be said of many of the target countries with whom the Western intelligence agencies are most concerned. Although this appears to place these agencies at a disadvantage, forcing them to put more of their increasingly expensive resources, like the spy satellites, into the collection of detailed information, it does make it much easier for them to gauge the intentions of the target governments, since the media in closed societies will invariably reflect official thinking or, where discordant views appear, power struggles and possibly impending changes that will be of interest to the consumer.

The retasking of Britain's intelligence services has, surprisingly, led to far more openness about their roles. The 1989 Security Service Act, which put MI5 on a statutory footing, was followed by the 1994 Intelligence Services Act, designed to perform the same function for GCHQ and MI6, whose well-publicized existence previous British governments had consistently refused to confirm. Having named all the main officials involved in Britain's intelligence community, the government then published outlines of how they operated, in an astonishing reversal of the previously held position which was epitomized by the farcical *Spycatcher* affair, in which the Thatcher government sought frantically to prevent the publication of a book which, once read, few believed.

The Intelligence Services Act also set up a committee of nine MPs to provide the first parliamentary oversight of the activities of Britain's intelligence community since its creation in the Middle Ages. The committee, which was set up 'to examine the expenditure, administration and policy' of MI5, MI6 and GCHQ, meets once a week – 'inside a ring of secrecy' – in Room 130 of the Cabinet Office. It produces an annual report to Parliament through the Prime Minister, who under the Act is entitled to censor any part of the report if its publication 'would be prejudicial to the continued discharge of the functions' of any of the services involved.[9]

If politicians hoped that the reorganization of the secret services would lead to major cuts in the intelligence budgets, they were very quickly disabused of the idea. While the major focus of the spies on both sides of the old Cold War has clearly gone, their governments' needs for intelligence has not. If anything the Western agencies now find themselves facing far more complicated and less easily quantifiable problems.

The future of many old Warsaw Pact countries remains uncertain, a situation aggravated by the continuing turmoil in the various independent republics of the former Soviet Union and by the rapidly escalating influence of organized crime. The increasingly desperate economic situation for many ordinary people as the old Communist states attempt, with widely varying degrees of success, to adapt to capitalism has provided fertile ground for extremist politicians whose foreign policies may be more dangerous than the extremely conservative, and therefore highly predictable, stances of their Communist predecessors. The governments of the smaller republics are also extremely vulnerable to organized crime, since the profits, particularly from drug trafficking, are so large and the number of people who need to be bribed is so small.

With such uncertainty over who is, or will be, in charge, the West still needs detailed intelligence on Russia's military strengths and, as has been shown by the apparent ease with which nuclear material stolen from the former Soviet Union can be purchased on the open market, its nuclear capabilities. In spite of the various treaties on arms control and destruction, there are still thousands of nuclear missiles in the former Soviet Union, all of which would be available to any future leader.

The situation in the Third World is no less volatile. Under the old superpower system, the Soviet Union and the United States were able virtually to dictate the foreign policies of their allies. Few such restraints now apply, particularly among former Soviet client states over whom Russia has little or no control. The risk of being dragged into war – either directly, as in the Gulf, or indirectly, as in the former Yugoslavia – remains high. Even where Western countries do not become embroiled directly in such conflicts, they will need intelligence to ensure that they can protect or rescue their own nationals, or, as in Bosnia, mount effective peace-keeping missions.

Nuclear proliferation in the Third World also creates an increasing risk of a cataclysmic conflict between traditional enemies, such as Iran and Iraq, India and Pakistan, or North and South Korea. In such situations, counter-proliferation comes into its own, with good intelligence making the difference between detecting a nuclear-weapons programme in its early stages, when it can be curtailed by concerted diplomatic pressure or, if necessary, covert action, and having to respond to a new nuclear power by introducing costly modifications to nuclear-deterrent systems.[10]

Clearly, the need for intelligence in such areas will not diminish, and if the evidence of the past is anything to go by the quality of the information will have to be significantly better than before. Robert Gates, Director of Central Intelligence under George Bush, has admitted that the intelligence community drastically misread the situation in Iraq in the run-up to the 1990 invasion of Kuwait, telling Bush that Saddam

Hussein's military resources were too exhausted following Iraq's ten-year war with Iran to allow him to launch another attack for 'two or three years'.[11]

In Britain, the 1994 Intelligence Services Act legalized a number of activities already undertaken by both GCHQ and MI6 which before the removal of the Soviet threat had not featured high in the public's perception of these agencies' work. These include not only counter-proliferation and counter-terrorism – a role in which MI5 takes the lead – but perhaps less obviously the combating of serious crime and involvement in gathering economic intelligence.[12] The latter has been widely touted as the new justification for the intelligence services, although in reality it has been undertaken in various forms for a considerable time. Nevertheless, there is no doubt that, as the old superpower system is replaced by a new world order based largely on economic strength, the agencies' 'consumers' are becoming increasingly interested in the type of economic information the intelligence services can provide.

A review of US government intelligence requirements undertaken in 1992 by America's policy-making National Security Council revealed that about 40 per cent of the information required by policy-making departments was 'economic in nature'.[13]

James Woolsey, Director of Central Intelligence from 1993 to 1995, said that, while the CIA would keep 'a rather careful eye on some foreign companies' and countries' efforts to bribe their way to contracts', it would 'not engage in industrial espionage to help American companies get a leg up on the competition'.[14] His words were echoed by Sir Gerry Warner, Britain's former Intelligence Co-ordinator, who said 'we are not businessmen' – adding in a peculiarly English fashion that such activities were 'not the right way' to go about advancing British business.[15]

But the new national intelligence priorities set by Britain's Joint Intelligence Committee (JIC) clearly indicate the increasing importance of economic intelligence. Although the continuing fears of a resurgent nuclear threat mean there is still a great deal of interest in the former Soviet Union – in particular the unstable republics of central Asia – there is as much if not more interest in Britain's economic rivals in western Europe than in the adversaries turned friends of eastern Europe. The real pointer to an increased interest in matters financial is in the priorities for the Far East, where the countries of the Pacific Rim – the so-called Tiger economies – are deemed to be as important as the Communist dinosaurs of China, North Korea and Vietnam.[16]

The inclusion in Britain's Intelligence Services Act of a reference to 'the detection of serious crime' has led senior police officers to express concern that, in an attempt to justify their continued existence, the intelligence services will 'trample on our patch'. However, Sir Gerry said the role of MI6 and GCHQ in this regard, although not that of MI5, was limited to terrorism, drugs and money-laundering – the last since it plays such a large part in raising funds for the first two and in concealing the profits from drug trafficking.[17]

But the arguments in Britain between the intelligence services and the police have been as nothing to the increasingly bitter battles that have broken out in the United States between the FBI and the CIA in the wake of the Cold War. Lieutenant-General William E. Odom, a former NSA Director, said the two agencies were embroiled in 'a turf war over counter-intelligence only slightly less bitter than the war in Bosnia'.[18]

National intelligence agencies are notorious for the bitter rivalries that rage between them. The relationship between the various American spy organizations has been so bad at times during the past fifty years that they have had far better relations with their British counterparts than they have enjoyed with each other.

Ever since the beginning of the Second World War there has been a close link between the British and American agencies, based at first mainly on signals intelligence but also embracing other areas such as covert action.

In July 1940, at the height of the Battle of Britain and seventeen months before America entered the war, Churchill ordered Lord Lothian, the British ambassador in Washington, to begin negotiations on an exchange of information. Having promised to send British scientists to America to discuss what Britain had to offer, Lord Lothian concluded, 'His Majesty's Government would greatly appreciate it *if* the United States Government, having been given the full details of any British equipment or devices, would reciprocate by discussing certain secret information of a technical nature, which our experts are anxious to have urgently.'[19]

The work of GC&CS was deemed too secret and too crucial to the outcome of the war to be part of the deal. But in late 1940, when he became aware of America's own successes with Japanese diplomatic cyphers, Churchill sanctioned a secret exchange deal covering intercepts of German, Japanese and Italian communications. In February 1941 he authorized Bletchley Park to brief a visiting American delegation on 'the progress made on the Enigma machine', to decypher German communications. Stewart Menzies, the MI6 Director, assured the British Prime Minister that discussion was 'confined to the mechanised devices we utilize and not to showing our results' – a decision that almost certainly reflected concern that the Americans should not discover that the British were reading their diplomatic traffic, and had been for the past twenty years. Nevertheless, the Americans were impressed. GC&CS noted that 'complete co-operation on every problem is now possible' and asked that a senior member of MI6 be sent to the British Embassy in Washington to liaise with the Americans.

Intelligence co-operation between the two sides inevitably grew, extending in 1942 to an agreement between the two special operations bodies, the Office of Strategic Services (OSS) and the Special Operations Executive (SOE), splitting up the world into traditional spheres of influence and thereby ensuring that neither side trod on the other's toes. Those two deals were to form the basis of the close working relationship between British and American intelligence that continues to this day.[20]

The arrangement was not without its initial difficulties. Although the Americans gave the British two of the electronic Purple machines which the Japanese used to encypher their communications, Lord Halifax, the British Foreign Secretary, vetoed any reciprocal delivery of the equivalent German machine, Enigma.[21] The US Army meanwhile was deeply suspicious of the conservative, class-ridden British and saw no reason why it needed to co-operate with a country so lacking in technological vision.[22]

By 1943 the exchange of signals intelligence had become so well-established that neither side could have operated effectively without it. An American delegation visiting Bletchley Park in mid-1943 was given a full briefing on the advances made since May 1940, when Hut 6, the section that covered the Wehrmacht, the German army, and the Luftwaffe, the German air force, made the first breaks in the Enigma cypher. By 15 July the two sides were ready to sign a formal exchange agreement – the BRUSA Accord – linking their signals intelligence services.

The first three clauses of the accord summarized its intent:

1. Both the US and the British agree to exchange completely all information concerning the detection, identification and interception of signals from, and solutions of codes and cyphers used by, the Military and Airforces of the Axis powers, including secret services (*Abwehr*).
2. The US will assume as a main responsibility the reading of Japanese Military and Air Codes and cyphers.
3. The British will assume as a main responsibility the reading of German and Italian Military and Air Codes and cyphers.[23]

Quite how interdependent the two sides were to become was evident when the two sides began to consider the post-war intelligence requirements. The agreement had given them access to a range of intelligence that it would have been virtually impossible for either side, and in particular Britain, to acquire on its own and which had made the analysis of enemy intentions child's play. There was no question but that it must continue.

A joint conference was held in London in September 1944 to discuss the shape of future SIGINT exchanges. By mid-1945 the War Office and the US War Department were exchanging intelligence on the Soviet Union, and the two sides' photographic reconnaissance organizations had begun to share imagery of various parts of the world.[24]

But by October of that year the JIC was reporting that America had banned any exchange of intelligence. Problems had begun to creep into the exchanges, with clear signs of an American reversion to isolationism – 'Although there are indications that the military authorities in Washington were not in sympathy with this policy which has probably been laid down by the State Department.' The McMahon Act, passed partly in reaction to the uncovering of the Soviet agent Alan Nunn May, a British scientist on the allied atomic-weapons programme, prevented virtually any exchange of atomic information, the top priority of British intelligence at the time.

But, despite the official policy, behind the scenes the close co-operation continued, partly as a result of the close personal relationships built up during the war but mainly because the two countries' intelligence systems were now inextricably intertwined. Any attempt by either side to withdraw from the BRUSA relationship would have seriously damaged the intelligence-gathering capabilities of both. Not only would their coverage of the world be seriously diminished, but, since each knew the other's most vital secrets, the two sides must for security reasons remain permanently bound together.[25]

Following a meeting of the British Chiefs of Staff held in late 1945 to examine the close relationship, Andrew Cunningham, the then Chief of Naval Staff, recorded in his diary that there had been 'much discussion about 100% co-operation with the USA about SIGINT. Decided that less than 100% was not worth having.' This was a feeling shared at the highest level on the other side of the Atlantic. The American military's willingness to continue with the relationship, despite its opponents, was bolstered not just by personal relationships but by a Top-Secret presidential edict which gave the joint chiefs of staff *carte blanche* 'to extend, modify or discontinue this collaboration, as determined to be in the best interests of the United States'.[26]

So the relationship grew, and in 1948 the new Soviet threat led to the signing of the UKUSA Accord, a landmark agreement under which the two sides, joined as junior partners by Britain's imperial allies, Canada, Australia and New Zealand, carved up the world between them, with the United States taking responsibility for the Americas and much, although not all, of the Far East, while Britain covered its traditional spheres of influence in Africa, the Middle East and subcontinental Asia. The most important target areas – eastern Europe and the Soviet Union – were shared between Britain and America.[27]

The extent of the interdependency was evident in a report prepared by the US State Department's Bureau of Intelligence and Research in advance of a 1968 visit to America by the then Labour Prime Minister, Harold Wilson. The report, prepared for Dean Rusk, the American Secretary of State, said:

> In the intelligence field, the US and the UK give each other a greater volume and wider variety of information than either does to any of its other allies. The arrangements provide for exchange of information gathered both from overt and covert sources; for the swapping of estimates; and for the preparation of joint estimates. There is a division of labor in certain geographic and functional fields, and on some areas and subjects, each nation is dependent for its intelligence mainly on the other.[28]

But the ability to acquire such large amounts of intelligence does not necessarily aid consumers. Indeed, if too much information is passed on, it will only hamper their efforts to understand what is going on. So the raw intelligence information is analysed and reports are written. These are then passed further up the line, where they are in turn analysed in conjunction with material from other sources. Fresh reports are then compiled, pulling together all the available intelligence and presenting it to the consumers in a way that will provide them with only the information that they need to make policy decisions and not take up their time with material that is irrelevant to the decisions to be made.

The maxim 'need to know' is primarily concerned with security: the fewer people who know about any individual source or the information it is providing, the safer it is. But it is also important that both consumers and initial analysts are not burdened with information they do not 'need to know'.

If an intelligence reporter assessing the significance of a piece of information at the primary level of collection were to bring in material from a separate source his report would become tarnished, making it far more difficult for the analyst producing the final report for the consumer to assess the relative value of the information at his disposal. One source would gain extra credence by appearing to be backed up by information emanating from another. The effect would be like Chinese whispers, with inaccuracies introduced into the information on which the final intelligence assessment was made.

For this reason, an intelligence-reporting network has to be very carefully integrated. The British system has been repeatedly changed in response to perceived intelligence failures, and began to evolve into its present relatively well-integrated form shortly before the Second World War.

Until the mid-1930s Britain had no system for co-ordinating the work of its various intelligence bodies or for providing assessments that drew together information from all available sources.[29] But in January 1936 the War Ministry produced a report entitled *Central Machinery for the Co-ordination of Intelligence* which recommended the setting up of a special body to perform precisely that function. Originally called the Inter-Service Intelligence Committee (ISIC), it was made up of senior members of the three service intelligence branches. But these organizations were themselves largely disorganized and the system was at best haphazard. Within six months came the first of many attempts to fine-tune it, with the ISIC made directly subordinate to the Chiefs of Staff and renamed the Joint Intelligence Committee.[30]

The new system worked little better and there was a further reorganization in July 1939, two months before the start of the Second World War, with the JIC coming under Foreign Office chairmanship. Its role was 'the assessment and co-ordination of intelligence' in order to improve 'the intelligence organization of the country as a whole'. But it remained hampered by the fact that it had no intelligence analysts of its own.[31]

Far from co-ordinating and editing the incoming intelligence to produce a more accessible product, the JIC became overburdened by a variety of demands from various customers and ended up putting out bland and uninformative assessments, at one point adding to a particularly uninspired list of possible moves by the Germans the distinctly unhelpful caveat: 'which of these courses the enemy will select will depend less on logical deduction than on the personal and unpredictable decision of the Fuehrer'. The committee was also distinctly amateurish in its approach. One JIC subcommittee, charged with getting under the skin of the enemy, produced reports which ended with the words 'Heil Hitler'.[32]

But in May 1941 this subcommittee was replaced by the Joint Intelligence Staff, which provided the JIC with its first professional intelligence assessments staff. There was an immediate improvement in the standards of reports – helped in no small part by the fact that Ultra was beginning to come on stream in a big way and by the introduction of more free-thinking civilian analysts. From then on most of the reports produced by the JIS could be passed on to the War Cabinet as so-called 'finals', without amendment. Assessing the reasons why Germany lost the war, the JIC pointed among other things to a failure of intelligence. 'The weakness and failure of the war were due to an ill-directed, badly organized and corrupt *Abwehr*. . . and to the absence of any inter-service staff for the co-ordination and appreciation of intelligence.'[33]

After the war the JIC continued in its role as an intelligence clearing-house, undergoing a number of changes before reaching its present form. The most important of these were the 1957 decision to bring it into the Cabinet Office and therefore closer to the decision-making process; the creation, in 1968, of the post of Intelligence Co-ordinator and of an assessments staff to write consolidated reports; and the removal, following the Falklands conflict, of Foreign Office chairmanship, in order to give the JIC 'a more independent and critical role'.[34]

The JIC sets Britain's national intelligence requirements, reviewing them annually, and oversees the whole of the UK intelligence community to ensure that the target areas are covered as efficiently as possible. It co-ordinates intelligence from all the available sources, including the media, as part of its brief 'to monitor and give early warning of the development of direct or indirect foreign threats to British interests, whether political, military or economic . . . to assess events and situations relating to external affairs, defence, terrorism, major international criminal activity, scientific, technical and international economic matters'.[35]

According to Sir Percy Cradock, a former JIC Chairman, 'The committee gathers together all the information, secret and non-secret, and produces assessments of situations abroad or sometimes at home which are likely to be threatening to affect British interests – for example Iraq, the former Soviet Union, terrorist threats of various kinds.'

Intelligence from all sources is disseminated to a variety of customers, many of whom will have made specific requests for a certain type of information and will need very detailed reports on those issues. But if that detail were to be sent to every customer it would simply overload the system, so most reports also go to one central point, the offices of the Joint Intelligence Committee. 'The total number of intelligence reports is indeed huge,' John Major told the Scott Inquiry. 'The amount of intelligence reports reaching the Foreign and Commonwealth Office, for example, would be around 40,000 a year, and that would probably be – GCHQ and SIS split down – about two-thirds GCHQ and one-third SIS.'

The reports from the various agencies and outstations are then examined by the JIC's assessments staff. 'Some of that intelligence would be extremely valuable, some not so,' Mr Major said. 'Quite a strong filtering process is needed. It is clearly absurd that ministers should read 40,000 pieces of intelligence, but it would be filtered through the appropriate machinery and, where intelligence was thought to be relevant, validated and reliable – reliable being a key point – the officials would endeavour to put that before ministers.'

Clearly if a piece of intelligence is of urgent interest it will be put before the relevant minister as soon as possible. But, in terms of general strategic intelligence, the assessments staff collate it, analyse it, and where appropriate incorporate it into draft JIC reports. These include special evaluations of a particular situation or topic and the Weekly Survey of Intelligence for ministers known as the Red Book. But there will also be daily or more frequent reports on situations where Britain has a special interest, such as Bosnia, and occasionally, as in the Gulf War, an unlimited number dependent only on the relative importance of the new information.[36]

The drafts of the long-term and weekly reports are examined and, where appropriate, amended by Current Intelligence Groups, JIC subcommittees made up of specialists and experts on various areas or fields of interest, many of them seconded from other government departments. 'These groups tend to be geographical, for example, one on the Middle East, one on the Far East, one on the former Soviet Union,' Sir Percy Cradock said. 'But there are also functional ones dealing with terrorism and also dealing with economic matters. There is a staff of perhaps forty people plus a very high-powered secretariat to get the reports out in short order.' The long-term and weekly reports are then passed on to the JIC, which will decide how and to whom they should be disseminated.[37]

The full JIC normally meets once a week in the Cabinet Office and is made up of senior Foreign Office and Treasury Department officials; the heads of MI5, MI6 and GCHQ; the Chief of Defence Intelligence and his deputy; the Intelligence Co-ordinator and the Chief of the Assessments Staff. 'It tries to answer the first question in any crisis: namely, What is the nature of the problem? What is the nature of the threat? Leaving it to ministers to decide the second question, which is, What is the policy response to it?' Sir Percy said. 'It is a very flexible and efficient machine which serves British interests well and is much admired by our allies.'

Ministerial control over the intelligence machine is exercised by a Cabinet subcommittee, the Ministerial Committee on the Intelligence Services, comprising the Prime Minister, the Foreign, Defence and Home Secretaries, and the Chancellors of the Exchequer and the Duchy of Lancaster. Within the permanent government – the Civil Service – the top intelligence body is the Permanent Secretaries Committee on the Intelligence Services, chaired by the Cabinet Secretary and including the permanent under-secretaries at the Foreign and Commonwealth Office, the Ministry of Defence, the Home Office and the Treasury. But the day-to-day running of British intelligence is carried out by the JIC's secretariat and by the Intelligence Co-ordinator. The committee reports to the Cabinet Secretary or, where military issues are directly involved, the Armed Forces Chiefs of Staff. But the Intelligence Co-ordinator has direct access to the Prime Minister, as do the JIC Chairman and the heads of MI5, MI6 and GCHQ.[38]

The intelligence has arrived on the desk of the policy-makers, but how much influence it exerts on their decisions depends on a number of factors. A report will need to be easily accessible merely to ensure that it is read. Whether or not they are always busy, politicians see themselves as such, and any analysis that does not immediately make its point is likely to be discarded. Few people reach the elevated position of national policy-making without having a high opinion of their own abilities. Poorly worded reports will result in the consumers deciding that their own assessments are better informed. The best-known example of this was Winston Churchill, who at one point in the Second World War became so frustrated with the standard of reports he was receiving that he offered to do the analysis of the raw intelligence himself.[39]

The Scott Inquiry into the Matrix-Churchill affair revealed a worryingly low regard for intelligence reports among British Cabinet ministers. 'They were significantly less riveting than the novels would have you believe,' said David Mellor, who as a former Home Office and Foreign Office minister would have had dealings with both MI5 and MI6. 'They were not as interesting as metal boxes marked "eat after reading".' Lord Howe, Foreign Secretary under Margaret Thatcher, recalled, 'In my early days, I was naïve enough to get excited about intelligence reports. Many look, at first sight, to be important and interesting and significant. Then when we check them they are not even straws in the wind. They are cornflakes in the wind.'[40]

But while policy-makers frequently point a finger at the analyst for getting it wrong – and it could be argued ministers involved in the Matrix-Churchill affair had a vested interest in doing so – the commonest failures of intelligence occur because it is disregarded by the consumer or because the policy it sought to help was itself wrong. Intelligence, however accurate it may be, will have little or no beneficial effect if basic foreign or defence policy is flawed.

The intelligence reporter is in a no-win situation. If he is right and his analysis is accepted, policy will be changed and his 'negative' assessments will be shown automatically to be incorrect. If he is wrong, or if his assessment does not coincide with considered opinion, he becomes a convenient whipping-boy for those in charge.[41] The inevitable result is that too often intelligence is diluted at various stages in the analysis process merely to match the perceptions rather than the requirements of the consumer.[42]

It was ever thus. During the Israelites' exodus from Egypt, God told Moses to send spies into Canaan to discover whether it was safe to settle there. They returned with reports of 'a land flowing with milk and honey' but disagreed over the danger posed by the Canaanites. Caleb, the leader of the spies, reported that there was no significant threat, but the majority of the Israelites were afraid and Moses ignored his spymaster's advice in favour of popular opinion. His failure to trust the intelligence assessment led to the Israelites spending the next forty years wandering in the wilderness. It is unlikely to have been the first time that the word of a spy was distrusted. It was certainly not the last.[43]

# CHAPTER 3

# Discarding Morality

'Nothing is more revolting to Englishmen than the espionage which forms part of the administrative system of continental despotisms.'

Erskine May, *Constitutional History of England*, Vol. 2, 1863

During the early part of the nineteenth century, British intelligence went into decline.[1] But the resurgence of Irish nationalism in the mid-1860s led the Home Office to mount a number of 'secret service' operations, successfully infiltrating numerous agents into the republican movement and ensuring that an attempted rebellion in March 1867 was thwarted. The Fenians then took their campaign to the mainland, killing thirteen people, including a police sergeant. Fearing the start of a widespread bombing campaign, the Home Office set up its own fully fledged 'Secret Service Department' under a young Anglo-Irish lawyer called Robert Anderson.

By pure chance, Anderson was able to recruit a Briton who had close contacts with the Fenians in America to infiltrate their ranks. Thomas Billis Beach adopted the alias of Henri le Caron and set up a Fenian camp in Lockhart, Illinois, with himself as camp commandant. He was rapidly promoted, first to Military Organizer of the Irish Republican Army and later to Inspector-General, feeding Anderson with every detail of the IRA's operations.[2]

In the early 1880s the Fenians began a new bombing campaign on the mainland, killing a seven-year-old boy and leading the Metropolitan Police Criminal Investigation Department to set up a Fenian Office. The rebel campaign escalated in 1882 with the assassination of Lord Frederick Cavendish, Chief Secretary for Ireland, and Thomas Burke, his permanent under-secretary, as they were walking through Phoenix Park in Dublin, and it reached its peak in the Dynamite War of 1883, when some ten bombs exploded in London alone.

Sir William Vernon Harcourt, the Home Secretary, called for the creation of what was eventually to become the Special Branch. 'This is not a temporary emergency requiring a momentary remedy,' he wrote.

'Fenianism is a permanent conspiracy against English rule which will last far beyond the term of my life and must be met by a permanent organization to detect and to control it.'[3]

In March 1883 the Metropolitan Police set up an Irish Bureau with a network of agents and informers run by Major Nicholas Gosselin, whose main qualification for the job was that 'he understands these Irish scoundrels and can talk to them'. It did not have an auspicious start. Just over a year after its creation, in direct response to a series of mainland bomb attacks by Fenian Dynamitards, a bomb in the public lavatory below its Scotland Yard offices destroyed a large section of the building and caused considerable injury. But the bureau survived, and four years later it became the Special Branch, with responsibility for all political crime.[4]

British attempts at intelligence-gathering abroad remained essentially amateurish. In an 1893 report on the threat from France, the then British Director of Military Intelligence, General E. F. Chapman, wrote, 'Neither the Naval nor the Military Intelligence Departments have any system or machinery for securing secret information from abroad such as is possessed by the corresponding departments of every great state in Europe.'[5] This belief that intelligence needed to be better organized was echoed two years later in the publication, by Colonel G. A. Furse, a British Army officer, of the book *Intelligence in War*. 'The intelligence service in war does not appear to us to have met with all the attention it rightly deserves,' he wrote:

The very term 'spy' conveys to our mind something dishonourable and disloyal. A spy, in the general acceptance of the term, is a low sneak who, from unworthy motives, dodges the actions of his fellow beings to turn the knowledge he acquires to his personal account. His underhand dealings inspire us with such horror that we would blush at the very idea of having to avail ourselves of any information obtained through such an agency.

This distaste for the whole business of espionage had to be put aside, Furse said. 'In war, spies are indispensable auxiliaries and we must discard all question of morality. We must overcome our feelings of repugnance for such an unchivalrous measure because it is imposed on us by sheer necessity.'[6]

The Boer War brought a new respectability to spying – at least within the military. Despite some initial criticism of the War Office Intelligence Branch for an alleged lack of preparation for the war – an allegation that was subsequently shown to be unfounded – it was raised in status to an Intelligence Division and a new section was formed with special responsibility for counter-intelligence and 'secret service'. Its budget was increased to £32,000, and a Field Intelligence Department was set up in South Africa, employing at its peak a total of 132 officers and 2321 civilians.

One of the Field Intelligence Department's most famous agents was Lord Baden-Powell, the founder of the Boy Scout movement, who as a young subaltern treated spying rather like cricket, a game for the gentleman amateur. His attitude was typical of the intelligence officers of the time. 'The best spies are unpaid men who are doing it for the love of the thing,' he wrote in his book *My Adventures as a Spy*. 'It is that touch of romance and excitement which makes spying the fascinating sport it is.'[7]

When the Boer War came to an end, the Intelligence Division, by then based at Winchester House, St James's Square, in the heart of London's clubland, was again wound down. But the success of the Field Intelligence Department was to lead eventually to the creation of the British Army's Intelligence Corps.

Lieutenant-Colonel David Henderson, Director of Military Intelligence, South Africa, returned to England to write 'an intelligence handbook' which he called *Field Intelligence, Its Principles and Practices*. It was used as the basis for the *Regulations for Intelligence Duties in the Field*, published by the War Office in August 1904.[8] The most significant part of Henderson's handbook was his recommendation, which would be implemented at the outbreak of the First World War, that 'all persons, except staff officers and secret agents, permanently engaged on intelligence duties in a campaign should be formed into an Intelligence Corps'.

Henderson painted a picture of the ideal intelligence officer. 'He must be cool, courageous and adroit, patient and imperturbable, discreet and trustworthy,' he wrote:

> He must have resolution to continue unceasingly his search for information, even in the most disheartening circumstances and after repeated failures. He must have endurance to submit silently to criticism, much of which may be based on ignorance or jealousy. And he must be able to deal with men, to approach his source of information with tact and skill, whether such source be a patriotic gentleman or an abandoned traitor.

*Field Intelligence* also contained an interesting contribution on the work of female intelligence operatives. 'When women are employed as secret service agents, the probability of success and the difficulty of administration are alike increased,' Henderson claimed:

> Women are frequently very useful in eliciting information. They

require no disguise. If attractive, they are likely to be welcome everywhere and may be able to seduce from their loyalty those whose assistance and indiscretion may be of use.

On the other hand, they are variable, easily offended, seldom sufficiently reticent, and apt to be reckless. Their treatment requires the most watchful discretion. Usually they will work more consistently for a person rather than a principle and a lover in the Intelligence Corps makes a useful intermediary.[9]

During the later part of the nineteenth century and even into the early twentieth century, the main threats to Britain were seen as France (the traditional enemy) and Russia. As late as February 1903 the Foreign Office was fighting off Treasury attempts to cut the Secret Service Vote, which following the Boer War had risen to £65,000, by arguing that 'most of our troubles are at present in Oriental countries where money is such a potent factor and our principal antagonist is Russia where such large sums are available for purposes of this kind'.[10] Russia, France and the Fenians were all seen as far more dangerous to Britain than Germany. The threat from the IRA was at the heart of the close links between the War Office Intelligence Division, run by Sir John Ardagh, and Scotland Yard's Special Branch, led at the turn of the century by Superintendent William Melville.

General Ardagh believed that the main threat lay in a French invasion timed to coincide with an uprising in Ireland. 'The Irish Revolutionary Party, which has recently been very active in Paris, has in view the obtaining of French aid for a rising in Ireland in the event of a war with England,' he wrote in early 1901. 'There is reason to believe that such a project would command more support in France than it has done for many years past,' he added. The most likely route for the French invasion was via 'waters which cannot be so effectually observed', he said. 'This naturally leads to the conception of an expedition starting from ports south of Brest with a destination west of Scilly, say to the west coast of Ireland.'[11]

It was during this period that the legendary Sidney Reilly is supposed to have begun his long career as a spy, providing information on the Russians while working undercover for British Naval Intelligence as a businessman in Port Arthur in the Russian Far East. Certainly the Russians and the British were still engaged in a full-scale espionage war – the Okhrana, the tsarist predecessor of the KGB, even had a mole in the British Embassy in St Petersburg providing it with secret documents – but there is little evidence to back up Reilly's claims to be heavily involved in spying, at least for the British, at this early stage in his career, and former MI6 officers who have examined the files say he was not recruited until 1917.[12]

British intelligence from the Russian Far East was very poor at this time and dependent on an ad hoc exchange accord with the Japanese, concluded in 1903. 'The Japanese military attaché called the other day and left an elaborate memo on a joint system of secret service,' Colonel Francis Davies, the department head, told the Foreign Office:

> He mentioned in conversation that the Japanese could travel anywhere in China and Korea but that they were marked in Europe. It appears to me that we can only work with the Japanese by giving them some of our information in exchange for theirs. We are now working on those lines, giving to the Japanese military attaché some confidential, not secret, details and we have received from them some matters of importance, including plans of Port Arthur and Vladivostok.[13]

It seems unlikely that the British would have been grateful for a map of Port Arthur if they had their own secret agent there (although this could of course be an early, and somewhat extreme, example of inter-service rivalry hampering intelligence collection).

There appears to have been no such competition between the War Office Intelligence Division and Special Branch. The close links between the two were demonstrated by the fact that the division's agents were run by Major Nicholas Gosselin, the same man who controlled a network of Special Branch agents among the Irish rebels.

In 1901, in a successful application for the ID handler's job, Gosselin gave a brief description of his role with Special Branch: 'My work has been hitherto entirely or almost so with Irish Secret Societies in Europe and America. During the early stages of the dynamite scare, a good many Irish Constabulary and secret agents (private detectives) were employed.'[14]

Two years later, when Gosselin decided to leave to concentrate on the Irish network, he was replaced by Superintendent William Melville, the head of Special Branch. Despite Melville's initial role as the 'controller' for the War Office agents and the fact that he was already in his early fifties, it was he and not Reilly who appears to have been the main British secret agent in the period before the First World War.[15]

Born at Sneem in County Kerry, Melville was one of a long line of Irishmen recruited to watch their own. His enthusiasm for the job was not in doubt – he was very keen on disguises, his favourite being that of a sanitary inspector – but his methods were sometimes dubious.

Melville had come to prominence in 1892 with the capture of the Walsall Bombers. The affair began with the arrest in London of Joseph

Deacon, an anarchist from Walsall in Staffordshire, who had been under police observation for some time. Melville, then an inspector, was sent to Walsall to investigate the alleged ring of anarchists run by Deacon. He found bomb-making instructions, fuses and anarchist pamphlets, and five other men were arrested. Four of them were subsequently convicted of anarchy and imprisoned for up to ten years.

The convictions ended the drive to cut back on the Special Branch, leading to widespread suspicion that those convicted had been set up by a police *agent provocateur*. At their trial, the anarchists claimed that the order for the bombs they were making had come from one of their number who turned out to be a paid agent of Melville.

William Melville

The incident did no harm to Melville's career – rather the reverse: within a year he had been made head of Special Branch – but it may have coloured the response of Edward Henry, the Metropolitan Police Commissioner, when he was asked by the War Office to comment on Melville's suitability for the post of 'intermediary for the employment of secret service agents'.[16] Henry said:

He is shrewd, resourceful and although he has a tendency towards adventuring, he can keep this in check when it suits his interest to do so. For the purpose for which he is needed, to be an intermediary, no better person could be secured – probably no one nearly so good for the money. The Intelligence Dept will make it clear to him that he must abstain from taking a line of his own. We must arrange that he severs his connection with Scotland Yard as quietly as possible. His utility to WO would be much lessened if it became known that he had taken service with them.

The need for secrecy was paramount since Melville had become a popular hero for the Victorian press, which took delight in chronicling the activities of 'the ever-watching Chief Inspector' in his fight against anarchists and Fenians. The *Golden Penny* noted in July 1898 that 'To the journalist seeking information for publication, Mr Melville's lips are as a sealed book.' This may have made it necessary to fill in the odd gap. The most famous of his exploits, for example, was the arrest on Victoria Station in April 1894 of the French anarchist Theodule Meunier, who, according to the *Dublin County Telegraph*, shouted out as he was grabbed, 'To fall into your hands, Melville! You, the only man I feared, and whose description was engraved on my mind!'

Melville, who was already receiving a police pension of £280 a year, was paid an annual salary of £400 by the War Office plus an allowance of 30 shillings a week for out-of-pocket expenses. He was also provided with enough funds to set up 'a small office doing the ostensible business of a general agency and making enquiries nominally on behalf of commercial firms' as a cover for his activities. As well as acting as general controller for the War Office agents in Africa, Germany and Russia, Melville, who to disguise his identity was known only as 'M', took on a role as a London-based 'fireman', undertaking a number of secret missions of his own around the world.[17]

Just over a year later he was given a pay rise of £50 a year after complaining that Henry Long, his African-based agent, was better paid than he was. 'This last is an unfortunate circumstance and one which I always hoped he might not discover,' Colonel Davies said:

It evidently rankled that a subordinate of comparatively little experience should get more than he does. He also fears that a change of Government might lead to his dismissal and he has got it into his head that a Liberal minister might disapprove of anyone being employed on such work as he is doing.

In my opinion, 'M' has worked very satisfactorily and I doubt very much if we could get anyone else for the money who would do as well. He is very resourceful and has a great capacity for picking up suitable persons to act as agents. Further he has a really good working knowledge of French, which is uncommon in men of his class and is most useful, in fact almost indispensable. His accent would certainly appall you but he is quite fluent and fully capable of transacting business in French.[18]

A typical depiction of Melville's exploits in the Victorian press shows
the then head of Special Branch arresting the French anarchist
Theodule Meunier in 1894

Few details of Melville's 'secret missions' survive. But by the beginning
of the First World War, when he had transferred to the recently formed
Secret Service Bureau, he had accumulated an impressive list of foreign
decorations for his work on 'secret service', including the French Légion
d'Honneur, the Crown of Italy, Spain's Order of Isabel la Catolica, the
Order of Christ of Portugal, and the Danish Order of Danneborg. One
contemporary said Melville had spent the period between 1903 and 1914
on 'responsible and spectacular duties which entailed extensive travel on

the Continent during which he played an active part in the suppression of anarchism'.[19]

On his death, in 1918, his obituary in *Police Review* referred only obliquely to his post-police career. 'When he retired from the "Yard" his services to the state did not cease,' it said. 'They continued on most confidential matters until almost the day of his death. It would probably surprise some people to discover that their whole history during the course of the present war had been investigated by this officer.'[20]

The status of military intelligence was dramatically downgraded in 1904 under a radical reorganization of the War Office which abolished the post of Director of Military Intelligence and subordinated it to a new Directorate of Military Operations split into four sections of which only two were concerned with intelligence – MO2, the Foreign Intelligence section, and MO3, whose role was described as 'Special Duties' (a euphemism for covert intelligence activities).[21]

By now the main potential threat was increasingly seen not as France or Russia but as Germany, and in 1905 the War Office was drawing up plans for a secret service in the event of 'a war in Europe'. Although no mention was made of Germany, details of the scheme were circulated among consular and diplomatic staff in Scandinavia and Switzerland, leaving little doubt as to the identity of the 'enemy territory' between them.

'Observers' based there were to collect intelligence which they would then hand on to 'carriers' – people who might travel in and out of the country without arousing suspicion, such as 'commercial travellers, gypsies and women'. The 'carriers' would take the information to the 'collectors', intelligence officers based in neutral countries, who would then pass it back to London via the local British consulates and embassies.

The plan caused alarm among some of the recipients. One diplomat in Denmark baulked at the idea of becoming involved in any way with such a scheme. 'I have always thought it undesirable that members of His Majesty's Embassies and Legations should be in any way connected with espionage,' he wrote. 'With earnest desire to be of every possible use to England, I think that the embassies and legations should have as little as possible to do with such matters which should be left to specialists.'[22]

That attitude still permeated Britain's foreign service. In July 1901 Sir Ernest Satow, Britain's ambassador to China, wrote the following note to Sir Thomas Sanderson, then the permanent under-secretary at the Foreign Office in charge of the Secret Service Vote.

My Dear Sanderson,

You know how often it has been said that this legation was not well informed as to what was going on and that it had no Secret Service. It seems to me quite natural that it should be so. The Chinese secretary is fully occupied with translations of notes and interviewing people. He cannot go around picking up information.[23]

Even those Army officers posted as military attachés to Britain's embassies abroad saw espionage as below their station. Charles à Court Repington, who served as attaché in Brussels and The Hague in the early 1900s, wrote:

I would never do any Secret Service work. My view is that the military attaché is the guest of the country to which he is accredited, and must only see and learn that which is permissible for a guest to investigate. Certainly, he must keep his eyes and ears open and miss nothing. But Secret Service is not his business and he should always refuse a hand in it.

With war now inevitable, no such scruples were open to Sir William Everett, the British military attaché in Berlin. But when asked by the Intelligence Branch to continue in secret service after leaving Germany, he declined:

You will not have forgotten when we talked this matter over some months ago, that I mentioned how distasteful this sort of work was to me and how much more distasteful it would be to me when it no longer formed a necessary part of my duties. I so dread the thought of being compelled to continue in communication and contact with the class of man who must be employed in this sort of work, while the measures to which we are obliged to resort are repulsive to me.[24]

The Admiralty shared Everett's disparaging view of espionage. The Royal Navy had only reluctantly formed a Foreign Intelligence Committee in 1883, and even more reluctantly, on the orders of Lord Salisbury, the Prime Minister, had expanded it four years later into the Naval Intelligence Department. It was given the somewhat less than inspiring mission 'to collect, classify and record with a complete index all information which bears a naval character or which may be of value during naval matters, and to preserve the information in a form available for reference'.[25]

By 1908, the NID was asking all British diplomatic and consular staff abroad to look out for intelligence on:

publications and printed matter such as the annual reports of the ministers of war and marine; lists of officers and ships of the Navy, Navy and Army estimates; code-lists of merchant-ships; progress reports of naval or military works; items of local or general interest having any connection with naval and military forces, fighting ships or permanent defences; and any change with regard to these either in equipment numbers or disposition.[26]

It was also sending officers to the main German ports to gather intelligence on 'naval policy, mobilization, fleet dispositions and the like', according to a series of articles by 'A Former Member of the Secret Service' in the *Daily Telegraph* in September 1930.

'Although the writer feels some difficulty in praising his old service, he is satisfied that the British Naval Intelligence was incomparably superior to the much more elaborate, widespread, and expensive system of espionage which Germany built up in this country,' one article said. 'At any given moment, our Admiralty could have announced the number of submarines on the stocks or completing at Danzig, together with the salient features of each craft.'

But the Navy's low regard for intelligence was still evident. 'The work of our Intelligence correspondents in pre-war years was severely handicapped by the exiguous funds available,' the writer complained:

Compared with the Secret Service budgets of the Continental powers, our expenditure on this branch was very small indeed.

For reasons which to the writer are inexplicable, Intelligence work, however hazardous it might be, and however valuable the results, was never sufficiently recognized by our home authorities as deserving of reward. It may be that this pointed neglect is due to an inherent prejudice against the whole business of espionage.[27]

By the beginning of 1909 the Special Duties section of the Directorate of Military Operations – by then known as MO5 – was busy building up a network of agents in Germany. Melville recruited 'a retired officer of the army of a friendly power who is resident in Germany', on a salary of £600 a year, and redeployed one of the junior agents from Russia to join Byszewski, the controller of the Russian network, who was based in Berlin.[28]

At home, a full-scale anti-German scare was in progress, orchestrated by the author William le Queux, who produced a series of books with titles like *The Invasion of 1910* and *Spies of the Kaiser: Plotting the Downfall of England*. He protested vigorously to anyone who would listen – and many influential people did – that the authorities were negligently ignoring the German threat. Lord Harmsworth, proprietor of the *Daily Mail*, serialized *The Invasion of 1910* in his newspaper, carefully re-routing the hypothetical marauding Hun troops through towns and villages where the *Mail*'s circulation was high.

'Among the thousands of Germans working in London, the hundred or so spies, all trusted soldiers, had passed unnoticed,' le Queux wrote in a work which deliberately set out to blur the lines between fact and fiction. 'But, working in unison, each little group of two or three had been allotted its task and had previously thoroughly reconnoitred the position and studied the most rapid or effective means.'[29]

As the public excitement grew, so too did the number of German spies. Lord Roberts, taking up the theme in Parliament, said, 'It is calculated, my Lords, that there are 80,000 Germans in the United Kingdom, almost all of them trained soldiers. They work in many of the hotels at some of the chief railway stations, and if a German force once got into this country it would have the advantage of help and reinforcement such as no other army on foreign soil has ever before enjoyed.'[30]

In fact, Gustav Steinhauer, the officer in charge of the German intelligence network, had relatively few spies in Britain. Poorly paid and amateurish, virtually all of them were successfully rounded up before the war began. 'Each German agent in this country received a small retainer, and the news he supplied was paid for according to its supposed value,' one British intelligence official later recalled. 'It is safe to say that 99 per cent of their reports were utterly valueless, but our own authorities, having access to the correspondence of most of these agents, may sometimes have found it convenient to insert items so circumstantial and convincing as to be calculated to deceive the shrewdest heads on the German naval staff.'[31]

But the momentum of the German spy scare was such that trivial matters of fact became inconsequential. Even military intelligence was convinced by le Queux's claims, not least because Lieutenant-Colonel James Edmonds, the head of MO5, was his close friend. Edmonds asked the police what could be done about 'the systematic visits to this country by Germans who locate themselves with clergymen, farmers, and private persons' ostensibly to learn English.

Unlike the military, Special Branch was unconvinced by reports that German visitors to Britain were 'assiduous in collecting other information concerning the topography of the country, roads, dockyards, military magazines, which might be considered of value from the military point of view'.

'It seems doubtful that these visitors are really a source of danger,' the Branch told Edmonds:

The really dangerous person is the foreigner possibly naturalized, settled in and British and carrying on some business or pursuit which shields him from suspicion, who has opportunities of collecting information and of transmitting it, probably at a time when it could be useful to some other country. If we could exercise some impression over these latter, it might be useful, but we cannot.[32]

But Edmonds and his direct superior, General John Ewart, Director of Military Operations, continued to lobby hard for some form of action, and in March 1909 Herbert Asquith, the British Prime Minister, instructed the Committee of Imperial Defence 'to consider the dangers from German espionage to British naval ports'.

A subcommittee was set up, chaired by R. B. Haldane, the War Secretary, and including the Home Secretary, the Metropolitan Police Commissioner, the Postmaster-General, the First Lord of the Admiralty, the Director of Naval Intelligence, the Director of Military Operations, and the permanent under-secretaries at the Treasury and the Foreign Office who between them administered the Secret Service Vote.[33]

At first, many of the subcommittee members were rightly sceptical of the alleged German threat. Edmonds, who described himself as 'employed under the DMO on secret service', was dismissed by Lord Esher, the Postmaster-General, as 'a silly witness from the War Office'. Esher asked Edmonds sarcastically if he was not worried about 'the large number of German waiters in this country' and noted in his diary that 'Spycatchers get espionage on the brain.'

But the subcommittee was bombarded with a welter of reports of German spies, albeit largely unsubstantiated and highly circumstantial. On 24 July 1909 it reported:

> The evidence which was produced left no doubt in the minds of the sub-committee that an extensive system of German espionage exists in this country, and that we have no organization for keeping in touch with that espionage and for accurately determining its extent or objectives.
>
> We have considered the question of how a Secret Service Bureau could be established to deal both with espionage in this country and with our own foreign agents abroad, and to serve as a screen between the Admiralty and the War Office on the one hand and those employed on secret service, or who have information they wish to sell to the British Government on the other.

The subcommittee also set the tone for the refusal of subsequent governments to acknowledge that Britain had any form of secret service, publishing only one copy of its detailed recommendations and calling for the passing of a new Official Secrets Act to allow spies to be prosecuted for revealing any information 'prejudicial to the security of the state'. 'The detailed recommendations of the sub-committee regarding the establishing of the Secret Service Bureau are of so secret a nature that it is thought desirable that they should not be printed or circulated to the members,' the report said. 'These recommendations have been considered by the sub-committee, and a single typed copy has therefore been made and handed over to the custody of the Director of Military Operations.'[34]

On 1 October 1909 the Secret Service Bureau was set up jointly by the War Office and the Admiralty, and made subordinate to the War Office's Directorate of Military Operations and Intelligence. According to popular mythology, the bureau consisted solely of Captain Vernon Kell, an officer in the South Staffordshire Regiment who would later become the first head of MI5. In fact it was slightly, although not much, better staffed than that.

The two principal members of staff were Kell and Captain Mansfield Cumming of the Royal Navy. Since the Admiralty's main requirement was for information on the Kaiser's rapidly growing navy, the naval section commanded by Cumming – or 'C', as he became known for security reasons – concentrated on gathering intelligence overseas, while the military section – under Kell, or 'K' – took responsibility for counter-espionage within the British Isles, recruiting several new agents, one of whom was William Melville.

In January 1916 a new Directorate of Military Intelligence was set up within the War Office. Cumming's foreign department was designated MI1c – it was only later that it would become MI6. Kell's home department was renamed MI5.[35]

# CHAPTER 4

# Learning from the Crook

Security is the mother of danger and the grandmother of
destruction.
Thomas Fuller, *The Holy State and the Profane State*, 1642

A mong the mixture of real and imaginary evidence of German treachery which Edmonds used to justify the creation of the Secret Service
Bureau was a map on which he marked the whereabouts of all the Kaiser's
known spies.

'I made a map of England showing the positions of various spy locations
which had considerable effect upon the Committee of Imperial Defence,'
he wrote. 'I was opposed to the arrest of even undoubted espionage
agents: it was better to let Germany live in a fool's paradise that we had
no counter-espionage system. This was accepted: the agents were marked
down and all but one (on leave) seized on declaration of war.'[1]

Sir Eric Holt-Wilson, Kell's deputy, recorded that Gustav Steinhauer's
network was uncovered after a chance remark on a train by a loose-
tongued German admiralty official. The home section of the Secret Service Bureau discovered the agent whose barber's shop was used as the
central 'post office' for the German network, and blanket interception
of his mail allowed it to compile a complete list of Steinhauer's twenty-
two spies.[2]

Edmonds and Kell agreed to keep the bulk of Steinhauer's network in
place, watching their movements and intercepting their correspondence
until the very day war was declared, when the network was rolled up,
bar that one agent who had the good fortune to be on leave in Germany
at the time. It is still regarded by the Security Service as one of its greatest
coups.

'This sudden action had the effect of destroying the complete spy
organization built up by the enemy in peacetime,' wrote Holt-Wilson:

As a proof of this statement, a German order came into our hands
early in the war which disclosed the fact that as late as the 21st August
[seventeen days after war was declared] the German Military commanders were still ignorant of the despatch or movements of our main

expeditionary force, although this had been more or less common knowledge to thousands in this country.

MI5 discovered many more spies during the war, thirty-five of whom were brought to trial. Nineteen of these were condemned to death, although a number were later reprieved. Kell was somewhat irate to find that in the first of these cases it was because the condemned was a woman. He protested strongly, arguing that once the Germans realized that the British would not kill women they would flood the country with female spies.[3]

Vernon Kell, Director-General of MI5 from its creation in 1909 (as part of the Secret Service Bureau) to 1940

The First World War saw a massive increase in the resources allocated to Kell's section, which was based in Victoria Street, Westminster. At the start of the war it had four officers, three detectives and seven clerks. By the time of the Armistice there were almost 850 employees. Their activities had been bolstered by the catch-all phraseology of the 1914 Defence of the Realm Act, which effectively turned Britain into a military-controlled state and allowed unparalleled surveillance of the population, including the widespread interception of postal communication.

Although Kell insisted that MI5 should stay 'foursquare' within the law, Inspector William Melville lectured new recruits on how to pick locks and break into houses. His course included practical training using the safe of the embassy of 'a so-called neutral power' and the services of 'a very experienced assistant who is out on a kind of compassionate leave from Parkhurst so that he can put his shoulder to the war effort for a few days'. The aims of the operation were not to be compared to those of the common thief, as one of the trainees recorded in his diary:

> Melville paused. 'So much', he said, 'for the needs of the average crook.' But if the same 'operation' were to be envisaged by MI5 the whole pattern of the undertaking would need to be changed. The accent would no longer be on lifting the swag but on the identification of documents. When located they were likely to be photographed there and then and afterwards replaced so that they appeared to have been undisturbed. Finally in leaving the premises the marauders would need to obliterate every possible trace of their entry.
>
> The guiding principle, so far as an operation in this country was concerned, would not be the avoidance of conflict with the police but a clash with the vigorous security precautions made by the 'other side' which could come into action at many points and nullify the exploit. This would lead at best to a showdown and at worst to the embarrassment of the Cabinet. Nevertheless, a house-break was always a house-break and there must remain much that the MI5 could learn from the crook.

Melville warned his students against using the tricks they had learned for any more profitable activities:

> In case any of you should be tempted after the war to act up as a 'gentleman burglar', I believe that is the term, I think I should point out that there is precious little in it for you. What you do for MI5 in wartime is strictly privileged. You may have to face risks because you are dealing with men who are potentially desperate. But there are positively no legal penalties, even if very occasionally you shoot to kill. In contrast, the peacetime 'screwsman' can expect no government sponsorship and certainly no police protection . . . sooner or later he gets convicted.[4]

With the help of the police, Kell had spent the pre-war years drawing up a list of 30,000 aliens. The Central Registry was a card index in which the subjects were classified on a bizarre scale that ran from AA for the least dangerous to BB for the most. AA was Absolutely Anglicized or Absolutely Allied, denoting someone who was definitely supportive of the British cause. A was Anglicized or Allied, i.e. supportive. AB was Anglo-Boche – allegiances unclear, but probably pro-British. BA was Boche-Anglo – allegiances also unclear, but probably pro-German. B was Boche, i.e. hostile. Where a subject's hostility to the British cause was not in doubt, he or she was graded BB or Bad Boche.

Once the war began, the number of registered enemy aliens swelled to an unlikely 100,000, of whom 32,000 were eventually interned and a further 25,000 deported. Nor was it just the, mostly imaginary, German spies who provided scope for Kell's inveterate empire-building. From 1916, the Home Section – now officially known as MI5 – and Special Branch became increasingly involved in countering 'subversion', either from pacifists or from the left. This fuelled the growing rivalry between the two organizations, and Kell and Basil Thomson, the head of Special Branch, both lobbied furiously for control of what was expected to be the new post-war threat – the fight against Bolshevism.

MI5 officers had become openly resentful of Special Branch, complaining that, no matter how much work they put into uncovering German spies, Thomson always managed to take the credit for his own men. Captain Reginald Drake, the head of MI5's counter-espionage department, wrote, 'BT [Thomson] did not know of the existence, name or activity of any convicted spy until I told him; but being the dirty dog he was he twisted the facts to claim that he alone did it.' It was to be the beginning of a long-running feud that has continued through to the present day.[5]

Fears that industrial unrest would disrupt the war effort led to the creation of a 'Labour Intelligence' department within the Ministry of Munitions. Set up in 1916 with Kell's assistance, it was given the cover-name Parliamentary Military Secretary Department No. 2 Section (PMS-2) to disguise its real role. But its amateurish attempts to capture alleged union subversives by using *agents provocateurs* served only to show the lack of any credible subversive threat and brought the intelligence services into public disrepute. PMS-2 was soon absorbed back into MI5, having tarnished not only its own reputation but that of Kell, who lost control over the fight against subversion to Special Branch at a crucial time – just months before October 1917 and Russia's Bolshevik Revolution.[6]

By the end of the war, Thomson and Special Branch had become the prevalent force in British domestic intelligence operations and Bolshevism the principal threat. When the government, fearful that Bolshevism was more rampant in Britain than anyone realized, set up a Directorate of Intelligence in March 1919, it was Thomson and not Kell who was appointed to head it.[7]

At the same time MI5 lost control of its Military Control network, the system of monitoring the movements of aliens. This was modified 'to exclude Bolshevik agents from the United Kingdom'; renamed the Passport Control Department; and handed over, together with the MI5 men who ran it, to the Secret Intelligence Service.[8] To Kell's dismay, MI5's role was limited to military counter-espionage and preventing the spread of Bolshevism within the armed forces, and his budget was cut from £100,000 a year to £30,000.

Despite seeing his staff slashed by more than 800 to just 30, Kell fought a rearguard action to keep MI5 alive. He centred his activities around his registry of undesirable aliens, now renamed the Precautionary Index, using this to monitor the activities of all Russians and their sympathizers in Britain. MI5 expanded the list to include anyone who held or was suspected of having held left-wing views and might therefore pass them on to unsuspecting soldiers, sailors and airmen.[9]

In the mid-1920s Kell successfully beat off an attempt by MI6 to absorb MI5. But his main turf battle remained with Special Branch over who should control civilian counter-espionage. 'The work of British MI5 is now carried on under the plea that revolutionary agents are attempting to create trouble in the British Army,' Major R. F. Hyatt, the deputy US military attaché, reported back to Washington in December 1920. 'Officially, MI5 is only concerned with civilian activities as they affect the army, but in reality and especially recently, they have concerned themselves in general with revolutionary and Bolshevik agents, using the Suspect List, built up during the war and since added to, as a basis for operations.'[10]

As he strove to rebuild his empire, Kell made common cause with the private intelligence organizations set up by right-wing groups in the 1920s to counter the 'Bolshevik threat', even recruiting one of his most successful agent-runners, Maxwell Knight, from the British Fascisti, where he was Director of Intelligence.[11]

But the most significant link between MI5 and private intelligence agencies was that with Conservative Central Office, and it was this that led to the disclosure of the so-called Zinoviev Letter. The letter, supposedly written to the Communist Party of Great Britain by Grigori Zinoviev, President of Comintern, the international body set up by the Soviet Union to co-ordinate Communist activity, called for the mobilization of sympathetic forces in the Labour Party and the intensification of 'agitation-propaganda work in the armed forces'. It was leaked to the *Daily Mail*, which published it shortly before a general election called by Labour Prime Minister Ramsay MacDonald for 29 October 1924.

The motive for leaking it was a feeling within the intelligence services that the Labour Party was soft on Bolshevism. This belief was fuelled by MacDonald's signing of two treaties with Russia – one of which aimed at settling Russian debts, was dubbed 'Money for Murderers' by the popular press – and by the decision not to prosecute John Campbell, a Communist journalist accused of preaching sedition to the armed forces.

Much remains uncertain about the Zinoviev Letter – not least whether or not it was genuine and if it had any significant effect on the election, which the Labour Party had anyway seemed certain to lose. But the greatest mystery surrounds the leak itself, which confirmed the right-wing nature of the intelligence services at the time, placing them firmly in collusion with Conservative Party Central Office.

The key players in the affair were Thomas Marlowe, the *Daily Mail* editor; Colonel Frederick Browning, the former deputy head of the SIS; and Donald im Thurn, a former MI5 member. But at least three other serving or former intelligence officials were also involved: Kell himself; Admiral Hugh Sinclair, the head of SIS; and Admiral Reginald 'Blinker' Hall, the former Director of Naval Intelligence, who was by now Unionist MP for Eastbourne and had strong connections with Central Office, the headquarters of the Opposition Conservative Party.

The precise roles of each of the men are far from clear, but Central Office had offered to pay im Thurn £5000 to pass the letter to the press. Either Hall or Browning was almost certainly a man described by the *Daily Mail* editor as the 'old and trusted friend' who first told him of the letter's existence, while the other was the other 'friend' who confirmed its authenticity.

According to im Thurn's diary, both Kell and Sinclair were involved in the decision as to when the letter should be leaked, with Kell pressing for its early release and Sinclair in favour of holding it back. Further proof of the close links with Central Office was to come in January 1927, when Joseph Ball, a senior member of MI5 who had been involved in black propaganda and is believed by some to have been the architect of the Zinoviev affair, resigned to take up a post as the Conservative Party's Director of Publicity.[12]

How much effect all this had on Kell's rearguard action is difficult to say, but in 1931 he won a major victory in the long turf battle with Special Branch. MI5, which was by then based in Cromwell Road, Fulham, west London, took control of civil and military counter-espionage throughout the United Kingdom and the British Empire. Scotland Yard's civil intelligence staff was absorbed into Kell's organization, and a new title, the Security Service, was adopted, although in practice the service was still known as MI5. Special Branch was left with the role of merely carrying out arrests and surveillance when MI5 directed. The new MI5 organization consisted of four divisions: A – Administration; B – Counter-espionage; C – Security; and D – Liaison with the Military.[13]

From an outstation in an expensive apartment block at Dolphin Square in Pimlico, B Division built up a network of moles in the Communist Party. They were controlled by Maxwell Knight. An eccentric man with a passion for natural history, Knight would later present a BBC radio programme for children as 'Uncle Max'. But his fame within the intelligence services was based on a willingness to wait years for the 'sleeper' agents he placed inside the Communist Party to gain positions of influence.

The most successful of his operations against the Communist Party involved the use of Olga Gray. In a typical Knight ploy, the nineteen-year-old began attending meetings of the Friends of the Soviet Union and in 1932 started working for the Anti-War Movement, a Soviet front organization, as a typist. Eventually, four years into the operation, she had won the confidence of Harry Pollitt, the British Communist Party leader, who sent her on a secret mission to India.

Knight was insistent that at no stage was Gray to initiate a move deeper into the Communist organization: advance was always to come at the invitation of the party. This patient approach paid dividends, and in 1938, seven years after first being recruited, Gray uncovered the Woolwich Spy Ring which was smuggling details of the Army's 'Most Secret' weaponry to the Soviet Union. Percy Glading, the Communist agent running the spy ring, and two co-conspirators were jailed after being convicted on the evidence given by Gray who was known throughout the trial only as 'Miss X'.[14]

Despite his previous membership of the British Fascisti, from which he resigned only in 1930, Knight was equally successful at infiltrating right-wing extremist groups. Following the 1933 Home Office decision that the intelligence services should begin collecting data on Fascist movements, MI5 infiltrated a number of agents into Sir Oswald Mosley's British Union of Fascists, including James McGuirk Hughes, who under the pseudonym P. G. Taylor became the BUF's head of intelligence and in an interesting side-operation used a number of BUF activists to burgle confidential documents from the home of a suspected Communist.[15]

This was by no means the only skulduggery in which MI5 was involved at the time. During the Second World War, Anthony Blunt, later revealed as the Fourth Man, was briefly part of a unit which, since before the war and with the help of a secret department in the Post Office, had been routinely opening diplomatic bags.[16]

MI5 had moved to Horseferry Road, Westminster, in 1937. Shortly before the outbreak of the Second World War it transferred its headquarters to Wormwood Scrubs Prison in north-west London. But the Victorian prison was not an ideal location, and in May 1940 all non-essential sections were transferred to Blenheim Palace in Oxfordshire, while those that had to stay in London moved to 58 St James's Street in Mayfair.[17]

In the same month Knight had success with another of his operations.

Joan Miller had been told to infiltrate the Right Club, an anti-Semitic organization set up by Captain Archibald Maule Ramsay, the Conservative MP for Peebles, who blamed the Jews for the war and wanted to reach an accord with Hitler. Knight succeeded in placing three female agents inside the Right Club: Miller herself; Marjorie Mackie, whom Miller described as 'a cosy middle-aged lady who will always remind me of Miss Marple'; and a young Belgian girl called Helene Louise de Munck.

Miller discovered that Anna Wolkoff, a Russian émigré who was a member of the Right Club and, perhaps worryingly for the government, a dressmaker for the Duchess of Windsor, was passing the Italians details of secret communications between Winston Churchill, the British Prime Minister, and Franklin D. Roosevelt, the American President, which she had been given by Tyler Kent, a cypher clerk at the American Embassy. The affair fuelled fears of attempts to replace King George VI with the Duke of Windsor and install a government willing to make peace with Hitler. A number of alleged Nazi sympathizers, including Mosley and Ramsay, were interned.[18]

Despite the success of the operation against the Right Club, Churchill, who was singularly unimpressed by MI5's failure to detect a mythical German fifth column largely dreamed up by the *Daily Mail*, set up a Security Executive to ensure that British intelligence was operating efficiently. It was to be chaired by Lord Swinton, a former Air Minister, with the former MI5 member Sir Joseph Ball, now Director of Information at Conservative Party Central Office, as Vice-Chairman.[19]

The Security Executive discovered that MI5 had been ill-prepared for the heavy workload the war would bring. In early 1939 it had only thirty officers and its surveillance section comprised just six men. Its problems had been exacerbated by the destruction of much of the Precautionary Index in a bombing raid.

Within weeks of Swinton being appointed, Churchill ordered that Kell be sacked. The man who had created MI5 and had run it for thirty-one years was sixty-seven years old. He died less than two years later at his small rented cottage in Emberton, Buckinghamshire, a broken man.

For six months, the Security Service was in disarray as it sought to fight off attempts by the 'abrasive' Swinton to modernize it. In November 1940 Churchill, having heard of the low morale within MI5 through his own sources, brought in Sir David Petrie, a retired Indian police officer who had been in charge of the Indian Political Intelligence Bureau, to oversee the reorganization, and in March 1941 Petrie was appointed Director-General.[20]

With MI5 looking over its shoulder at the Security Executive, there ensued a determined campaign to ensure that a Nazi fifth column could not operate. In what was by any standards one of the sorriest episodes in the history of British intelligence, the Security Service supervised the incarceration of 22,000 Austrian and German citizens and a further 4000 Italians, the vast majority of whom had fled to Britain to escape the very regimes they were now being accused of supporting.

Brigadier H. I. Allen, the MI5 representative on the JIC, told his fellow committee-members that there were 'a large number of Italian waiters employed in London restaurants and that a number of these were anti-British. These waiters were in an excellent position to overhear scraps of conversation from members of the government and others.' The JIC issued a report backing MI5's call for tougher action. 'We fully realize that high political considerations arise in regard to taking firm action against aliens or interfering with the liberty of British subjects. Nevertheless, in our opinion the safety of the State must come first.'

Both the Home Office and the Foreign Office opposed the detentions. One Foreign Office official accused the service of using 'arbitrary rules of thumb which led to injustice and chaos'. The MI5 officers supervising the internment were displaying 'a notable incapacity for weighing evidence and a tendency to conceal this incapacity by unnecessary recourse to secrecy'.

An inquiry into the intelligence services carried out by Lord Hankey, the former cabinet secretary now a minister without portfolio, backed MI5's actions. 'We simply cannot afford to take any risks,' Hankey said. 'Any injustices to which such precautions may give rise are of minor importance compared with the safety of the State.'

But Churchill, having initially encouraged 'a very large round-up', began to have serious doubts over the political wisdom of what he now described as 'the witch-finding activities of MI5', and by the end of 1941 most internees had been ordered to be released, although some were held until the end of the war. A number of them died – up to 650 of them when the liner *Arandora Star*, taking them to Canada, was sunk by a German U-boat. Some committed suicide during their incarceration; others became seriously ill. Yet, save for their ethnic origins, in only a very few cases was there any real evidence that they were serious members of an enemy fifth column.[21]

Paradoxically, at the same time as it was indulging in these 'witch-finding activities', MI5 was also setting up the major wartime triumph of British human intelligence – the Double-Cross system – working closely with Section V, the counter-espionage section of MI6.

'In the earlier years, the main aim was to block German attempts to infiltrate the UK with their spies,' said Kenneth Benton, one of the MI6 officers involved in the project:

But it became clear that as well as keeping the Abwehr case officers content with their apparent coverage of events in wartime Britain, we could use our Abwehr agents for a process of strategic deception.

The object was not only to stop an enemy agent from operating, but where possible to 'turn' him. He could be given the simple choice of either being tried and shot as a spy or agreeing to work entirely under the orders of the MI5 case officer. When a spy was successfully turned the profit was twofold. On the one hand the Abwehr case officer would believe that he had a useful agent on his books and thus have less need to recruit others. On the other, the false information which the British case officer would send to Germany through his agent's communication – e.g. radio messages or secret ink letters – could be useful for strategic deception.

The first opportunity to turn a German agent came when Arthur Owens – a businessman and part-time MI6 agent or 'stringer' – was found to be working for German military intelligence, the Abwehr. Owens was arrested and agreed to work as a double agent under the cover-name of 'Snow'. His controller was Lieutenant-Colonel Tommy 'Tar' Robertson.

By December 1940 Robertson had expanded the Double-Cross system to include twelve other agents run by his MI5 unit, B1(a). An organization known as the Wireless Board – comprising Guy Liddell, the director of B Division; Sir Stewart Menzies, the head of MI6; and the directors of military, naval and air intelligence – was set up to decide what information should be fed back to the Germans. But, since this was rapidly becoming an all-consuming task, day-to-day co-ordination was left to a subcommittee run by J. C. Masterman, an academic from Christ Church, Oxford.[22]

The Radio Security Service managed to intercept the Abwehr's messages to its spies, which were then decyphered by GC&CS at Bletchley Park. The German agents were infiltrated into Britain via Spain or Portugal; Section V of MI6 placed officers in Madrid and Lisbon to identify them as they arrived and where possible to make the initial contact before handing them over to an MI5 case officer.

Working together, B1(a) and Section V succeeded in turning more than forty Abwehr agents. 'We actively ran and controlled the German espionage system,' Masterman would later write.

One 'XX' agent was 'Tate', Wulf Schmidt, a Dane who parachuted into East Anglia in September 1939 and was given his cover-name because of a striking resemblance to the famous music-hall artist Harry Tate. Schmidt continued operating until Hamburg fell in May 1945. He was so successful that the Abwehr described him as 'the pearl' in its British network and awarded him two Iron Crosses.[23]

Another agent was Dusko Popov ('Tricycle'), an urbane, womanizing Yugoslav who is thought to have been the model for James Bond. Popov had been recruited before the war by MI6 and was later to claim controversially that the FBI ignored intelligence he provided which indicated that an attack on Pearl Harbor was being planned.[24]

Perhaps the most important use of the Double-Cross system was in Operation Fortitude, the deception campaign to persuade the Germans that the Normandy landings were merely a feint for a main D-Day invasion which was to take place in the Pas-de-Calais. 'Garbo', the Spaniard Jean Pujol, warned the Germans of the D-Day Normandy landings too late to allow them to prepare adequate defences, but in so doing he persuaded them that his intelligence on the landings was accurate.

A week later, as the allied advance faltered and with the élite 1st SS Panzerdivision on its way, together with another armoured division, to reinforce the German defences, 'Garbo' told his control that 'the present operation, though a large-scale assault, is diversionary in character'. On reading the message, Hitler ordered the two divisions back to the Pas-de-Calais to defend against what he expected to be the main invasion thrust and awarded Pujol the Iron Cross. Had the two divisions continued to Normandy, the allies might well have been thrown back into the sea.[25]

Yet for all its success against Germany, detecting some two hundred of Hitler's agents in Britain, MI5 never uncovered the presence deep inside the British Establishment throughout the war of a ring of five top KGB agents including its own agent Anthony Blunt. Claims by Maxwell Knight, the veteran anti-Communist campaigner, in a 1941 report entitled 'The Comintern is not Dead', that there was a Soviet agent inside MI5 were ignored at an horrific cost.[26] The Double-Cross system was an unqualified success, but it did nothing for MI5's reputation. By the time the details emerged, that had already been damned by the failure to detect the Cambridge spy ring.

As the war came to an end, there were repeated mutterings about MI5 – even among those who were aware of its wartime success – possibly as a result of the knock-on effect from the earlier 'witch-finding'. One MI5 officer noticed 'a strong current of prejudice against MI5 in many prominent circles' and Lord Alanbrooke, the Chief of the Imperial General Staff, wrote in his diary that there was a 'grave danger of it falling into the clutches of unscrupulous political hands of which there are too many at present'.[27]

MI5 was deeply distrusted both by the Labour Party, which still harboured bitter memories of the Zinoviev Letter, and by the Conservatives. During the 1945 election campaign Churchill played on fears of the idea of a British secret police, warning that a Labour government 'would have to fall back on some form of Gestapo'.[28]

When Clement Attlee came to power, he ignored the internal favourite, Guy Liddell, and appointed Sir Percy Sillitoe, the Chief Constable of Kent, to head the service. No doubt it was a reassuring choice for the Labour leader. In his introduction to Sillitoe's autobiography, Attlee wrote that one of the key requirements for a Director-General of MI5 was 'a very lively appreciation of the rights of the citizen in a free country'. R. V. Jones, who, as Director of Scientific Intelligence, sat on the JIC with Sillitoe in the early 1950s, recalled once asking him if he would like support for more draconian powers. 'No,' he replied. 'If I had more power, it would turn Britain into a police state. That would be the worst thing for England.'[29]

Less reassuring was the secret report of the inquiry by Brigadier Sir Findlay Stewart, Chairman of the Security Executive, into the future of the intelligence services. 'The purpose of the Security Service is the Defence of the Realm and nothing else,' it said. 'From the very nature of the work, need for direction except on the very broadest lines can never rise above the level of Director-General . . . There is no alternative to giving him the widest discretion in the means he uses and the direction in which he applies them – always provided he does not step outside the law.'[30]

The London headquarters of MI5 had by now moved to Leconfield House in Curzon Street, Mayfair, and the staff evacuated to Blenheim during the war transferred there. It was to be the service's main base until 1972.[31]

One of MI5's biggest post-war headaches was the number of refugees coming in from Europe, many of whom were expected to be Soviet agents. Between 1950 and 1952 the service carried out a mass investigation into their backgrounds, interrogating more than 200,000 émigrés, the vast majority of whom had come from what had become the Soviet Bloc. Of those interrogated, 3023 were earmarked for internment should there be war with Russia. Operation Post Report was not just about looking for Soviet spies: MI6 was keen to send some of the refugees back into the Soviet Union as British agents. What it was definitely not about, however, was finding war criminals. In order to encourage the émigrés to tell the truth, they were given an assurance that they had 'nothing to fear by disclosing the facts about their past history and true identity'.[32]

With the defection of Igor Gouzenko, a cypher clerk at the Soviet Embassy in Ottawa, and a failed attempt at defection by Konstantin Volkov, the NKGB's deputy *Rezident* in Ankara, the end of the war also brought the first details of the extent to which the British Establishment had been penetrated by the Soviet intelligence services. Volkov claimed to have the names of seven Soviet wartime moles in British intelligence, and Gouzenko revealed that Alan Nunn May, a British atomic scientist, was working for the GRU, Soviet military intelligence. The fact that Nunn May, a Communist, had been allowed to work in such a secret field and the resultant American fears over poor British security led to the United States Congress passing the 1946 McMahon Act, which severely restricted exchanges of atomic information.[33]

In 1947 Attlee set up a Cabinet committee on subversive activities, GEN 183, and this began the process of weeding out Communists and Fascists from sensitive government posts. But it was a slow job, and even after the 1950 discovery of another atom spy, Klaus Fuchs, Attlee refused to sanction stronger measures. It was not until 1951 that the defections of Donald Maclean and Guy Burgess led to the more comprehensive process of 'positive vetting' being introduced for all sensitive posts.[34]

At the same time a re-examination of MI5's role by Sir Norman Brook, the Cabinet Secretary, recommended that the service be made responsible to the Home Secretary, ending an anomaly under which it had been responsible to no single government ministry and at the mercy of inter-departmental wrangles – in the words of Brook's predecessor, Maurice Hankey, 'something of a lost child'.[35]

Informing Sir Percy Sillitoe of the change, on 24 September 1952, Sir David Maxwell Fyfe, the new Conservative Home Secretary, laid down the ground rules which were to apply to MI5 until the Security Service Act was passed in 1989. 'The Security Service is part of the Defence Forces of the country,' he said. 'Its task is the Defence of the Realm as a whole, from external and internal dangers arising from attempts at espionage and sabotage, or from actions of persons and organizations, whether directed from within or without the country, which may be judged to be subversive to the State.'

Although the Maxwell Fyfe directive stressed that the Director-General should ensure that MI5's operations were apolitical and limited to what was absolutely necessary, it left the decisions on what actually constituted subversion or a threat to the Defence of the Realm entirely up to MI5 itself. It said, 'You and your staff will maintain the well-established convention whereby Ministers do not concern themselves with the detailed information which may be obtained by the Security Service in particular cases, but are furnished with such information only as may be necessary for the determination of any issue on which guidance is sought.'[36]

While many of Peter Wright's allegations in *Spycatcher* were simply not credible, his description of MI5 in the immediate wake of the 1952

Maxwell Fyfe directive certainly was. The training he received on joining the service in 1955, which included 'regular classes run for MI5 and MI6 in its lockpicking workshop', seemed remarkably similar to that given to earlier recruits by Inspector William Melville.

Although the very broad outlines of the Maxwell Fyfe directive may have been adhered to in Wright's MI5, Sir Findlay Stewart's exhortation that the Director-General should not 'step outside the law' clearly was not. Sir John Cuckney, who went on to become chairman of a number of prominent British companies, including Brooke Bond, Thomas Cook and Royal Insurance, began the training with a lecture on MI5's legal status, Wright recalled:

> 'It hasn't got one,' he told us bluntly. 'The Security Service cannot have the normal status of a Whitehall department because its work very often involves transgressing propriety or the law.' He made it very clear that MI5 operated on the basis of the 11th Commandment – 'Thou shalt not get caught' – and that in the event of apprehension there was very little that the office could do to protect its staff.[37]

Wright's description of how, in Operation Party Piece, his colleagues burgled the British Communist Party's membership files from a flat in Mayfair to photocopy them may appear scandalous today. But, with Churchill's Iron Curtain speech still ringing in people's ears, the operation doubtless seemed entirely reasonable to the 'pompous bowler-hatted civil servants' of the early 1950s.

Communism was seen as the main threat to the Defence of the Realm. The next two decades were to be dominated by Soviet penetration of the British Establishment and even of the intelligence services themselves. That was of far greater public concern at the time, and questions would more likely have been asked if MI5 had not 'bugged and burgled its way across London' to prevent it.

The service's reputation was badly damaged by a series of spy scandals in which it was seen as not doing enough to stop Soviet penetration. Between the defections of Guy Burgess and Donald Maclean in 1951 and that of Kim Philby twelve years later came the arrests of the Portland Spy Ring which was passing on submarine secrets from the Portland naval base; George Blake, an MI6 officer 'turned' by the Russians; and William Vassall, a homosexual Admiralty official blackmailed into passing secrets to the KGB. There was also the Profumo affair, when an MI5 operation to recruit the Soviet naval attaché in London became embroiled in the public scandal surrounding the relationship between Christine Keeler, a call-girl, and John Profumo, the Defence Secretary.[38]

There were some successes, during the counter-insurgency campaigns that marked the retreat from empire in the late 1940s and the 1950s. But these were mainly orchestrated by MI5's security liaison officers in its colonial outposts – Security Intelligence Middle East (SIME) in Cairo and Security Intelligence Far East (SIFE) in Malaya – and were anyway seen as being successes for the British Army rather than for MI5, which until the Denning Report into the Profumo affair was not even officially acknowledged to exist.[39]

Dick White, MI5 Director-General from 1953 to 1956, instigated a major reorganization of the Security Service. Henceforth the divisions would be known as branches. Technical support – including the 'watchers', the officers in charge of target surveillance, remained the responsibility of A Branch; B Branch became Personnel; C Branch was Security; D Branch took over Counter-espionage; E Branch was in charge of Security and Intelligence in the Colonies, which under the so-called Attlee Doctrine was solely an MI5 responsibility; and F Branch was charged with Counter-subversion, with orders from White to infiltrate left-wing organizations, including the Labour Party and the trade unions.[40]

White, who as head of both MI5 and MI6 and later as Britain's first Intelligence Co-ordinator dominated post-war British intelligence, had hoped that the reorganization would expunge the memory of the failures of the post-war era and restore morale within the service. But it was not to be. The Cambridge spy ring was to haunt MI5 for years to come. Following the defection in December 1961 of Anatoly Golitsyn, a KGB officer who told startled British intelligence officers that there were not three members but five, and the 1964 discovery that Anthony Blunt, a wartime member of MI5, was one of the so-called Ring of Five, the service turned in on itself in a series of investigations supervised by a joint MI5–MI6 working party known as the Fluency Committee. If the KGB had been happy to let Blunt leave MI5 at the end of the war, the mole-hunters reasoned, they must have had another Soviet agent in place.[41]

A number of the committee's mole-hunters – Wright among them – became inordinately influenced by the views of James Angleton, the head of the CIA's counter-espionage division, sharing his obsession that the British intelligence services were riddled with Soviet agents. Their main suspicion, that Roger Hollis, Director-General of MI5 from 1956 to 1965, was a long-term KGB agent, was eventually ruled out. It was Wright's refusal to accept the vindication of Hollis that eventually led to the publication of *Spycatcher*. But Wright was by no means alone in his continued belief that Hollis was a spy. Oleg Gordievsky, a former KGB colonel and long-term MI6 double agent, recalled that 'when the

KGB saw the chaos caused by the allegations against Hollis, their laughter made Red Square shake'.[42]

The service fought back, however, and, following the defection in 1971 of Oleg Lyalin – a KGB officer charged with identifying British targets for Spetsnaz (Soviet special forces) sabotage squads – succeeded in persuading the Foreign Office to expel ninety Soviet diplomats and exclude a further fifteen who were on leave. The expulsions were made on the grounds that the diplomats were *personae non gratae* – the traditional code for spies. The bulk of the KGB's London *Rezidentzura* had gone.

'In 1971, the golden age of KGB operations came to an end,' Gordievsky claimed later. 'The London residency never recovered from the expulsions. Contrary to the popular myths generated by media "revelations" about Soviet moles, during the next fourteen years . . . the KGB found it more difficult to collect high-grade intelligence in London than in almost any other Western capital.'[43]

# CHAPTER 5

# Subversion, Terror and Crime

> MI5's political surveillance role involves above all a fine judg-
> ment between what is subversion and what is legitimate dissent,
> which in my experience is unlikely to be found in those who
> live in the distorting and *Alice-through-the-Looking-Glass* world
> in which falsehood becomes truth, fact becomes fiction, and
> fantasy becomes reality.
>
> Roy Jenkins, former Home Secretary, speaking in 1993
> on his impressions of MI5

If MI5 was looking around for something to compensate for the
dearth of Russian spies, it soon found it. Within months of coming
to power in June 1970, the Conservative government of Edward
Heath was engaged in a bitter battle with the trade unions, declaring
a state of emergency in response to strikes by dockers and power
workers.

The 1971 Industrial Relations Act, designed to curb union power,
merely precipitated further stoppages, and more days were lost to strikes
in 1972 than at any time since 1919. When the 'flying pickets' deployed
during the 1972 miners' strike prevented coke from reaching the power
stations and Britain's industry had to be placed on a three-day week, the
government was close to panic.[1]

'At this time, many of those in positions of influence looked into the
abyss and saw only a few days away the possibility of the country being
plunged into a state of chaos not so very far removed from that which
might prevail after a minor nuclear attack,' Brendan Sewill, a special
adviser to Anthony Barber, the then Chancellor of the Exchequer, would
later recall.

> If that sounds melodramatic I need only say that – with the prospect
> of the breakdown of power supplies, food supplies, sewage, communi-
> cations, effective government and law and order – it was the analogy
> that was being used at the time. This is the power that exists to hold
> the country to ransom: it was fear of that abyss which had an important
> effect on subsequent policy.[2]

One of the measures taken by the Heath government was to ask MI5, which was in the process of moving its headquarters to Gower Street, Euston, North London, to increase surveillance of the trade unions and left-wing organizations. Sir Michael Hanley, the new Director-General of MI5, called a meeting of key members of F Branch, the counter-subversion department, 'to discuss the changing shape of MI5's priorities', Peter Wright would claim.

> The meeting began with a presentation from Hanley on the climate of subversion in the country and the growth of what he termed the 'far and wide left'. The prime minister and Home Office, he said, had left him in no doubt that they wanted a major increase in effort on this target. Hanley began to pour resources and men into F Branch and away from K Branch. Obtaining intelligence about domestic subversion, as opposed to catching spies, became our overriding priority.[3]

The Maxwell Fyfe directive, which still ruled MI5's operations, allowed it to act against 'persons and organizations, whether directed from within or without the country, which may be judged to be subversive to the State'. But by the mid-1970s there was growing concern over what exactly constituted subversion in MI5's eyes.[4] Unlike many of Peter Wright's allegations, the expansion of activities against 'subversive' organizations and individuals had already been confirmed by other former MI5 officers.[5]

Periodic claims, mainly in the left-wing press, that MI5 indulged in widespread bugging of the telephones of union leaders and organizations like the National Council for Civil Liberties were largely unsubstantiated and dismissed by most people as 'conspiracy theory'. One of the more bizarre claims was an allegation made by Sir Harold Wilson that, while Prime Minister, he had been the subject of a smear campaign by a group of right-wing MI5 officers. A subsequent claim that Wilson's office in 10 Downing Street had been bugged led to the whole story being dismissed as yet another conspiracy theory.[6]

But in April 1984 a spectacular court case set in train a series of revelations which showed that not every allegation made against MI5 could so easily be dismissed. Michael Bettaney, a young K Branch officer, was found guilty of attempting to pass secrets to the Russians. He had been arrested the previous September, having made three unsuccessful attempts to offer himself as a potential double agent, contacting Arkady Guk, the KGB's London *Rezident*, or head of station, directly.[7]

In messages dropped through the letter-box of Guk's London home, Bettaney employed typical agent tradecraft to lay out a complicated system of dead-letter-boxes and methods of communication that were to be used should Guk decide to accept his offer. In the first letter, Bettaney 'instructed Guk that he would find in the first-floor gents lavatory at the Academy One Cinema in Oxford Street, taped under the lid of the cistern, a canister containing exposed film of classified information', Sir Michael Havers QC, the British Attorney-General, told Bettaney's Old Bailey trial:

> If he did decide to accept, he was to place a drawing-pin (any colour) at the top of the right-hand banister of the stairs leading from platforms three and four at Piccadilly Underground Station. When the defendant checked the banister at Piccadilly Underground, there was no drawing-pin and he concluded 'that after consultation with the KGB's head-quarters in Moscow a decision had been taken that my offer should not be accepted'.[8]

In fact Guk had decided that Bettaney's approach was an attempted MI5 provocation, and he ignored both it and the next two attempts. But he mentioned it to fellow KGB officers, including Oleg Gordievsky, a long-term MI6 agent. Gordievsky informed his British handlers, and Bettaney was subsequently arrested.

Following his conviction, Bettaney issued a prepared statement which, among other things, alleged that MI5 'cynically manipulates the definition of subversion and thus abuses the provisions of its charter so as to investigate and interfere in the activities of legitimate political parties, the Trade Union Movement and other progressive organizations'.[9] The statement, which was full of pseudo-Soviet rhetoric, was widely discounted as an attempt by Bettaney to justify his attempted treachery and sparked little debate. But there was considerable discussion of the way in which senior MI5 officers had apparently ignored Bettaney's serious drink problem and the fact that he had become disillusioned to the point where he was openly denouncing MI5's activities to his colleagues. The Security Commission, set up in the wake of the Profumo affair to investigate such scandals, subsequently ordered a comprehensive overhaul of the service's personnel system.[10]

The debate led two of Bettaney's former colleagues to complain that he was not alone. There was widespread disillusionment among the service's younger officers, partly due to the intractably right-wing attitudes of its senior officers but mainly as a result of the role of F Branch.

Miranda Ingram, a former colleague of Bettaney's in K Branch, wrote that while the counter-espionage branch is 'the acceptable face of MI5 . . . it is in the area of domestic surveillance that problems can occur. This comes under F Branch. Working here means monitoring one's fellow-citizens.' There was concern among some officers over what was considered to be subversion, she said. But, 'in the prevailing right-wing atmosphere, an officer who dissents from the official line does not feel encouraged to voice his concern. He feels that it will be futile or detrimental to his career.'[11]

Ingram expanded on the theme in a subsequent newspaper article. 'Then come the doubts about the nature of your work,' she wrote:

> Reading private letters, listening to telephone calls – which to some is distasteful. Suddenly, at the age of 24, you have to decide whether to open a file on a fellow citizen. Your vetting assessment may ruin somebody's career. There are doubts about the legality of some of the work. It can be alarming for a recruit to be party to deliberate law-breaking, and particularly worrying to discover that it is 'wrong' to question such activity.[12]

The second officer, Cathy Massiter, had herself served in F Branch but had left after becoming 'increasingly at odds with myself over the nature of the work and its justifications'. Massiter alleged that she and other MI5 officers had been 'violating' the rules on political bias in an operation against the Campaign for Nuclear Disarmament.[13]

In March 1983 Michael Heseltine, the Defence Secretary, had set up an organization called Defence Secretariat 19, or DS19, to counter CND unilateralist propaganda. The unit approached MI5 for information on CND activists, and Massiter was ordered to help it. She expressed the view that it contravened the Maxwell Fyfe order to be 'absolutely free from any political bias or influence', but was told to get on with the job.

'It did begin to seem to me that what the Security Service was being asked to do was to provide information on a party political issue,' she said.

> Unilateral nuclear disarmament had been adopted as a policy by the Labour Party, a general election was in the offing, and it had been clearly stated that the question of nuclear disarmament was going to be an important issue there. It seemed to be getting out of control. This was happening not because CND as such justified this kind of treatment but simply because of political pressure. The heat was there for information about CND, and we had to have it.

Massiter described how any union taking strike action would routinely be subjected to MI5 surveillance. 'Whenever a major dispute came up – something at Fords or the mines, or the Post Office – immediately it would become a major area for investigation: What were the Communists doing in respect of this particular industrial action? And usually an application for a telephone check would be taken out on the leading comrade in the particular union concerned.'

She also revealed that two prominent members of the National Council for Civil Liberties, Harriet Harman, who has since become a leading Labour politician, and Patricia Hewitt, had been the subject of MI5 surveillance. Files would be routinely opened on anyone who was active within the NCCL.[14] Her revelations led the NCCL (now known as Liberty) to take the government to the European Court of Human Rights and – indirectly, since the government anticipated that the court would rule MI5's activities illegal – brought about the 1989 Security Service Act.[15]

It was clear from the testimony of Massiter and Ingram that not only was MI5 bugging people's telephone calls and opening their letters but many of those put under surveillance were not even guilty of the very broad definition of subversion that the service was using as a benchmark.

'You couldn't just concentrate on the subversive elements of CND,' Massiter said:

> You had to be able to answer questions on the non-subversive elements, and the whole thing began to sort of flow out into a very grey area. It highlights very clearly this extreme ambivalence between what the Security Service is there to do – what it perceives itself as being there to do: to study subversion – and what actually happens in practice, which is in effect to broaden this study quite a long way beyond those basic guidelines.[16]

Her allegations led to Leon Brittan, the then Home Secretary, admitting that people did not have to be behaving illegally or even contemplate doing so to find themselves the subject of an MI5 surveillance operation. 'Tactics which are not in themselves unlawful could be used with the aim of subverting our democratic system of government,' Brittan said.[17]

With MI5's reputation at an all-time low, it emerged that further revelations would appear in a new book by a former MI5 officer. Peter Wright's motives for writing *Spycatcher* were not to expose alleged 'dirty tricks' – far from it. Despite starting his career in 1955 as a scientific officer, apparently producing useful gadgets much in the manner of James Bond's fictional colleague 'Q', Wright had chaired the Fluency Committee and remained convinced that Hollis was a long-term Soviet agent. But when *Spycatcher* was finally published, after a protracted and, for the British government, ignominious battle through the Australian and British courts, it was Wright's allegations of an MI5 plot to destabilize Harold Wilson that made the headlines rather than the oft-repeated claims against Hollis.

Wright and Arthur Martin, the two leading mole-hunters, had given considerable credence to a claim by the KGB defector Anatoly Golitsyn that Hugh Gaitskell, Wilson's predecessor as Labour Party leader, had been murdered to allow Wilson to become Prime Minister. But the allegations of a plot against Wilson were damaged by Wright's own subsequent testimony. Interviewed by the BBC, he admitted that the *Spycatcher* claims of a plot were 'unreliable'. Asked about the figure given in the book of thirty officers who approved of the plot, he conceded that it was 'exaggerated'. 'The maximum number was eight or nine,' he said. 'Very often, only three.' Wright, who had written in *Spycatcher* that he was not involved in the plot, was then asked, 'How many people, when all the talking died down, were still serious in joining you in trying to get rid of Wilson?' He replied, 'One, I should say.'[18]

Even taking Wright's admission of exaggeration into account, *Spycatcher* only added to the impression of a Security Service that if not totally out of control was already a good way along that road. The inevitable concentration on the alleged Wilson plot and the fact that Massiter had already blown the whistle on F Branch's counter-subversion activities meant that little attention was given to Wright's account of the 1972 Hanley order to root out the 'far and wide left'.

But several senior politicians who had direct experience of working with MI5 while in government during the 1970s and had no record of subscribing to conspiracy theories expressed serious doubts over what was going on. Roy Jenkins, Home Secretary from 1974 to 1976, called for MI5 to 'be pulled out of its political surveillance role'.

'I had been doubtful of the value of that role for some time,' he told a 1989 House of Commons debate prompted by the *Spycatcher* allegations. 'I am convinced now that an organization of people who live in the fevered world of espionage and counter-espionage is entirely unfitted to judge between what is subversive and what is legitimate dissent.'

Even Edward Heath, who as Prime Minister had ordered the increase in the surveillance of 'subversives', said there were officers within MI5 'whose whole philosophy was ridiculous nonsense. If some of them were on the tube and saw someone reading the *Daily Mirror*, they would say, "Get after him, that is dangerous. We must find out where he bought it."'[19]

The politicians and the public had lost faith in MI5, and within the service itself there was widespread dismay both at the low esteem in which it was held and at its inability to respond to the various allegations being made in the press. John Day, a former K Branch officer who had left the service in 1982, described many of the allegations made at the time as 'stupid rubbish', adding that, 'while some of the criticism levelled at MI5 was undoubtedly deserved, often it was ill-informed.'[20]

Following the Bettaney case, Prime Minister Margaret Thatcher had

appointed Sir Antony Duff, the Chairman of the Joint Intelligence Committee, the body which co-ordinates British intelligence assessments, to
be the new Director-General of the Security Service, with a brief to
stop the rot. He spent the next two years replacing the emphasis on
counter-subversion with a major drive against terrorism. He also began
pushing for a more clear-cut system of legal accountability and some
form of oversight.[21]

Duff's reforms, with their avowed emphasis on dragging the Security
Service out of the old-boy network and into the real world, included the
recruitment of more young people and promoting women to senior posts
– among them Stella Rimington, who, ironically, had distinguished herself
as an assistant director in charge of monitoring 'subversive trade-union
activity' during the 1984–5 miners' strike and who was appointed to
the prestigious post of Director of K Branch, in charge of counter-
espionage.[22]

Mrs Thatcher was adamantly opposed to any suggestion that the intelligence services should be subjected to parliamentary oversight. Even
getting her to set up the Franks Committee which looked into intelligence-gathering during the Falklands War had, according to David
Owen, the former SDP leader, been 'like dragging teeth'. She did agree
to the Security Service Act – which was seen as imperative, given the
NCCL's case in the European Court – but insisted there should be no
further moves towards openness. 'I believe we should continue to enable
the security services to run in a secret way,' she said. 'After all, those
against whom they operate have the benefit of secrecy.'[23]

The Security Service Act reiterated that MI5 was responsible to the
Home Secretary and laid out its role as being 'the protection of national
security and, in particular, its protection against threats from espionage,
terrorism and sabotage, from the activities of agents of foreign powers
and from actions intended to overthrow or undermine parliamentary
democracy by political, industrial or violent means'.

While that was a reiteration of MI5's traditional role, two other parts
of the Act would later lead to further debate over MI5's future role.
These were an additional task to 'safeguard the economic well-being of
the United Kingdom' and a reference to passing on, presumably to the
police, any information that the service might come across which might
be useful in 'preventing or detecting serious crime'.

The Act also included an immunity clause to the effect that 'no entry
on or interference with property shall be unlawful if it is authorized by
a warrant issued by the Secretary of State' and, in a limited move towards
oversight, provided for a Commissioner and a tribunal of three lawyers
to investigate complaints. They would have to meet in camera and,

although the Commissioner had the power to award compensation against the Home Secretary, the government was not obliged to take any notice of what the tribunal decided. Nevertheless, the report would be published and, if adverse, might be expected to lead to criticism from politicians and the media.[24]

Sir Patrick Walker, who took over from Duff in 1987, had maintained his reforms.[25] MI5 was reorganized, with the responsibilities of the old F Branch, by now the basis of most of MI5's work, forming three separate branches: Counter-Terrorism (International); Counter-Terrorism (Irish and Other Domestic) and Counter-Subversion. The new role of counter-proliferation was included among the tasks of the Counter-Espionage Branch, and the old A Branch, which provided technical support, such as expertise in breaking and entry, bugging, and surveillance – the 'watchers' – remained much as it had been before.[26]

MI5's computer records were soon shown to be little better than Kell's Precautionary Index. In an operation reminiscent of the Second World War 'witch-finding activities' against German, Austrian and Italian refugees, the threat of Iraqi terrorism during the Gulf War led to deportation notices being served on a total of 167 Iraqi, Jordanian, Lebanese and Yemeni nationals.

No doubt a number of the Arab nationals served with the notices had represented some form of risk. Eight were Iraqi diplomats, among whom were almost certainly members of Da'Irat al Mukhabarat al Amah, the Iraqi intelligence organization. But, as in 1940, the vast majority were innocent. A total of 81 left Britain without exercising their option to appeal. Most of the remaining 86 were held either in police cells or behind barbed wire on Salisbury Plain until they were released on appeal, which occurred in 33 cases, or until the end of the war. Their quasi-internment raised a political storm when the paucity of the evidence against them began to emerge.[27]

Sir Philip Woodfield, the Security Service Commissioner, held an inquiry into the affair. His report was kept secret, but the Foreign Office, which had bitterly opposed the detentions, let it be known that he had been severely critical of MI5 over the poor quality of information in its files on the detainees.[28]

The controversy over the Gulf War internments was an embarrassing glitch amid the internal changes that were intended to modernize MI5 and ensure there was no repeat of the public-relations débâcle of the mid-1980s. The second stage of that rehabilitation process was not to be enacted until Sir Patrick's successor, Stella Rimington, took over as Director-General in 1992. Her appointment was the first to be announced publicly, and she issued a statement saying that, despite the end of the

Cold War, the service still had a difficult job to do. She was pleased to have been given 'the responsibility of leading the service in facing up to the challenges which the coming years will bring'.[29]

The first challenge MI5 faced if it were to maintain its empire in the post-Cold War world was to find a new lead role. Counter-terrorism, and in particular the fight against the IRA, seemed to fit the bill. The Security Service had for some time been lobbying hard to take control of all activities by the police, military and intelligence services directed against Irish terrorism. Amid complaints of chronic lack of co-ordination between the various factions fighting the IRA and its 'loyalist' counterparts, the Home Office had been considering taking responsibility for counter-terrorism intelligence operations on mainland Britain away from the police and giving it to MI5.

Several times the move was rejected, but with a full-scale turf battle being waged in the pages of the national press, and following substantial private lobbying by Mrs Rimington herself, MI5 won control over all operations against the IRA both at home and abroad. In May 1992 Kenneth Clarke, the Home Secretary, told the House of Commons that 'political change' – an apparent euphemism for the collapse of the Warsaw Pact and the resultant drop in espionage activity – had made it possible for MI5 to devote more resources to countering the IRA. There would be no conflict with the police, who would remain responsible for the collection of evidence and the arrest and prosecution of suspects. MI5 would share its intelligence on IRA activities with the Special Branch and the Anti-Terrorist Squad, Clarke said. It had been important to draw a line in the sand to prevent relations between MI5 and Special Branch 'festering'.[30]

With the battle to keep its resources secured, MI5's management board moved on to the next stage in the rehabilitation process. On 16 July 1993 Mrs Rimington held a press conference to launch a government brochure describing the role of MI5 and how it worked. In the introduction, she admitted the information it provided on the service was limited. 'There is, of course, a clear limit to what can be made public without either undermining its [MI5's] effectiveness, or else endangering its staff, and others who work closely with it.' But the brochure was being published 'to dispose of some of the more fanciful allegations surrounding its work'.

In fact the booklet, which looked for all the world like a company prospectus, did not do very much to dispel the 'fanciful allegations', apart from a specific denial that MI5 monitored the behaviour of people just because they were well-known or held positions of responsibility – presumably a reference to the royal family and the so-called 'Squidgy tapes'

Stella Rimington, who as Director-General from 1992 to 1996 gave MI5 a more public face

of telephone conversations between the Princess of Wales and a male friend – and a denial of Wright's allegations of a plot against Harold Wilson.

Nevertheless, the fact that only 5 per cent of the service's resources were taken up with subversion – a figure that was later reduced to just 3 per cent – would have gone a long way towards reassuring left-wing and trade-union activists. The remainder of the cake is split between: counter-espionage and counter-proliferation, 25 per cent; international terrorism, 33 per cent; and Irish and domestic terrorism, 39 per cent.[31]

Even former MI5 officers conceded that the booklet was a step in the right direction. 'If MI5 is moving towards more openness, two cheers,' said one. 'It may be a public relations exercise but if it makes the public aware of the good things the service is doing what is wrong with that? At least this might bring worthwhile criticism instead of the stupid rubbish that appeared during the *Spycatcher* episode to which nobody in the service could respond.'[32]

Clarke's hopes that giving the Security Service primacy in the battle against terrorism would prevent a 'festering' rivalry between MI5 and the police had meanwhile proved to be false. During a 1991 visit to Moscow, when she was Deputy Director-General (Operations), Mrs Rimington had held detailed discussions with her Russian opposite numbers on what the TASS news agency described as 'the fight

against international terrorism and drug trafficking'.[33] The reference
to 'drug trafficking' had set alarm bells ringing among senior police
officers, a number of whom, having noted the clause in the Security
Service Act on 'preventing or detecting serious crime', already suspected
that Mrs Rimington had a hidden agenda to turn MI5 into a British
version of the FBI.

Both the Home Office and Mrs Rimington herself denied that there
were any plans for MI5 to become involved in the investigation of organized or drugs-related crime. But the service's involvement appeared to
be confirmed by Baroness Park, a former member of MI6, who in
December 1993 told the House of Lords that both MI6 and MI5 were
reporting on 'the potentially destabilizing threat posed to our economy
and that of some dependent territories by drug trafficking and the conse-
quent laundering of dirty money'.[34]

As the moves towards greater accountability continued, with the
announcement that a new cross-party committee of privy counsellors
would provide a limited form of oversight of MI5's activities, Mrs Rimington kept up her efforts to improve the service's public reputation, appearing on television to give the 1994 Richard Dimbleby Lecture. It was a
careful mix of candour and Civil Service-speak which flitted between the
past and present tenses in order to put the best possible gloss on the
service's image and also included touches of dry humour.

Mrs Rimington worked hard in her lecture at dispelling the lingering
'fanciful allegations'. The service now always operated within the law,
she said. It did not keep watch on people simply because it disagreed
with their politics, nor did it subcontract operations out to evade legal
controls or monitor the activities of people with a high public profile 'on
the off chance ... that they might be at or even pose a risk'. This was
all said in the present tense, of course – and, given MI5's dubious past,
much of it could only have been honestly stated if it were.

She acknowledged this briefly, conceding that, yes, there may have
been occasional 'rotten apples' in the past, but in her MI5 there was no
group of 'mavericks' pursuing its own agenda, she said. Nor was the
service using the resources previously deployed in the Cold War to turn
its attention to the general public 'or for that matter anyone else about
whom we, or perhaps the government, feel uncomfortable. The idea is
quite frankly ludicrous. Just as ludicrous as the allegation that the service
carries out murder.'

In the only apparent allusion to the counter-subversion activities of the
1970s and early 1980s against organizations like CND and the National
Council for Civil Liberties, she said simply, 'The allegation that the
service investigated organizations which were not in themselves subvers-

ive is quite untrue. Our interest was in the subversives, not in the organizations they sought to penetrate.'[35]

At best that last statement was highly subjective. It scarcely squared
with Massiter's sworn affidavit on the work of the old F Branch. Nor
presumably would it have met with much sympathy from Roy Jenkins,
who had a few months earlier told Parliament that he retained grave
doubts over the service's ability to distinguish between subversion and
legitimate dissent. 'I experienced in the Security Service what I can best
describe as an inherent lack of frankness, an ingrowing monoculture
and a confidence-destroying tendency to engage in the most devastating
internal feuds,' he said. The political surveillance role involved 'a fine
judgement . . . which in my experience is unlikely to be found in those
who live in the distorting and *Alice-through-the-Looking-Glass* world in
which falsehood becomes truth, fact becomes fiction, and fantasy becomes
reality'.

But, in the real world of spin-doctored public relations, it was not what
Mrs Rimington or anyone else said that mattered. It was the fact that
she had been prepared to stand up in front of the television cameras and
justify her existence – albeit without anyone questioning her statements
– that would grab the headlines, take MI5 a step further down the road
to public rehabilitation and, perhaps more importantly, improve her stock
still further among the politicians and senior civil servants who would
decide the service's future role.

For, as Mrs Rimington would already have known, covert negotiations
on a peace settlement with the IRA were by now well advanced, and,
with some 40 per cent of the service's resources devoted to domestic
terrorism, peace in Northern Ireland represented a considerable threat
to MI5's future. The announcement of the IRA cease-fire and the official
start of the Northern Ireland peace process, in September 1994, brought
renewed speculation that the service was about to move into the area of
serious crime and on to the police's patch.[36]

As MI5 prepared to move from the various offices it had occupied
during the past thirty years, mostly dotted around its Gower Street headquarters, into the new home at Thames House on Millbank, which had
been refurbished and specially kitted out at a cost of £245 million, it
found itself at an important watershed.[37]

There were inevitable parallels between similar situations in 1919, 1946
and 1972. On all three occasions MI5 had lost a major part of its work
at a stroke: in 1919 and 1946 by the end of the two world wars, and in
1972 by the expulsion of the bulk of the KGB's London *Rezidentzura*.
In 1972 the fear of left-wing subversion had provided a replacement
activity for MI5; in 1946 it was the Soviet threat and the coming Cold

War. The salutary lesson, to be avoided at all cost, was 1919, when the new role of countering Bolshevism had gone to the police Special Branch – albeit in the guise of Basil Thomson's Directorate of Intelligence – leading to horrendous cuts in MI5's budget and staff.

The Security Service now found itself under a similar threat. The drop in counter-espionage activities resulting from the end of the Cold War had been adequately compensated for by the increase in counter-terrorism and the 1992 take-over of the war against the IRA. But, with both the republicans and the government apparently moving inexorably towards a peace agreement, it was clear that MI5 had the choice of making drastic cuts in staff or finding a new role.

In November 1994 Mrs Rimington emerged from the shadows again, to deliver the 1994 James Smart Lecture – and with it the first shots in a campaign to ensure that this time MI5 did not lose out to the police. Addressing an audience of senior police officers, she suggested a more expanded role for MI5 in areas that would normally be the territory of the police.

Senior police officers defended their patch by stressing that their role of collecting evidence and then making arrests was very different from that of the Security Service, which tends to keep suspects in place rather than have them arrested. Intelligence officers regard having a comprehensive picture of what is going on as more important than preventing crime, and have a poor record of collecting evidence. But Mrs Rimington said it was wrong and misleading to make too sharp a distinction between the

Thames House, the current home of MI5

spy and the detective. 'The Security Service is fully committed to supporting the police in detecting and preventing crime and preserving law and
order,' she said. 'Criminal investigation can be a valuable focus for intelligence work, and equally intelligence can be converted into evidence.'[38]

It was those two carefully phrased sentences which convinced senior
police officers that she aimed to move into other areas such as combating
organized crime, drug trafficking and money-laundering. They knew they
were vulnerable to attack. Mrs Rimington had proved to be an extremely
effective Whitehall infighter, and she was able to argue with justification
that, like the various agencies fighting the IRA before the 1992 MI5
take-over, police intelligence was poorly co-ordinated, with no acknowledged overall supremo.

Their concern was not eased by an endorsement from Michael Howard,
the Home Secretary, of Mrs Rimington's sentiments. While the Secret
Service and the police had distinct roles and functions 'these differences
should not be exaggerated,' he said. 'The two services should be seen as
complementary and ... operating in a broadly similar field.' A secret
Home Office report had just denounced the National Criminal Intelligence Service, which was supposed to be co-ordinating police intelligence, as ineffective and impotent, dependent on other parts of the police
force to carry out actual operations.[39]

But police officers argued that the MI5 officers they had worked with
seemed to have no real understanding of what would be required in terms
of evidence if a case were to come to court.[40] Mrs Rimington had assured
senior police officers that MI5's procedures for gathering, recording and
collating intelligence had been tightened to ensure it could be used effectively as evidence. But Special Branch officers said that, despite Kenneth
Clarke's 1992 insistence that the police would remain in charge of evidence, attempts to give the increasingly young and highly ambitious
MI5 desk officers advice on the difficult process of collecting evidence
frequently led to 'friction'.[41]

In the mid-1990s another reorganization split responsibility for the
service's work between two deputy director-generals: one in charge of
intelligence operations, and the other covering administration. But in
early 1996 one of these posts was abolished, leaving the other deputy
controlling four operational branches. A Branch, intelligence resources
and operations, now provides technical support, such as expertise in
breaking and entry, bugging, and surveillance. D Branch, counter-
espionage and all other non-terrorist threats, covers areas such as organized crime, subversion and proliferation. (This branch also deals with
protective security, providing vetting for government departments and
defence contractors, advising on computer security, and investigating

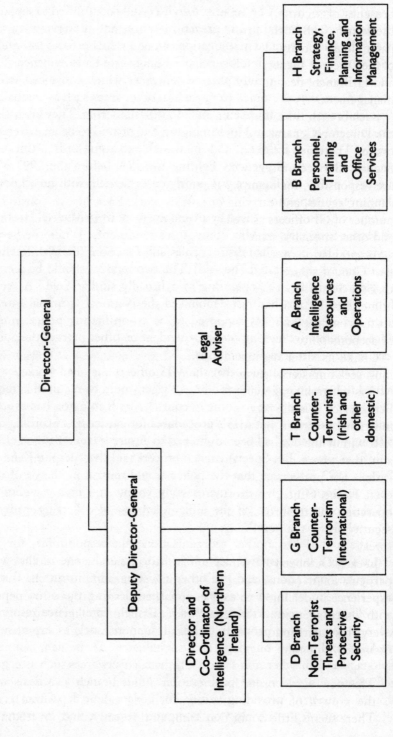

Organization of MI5

Director-General

Deputy Director-General

Legal Adviser

Director and Co-Ordinator of Intelligence (Northern Ireland)

D Branch Non-Terrorist Threats and Protective Security

G Branch Counter-Terrorism (International)

T Branch Counter-Terrorism (Irish and other domestic)

A Branch Intelligence Resources and Operations

B Branch Personnel, Training and Office Services

H Branch Strategy, Finance, Planning and Information Management

*Source:* Security Service, January 1996

breaches of security.) G Branch handles international terrorism; while the fourth, T Branch, covers domestic terrorism and in particular Irish paramilitary activity. Two other branches come under the direct control of the Director-General: B Branch, personnel, training and office services; and H Branch, dealing with strategy, finance, planning and information management.

Each branch is headed by a director, and these directors together with the Director-General and his deputy make up the service's management board. There are a total of 340 'General Intelligence' staff – the actual Security Service officers who form the core management structure and are responsible, for example, for monitoring intelligence investigations, running agents, and carrying out policy work. Each branch consists of a number of GI officers as well as a wide range of administrative, technical and other specialist staff.[42]

As speculation over MI5's search for new roles mounted, Deputy Assistant Commissioner John Howley, the head of Special Branch, accepted that the Security Service had a part to play in the investigation of serious crime. But he insisted that 'There would need to be a difference of attitude on the part of MI5 in coming to terms with the different standards of accountability.'[43]

Unlike its sister organization, the Secret Intelligence Service, which must seek ministerial permission before undertaking any new operations, MI5 is self-tasking. Having been given its remit in terms of the Security Service Act, it is the service's own management board that sanctions the individual branches' proposed operations, having satisfied itself that each falls within the Act, that it is a cost-effective method of achieving the aim, that where necessary the evidence will stand up in court, and that it does not pose unnecessary risks.[44] But the lack of any ministerial, or even Home Office, control over the decision to undertake a specific operation and the broad, if not open-ended, mandate to protect national security leave the service itself to decide what constitutes a security threat.

In early October 1995 Mrs Rimington again laid out her stall for MI5's participation in operations against organized crime, stressing the service's experience in dealing with transnational terrorism through co-operation with other agencies. 'The changing international climate means that everywhere perceptions of the threats to national security are being re-examined,' she said:

This new world order has created conditions which also encourage the growth of what is increasingly being called 'organized crime'. There seems little doubt that crime of this sort will grow, feeding on the increasing ease and speed of communications and travel and the weakening of controls.

Countering the threat successfully will require the same methods which have been developed to deal with the more familiar threats such as terrorism. This means the same strategic approach, the same investigative techniques. But above all it means the same close national and international co-operation between security intelligence and law-enforcement agencies.

It later emerged that those comments had also been designed to reinforce the case for her chosen successor, Stephen Lander, amid suggestions that a senior police officer might better cope with the changes required if MI5 were to take on organized crime. Mr Lander, as a former director in charge of counter-terrorism, had been responsible for setting up the close links with other agencies that Mrs Rimington said would be vital in combating serious crime.[45]

A week after Mrs Rimington's lecture, John Major announced that the government was planning to change the legislation to give the Security Service the role it wanted in fighting crime, working with the National Criminal Intelligence Service under the control of the newly created Home Office Directorate of Organized and International Crime. In fact, despite the lack of adequate legislation, MI5 had already mounted a number of criminal operations in support of the police.[46]

The willingness of the Home Office – which, while it appears to have only very loose control over MI5, does at least have a firm grip on NCIS – to allow this to occur in advance of legislation is not reassuring. Nor is the new Act itself. MI5 may now investigate crime if it:

> involves the use of violence, results in substantial financial gain or is conduct by a large number of persons in pursuit of a common purpose; or the offence or one of the offences is an offence for which a person who has attained the age of 21 and has no previous convictions could reasonably be expected to be sentenced to imprisonment for a term of three years or more.

There may just be a few too many ors in that brief, since it appears to sanction operations against a wide variety of criminals, including wife-batterers and bosses with their fingers in the company pension fund – people few would regard as a threat to the security of the state.

There are also legitimate concerns over MI5's large armoury of highly sophisticated electronic surveillance equipment, most of which is so Top Secret that it has to be protected in court by the use of public immunity certificates – the so-called gagging orders which featured so heavily in the Scott Inquiry into the Matrix-Churchill affair. How far do these new high-tech surveillance gadgets infringe on our civil liberties? Telephone taps and postal intercepts are authorized by government ministers under the 1985 Interception of Communications Act and their use is recorded in an annual report. But what controls are there over these new electronic surveillance techniques? Who is watching the watchers now?

Mrs Rimington has made great play of the fact that only 3 per cent of MI5's resources is used against what she judges to be 'subversives'. But 3 per cent of a budget estimated at between £50 million and £200 million will pay for an awful lot of surveillance, and Mrs Rimington's explanation of the CND and National Council for Civil Liberties operations displayed a rather broad view of what might be acceptable in terms of monitoring such activities.[47]

In addition, it is clear from the cases that have so far come before the courts that many of those people who come under MI5 surveillance are totally innocent of any crime. In Mrs Rimington's own words, 'It is almost inevitable that national security intelligence work which is based on the use of covert sources and techniques will involve some infringement of the civil liberties of those who are under investigation.' She has dismissed suggestions that an underemployed MI5 has turned its attention to the general public, but that does not mean that individual members of the public might not from time to time find themselves caught innocently in an MI5 surveillance operation on one of its legitimate targets.[48]

One former MI5 officer argued persuasively that this was to some extent inevitable. 'Spies, subversives and even terrorists do not suddenly appear in their true light, crying out to be investigated,' he said:

> In an espionage case, information may point to half a dozen individuals who, to some degree, fit the often meagre criteria available. So all six have to be investigated. If the real spy is identified the others are innocent and in due course their records will be destroyed. If there is no firm identification, the records of the six will have to be retained in case a new lead comes to light in the future. The young man collecting funds in a north London pub for Sinn Fein may be no more than an Irish nationalist. But one day he may be involved in planting a bomb. Do you ignore this possibility?

MI5's new enemies already include those members of Britain's Irish, Asian and Arab communities it suspects of supporting terrorism, foreign students on courses that might improve their countries' military might, and refugees from east-European states still active in the espionage field, not to mention those groups on the far left and far right still deemed to be subversive. A full-blooded extension of this already large group to include all those involved in 'serious' crime would leave few areas of British life free from surveillance, and large numbers of innocent members of the public would find themselves subject to Mrs Rimington's 'almost inevitable' infringement of their civil liberties.[49]

The Security Service Act may give MI5 a new cloak of respectability, but behind it there is ample opportunity, whether or not it is being taken, to wield the same old dagger. The Act was largely welcomed by MI5 officers, but not the least of the reasons for this was the fact that those of their activities which might previously have been regarded as illegal now had official rather than unofficial sanction. 'These were not some private initiatives by MI5 but were accepted by all governments in the past,' one said. 'Thank goodness they are now publicly acknowledged by the immunity clause in the Security Service Act.'[50]

MI5's need for a new role is not urgent. After an initial post-Cold War lull, the activities of the Russian intelligence services in Britain have again increased, and even if the peace process were to succeed it would be a long time before there could be any reduction in intelligence activities against the IRA. There would also be maverick hardliners on both the loyalist and the republican sides who would need to be kept under surveillance.[51]

Ministers and civil servants could easily find they have made a mistake in allowing the Security Service to increase the scope of its activities without a corresponding increase in its accountability. John Alderson, the former Chief Constable of Devon and Cornwall, suggested in the wake of Mrs Rimington's James Smart Lecture that her attempts to muscle in on crime could easily turn MI5 into a 'secret police':

> These proposals are but tiny steps towards the fashioning of a police instrument which ultimately could damage even democracy itself. To minimize the differences between the political police and the ordinary civil police in a democracy gives hostages to fortune. Political police seek to infiltrate agents and informers into all aspects of social and political life. What we could end up with is a secret police force.[52]

# CHAPTER 6

# Sharp Practice and Green Ink

Between the wars, the profession and practice of espionage did not much change. Invisible inks and false beards were still standard issue.

Robert Cecil, 'C's War', in *Intelligence and National Security*, Vol. 1, No. 2 (May 1986)

The head of the Secret Service Bureau's foreign department, Captain Mansfield Cumming, set up his headquarters in Whitehall Court, off Trafalgar Square. 'A lift whisked us to the top floor, above which additional superstructures had been built for war emergency offices,' wrote Sir Paul Dukes of his recruitment as a spy. 'I had always associated rabbit warrens with subterranean abodes, but here in this building I discovered a maze of burrow-like passages, corridors, nooks and alcoves, piled higgledy-piggledy on the roof.'[1]

Cumming was known only by the initial letter of his surname. Like the majority of 'C''s officers, Dukes regarded him with a great deal of affection, despite his abrupt manner and numerous eccentricities, which included a predilection for writing all his memos and instructions in green ink.

'This extraordinary man was short of stature, thick-set with grey hair half covering a well-rounded head. His mouth was stern and an eagle eye, full of vivacity, glanced – or glared as the case may be – piercingly through a gold-rimmed monocle,' Dukes wrote. 'Awe inspired as I was by my first encounter, I soon learned to regard "the Chief" with feelings of the deepest personal admiration. He had only one leg, but this did not deter him from driving his high-powered car at breakneck speed about the streets of London to the terror of police and pedestrians alike.'[2]

Initially, the highest priority was to obtain intelligence on German naval activity, and the foreign department was subordinated to the Admiralty. But one officer claimed that the work was 'severely handicapped by the exiguous funds available' and by the hostility of the Foreign Office, which remained reluctant to allow its staff abroad to involve themselves in secret service work. But, in spite of this handicap, the British intelligence system was, 'on the whole, wonderfully efficient ... every "surprise" which the Germans sprang upon us at sea was foretold and elucidated in full detail'.

The German network was based around three or four British officers and a network of stringers whose work was 'by no means as melodramatic as certain writers have pictured them', the former officer explained to readers of the *Daily Telegraph* in a series of articles on the 'Work of the Secret Service':

> A great deal of information, and that not the least valuable, was collected by perfectly legitimate means. The newspapers often contained, in spite of careful censorship, service news which conveyed useful facts to the trained reader. Again a trip round Kiel harbour, or along the waterfront of Hamburg or Bremen, where the great shipyards are situated, rarely failed to bring to light some new development of importance.
>
> Occasionally, however, it was necessary to resort to less overt measures.[3]

Cumming had four agents based in Brussels, controlled by Henry Dale Long, or 'L' – an experienced officer who had previously served under Melville as the military intelligence department's man in Africa. There was also a Rotterdam bureau headed by Richard Tinsley, or 'T', the owner of a successful shipping business. When war broke out in August 1914, the networks in Brussels and Germany collapsed and T's Rotterdam base became the centre of the European operations, although 'there still remained in the enemy's country a few courageous men, who taking their lives in their hands continued to keep German and Austrian naval affairs under observation'.[4]

The problems caused by the loss of most of 'C''s European networks were exacerbated when he was involved in a serious car crash while driving back from a visit to the headquarters of the British Expeditionary Force in France. Cumming's son was killed, and he himself was so badly injured that one of his legs had to be amputated, putting him out of action for several months. In his absence both the Army and the Navy set up their own independent 'secret services', and by the time Cumming had recuperated there were three separate and largely uncoordinated bodies all vying with each other to produce intelligence.[5]

He set about rebuilding his own intelligence system, with networks in Holland, Belgium and Switzerland supplementing the information provided by those agents left behind in Germany.

The author Somerset Maugham, one of the British spies based in Switzerland, created the fictional hero Ashenden based on his wartime service. Ashenden, who shared a cover-name, a London address and a number of agents with his creator, was based in Geneva, sending freelance stringers into Germany to collect information from which he compiled 'long reports which he was convinced no-one read, till having inadvertently slipped a jest into one of them he received a sharp reproof for his levity'.[6]

Captain Mansfield Cumming, the first head of MI6 and the original 'C', as depicted in a portrait which still hangs in his successor's office

If the intelligence reports were at least read, they were seldom passed on to the departments that needed them. Even when they were, the intelligence was frequently not believed. When one agent based in Germany reported, entirely accurately, that the Kaiser's naval gunners had developed a superior new targeting system, the Admiralty was dismissive, claiming that 'shooting of the quality detailed in his report was absolutely impossible . . . and that, in effect, he had been hoodwinked'.[7]

Cumming's department also maintained a number of agents in the United States, where, despite a Royal Navy blockade, the Germans were attempting to obtain supplies and war *matériel*. Controlled by Sir William Wiseman, the station chief in New York, and his deputy, Major Norman

Thwaites, the British spies kept a close watch on German commercial activities and the cargo ships trapped inside the blockade.

'Persons in the employ of the British Intelligence Service were stationed at every port on the Atlantic coast of the United States and in consequence no movement of any enemy ship could take place without almost instant notification to British headquarters, the locality of which had better not be divulged,' the former agent wrote:

> Many of the people who kept watch and ward at these ports were humble individuals who performed a very dangerous duty from purely patriotic motives. The writer has in mind one person who was responsible for observing enemy shipping at a port not a hundred miles from New York.
>
> Although a working man, his despatches and memoranda sent to headquarters were standard examples of terse English, reflecting the keenest powers of observation. For two and a half years, he performed his duties admirably, though in constant danger from the machinations of the Central European agents, who swarmed in the Eastern States. Then one morning, his body was found floating in the dock, riddled with bullets.[8]

Wiseman developed close relations with both American intelligence and President Woodrow Wilson, pioneering the links formalized during the Second World War and which still exist to this day.'[9]

In January 1916 the War Office had reorganized its intelligence operations, absorbing Cumming's 'Secret Service' into its Directorate of Military Intelligence. But by the end of the war, although still being referred to by its military intelligence designation of MI1c, the service was subordinated to the Foreign Office, where it had become known as the Secret Intelligence Service. The main target for its operations was now Russia, where its agents included Dukes and the legendary Sidney Reilly.[10]

Dukes, a fluent Russian speaker, managed during a brief ten-month mission to the Soviet Union not only to join the Communist Party but also to pass himself off as a member of the Tcheka, the early Soviet predecessor of the KGB. He had been talent-spotted during a spell as a diplomat in the Soviet Union, and he described how he was shipped back home to be recruited by Cumming's deputy, Lieutenant-Colonel Freddie Browning:

> The Colonel, to my stupefaction, informed me immediately that I had been recalled to London because I was to be invited to work in the Secret Intelligence Service. 'We have reason to believe that Russia will not long be open to foreigners,' he explained. 'We want someone to

remain there to keep us informed of the march of events.' Besides general conditions, he told me, I should have to report on changes of policy, the attitude of the population, military and naval matters, what possibilities there might be for an alteration of regime, and what part Germany was playing. As to the means by which I should re-enter the country, under what cover I should live, and how I should send out reports, it was left to me to make suggestions.[11]

Although Dukes was probably regarded by Cumming as his best agent in post-revolutionary Russia, the most famous was undoubtedly Sidney Reilly. Despite his Irish name, Reilly was in fact born in Odessa in March 1874. He came to Britain in his twenties, acquiring a British passport and his new identity by claiming to be the son of an Irish father and a Russian Jewish mother. By the early 1900s he was combining extremely dubious business activities with even more dubious espionage activities on behalf of a variety of governments. There have been suggestions that at one time or other between 1903 and 1917 he worked for the Japanese, Russian, German and British governments – in some cases simultaneously.[12]

Reilly's activities – in government service, in business and in love – were exaggerated beyond belief, both by himself and by his biographers. But they were nevertheless colourful. 'He's been written off by historians by and large,' one former SIS officer said:

But he has been greatly underrated. He was very, very good – a very able agent and a far more serious operator than the impression given by the myth. Historians do have this tendency to write off something that has been made to appear glamorous. He was unusual but I don't think he was glamorous. He was a bit of a crook, you could almost say, certainly sharp practice. But as an agent he was superb.

After spending the years before the war in St Petersburg – allegedly combining the job of Russian agent for a firm of German shipbuilders with intelligence work for the British – Reilly had sailed for America, where he appears to have spent much of the war mixing weapons procurement for the tsarist government with sabotage operations against US factories that might be blamed on German agents and thereby hasten America's entry into the war.

When Wiseman was asked by American intelligence in July 1917 what he knew of Reilly, he replied:

[he] claims to be a British subject but doubt has been cast upon this. For the last two years, he has been mixed up with various scandals

in connection with the purchase of Russian munitions here and his reputation is a bad one. Reilly is said to have been at Port Arthur in 1903 where he is suspected by the Russians of acting as a spy for the Japanese. While in this country, during the present war, he has been mixed up with various undesirable characters and it would not be the least surprising if he was employed by enemy agents in propaganda or other activities.

Sydney Reilly

Since the available evidence suggests that by now Reilly was, at the very least, in close contact with MI1c, this could only be disinformation and strongly suggests that his sabotage activities were undertaken on behalf of the British. So too does the fact that, with America now having entered the war, Reilly returned to London with the assistance of Thwaites and within months was in Russia working for Cumming as agent ST-1. The October Revolution had ended Russia's part in the war, allowing the Germans to concentrate on the western front, so the British were anxious to bring the new government back on board.[13]

'In the spring of 1918, on returning from a mission, I found my superiors awaiting me with some impatience,' Reilly wrote:

I was instructed to proceed to Russia without delay. The process of affairs in that part of the world was filling the allies with consternation. My superiors clung to the opinion that Russia might still be brought to her right mind in the matter of her obligations to her allies. Agents from France and the United States were already in Moscow and Petrograd working to that end.[14]

Reilly was having none of it. Fanatically anti-Communist, and ever anxious to increase his own importance, he reported back to Cumming that defeating Germany was of minor significance compared to preventing the spread of Bolshevism. 'Will the people of England never understand?', he wrote:

The Germans are human beings; we can afford to be even beaten by them. Here in Moscow there is growing to maturity the arch enemy of the human race . . . At any price, this foul obscenity which has been born in Russia must be crushed out of existence. Peace with Germany? Yes, peace with Germany, peace with anybody. There is only one enemy. Mankind must unite in a holy alliance against this midnight terror.[15]

Robert Bruce Lockhart, the head of the British mission to Russia, was horrified when Reilly sparked off a diplomatic incident by marching up to the Kremlin gate and demanding to see Lenin. 'Asked for his credentials, he declared that he had been sent specially by Mr Lloyd George to obtain first-hand news of the aims and ideals of the Bolsheviks,' Bruce Lockhart wrote. 'The British government was not satisfied with the reports it had been receiving from me. He had been entrusted with the task of making good the defects.'

Told of the incident by a furious Bolshevik Commissar for Foreign Affairs, Lockhart at first thought that Reilly must be a madman masquerading as a British agent, but promised that he would investigate. 'That same evening, I sent for [Lieutenant Ernest] Boyce, the head of the Intelligence Service, and told him the story. He informed me that the man was a new agent who had just come out from England. I blew up in a storm of indignation.'[16]

Nevertheless, Lockhart and Reilly were to become involved in one of the greatest spy scandals of all time – the so-called Lockhart Plot. The British head of mission confessed to a grudging admiration for Reilly's style. 'He was a man of great energy and personal charm, very attractive to women and very ambitious. I had not a high opinion of his intelligence. His knowledge covered many subjects, from politics to art, but it was superficial. On the other hand, his courage and indifference to danger were superb.'[17]

By mid-1918 most of the allied representatives in Russia had given up all hope of persuading the Bolsheviks to join the fight against Germany, and a number of plans were being made to try to subvert the new government. Two Latvian soldiers then made contact with the British naval attaché in Petrograd asking for British support for the anti-Bolshevik underground.[18]

The two 'walk-ins' were sent to Lockhart, who claims to have simply passed them on to Reilly. The full extent of Lockhart's involvement is far from clear. His own published account seeks to distance him from the whole affair – and indeed from anything but the most insubstantial involvement in espionage and covert operations – but his reports to the Foreign Office portray a different picture, recording various attempts to fund and support the anti-Bolshevik underground.[19]

Since the Latvian regiments were being used to police Moscow, Reilly saw the two officers as a golden opportunity and held a series of meetings with them, trying to persuade them to help overthrow Lenin. Lockhart, who admitted discussing the plans with his French counterpart, claimed to have 'categorically turned down' any such suggestion. 'Reilly was warned specifically to have nothing to do with so dangerous and doubtful a move.'[20]

But this seems to have been another in a long history of 'deniable operations' carried out by the intelligence services – a tactic in which Reilly clearly specialized. Lockhart was in fact present at a number of meetings with the two Latvian officers, and it was his request to meet a senior officer of Moscow's 'praetorian guard' which drew the British irrevocably into a Russian trap.

For the two Latvian 'walk-ins' were in fact Tcheka *agents provocateurs*. Their mission had been to infiltrate the underground, but by now Feliks Dzerzhinsky, the head of the Tcheka, had spotted an opportunity to dismantle not only the resistance but also the allies' spy networks by means of a 'provocation', a sting operation designed to entice foreign agents into illegal activities that could be used to discredit their employers.

In theory, Dzerzhinsky had himself banned such practices, chiefly because of their widespread use against the Bolsheviks themselves by the Okhrana, the tsarist secret police. But with both Reilly and Lockhart convinced that the Latvians were genuine the opportunity was clearly too good to miss. When Lockhart demanded to speak to a senior officer, another Tcheka agent, Colonel E. P. Berzin of the Latvian Special Light Artillery Division, was brought into the scheme with a brief to draw the conspirators into a plot to assassinate Lenin.[21]

There is some evidence to suggest that British intelligence seriously considered killing the Russian leader, although George Hill, a War Office agent who was also involved in the plot, claimed Reilly was insistent that, if at all possible, none of the Bolshevik leaders was to be killed. 'He proposed to march them through the streets of Moscow bereft of their lower garments in order to kill them by ridicule.'[22]

Whatever the extent of Reilly's real plans, Dzerzhinsky's were brought to a premature halt by an apparently unrelated, but very nearly successful, assassination attempt on Lenin. The Tcheka began rounding up all those involved in the plans to overthrow the Bolshevik leader. Reilly and Hill both evaded capture and made their way back to Britain on false passports. But their Russian agents and the counter-revolutionary underground were less lucky. The Tcheka executed many hundreds of opponents of the regime and wiped out all of Hill's fourteen agents and couriers.

Meanwhile, *Pravda* announced the discovery of a widespread Anglo-French conspiracy to overthrow the Bolsheviks, shoot Lenin and Trotsky, and set up a military government allied to the West and hostile to Germany. Lockhart had provided a total of 1,200,000 roubles to fund a counter-revolution, *Pravda* said. 'The intention of the allies as soon as they had established their dictatorship in Moscow was to declare war on Germany and force Russia to fight again.'[23]

On their return to Britain, Reilly was awarded the Military Cross and Hill the Distinguished Service Order. Lockhart meanwhile set about distancing himself from the whole affair. 'My experiences of the war and of the Russian revolution have left me with a very poor opinion of secret service work,' he wrote. 'Doubtless, it has its uses and its functions, but political work is not its strong point. The buying of information puts a premium on manufactured news. But even manufactured news is less dangerous than the honest reports of men, who, however brave and however gifted as linguists, are frequently incapable of forming a reliable political judgement.'

MI1c believed that Bruce Lockhart was to blame for the collapse of the scheme. 'He very quickly involved the French and there seems little doubt that the French then brought in a French correspondent who was actually in touch with the *Tcheka*,' a former SIS officer who had studied the files said.

In a sense, Reilly was landed in it by Bruce Lockhart. I think Bruce Lockhart was very glad to have got away and not got tarred with Reilly's brush as it were. There is a slight smell around that whole period. The French were probably the culprits in that they were very slack about security and they produced this correspondent who was supposedly working for them but was also working for the Russians. It all came unstuck then.

Despite his MC, Reilly found that he was no longer held in high regard either by the Foreign Office or even by Cumming. His rampant anti-Bolshevism and his taste for *Boy's Own* schemes made him at best unreliable, at worst dangerous. Reilly applied for a full-time post with MI1c, telling Cumming, 'I venture to think that the state should not lose my services. I would devote the rest of my life to this wicked work.' But his offer was declined, and he spent the next seven years mixing his business schemes with intermittent freelance jobs, mainly involving further hopeless plots to overthrow the Soviet government which – despite a consistent record of failure – convinced the Russian intelligence service, by then known as the OGPU, that he was a top British agent.

Seven years after the Lockhart Plot, Soviet intelligence lured Reilly into a second, and this time fatal, deception operation. The Trust – supposedly a secret White Russian opposition group – had been created by the OGPU in order to penetrate the pro-monarchist émigré groups, to control their activities and to uncover the remaining opposition contacts inside Russia. Reilly, working with Ernest Boyce, now the secret service station chief in Helsinki, agreed to cross the border into Russia to meet the Trust's leadership. What happened is still not clear, but there seems little doubt that at some point Reilly was shot dead – possibly resisting arrest, since a show trial featuring Britain's 'master spy' would have had inestimable value for the Russians.[24]

In 1921 a Secret Service Committee set up to consider the post-war future of intelligence handed control over all foreign espionage operations to Cumming's department, still nominally subordinate to the Foreign Office, although now using the military covername MI6 by which it was to become more commonly known.[25]

The interests of the two main consumer departments – the War Office and the Admiralty – were protected by ensuring that they would take turns in providing the Chief of the Secret Service, and by giving them a formalized presence within the service in the shape of the liaison sections which informed 'C' of their requirements and then passed back intelligence to their respective masters. It was also tasked to collect political intelligence – but only at the request of the Foreign Office, which also had its own liaison section within the service.[26]

All this had the theoretical advantage of ensuring that MI6's operations were consumer-led. But, with various departments vying for its services and budgets being slashed each year as memories of war grew dimmer, MI6 found itself unable to cope with the competing demands of its consumers and without the authority to allocate higher priority to one set of requirements at the expense of another. Little attempt was made to analyse the product collected on behalf of the consumer departments, raw intelligence being passed on direct without interpretation.[27]

The Secret Service Committee also placed MI6 in charge of the Passport Control Department, thereby providing its overseas heads of station with some form of cover, although no diplomatic status. But just as Boyce remained remote from Reilly's activities in Russia, the station heads acted as little more than postboxes while 'the secret service work itself continued to be carried out by private individuals paid out of Secret Service funds' and by members of the service acting under commercial cover. The operations were controlled by 'C' from London with the assistance of a small group of assistants known as G officers.[28]

Cumming died in 1923 and was succeeded not, as he should have been under the inter-service rules, by an Army officer, but by Rear-Admiral Hugh 'Quex' Sinclair, Director of Naval Intelligence, who was appointed Head of the Secret Service and at the same time acquired control of the Government Code and Cypher School, the predecessor of GCHQ. In Cumming's memory, Sinclair kept his title 'C' and the practice of writing all memos in green ink – a tradition that continues to this day.

Although Cumming had resisted an earlier attempt to amalgamate the various British agencies, Sinclair saw counter-espionage as a valuable tool in the intelligence battle against the Soviet Union and lobbied hard to be allowed to absorb MI5 into his operations. When this failed, he set up his own counter-espionage section under a former Indian police officer, Valentine Vivian, with a brief to obtain advance notice of espionage operations mounted against Britain from abroad. He also set up a unit known as N, the existence of which is still not acknowledged, to gather intelligence by intercepting diplomatic bags.[29]

SIS and GC&CS moved to Broadway Buildings, at 54 Broadway, Westminster, in 1925, but the headquarters operation of MI6 itself was relatively small, with only about twenty officers collecting intelligence on an ad-hoc basis as required by the customer departments. In addition to Sinclair and his small coterie of G officers controlling the collection process, there were three liaison or circulating sections: Political Intelligence, working for the Foreign Office; Military Intelligence, for the War Office, using the old cover-name of MI1c, and Naval Intelligence, for the Admiralty, where it was known as NI1c. An Air Intelligence section, AI1C, was set up in 1929. The only other headquarters elements were Vivian's counter-espionage department, the diplomatic-bag interception unit, a financial and administration section, and the Passport Control Department based in Queen Anne's Gate at the back of Broadway Buildings.[30]

MI6 remained badly underfunded. The disdain felt within the Foreign Office for anyone involved in the 'dirty business' of intelligence continued until the Second World War. Many diplomats still refused to sanction an MI6 presence in their missions.

'Right up to the outbreak of war, cases had occurred in which a head of mission was hostile to secret intelligence and other arrangements had to be made,' said Robert Cecil, a Foreign Office official who spent much of the war as personal assistant to 'C'. 'Hostility arose partly because some heads of mission objected to transmission of intelligence to London from an unknown source and partly because of fear that the activities of the passport control officer might land the mission in trouble, even though in friendly countries he was supposed to cooperate with local counter-espionage authorities.'[31]

The work of the heads of stations was also hampered by the fact that they had to carry out passport control on top of their own duties, often with little or no knowledge of either consular duties or indeed espionage. When Leslie Nicholson was sent to Prague in 1930 to run MI6 operations there, he was given no training in tradecraft and had not the faintest idea of how to run a network of agents. 'Nobody gave me any tips on how to be a spy, how to make contact with, and worm vital information out of, unsuspecting experts.'

An attempt by Nicholson to draw on the experience of Captain Thomas Kendrick, the Vienna station chief and allegedly one of the service's top field men, provides a useful insight into the abilities of many of the MI6 old hands. Asked if there were any standard rules or practical hints he could pass on, Kendrick replied, 'I don't think there are really. You'll have to work it out for yourself.'[32]

Perhaps unsurprisingly, few MI6 customers were satisfied with the service they received. 'It is beyond question that the system produced frustration in the user departments,' noted the official historian with a measure of understatement. 'There was some substance in the departmental criticisms.'[33]

CHAPTER 7

# Turning on the Tap

Of the great intelligence triumphs of the war, not one was
directly or exclusively due to the Secret Service proper.
Hugh Trevor-Roper, *The Philby Affair*, 1968

The main cause of MI6's inefficiency in the inter-war period was a
severe lack of funds.[1] The impossibility of running an efficient service on the resources that were being allocated came to a head in 1935,
when Sinclair complained that the SIS budget was 'so reduced that it
equalled the normal cost of maintaining one destroyer in Home Waters'.
A report on the parlous state of affairs noted that demands on MI6 were
increasing as awareness of the Nazi threat grew. If its budget was not 'very
largely augmented, this country will be most dangerously handicapped'.[2]

The urgent call for funds brought a virtual doubling in the size of the
Secret Service Vote, from £180,000 to £350,000, allowing Sinclair to
increase his preparations for war against Nazi Germany.[3] With the passport control officers swamped by the mass exodus from the Third Reich,
and anticipating (correctly) that many of its European agents were already
compromised, Sinclair authorized the 1935 creation of a series of parallel
'fallback' networks in Germany and Italy – the Z Organization.

Its members were recruited by Colonel Claude Dansey, the former
station head in Rome, who was believed by everyone except Sinclair to
have been sacked over one of the many financial scandals that bedevilled
the passport control offices.

But where some were willing to take financial advantage of the Jewish
exodus, Frank Foley, the passport control officer in Berlin from 1923
until the outbreak of war, went out of his way to help as many as he
could, leading to him being described as 'Britain's Oskar Schindler'. From
the MI6 station in Tiergartenstrasse, Foley provided tens of thousands
of Jews with documents allowing them to go to British territories, even
walking into concentration camps to gain their freedom.

Ze'ev Padan's father had spent two years in Sachsenhausen concentration camp when he was amazed to be told that he had a visitor. He
was given a coat to hide the wounds caused by repeated beatings and was

taken to an office where a small man with glasses and white hair told him, 'My name is Foley. I am from the British Consulate.' Two days later, the Padans were on their way to Palestine. 'I don't know how he did it,' said Padan. 'He would always go to the right Nazi office and get a file placed on the top of the list.'

Ann Forbes-Robertson, who worked for Foley in the Passport Control Office, said, 'He was a most charming man, interesting and erudite. Years later, Captain Foley was mentioned in the Eichmann Trial in Israel in 1961, when it was stated that "Captain Foley singlehanded saved more Jews than any other person, he was the Pimpernel of Jewry."'

One wartime SIS officer said of Foley:

He was a quite outstanding character. Schindler pales into insignificance besides his work on getting Jews out of Germany and he was also an outstanding officer.

There would be lots of people waiting for Major Foley to hand out the visas so the Gestapo would come round and try and frighten them away. Foley would come out and say: 'You gentlemen have come to apply for a visa I suppose. Could you join the queue?' And when they said: 'No we haven't,' he'd reply: 'Well, could you kindly get out because this room's a bit crowded.'

He went on to Norway and organized the evacuation of the Norwegian Royal Family and then got out himself. He was later involved in running operations into Norway and he interrogated Hess, whom he already knew. A very, very able man, who I don't think ever got the recognition he should have done, outstanding.

At the end of the war, Foley wrote to a friend:

We are now reading about and seeing photographs of those places, the names of which were so well known to us in the years before the war. Now the people here finally believe that the stories of 1938–39 were not exaggerated. Looking back, I feel grateful that our little office in Tiergartenstrasse was able to assist some far too few to escape in time.

Dansey used the commercial cover of an export agency to recruit a number of agents across Europe, most of them already well-established businessmen.[4]

Sinclair used the rest of the money to set up a number of special departments, including Section D – the D allegedly standing for 'destruction' – to investigate 'every possibility' of carrying out 'irregular' warfare (a euphemism for terrorist attacks) behind enemy lines. A further circulating section was added to process economic intelligence. Richard

Gambier-Parry was recruited from Philco to set up a communications department, and Sinclair also encouraged the air section, run by Frederick Winterbotham, to carry out a series of secret Anglo-French aerial photo-reconnaissance missions across Germany and the Mediterranean under the cover of civilian flights on behalf of a front organization called the Aeronautical Research and Sales Corporation.[5]

By mid-1938 repeated SIS reports that a German invasion of Czechoslovakia was imminent had paradoxically improved its reputation politically, the fact that the invasion did not come being put down to a subsequent British 'hands-off' warning rather than to faulty intelligence. Thereafter, Sinclair found himself a valued adviser to Chamberlain, and in a report dated 18 September 1938, entitled 'What Shall We Do?', he counselled a mixture of appeasement and rearmament.

'It seems undesirable to give Hitler any pretext for saying Germany is being encircled or that hostile combinations are being built up against her,' Sinclair wrote. Britain should aim to achieve a peaceful separation of the Sudetenland from Czechoslovakia 'and make the Czechs realize they stand alone if they refuse such a solution'.

A similar approach should be adopted over Germany's other territorial gains, the report suggested:

International steps of some sort should be taken, without undue delay, to see what really legitimate grievances Germany has and what surgical operations are necessary to rectify them. It may be argued that this would be giving in to Germany, strengthening Hitler's position and encouraging him to go to extremes. Better however that realities be faced and that wrongs if they do exist be righted than leave it to Hitler to do the righting in his own way and time.[6]

Despite Chamberlain's regard for Sinclair's advice, the service's ability to provide adequate intelligence cover of the events in Europe was dismal. The three armed services repeatedly complained that the SIS was unable to produce any reliable intelligence, with the Air Ministry discounting MI6 reports as 'normally 80 per cent inaccurate'. The situation was not helped by the arrest of Kendrick, the head of station in Vienna, while observing German troops carrying out manoeuvres on the Czech border. 'Kendrick had been double-crossed by two of his agents,' a former MI6 officer said. 'They told all to the Gestapo about his military reporting on the German Army in Austria.' His expulsion 'because proofs are to hand that he engaged in espionage' led Sinclair to recall temporarily the passport control officers in Berlin and Prague for fear that similar action might be taken against them.[7]

In the months leading up to the war, raw intelligence emanating from the SIS was dominated by false reports and rumours. Since Britain had no effective central analytical body, few customer departments were able adequately to assess the intelligence they were receiving. With the circulating sections passing on without comment what most consumers regarded either as 'rumours planted by international Jewry' or Abwehr disinformation, MI6 reports lost all credibility.[8]

Alexander Cadogan, Permanent Under-Secretary at the Foreign Office, defended MI6 against the repeated attacks. 'Our agents are of course bound to report rumours or items of information which come into their possession,' he wrote in an internal Foreign Office minute. 'They exercise a certain amount of discrimination themselves, but naturally do not take the responsibility of too much selection and it is our job to weigh up the information which we receive and try to draw more or less reasonable conclusions from it. In that we may fail and if so it is our fault, but I do not think it is fair to blame the SIS.'[9]

It was these problems that led in July 1939 to the reorganization of British intelligence to turn the Joint Intelligence Sub-Committee of the Chiefs of the Imperial Defence committee into a more dominant body chaired by the Foreign Office and with responsibility for collating and assessing the increasing amount of intelligence reports. But the move did little to improve MI6's reputation – particularly among the military – and worse was to come.[10]

Under pressure from the Foreign Office to find political intelligence on German opposition groups willing to form an alternative government to Hitler's, MI6 had gradually become drawn into an elaborate deception plan in which agents of the Sicherheitsdienst (SD), the Nazi Party's internal intelligence organization, posed as members of the anti-Hitler opposition. It was to be a disastrous mistake.

On the outbreak of the war Dansey had moved the 'Most Secret' Z operation – his fall-back system to the long-blown passport control officers – to Switzerland, to keep it secure. But, for reasons that remain inexplicable, headquarters at Broadway Buildings now decided to merge the two networks, apparently without consulting Dansey who was in Zurich working under diplomatic cover of consul.

Sigismund Payne Best – a First World War Intelligence Corps officer and the Z network's Dutch representative – had been trying to recruit the alleged opposition members. He was ordered to work with the passport control office in The Hague, which had been infiltrated by the Abwehr.

Best and Major Richard Stevens, the Hague head of station, were lured to a café at Venlo, on the Dutch–German border, for negotiations with opposition 'emissaries' and were smuggled across the border by an SD snatch squad. Not only did German intelligence claim a major propaganda victory by alleging that Best and Stevens were part of a British-led plot to assassinate Hitler, but, more crucially, the 'Most Secret' Z Organization was blown and many of MI6's European networks were compromised.[11]

In the middle of the Venlo débâcle, Sinclair died and Stewart Menzies, the head of the military circulating section, was put in charge – possibly in an attempt to improve MI6's poor reputation among the military. Dansey, who had rushed back from Zurich to put in his own bid for the job, was made Assistant Chief. But a combination of the Treasury's inter-war refusal to provide more funds and the successful SD interrogation of Stevens and Best left the service with insufficient agents across Europe and resulted in frantic attempts to set up stay-behind networks.[12]

Unsurprisingly, the service struggled to make an impact, with the military particularly scathing. An investigation into Britain's intelligence services reiterated the complaints of the service chiefs, although the Foreign Office and the Ministry of Economic Warfare were both reasonably happy with SIS product. On 25 May 1940 Cadogan wrote in his diary that Lord Hankey, had 'agreed to try and overhaul SIS, which wants it badly'.[13]

It was not until May 1940 that MI6 was given a seat on the JIC, against the advice of Major-General F. G. Beaumont-Nesbitt, Director of Military Intelligence.[14] When Beaumont-Nesbitt complained bitterly of the 'apparent meagreness of Secret Service reports', he was told that the German advance had left MI6 with few agents in Europe and no stations outside of the neutral capitals of Madrid, Lisbon, Berne and Stockholm. 'The work of this department has been very considerably complicated as a result of the capitulations of Holland, France and Belgium,' the JIC noted. 'As a result, comparatively little information is being obtained from agents from enemy and enemy occupied countries.'[15]

The service suffered a further blow when Section D was hived off to form the basis of the Special Operations Executive behind Menzies's back – a move that created an acrimonious relationship between SIS and SOE which persisted throughout the war. Philip Johns, who joined SOE from SIS midway through the war, said:

I was indoctrinated into the belief that SOE was rash and untrustworthy, lacking in security. I was briefed that in 'setting Europe ablaze' our own agents might well be compromised and endangered so that caution was the watchword with the Baker St irregulars. It was emphasized that their intelligence originated from sources untrained and consequently unreliable. In short, SOE was suspect.

The competition between the two extended to battles over transport needed to infiltrate agents into occupied territory. As a result of the disenchantment with MI6, both the RAF and the Royal Navy saw any assistance rendered to secret service work as a wasted effort, and the JIC was forced to insist that 'all possible priority should be given to any request from MI6 for transport facilities'.

At one stage, MI6 and the SOE were running rival private navies of French fishing-smacks and small motor-torpedo-boats, based a few miles from each other on the Cornish coast, in order to infiltrate agents into France. But these were eventually amalgamated under joint command at Helford, five miles south-west of Falmouth. For northern Europe, the two organizations made extensive use of the many Norwegian fishermen who had been at sea when Norway fell and had sailed into British ports. Operating from Lunna and Scalloway in the Shetland Islands, they ferried hundreds of agents in and out of Scandinavia on what became known as the Shetland Bus.[16]

MI6 rivalries were not just restricted to the service's relations with other secret service organizations. Having placed Dansey in charge of operations with the title of Assistant Chief, Menzies now created an additional position of Deputy Chief for Valentine Vivian, without ever giving him any precise responsibilities. As a result, Dansey and Vivian spent as much time feuding with each other as in attempting to produce intelligence.

But Dansey did persuade the Czech and Polish governments in exile

Major-General Stewart
Menzies, who was head of MI6
from 1939 to 1951

to turn their networks over to the SIS. He also 'supervised' MI9, the organization set up to collect intelligence from British prisoners of war. Although the principal aim was to get PoWs back to Britain, where they could be debriefed, intelligence was also provided from inside the prison camps, dispatched in coded letters home.

How much useful intelligence was collected from PoWs is not altogether clear, although as the Allies closed in on Germany the JIC said it had been of 'vital importance' and was reluctant to order prisoners not to escape for fear of losing their contribution. 'If escaping stopped there would be a certain loss of intelligence gained by men at large, for example on general conditions, on raid damage and on questions affecting the Ministry for Economic Warfare,' it said. But by then MI9 had evolved into far more than an intelligence-gathering organization, giving PoWs a vital sense of purpose and a feeling that, despite capture, they remained part of the overall war effort.[17]

Meanwhile, the counter-espionage unit, Section V, had won a tussle with MI5 over control of the Radio Security Service which monitored communications between German intelligence agents and their controllers. But the victory only led to increased rivalry between the two, largely because MI6 was fighting off an attempt by Sir David Petrie, the MI5 Director-General, to absorb Section V into his own organization.[18]

The creation in mid-1940 of British Security Co-ordination, a New York-based organization run by the pugnacious William Stephenson, one of Dansey's recruits, helped to ensure the service had strong links with American intelligence. This was due in no small part to Stephenson's close relationship with Colonel William 'Wild Bill' Donovan, who later founded the Office of Strategic Services, an American organization which combined the roles of Britain's SIS and SOE and was a predecessor of the CIA. By December 1941 the two sides were sharing intelligence extensively.[19]

British output was passed on either to a US liaison officer in London or to Donovan himself via a Washington-based Joint Intelligence Committee which included Stephenson among its members. However, the Americans were still not to be told 'our sources of intelligence and most secret methods of acquiring it'.[20]

The Americans do not appear to have been missing much. As late as January 1941 Air Chief Marshal Sir Robert Brooke-Popham, C-in-C Far East, was complaining of the poor quality of British intelligence in the region:

Weakest link undoubtedly is SIS organization. At present little or no reliance is placed upon SIS organization by any authorities here and little valuable information in fact appears to be obtained. I am satisfied that identity of principal officers at Shanghai, Hong Kong and Singapore is known to many. Their chief subordinates are in general local amateurs with no training in intelligence techniques nor adequate knowledge of military, naval, air or political affairs.

There were only a limited number of SIS officers in the Middle East at the start of the war. This and the fact that they were frequently required to cover both security and intelligence roles left them 'overworked and unable to devote adequate time and consideration to either role', and there were again complaints that their product was inadequate. The situation was improved by the creation of the MI5-controlled Security and Intelligence Middle East, based in Cairo, and an SIS organization known under the cover-name of Inter-Services Liaison Department.[21]

In 1942, with the services still calling for reform but apparently unwilling or unable to be specific about what changes should take place, Menzies agreed to the appointment of three deputy directors, one from each of the services, thereby relieving himself of some of the more onerous management duties while at the same time keeping the critics off his back. He also accepted a Foreign Office representative, initially Patrick Reilly, but later Robert Cecil, as personal assistant to 'C'. After the space of a year during which the service deputy directors – known within MI6 as the Commissars, because of their blatantly political role – were forced to experience at first hand some of the difficulties Menzies faced, their new roles were 'abandoned by mutual agreement' and each took over their respective service circulating section.[22]

By now the G officers had been replaced by production sections with precise geographical responsibilities numbered simply with Arabic numerals from P1 through to at least P8, which covered the Low Countries.[23] The circulating sections were allocated Roman numerals: I, Political; II, Air; III, Naval; IV, Military; V, Counter-espionage; VI, Economic; VII, Finance; VIII, Communications.[24]

Gradually the service's reputation began to turn around, helped partly by Section V's role in the Double-Cross system and partly by the gradual reconstruction of the networks in occupied Europe, but in the main by the increasing exploitation of special intelligence provided by the codebreakers of GC&CS at Bletchley Park and the extent to which they were prepared to go to ensure that the cracking of the German Enigma machine cypher was kept totally secret.

Each of the service circulating sections had elements based at Bletchley Park, in order to ease the process of assessment and dissemination. Decrypts were frequently sent out with a normal MI6 serial number, which routinely began with the digraph CX, and their origins were disguised by giving the impression that they came from human intelligence rather than communications intercepts.

R. V. Jones, who was in charge of scientific intelligence, said this resulted in a growing admiration for SIS abilities:

> At first those decrypts that were deemed important enough to justify some degree of circulation were disguised to appear as reports from secret agents operating under MI6, their cryptographic origin being disguised by some introduction such as 'A reliable source recovered a flimsy of a message in the wastepaper of the Chief Signals Officer of Fliegerkorps IV which read: . . .' Or, in the case of an incomplete decrypt, 'Source found a partly charred document in the fireplace of . . .' I can remember myself handing such a disguised decrypt to Air Commodore Nutting, the Director of Signals, who exclaimed: 'By Jove, you've got some brave chaps working for you.'
>
> Inevitably, there was speculation about the identity of the supposed secret agent or agents who were sending back such valuable reports. Gilbert Frankau, the novelist, who had a wartime post in the Flak Section, told me that he had deduced from internal evidence that the agent who could so effectively get into German headquarters must be Sir Paul Dukes, the legendary agent who had penetrated the Red Army so successfully after the Russian Revolution.

In early 1941, with the number of Bletchley Park reports growing to a level where it was beginning to be difficult to disguise them all as HUMINT, special liaison units were set up in all the key commands under the control of Section VIII, the communications section, to pass the reports on without disclosing their origin. But the continued assumption by those who were not indoctrinated into the Ultra secret that its product was the work of MI6 allowed the service to bask in the glory – albeit reflected – of what Menzies described as his 'Brains Trust', the assortment of academics and servicemen gathered together at War Station, as Bletchley Park was known within the service.[25]

But MI6 did not live entirely as a parasite. The close links with Czech and Polish intelligence services led to valuable information, particularly from the Czechs' Agent A-54, Paul Thuemmel, a senior Abwehr officer who provided comprehensive details of German plans before being arrested by the Gestapo in March 1942.[26]

There were also close relationships with Norwegian intelligence and with both the Vichy and Gaullist French services. Norwegian agents, ferried back into Scandinavia via the Shetland Bus or by Royal Navy submarine, located the *Tirpitz* and provided intelligence on the heavy-water plants.

The French networks provided useful details of German naval movements – particularly of the U-boats based on the French Atlantic coast – advanced notice of impending V-1 attacks on England, and vital intelligence for the British commando raids on Dieppe and Saint-Nazaire and for the D-Day landings. The Vichy intelligence service also passed on the product of Source K, a French telephone engineer called Robert Keller, who tapped into the long-distance telephone line between the German command centre in Paris and Hitler's headquarters in eastern Prussia.

In the run-up to the D-Day landings, MI6 devised Operation Sussex, a joint enterprise with the OSS and the Gaullist Bureau Central de Renseignements et d'Action in which two-man teams were dropped into Normandy to provide up-to-date tactical intelligence. French agents stole the plans for the Atlantic Wall and provided detailed sketches of the beaches where the landings were to take place.[27]

There was also some human intelligence from within Germany itself which among other things helped to locate the German air-defence radar system and to discover the V-weapons base at Peenemunde, long before the first V-bomb was ever launched at London.

The first information on Peenemunde had been sent anonymously to the British Embassy in Norway, in the so-called Oslo Report. It was subsequently discovered to have been written by the brave German scientist Professor Hans Ferdinand Mayer, who was later incarcerated in a series of concentration camps. Information on what was going on at the experimental rocket site in Peenemunde then began to come in from refugees arriving in Switzerland, said Sir Harry Hinsley, the official historian of wartime intelligence. 'We did not have an agent there,' Sir Harry said, 'but we did have these neutrals – Luxembourgers and Swiss – who were working there, some of them in Peenemunde, and information from them would come into Berne.'

Sverre Bergh, a Norwegian student studying at the Technische Hochschule in Dresden, was sent by MI6 to Berlin to make contact with Dr Paul Rosbaud, a dissident German scientist, who was prepared to talk about the work on the V-1 rockets taking place at Peenemunde. Rosbaud was unable to provide all the details of the test site the British required, so Bergh went himself to Peenemunde, preparing a report that was smuggled back to Stockholm station via the Swedish diplomatic bag.

But none of this information was given enough credence, and it was not until 1943 – nearly four years after the Oslo Report had been delivered

– that major air raids were launched against Peenemunde, forcing the Germans to pull the rocket base back into Poland.[28]

It is commonly held that SIS had no agents in Germany. But Bergh and the foreign workers were by no means the only SIS sources inside the Third Reich. Victor Hampton, an SIS officer based in Stockholm, apparently ran a number of intelligence networks in Berlin, Hamburg, Bonn, Königsberg and Vienna. The most extensive description available of these networks comes from the German interrogation of SIS agent R34. Carl Aage Andreasson, a Danish businessman who was able to travel in and out of Germany, was captured by German intelligence in January 1944. He told them that in Berlin alone there were four separate British networks, while in Hamburg Hampton had some eighty people working for him. Reports were sent in microfilm inside crates of goods exported to Sweden.

Some of the British agents were foreign workers; others were trade unionists. MI6 appears to have taken over links to the International Transport Federation set up by Naval Intelligence before the war, collecting large amounts of information, including details of weapons production.

A Norwegian agent run by the SIS station in Stockholm had such good contacts in Germany that he was given the run of its military facilities. Among the intelligence he supplied was the crucial report that the *Bismarck* was leaving the Baltic, allowing the Royal Navy to hunt her down. 'He has been given facilities to visit German military areas, Baltic provinces, naval ports, etc.' the naval attaché in Stockholm told London. 'On occasions this information has been of great value . . . including the passage of the *Bismarck* through the Kattegat in 1941.' But such was the reputation of MI6 that his report was initially ignored. 'It wasn't believed by the Admiralty,' a former SIS officer said. 'That was commonplace. Some of the best reporting we produced was not believed by the recipients.'[29]

But the prize source for information from inside Germany was Halina Szymanska, the Polish confidante of the head of the Abwehr, Admiral Wilhelm Canaris, and an MI6 agent. 'She was a very significant contact,' said a former MI6 officer:

Canaris was violently anti-Nazi and was involved in plotting against Hitler. He took a very dim view of what the Nazis were up to and as head of the Abwehr, where he could, he managed to commute death sentences to life sentences where agents were involved, including some British agents.

He had a penchant for attractive ladies. He is supposed to have placed four at various posts overseas. Madame Szymanska was the wife of the Polish military attaché in Berlin before the war. They were both very friendly with Canaris. She was rescued by him after her husband had been captured by the Russians during the Soviet occupation of Poland. Canaris was able to arrange for her and her children to travel in a sealed railway carriage across Germany from Poland to Switzerland, where he maintained contact with her. Indeed, he himself visited her in Berne a number of times.

On arrival in Berne, Madame Szymanska had reported her story to the Polish intelligence head of station. He passed it on to the head of Polish intelligence, Colonel Taduesz Wasilewski, who was then based in London with the government in exile. 'Wasilewski brought it to Dansey and said, "This is a very hot potato,"' another former MI6 officer said.

'It is the best I can ever give you and it is so secret that I don't trust my own people to handle it, so I am giving it to you,' he said. Dansey then sent Frederick Vanden Heuvel out to Switzerland and told him, 'Your number one mission in life is to handle this woman. Everything else is second class.' Canaris talked very freely to Madame Szymanska about German intentions. He was either extremely indiscreet or using her as an intentional conduit to pass information to the allies.

Dansey was determined to keep the information totally secure, and at the Berne station only Vanden Heuvel was briefed on what was going on.

Dansey kept the whole of the Swiss station and its activities in his own hands in headquarters. He wouldn't let the files go out. He wouldn't give them the general circulation that they should have. His story was: 'I started the Swiss station. It's my station and I'm running it from here.'

The most important item Szymanska reported was in January 1941, when she was able to tell us that an irrevocable decision had been made by Hitler, against the advice of his staff, to attack Russia in May of that year. At this time the main German military effort appeared to be preparing the invasion of England in the spring. This valuable nugget of intelligence foretold a relaxation of the pressures on England and a future sharing of the war burden with Russia. This information – suitably disguised, together with some other, probably Ultra, items on the subject – was passed to the Russians by Sir Stafford Cripps, our ambassador in Moscow. Unfortunately, Stalin discounted it as misinformation from the British intelligence service.

Szymanska's existence appears to have been revealed to the Germans by R34, who told his interrogators that the most important SIS agent was a woman who had a relationship with a senior German and who had provided the British with continuous information from inside Berlin, including warning of Operation Barbarossa, the invasion of the Soviet Union. It was on 12 February 1944, shortly after R34's arrest, that Canaris fell out of favour and Hitler ordered him to stay out of Berlin.[30]

Menzies believed to his deathbed that more use might have been made of Szymanska's links to Berlin, telling Winterbotham that Canaris had made an offer of talks that he had been ready to accept 'but Eden [the British Foreign Secretary] stopped me'. Shortly before he died, Menzies disclosed that he had hoped 'to open discussions with Adml Canaris on the removal of Hitler as a means of shortening the war and negotiating peace. But this biggest intelligence coup of all time ... was thwarted in certain Foreign Office quarters "for fear of offending Russia".'[31]

MI6 clearly had far better sources of information than it was ever given credit for. But the general opinion among its customers was that it had a bad war. Poorly prepared and frequently amateurish – agents were allegedly sent into Norway with their equipment wrapped in English newspapers – SIS took a long time to get up and running. Even then it was very largely sustained by the Ultra material produced by GC&CS at Bletchley Park – by far the most important element of Britain's intelligence system.

The Secret Intelligence Service did play a key role in the development of photographic intelligence – almost certainly the second most important element – but lost control of it to the RAF shortly after the war began. Its own collection responsibility – human intelligence – played a negligible part in the Second World War, although it is now clear that what part it did play might have been far greater had the reputation of MI6 among the consumer departments been better.

Certainly Robert Cecil was right to apportion a large part of the blame for this situation to the Treasury and the Foreign Office 'which did not understand that intelligence requires a long-term perspective and cannot be turned on, like a tap, when crisis impends'. But better organization, an earlier realization of the threat posed by Germany, and a willingness to cut the coat according to the cloth would surely have produced better results, and greater confidence among the consumer departments. As the Russians advanced inexorably across eastern Europe, there were those within the service and within its 'junior half-sister', the SOE, who were determined it should not be so badly prepared for the next war.[32]

# CHAPTER 8

# The Next Enemy

Long before the end of the War with Germany, senior officers
in SIS began to turn their thoughts towards the next enemy.
Kim Philby, *My Silent War* (1968)

British intelligence had been aware for some time, from messages intercepted by the Radio Security Service, that the NKVD, the predecessor of the KGB, was briefing its agents within the resistance movements on 'the next war'. Some British officials harboured grave reservations about an agreement by the SOE liaison mission in Moscow to infiltrate Soviet agents into western Europe, fearing that they would form the basis for post-war subversion and intelligence networks working to create Communist governments.[1]

A post-war British intelligence briefing on NKVD resistance operations confirmed their fears. 'Though resistance to the Germans was the unifying force in these movements, an equally important motive was to seize power from the ruling cliques on the defeat of Germany,' it said. 'Through their Communist leadership the partisans received encouragement from the Russians while Russian propaganda and the successes of the Red Army caused the partisans to look to Russia for inspiration and support when the time came to seize power.'[2]

But in 1942–3, the 'need to know' principle left many SOE officials unaware of the Soviet Union's Cold War preparations. In their eagerness to secure Moscow's co-operation for their own schemes, they were happy to back its repeated demands for British help in placing agents into various parts of the world.

In one particularly bizarre memo to the Foreign Office, the SOE even advocated placing NKVD agents at various strategic points of the British Empire like Singapore and Hong Kong, 'ensuring in the unlikely but always possible event of a collapse of the present regime in Russia there would be sufficiently senior NKVD officials at key points in British territory who would continue to control and direct for our purposes NKVD agents in various parts of the world'.

The Foreign Office pointed out the rather obvious dangers of helping

Soviet intelligence agents infiltrate the cornerstones of the empire, but Gladwyn Jebb, then executive head of SOE, defended the proposal. In a remarkably naïve assessment, Jebb said, 'These agents will not be Comintern men but agents of the Russian National State Police. I really do not think therefore that there need be any apprehensions.'

There was 'no intention that assistance shall be extended to the Soviets in furtherance of a long-term or post-war political policy,' the SOE claimed. But both the Foreign Office and MI6 rightly expressed considerable doubts about the whole enterprise. 'We must guard against requests which contribute nothing towards winning the war and are put forward only to further Russia's own post-war political aims,' one official wrote. 'We could be unwittingly building up an enemy organization under our very noses and far from collaborating in attack on the Axis, we may be subscribing to the doctrine of *hari-kari*.'

Stewart Menzies also expressed 'grave concern' at the effect it might have on the MI6 networks in France. As a result, the NKVD's activities in western Europe were severely disrupted, with SOE's Moscow mission – its own enthusiasm curbed by more sober heads in London – repeatedly stonewalling Russian demands for assistance in dropping agents into France, Belgium and Holland.[3]

MI6, its pre-war obsession with fighting Bolshevism suppressed but not forgotten, was quicker than the Foreign Office to realize the threat that would be posed by the Soviet Union once the war in Europe was over. 'Long before the end of the War with Germany, senior officers in SIS began to turn their thoughts towards the next enemy,' Kim Philby recalled. 'A modest start was made by setting up a small section, known as Section IX, to study past records of Soviet and Communist activity.'

Philby alleged that, on the orders of his NKVD controller, he conducted a concerted political campaign to ensure that he, and not his main rival, Felix Cowgill, was offered control of the new section. But his claim does not bear close scrutiny. Certainly, he was appointed head of Section IX in 1944, and no doubt this pleased the NKVD, but his version of the lead-up to his appointment does not tally with other contemporary accounts. It seems more likely that Valentine Vivian, who detested Cowgill and was a friend of Philby's father, was behind the appointment of his protégé.[4]

The British Chiefs of Staff were also quicker than the Foreign Office to realize that Russia was the next enemy, ordering the post-hostilities planning staff as early as August 1944 to consider 'realistically ... the best form of action which we should take to protect our strategic interests in the event of hostilities with Russia'.[5]

Despite the early enthusiasm of its Moscow mission for co-operation with the Russians, the SOE was if anything preparing even more vigorously for the Cold War. 'The chief threat to world peace is now the increasing divergence becoming evident between Russian aims and the policies of the western allies,' wrote Harold Perkins, head of the SOE's Polish section, in a confidential memo in October 1944. He suggested keeping the section's operatives in Poland in place and even sending others back to set up networks to collect intelligence and organize resistance to a Russian-controlled regime.

'There are very few Englishmen who possess a first-hand knowledge of Russia, of Russian mentality, and of Russian methods,' Perkins wrote. 'The Poles on the other hand have several thousand persons having those qualifications and being at the same time bitterly hostile to Russia, although friendly to us. In the event of war with Russia they would be of inestimable value to us. They represent an asset which should not lightly be discarded.'

The idea was taken up by Sir Colin Gubbins, the head of SOE, who ordered that a list of all its agents in central Europe be drawn up. 'It is considered most desirable', Sir Colin said, 'that contact should be maintained with them to form a nucleus of tried and experienced agents capable of rapid expansion in the event of another war.' Sympathetic businessmen were to be approached to provide the agents with cover as foreign representatives of British firms, he added. 'There are many people both within and outside SOE who have wide business and commercial contacts and will be willing and anxious to help in this scheme.'

The plans were co-ordinated with similar operations by MI6 and the American OSS. As the war in Europe drew to a close, Perkins travelled to Prague to contact its agents there. In signals back to London, he recorded their wartime cover and stressed that 'the continuity of the stories should not be broken'. Another SOE officer visiting agents in Hungary had clearly been briefed to consider the possibility of keeping networks in place. 'The few agents we had are blown,' he wrote. 'A new organization would have to be built up in cells initiated by our past agents and helpers. We must assume that in the event of trouble all our past collaborators would be arrested.'[6]

SIS began making exploratory attempts to infiltrate members of the anti-Russian resistance movements into the Baltic republics from Scandinavia. Menzies told the JIC that it was essential that Moscow 'should not become aware of the nature of the measures' – a somewhat vain hope given that Philby was head of Section IX and Major Anthony Blunt of MI5, another key member of the Cambridge spy ring, was a frequent participant in JIC discussions.[7]

With the end of the war, intelligence officers were needed *en masse* in

Germany to assess the information from Nazi files and interrogation of former German officers. The Nazi stay-behind units – the so-called Werwolf organization – failed to materialize in any strength[8] and it soon became clear that the main problem for those SIS officers posted to the British control commissions in Germany and Austria was the huge number of Russian espionage agents who had been infiltrated into the British sector. Intelligence exchanges with the Soviet Union were cut to an absolute minimum as the predictions of the post-war situation came to fruition. Officers working in Germany found their Russian counterparts at best uncooperative, while the JIC heard that Moscow was becoming 'truculent in political matters'.[9]

Menzies, negotiating with the service departments over their post-war intelligence requirements, was told by the JIC that its most urgent priority was information on the Soviet Union's attempts to produce an atomic bomb. SIS agents in Germany began recruiting scientists from the Russian zone. 'We are convinced there is an opportunity now to obtain high-grade intelligence from these men which will enable us to build up an almost complete picture of Russian scientific and technical activities in Germany and make it possible to forecast more accurately than we can at present the progress of Russian development of weapons during future years,' one official said.[10]

With the Cold War already under way in the occupied zones, Gubbins and Menzies made their peace. But SOE's independent attitude and its determination to 'resort to and encourage every form of terror' had made it unpopular within Whitehall, where the enthusiasm of SOE officers working with the British Control Commissions in Austria and Germany for freelance 'activities of a cloak and dagger variety' was viewed with undisguised horror. 'Their activities in Germany seem to me to be of a somewhat dangerous political character,' one official wrote. He also expressed alarm at an SOE plan to mount an operation into the Russian zone of Austria to 'lift' film of German rocket technology. 'We have to watch our step,' the official said. 'The Russians are watching us and we must be particularly careful not to allow any activities of a cloak and dagger variety to continue under our auspices.'[11]

Although the need for some form of slimmed-down peacetime special-operations branch was recognized, there were genuine fears that if SOE remained an independent body it would turn into a loose cannon. It was decided that special operations should be put back under 'C''s control.[12]

Even before SOE's 'liquidation' and absorption into SIS as the Special Operations Branch, in January 1946, SOE officers like Perkins began working effectively for their new boss, handing their networks over lock, stock and barrel to MI6.[13]

Harold Perkins,
the former
SOE officer
who became a
key figure in
early MI6 Cold
War operations

Perks, as he was generally known, subsequently became head of the Special Operations Branch, taking charge of a number of covert operations into eastern Europe. How successful his east-European networks were is not clear. But the Baltic operations were quickly compromised, and by May 1946 many of the SOE's former agents in Poland had been arrested by the NKVD. 'In many cases, we understand they are charged with being British intelligence agents,' one official noted. Harold Perkins was mentioned frequently during the show trials of alleged spies by the new regime in Warsaw.[14]

Having survived Lord Hankey's review of British intelligence, MI6 embarked on its own reorganization, in an attempt to turn the somewhat haphazard and amateurish pre-war organization into a professional service. Five separate directorates were created: Production; Requirements; Finance and Administration; Training and Development; and War Planning, which set up stay-behind units for use in the event of western Europe being overrun by Soviet forces.

The Requirements directorate, equating to the old circulating or liaison sections, remained much as before, although the roman numerals were dropped in favour of arabic and the importance of science – particularly in relation to atomic weapons – was reflected by its being given its own section, leaving R1, Political; R2, Air; R3, Naval; R4, Army; R5, Counter-Espionage (an amalgamation of Section V and Philby's Section IX); R6, Economic; R7, Scientific; and R8, GCHQ.

Production was split regionally on geographical lines under three chief controllers, the so-called Robber Barons: CC(E), covering Europe, split into North, East and West; CC(M) for the Mediterranean (the Middle East and Africa), and CC(P) for the Pacific (the Far East and the

Americas), with a fourth section covering operations carried out from the United Kingdom. It was only a step away from the chaotic system that had evolved by means of tacking departments here and there on to the old base of MI1c as needed, and it was certainly not the 'root and branch' reorganization that many within the service had hoped for.[15]

As a result of the propaganda of the war years, 'Uncle Joe' Stalin was still regarded with affection in the West. But the JIC assessed Communism as 'the most important external political menace confronting the British Commonwealth and likely to remain so in the foreseeable future'. On 1 March 1946 a JIC report on Russia's Strategic Interests and Intentions said, 'Russian policy will be aggressive by all measures short of war.' Stalin was unlikely to start a major war unless he unwittingly pushed America or Britain too far, but 'we cannot exclude the possibility that Russia may pursue a policy which will present the West with local *faits accomplis*'.[16]

Four days later, Churchill – now out of office but still well-briefed on intelligence matters – made a speech at Westminster College, Fulton, Missouri, that was to herald a radical sea change in the public perception of the Soviet Union. 'From Stettin in the Baltic to Trieste in the Adriatic, an Iron Curtain has descended across the continent,' he said:

> Behind that line lie all the capitals of the ancient states of central and eastern Europe. Warsaw, Berlin, Prague, Vienna, Budapest, Bucharest and Sofia, all these famous cities and the populations around them lie in the Soviet sphere and all are subject, in one form or another, not only to Soviet influence but to a very high and in some cases increasing measure of control from Moscow.[17]

Amid all this concern about the danger from the Soviet Union came a moment of pure farce, recalled by R. V. Jones, then head of the Scientific section:

> One morning just before a weekend, the Security Officer rushed round the MI6 offices telling everyone to take down all maps off their walls. It turned out that the MI6 offices were all rented and the landlord had heard that we were thinking of moving. Anxious to re-let the premises in such an event he had somehow made contact with the Russian Trade Delegation and he wished to take them round on the Saturday afternoon. Could it happen anywhere but Britain that representatives of its major prospective opponent should be allowed to tour the offices of its Secret Service?

By now, Menzies was already submitting proposals for special operations to the JIC. One of the earliest and, perhaps fortunately, more

short-lived was devised by Perkins in an attempt to stem the flow of Jews
to Palestine and involved planting explosive devices below the waterline
of ships that were to carry the refugees there from Italy. Only one ship
was blown up before the operation was abandoned.

But there was little doubt about the main target of the MI6 special
ops. Menzies told the JIC that he intended to make good use of a report
– compiled for the Germans by a captured Russian officer and inherited
by the British at the end of the war – providing 'suggestions for political
warfare against the Russians and containing plans and a map for military
action in support of this policy'.[18]

The first MI6 attempt to set up a network in Latvia took place shortly
after that country was annexed by Moscow in June 1940. Kenneth Benton
and his wife, Peggy, then posted to the service's Riga section, trained a
stay-behind agent to use a small wireless, but after sending three messages
detailing Russian activities he disappeared. 'There were no more messages
from our agent and we concluded that the Soviet police or NKVD had
traced his signals and located him,' Benton said.[19]

MI6 resumed its attempts to set up networks in the Baltic republics
in 1945. But unbeknown to Harry Carr, the MI6 Controller Northern Area, they were quickly compromised. Major Janis Lukasevics of
Latvian state security organized a deception operation. 'We had to
know the SIS plans and the only way we could do that was by successfully infiltrating our men into the SIS networks,' Lukasevics said.
Once the networks were infiltrated, they were to be left in place,
feeding back false information to London and providing Soviet intelligence with details of what the British were trying to do. 'There
was a decision not to touch them, to continue finding out what their
specific tasks were. Well, we quite quickly found out that their job
was not just spying but also to prepare the way for other spies, to set up
a link and new points of support and to establish contact with resistance
groups.'

More than thirty British agents – most of them émigrés – were dispatched to Lithuania, Estonia and Latvia over a period of ten years.
Anthony Cavendish, who as an SIS officer based in Germany, helped to
ferry some of them into Latvia, recalled that all the missions ended in
failure, as did similar attempts to link up with the Ukrainian nationalist
movement, the NTS, run from the Klagenfurt headquarters of the British
Control Commission (Austria). 'The operations must now seem nothing
more than a catalogue of disasters,' Cavendish said. 'However, there were
those in SIS headquarters who were not as gullible as the controller
of the operation, Harry Carr. The brilliant George Kennedy Young
scrutinized the whole operation in 1953 and realized that it was under

Soviet control. Young approached the Chief of SIS who agreed that the operations should be stopped.'[20]

None of this would have surprised those British and American intelligence officers who had worked in Germany at the end of the war. As they interrogated their German counterparts and Soviet defectors, it became clear that right back to the 1920s, most of the Russian, Ukrainian and Baltic émigré groups had been penetrated by Soviet agents. Arnold Silver, a US Army intelligence officer who served in Germany interrogating refugees, described the evidence of such penetration as 'staggeringly convincing'. It was 'astonishing' that both MI6 and the CIA nevertheless decided to use the émigré groups to set up networks inside the Soviet Union, he said:

> Given the scale of Soviet penetration of the groups, it could not be expected that such operations would benefit anybody but the KGB and of course CIA and MI6 suffered one disaster after another. There was not one successful operation. The mass of information militating against this kind of blindness on the part of those responsible for the decision to operate with émigré groups was simply ignored, resulting in many lost lives of émigré agents.[21]

Britain's Cold War activities against the Soviet Bloc were co-ordinated by a high-level Foreign Office committee, the Russia Committee, which in November 1948 decided on a more offensive policy, using limited 'special operations' that would stop short of all-out war. 'Our aim should certainly be to liberate the countries within the Soviet orbit by any means short of war,' the committee decided. Sir Ivone Kirkpatrick, the senior Foreign Office representative, suggested a joint US–British attempt to foment insurrection in Albania, again using émigrés to link up with resistance groups that were assumed to be operating inside the country.

'He thought that it would be best to start any kind of offensive operations in a small area and suggested for consideration, in this regard, Albania,' the minutes of the Russia Committee record. 'Would it not be possible to start a civil war behind the Iron Curtain?'[22]

With Philby as the SIS representative on the committee co-ordinating Operation Valuable, it was doomed to failure from the start. But even without his involvement it would surely not have worked. It was not only poorly conceived – there was no resistance group to link up with – it was also hampered by inter-service rivalry between the Americans and the British.

Over the next four years a succession of émigrés was ferried across the Adriatic or parachuted into Albania to stir up revolt. Most were discovered immediately by the secret police, the Sigurimi, and either were used to transmit false information back to their controllers or were executed. A few managed to make it across the border into Greece. 'The information they brought was almost wholly negative,' Philby wrote. 'It was clear, at least, that they had nowhere found arms open to welcome them.' The final phase of the operation – an 'invasion' by around 1,000 armed émigrés to firm up the revolt – like the uprising itself, never materialized.[23]

Another of the early Cold War operations occurred in Vienna, where in 1949 the British discovered they could tap into the telephone lines leading to the Imperial Hotel, the Red Army headquarters. In order to disguise these activities, MI6 dug a seventy-foot tunnel under the road to the telephone lines. 'We had a total of three tunnels at various times,' a former SIS officer said. 'They were important operations and the customers became very excited about them, particularly the defence establishment. They really thought they were in on something.'

The telephone-tapping operations continued until 1955, when the wartime allies withdrew from Austria. Simon Preston, who as a young Royal Marines subaltern was attached to MI6 in Klagenfurt, was involved briefly in one of the operations:

> In late 1952 I was sent up to Vienna for a week because they wanted someone to help in pretending to dig the road up. We were actually listening in on the Russian communications, which had to go through that part of our sector. We dug a hole, and a long way down there was a chap with earphones on tapping the Russian telephone lines.
>
> My job was simply steering people on the surface away – police, curious passers-by – and that went on every day for a week.
>
> I was working with an MI6 character in his mid-thirties. He and I were put up by an eccentric landlady in the south end of Vienna, and every day we used to come back covered in mud. For some reason he had told her that he played football, and she used to ask, quite incredulously, '*Wieder fussball spielen, Herr Oberleutnant? Wieder fussball spielen?*'

Peter Lunn, then station head in Vienna, repeated the phone-tapping operation in Berlin in 1955, on this occasion digging a 600-yard tunnel underneath the Soviet zone in conjunction with the CIA. For nearly a year it provided some information on the Soviet military and, most importantly, the news of Khrushchev's secret denunciation of Stalin at the Twentieth Congress of the Communist Party. But even here there was to be failure. The minutes of the meeting to set up the Berlin tunnel were recorded on the British side by George Blake, who was soon revealed as a Soviet agent.

'Blake had given the whole thing away from the beginning, and the

Russians knew perfectly well we were tapping these lines,' a former MI6 officer said:

> They probably said, 'Nobody's to say anything important and keep the buggers busy. It's a waste of their money and manpower mounting an operation like this.' And it was a tremendous operation. It was shared with the Americans – the CIA finance went to I should think about 75 per cent of the thing – and there was enormous manpower put into it on processing the results, which were brought back on tapes. We had something like fifty or sixty Russian émigrés assembled in two Georgian houses overlooking Regent's Park, going through all these tapes.
>
> But the truth of it is, they weren't good operations. We all thought they were. Everybody did. Foreign Office said, 'Very important, very important.' And so on and so on. But the Russians knew.

Throughout the late 1940s and early 1950s the British and Americans set up stay-behind units in western Europe in preparation for the expected Soviet invasion. Simon Preston and Michael Giles, another Royal Marine officer, were among those selected to take part in the operation and were sent to Fort Monckton, the MI6 training base on the Solent, where they were given instruction in codes, the use of a pistol, and covert operations. 'We were made to do exercises, going out in the dead of night and pretending to blow up trains in the railway stations without the stationmaster or the porters seeing you,' Preston said. 'We crept about and pretended to lay charges on the right part of the railway engine with a view to blowing it up.'

Not all the sabotage was simulated. Michael Giles took part in an exercise at the Eastleigh Marshalling Yards, part of the Southern Railway:

> We laid bricks inside railway engines to simulate plastic explosives. I remember rows and rows of steam engines all under thick snow, standing there in clouds of vapour. There were troops out with dogs. The guards came past and I was actually hiding among the cylinder blocks of these engines as they went past. We were also opening up the lubricating tops of the axle boxes and pouring in sand. What happens is that after about fifty miles the sand in the axle box starts to turn them red hot and they all overheat.

The fact that the locomotives were in public use was seen as irrelevant. 'That wasn't my problem. We were playing for real.'

Preston was dispatched to London for an additional course on tradecraft. 'I had to do a ten-day course in Greenwich, learning about following people in the street and shaking off people following me – the practicalities of being in the intelligence world.'

They were then sent to Austria, where MI6 and the CIA had set up a number of underground bunkers, filled with weapons, clothing and supplies. 'We spent a lot of our time up in the mountains, learning all about the terrain, learning German, meeting other potential agents, recruiting agents if possible, identifying and plotting dropping zones,' Preston said:

> The whole object was that we would all form the nucleus of a partisan or a guerrilla army should the Russians invade. It was thought that within five years there would be a conventional war. We would be dropped back into the area we knew and immediately we would be among friends. The food, arms and explosives would be all there in the bunkers.
>
> It doesn't take much imagination to work out that the Russian Army would have hunted us from pillar to post. It would have been a short but interesting life I suspect. But I can't remember ever worrying about that.
>
> There was one nasty moment. We'd been up in the mountains for about a week when early one morning there was an enormous number of explosions down in the valley which sounded like the beginning of something. It turned out to be some kind of saint's day, and the villagers were just letting off fireworks.[24]

The highlight of MI6's 'special political action' was Operation Boot, the overthrow of Mohammed Mossadegh, the Iranian Prime Minister, who in 1951 had nationalized the Anglo-Iranian Oil Company. The Great Game – Britain's rivalry with Russia for control of Persia – had continued into the Cold War, given added significance by the importance of oil to the Western economies. By August 1944 the JIC was identifying Iran and Iraq as the area where friction between the two sides might most easily arise, reporting, 'It is clear that if it came to war, Russia would be likely to strike at Persia and Iraq in order to gain depth of defence for the Caucasian oilfields, to deny us most important sources of oil and to secure an outlet to the Persian Gulf.'[25]

British interests in Iran were centred on Anglo-Iranian, in which Churchill had bought a majority stake for the government in 1914. As well as ensuring a steady supply of cheap oil, it was an important source of intelligence, and since 1946, when the refusal of Russia to withdraw its troops from northern Iran had sparked fears that this was to be the first of the JIC's predicted 'local *faits accomplis*', the company's employees had also included an MI5 officer.[26]

Although the British played up Mossadegh's left-wing sympathies, it was the loss of Anglo-Iranian that led to MI6 action. Montague Wood-house, the SIS chief of station in Tehran, hatched a plot under which Mossadegh was to be overthrown by the traditional Middle Eastern method of orchestrated street violence followed by a coup. With the plans well under way, Mossadegh broke off relations with the British, leaving SIS without a base in Iran, although its main agents, the influential Rashidian brothers, remained in place. Woodhouse flew to Washington to bring the CIA into the action.

'I decided to emphasize the Communist threat to Iran rather than the need to recover control of the oil industry,' he wrote.

> Two separate components were dovetailed into the plan, because we had two distinct kinds of resources: an urban organization run by the brothers, and a number of tribal leaders in the south.
>
> We intended to activate both simultaneously. The urban organiz-ation included senior officers of the army and police, deputies and senators, mullahs, merchants, newspaper editors and elder statesmen, as well as mob-leaders. These forces, directed by the brothers, were to seize control of Tehran, preferably with the support of the Shah but if necessary without it, and to arrest Mossadegh and his ministers. At the same time, the tribal leaders were to make a show of force in the direction of the major cities in the south.

For almost a week, mobs, incited by CIA dollars, ran riot through the streets of Tehran, trampling several hundred people to death. Behind the scenes, the Rashidian brothers and their influential contacts in the army and the police pulled the strings, ensuring that anyone who might oppose the Prime Minister's removal was quietly disposed of.

The operation was an undoubted success, although perhaps not an unqualifed one. The downside of bringing the Americans in was that Anglo-Iranian – renamed British Petroleum – was left with just 40 per cent control of the newly formed National Iranian Oil Company, with various American companies taking a further 40 per cent. The CIA also claimed the credit for the success of the operation. But the Shah, who was grateful for the removal of the left-wing threat, knew the real story, and right up until the 1979 Islamic Revolution, Woodhouse's successors were accorded privileged access to the Peacock Throne.

The Shah was not the only grateful party. The British and the French have always been able to make good use of oil companies as cover for their agents. There are few countries willing to turn down the potential revenue offered by an exploration team from a major oil company. Like their predecessor, Anglo-Iranian, BP was among a number of British companies that was to have close relations with SIS, to the extent that senior executives were on the distribution lists for its reports.[27]

Stewart Menzies had retired in 1951 and was replaced by his deputy, Sir John Sinclair, a former Director of Military Intelligence, 'to ensure that military intelligence was given proper priority'. Despite the success of Operation Boot, Sinclair's time in charge was to become known as 'the Horrors', largely due to the failures in eastern Europe and the knock-on from the Third Man affair. The Americans wondered if British intelligence was not riddled with Communist spies.

While there was a good deal of respect among individual American officers, dating back to the war years, there was also a lot of resentment at the patronizing, superior attitude of some of their British counterparts. As early as 1943, 'Wild Bill' Donovan, head of the OSS, had made it clear that, while he was 'perfectly willing to co-ordinate on a higher level', he was 'determined not to tolerate any tutelage' from the British. America's post-war tendency to isolationism and its determination to undermine the British position in the world as a means of improving its own had already strained the relationship. The Third Man affair brought it close to breaking-point.[28]

The lowest point of 'the Horrors' came in April 1956 with the Buster Crabb affair. Commander Crabb, a veteran frogman who had been used in the past by SIS for special jobs, was to dive into Portsmouth harbour to gather intelligence on the Russian destroyer *Ordzhonikidze*, which had brought the Soviet leader Nikita Khrushchev on a state visit to Britain. Following his second dive, Crabb failed to return. His body was not found for more than a year, by which time it was impossible for the coroner to determine the cause of death, although there was inevitable speculation that he had been murdered by the Russians. It was a nightmare moment for the service: Crabb's death came literally as the Russians uncovered the Berlin tunnel, and Khrushchev's prestigious state visit collapsed into acrimony. The Crabb affair grabbed the headlines for days, with the service inevitably depicted as a group of bungling amateurs, and Anthony Eden, the British Prime Minister, went so far as publicly to dissociate his ministers from the affair.[29]

Sinclair was 'allowed' to take early retirement and Dick White, the head of MI5, was switched across to replace him and clear up the mess. He was immediately presented with a further problem.

Eden, believing that Britain's control of the Suez Canal was 'the lifeline to the empire', had become obsessed with removing Gamal Abdel Nasser, the Egyptian President. With the military deeply sceptical of Eden's plans 'to knock Nasser off his perch', the premier's main instrument had become SIS, and in particular the Special Political Action Group. George

Kennedy Young, the Deputy Chief, and Patrick Dean, initially SIS Foreign Office Adviser but promoted mid-crisis to be Chairman of the JIC, told Eden what he wanted to hear: Nasser was a dangerous dictator who was taking arms from Moscow and was determined to overthrow the Middle East monarchies on which Britain depended for its influence in the region.

SIS recruited a senior Egyptian air-force officer, Squadron Leader Assam ul-Din Mahmoud Khalil, giving him valuable intelligence on Israel as cover for meetings with his controllers. Julian Amery, an MP and former member of SOE who had been heavily involved in the Albanian fiasco, was drafted in to find dissidents who could be counted on to form a pro-British government. A senior SIS officer, Nicholas Elliot, was sent to Tel Aviv to liaise with the Israelis, whose involvement in the affair was to be kept secret to all but a very few British officials. The Israelis were to invade Egypt across the Sinai. The British and the French would then intervene – ostensibly to separate the two warring sides; in reality as part of what was effectively a joint British, French and Israeli invasion force aimed at replacing Nasser with someone more amenable to all three.

For the British at least, deposing the Egyptian leader was not enough. Various schemes were devised to assassinate him – perhaps an exploding electric razor, or poison gas in the ventilation system; or of course there was always the straightforward hit squad. White vetoed them all. Young laughingly told one planning meeting that 'thuggery is not on the agenda'. It was. While the collusion with Tel Aviv was known to only a few, the suggestion that Nasser should be killed appears to have been widespread. After a meeting with one senior treasury official, Humphrey Trevelyan, the British ambassador to Egypt, complained, 'High officials in the Treasury seem to have been very free with their proposals on what to do with Nasser, which included the most extreme solutions.'

Meanwhile, Eden ordered the BBC to stop broadcasting even-handed reports of the crisis, and the SIS-owned Near East Arab Broadcasting Service, which ran a genuinely successful commercial radio station, Sharq al-Adna, from Cyprus, began pumping out blatant anti-Nasser propaganda so unsubtle that one commentator has suggested it 'could well have been conceived by Dr Goebbels'.

The SIS contributions were no more successful than the operation as a whole. Intelligence out of Cairo both before and during the crisis was at best highly optimistic if not downright misleading, particularly with regard to Nasser's popularity and the lack of any viable opposition. The main network, founded around another black-propaganda organization, the Arab News Agency, was rolled up by the Egyptian security police and a number of MI6 officers were arrested. To add to the British woes, Khalil turned out to be a double agent who had apparently kept Nasser well-informed of what the Egyptian leader subsequently dubbed 'the Restoration Plot'.

There was an element of irony in this failure, since Egyptian intelligence held MI6 in such high regard that its training school used James Bond books as textbooks in tradecraft. 'The Egyptians had a thing about 007,' a former SIS officer said:

> Their representative in London in the days of Nasser was instructed to go and buy every book by Fleming on James Bond because they wanted to have it as compulsory reading for the training course for their intelligence service. At that time, we happened to have a good connection with the Egyptian intelligence service of which they were not aware, and indeed this chap went and bought them all and was congratulated on subsequent visits to Cairo for having done so.[30]

The Suez Crisis served to draw MI6's attention away from events in eastern Europe, where, at the same time, the Hungarian uprising was taking place and food riots were sweeping across Poland. Although the immediate catalysts for these events could not have been predicted – most being associated with the de-Stalinization campaign that took place in the Soviet Bloc following Khrushchev's secret denunciation of his predecessor – MI6 had been active behind the scenes for some time providing covert assistance to potential Hungarian rebels and was aware that they were planning an uprising.

The mid-1950s were regarded by both British and American intelligence as the last chance to challenge the Soviet domination of eastern Europe. The Eisenhower administration had been elected on a platform of liberating the Soviet satellites – the so-called 'Rollback' policy – but in the ten years since the end of the war the Russians had considerably strengthened their hold over eastern Europe. All reports from inside the satellite states spoke of high levels of dissatisfaction, but the presence of 100,000 Russian troops held out little hope that any revolt was likely to succeed.

Nevertheless, American intelligence had stepped up its covert operations in eastern Europe in the twelve-month period leading up to the Hungarian uprising, training the 'Red Sox' teams of Polish, Hungarian, Czech and Romanian émigrés for covert action inside their home countries. Allen Dulles, the head of the CIA, told the National Security Council that 'developments in the satellites present the greatest opportunity for the last ten years both covertly and overtly to exploit the situation'.

Khrushchev's secret speech denouncing Stalin had a powerful effect across eastern Europe. Neither SIS nor the CIA had been able to get hold of the text of the speech, but a Mossad agent in Warsaw seduced a secretary working in the Polish Communist Party headquarters and persuaded her to let him make a transcript which the Israelis then passed to the Americans. Copies of the speech were run off in their thousands and were distributed clandestinely throughout eastern Europe, fuelling demands for reform, particularly in Poland and Hungary.

The British had been in close contact with dissident elements inside Hungary for some time, spiriting them across the border into the British zone of Austria for resistance training in preparation for a future uprising.

British intelligence had stumbled on a startlingly easy way of getting people out of Hungary and into Austria. An illegal frontier crosser admitted that her nephew, a driver on one of the trains taking Soviet staff officers from Hungary to their HQ in Austria, had smuggled her across the border in the cab. Since the Soviet officers were the train's only occupants, there were no document checks. 'From an intelligence point of view, it was like finding the Holy Grail,' one officer said. 'We had quite a traffic to and from Hungary. When our people had to return to Vienna it was a simple matter for them to make contact with the lady's nephew and "persuade" him to accommodate them.'

But the dissidents appear to have made their own way across the border rendezvousing with their contact in true Cold War fashion, often quite literally under a certain lamp-post in a backstreet of a border town. A military officer working for MI6 would then take them up into the mountains for a four-day crash course in a variety of military skills before they were infiltrated back into Hungary.

The expectation that an uprising would take place is surprising and – given that there were riots going on in Poland in support of reform at the same time – raises the possibility of outside co-ordination, even that some of Perkins's old networks were still in place. Certainly MI6 planned to support resistance fighters in both Hungary and Czechoslovakia. The SIS representatives in Prague and Budapest went out into the woods burying stay-behind packs like those that were being hidden in the Austrian Alps by Preston and Giles.

No one could have expected quite such propitious circumstances for an uprising as those caused in Hungary by the forced resignation in 1955 of the liberal Prime Minister Imre Nagy and the news a few months later of Khrushchev's denunciation of Stalin. As details of the secret speech became more widely known, the clamour for reforms began to grow.

On 23 October 1956 a student demonstration calling for free elections, the withdrawal of Russian troops and the return of Nagy brought a quarter of a million people on to the streets of Budapest. Large numbers of weapons began to appear in the crowd. Some came from the American arms caches in Austria and others almost certainly were British. Fighting broke out with the security forces. In an attempt to placate the demonstrators, Nagy was reappointed Prime Minister. There was sporadic fighting for several days, followed by a series of reforms introduced by Nagy, including the disbandment of the AVH secret police and the abandonment of the one-party system.

On 1 November the Red Army invaded Hungary. The uprising was suppressed. Nagy was arrested and the reforms were brought to an early end. Whether or not Western intelligence was aware that there was to be an attempted uprising, no one seems to have been expecting anything on quite the scale that occurred. Allen Dulles told the National Security Council, 'In a sense, what had occurred there was a miracle. Events had belied all our past views that a popular revolt in the face of modern weapons was an utter impossibility.'[31]

Throughout the Cold War, MI6 special operations were closely co-ordinated with the dissemination of if not black then at the very least grey propaganda. It was produced by the Foreign Office Information Research Department (IRD) – a direct descendant of an earlier secret Foreign Office department known simply as EH, because it was located in Electra House on the Embankment. At the start of the Second World War, EH had been amalgamated with Section D and a War Office special-operations organization to form the SOE. But it was soon hived off to form a separate psychological-operations department, the Political Warfare Executive, led by Sir Robert Bruce Lockhart, Sidney Reilly's co-conspirator in the Lockhart Plot.

At the end of the war, the PWE's intelligence-gathering responsibilities were taken over by the Foreign Office's Political Information Department. It was not until three years later that the propaganda function was reactivated, when Christopher Mayhew, then a junior Foreign Office minister, set up the IRD 'to discourage the Slavs from using the UN for blackguarding us, by occasionally pulling a skeleton out of their cupboard for a change'. It prepared briefs for politicians and journalists that were specifically designed 'to stimulate subversive activities in the Soviet orbits'.[32]

The Russia Committee had already enthusiastically advocated a co-ordinated policy of propaganda and special operations to counter Soviet influence in eastern Europe. 'We have a good analogy in our successful propaganda campaign during the war directed towards stimulating resistance movements in Europe,' Kirkpatrick recalled.

The V-sign was emblazoned all over the world. But at the same time we acted. We parachuted men, money and arms into occupied territory. We were not inhibited by fear that the Germans would find out what we were doing or that they might react, or that we might be criticized. Propaganda on the larger scale was co-ordinated with our policy. The result was success.[33]

The IRD's first use in conjunction with MI6 special ops came during Operation Valuable and the attempts 'to detach Albania from the Soviet Orbit'. But its attentions were soon attracted from 'the Slavs' to anywhere in the world where forces regarded as anti-British were operating. Long before Suez, Sharq al-Adna carried IRD-inspired news reports, as did the Arab News Agency, which had offices in all the major Middle East capitals and numbered most of the major Arab newspapers among its subscribers. Africa was flooded with IRD propaganda, while the department set up offices in Singapore and Hong Kong to further British influence in Malaya and the Far East.[34]

One of the most interesting aspects of the IRD's work with journalists was its relationship with the BBC, and in particular with the Overseas Service, whose director, Major-General Ian Jacob, was a member of the Russia Committee. Jacob had been drafted on to the committee after approaching the Foreign Office 'for guidance' on British policy towards Moscow. The committee's meetings were moved from Tuesdays to Thursdays to suit his schedule, and he took the key members of the IRD to lunch at the Café Royal to discuss policy. Thereafter the BBC was 'extremely helpful and co-operative'. Its coverage of the Soviet Bloc was 'tempered' so much that there were worries that if anything it was pushing propaganda too hard.[35]

In his twelve years in charge, White succeeded in moving MI6 away from what he regarded as the cowboy behaviour of the Robber Barons, who in the old days had met up every evening in the bar below Broadway Buildings to share a drink and dream up new targets for 'special political action'. Under a further reorganization which more sensibly reflected SIS coverage, four production directorates were formed, with the chief controllers becoming directors: DP1 to cover Western Europe; DP2, the Middle East and Africa; DP3, the Far East and the Americas; DP4, the Soviet Bloc and operations carried out from the United Kingdom.[36]

But there were to be two remaining hangovers from 'the Horrors' – the disclosure of George Blake as a long-term Soviet penetration agent and the 1963 defection of Philby to Moscow.

# CHAPTER 9

# The Ring of Five

It is possible to hate treason without making a caricature of a traitor.

Robert Cecil, *The Cambridge Comintern*, 1983

Walter Krivitsky, a Russian defector, arrived in London in early 1940 to tell MI5 what he knew of Soviet espionage against Britain. He brought with him a long list of NKVD agents, including 'a young English journalist' who had covered the Spanish Civil War for a London newspaper and a Foreign Office official – 'a Scotsman of good family' who had been educated at Eton and Oxford and worked for the Russians for idealistic reasons alone.

The journalist was Kim Philby, the Scots diplomat Donald Maclean. But neither case was followed up. The Krivitsky debriefing provided no information that could help in the war against Hitler. It was soon filed and forgotten.[1]

H. A. R. Philby had followed in the footsteps of his father, the noted Arabist Harry St John Bridger Philby, with an education at Westminster and then Trinity College, Cambridge. Shortly before coming down in 1933, he approached Maurice Dobb, one of his tutors and a well-known Communist, for advice. He had decided to travel in Europe and wanted to become a member of the party, How should he go about it? Dobb referred him to 'some French comrades who may be able to help you'. The 'comrades' were the members of an NKVD front organization, the World Committee for the Relief of Victims of German Fascism. They told Philby to go to Vienna to help the Communist underground.[2]

Philby's desire to become a Communist was not unusual at Cambridge. During the 1930s the effects of the depression, the overwhelming power of the British class system, and the rise of Hitler and Mussolini led many politically active undergraduates to see Communism as the only answer.

'The Wall Street Crash seemed to herald the end of capitalism,' said Robert Cecil, another graduate of Trinity in the 1930s and a contemporary of Philby at MI6:

In Germany and Italy fascism was in power and by 1936 was threatening to take control also in Spain. The USA remained aloof and in Britain and France the democratic trumpet gave a very uncertain and wavering sound. To this hard core of young intellectuals the schematic and revolutionary message of Marxism seemed to hold all the answers; it was a cause to which they could devote their idealism, a cause that would assuage their despair.[3]

Within months of Philby arriving in Austria the right-wing Christian Social government had organized a putsch, declaring the Social Democrats who controlled the city government in Vienna illegal. The private armies of the two political parties clashed on the streets of the capital, and more than a thousand people were killed. Philby worked as a courier for the Communists and helped those socialists and Communists who were on the government's wanted list to flee the country.

'I greatly admired Kim Philby,' one of those helping the refugees wrote:

Here was a young Englishman, determined to risk much to help the underground freedom movement in a small country which must have been of very limited interest to him. But doubts began to dawn on me when Philby appeared as a communist go-between and when he declared that he could provide all the money we needed for our work. The money which Philby offered could only have come from the Russians.[4]

Philby had not actually been recruited as a Soviet agent at this time, but his potential had been noted by Teodor Maly, a former Catholic priest who was now a Soviet intelligence officer based in Vienna. Philby then married Litzi Friedmann, his lover and a leading Communist activist, to get her out of Austria safely. She appears to have been under Maly's control, and once in Britain she got in touch with Edith Tudor-Hart, a British Communist, who made the actual approach to Philby to recruit him. A month before Philby returned to Britain, in May 1934, Maly had sent another KGB officer, Arnold Deutsch, to England to act as Philby's control.[5]

Tudor-Hart's role remains a matter of some controversy. But during the 1930s national Communist parties had close links to Soviet intelligence through the Comintern. Local Communist parties discouraged scientists, students, teachers and government employees from openly joining – ostensibly to protect their careers, but in reality to provide a ready source of well-placed agents. Selected local party members were frequently placed entirely at the disposal of the Soviet intelligence

*Rezident*, normally having been 'expelled' from the party some months earlier. Initial contact between the *Rezident* and his potential assistant was normally through an intermediary or 'cut-out', usually a woman, in case the target turned the offer down and went to the authorities.

Deutch sent Philby back to Cambridge with instructions to recommend a number of his former fellow students who would make good recruits for the NKVD. Top of his list was a young man who was about to join the Foreign Office. Donald Maclean was the son of a Liberal Cabinet minister. Tall, dark and athletic, he had won an exhibition at Trinity Hall, where he became part of a left-wing circle at Cambridge which

Donald Maclean

already included Philby, Guy Burgess and Anthony Blunt. It was Philby who made the initial approach to Maclean, who swiftly accepted the offer to work for Soviet intelligence.[6]

One of the other names on the list, almost as an afterthought, was that of Burgess, an Old Etonian who had won a scholarship in modern history to Trinity College. 'He had the reputation of being the most brilliant undergraduate of his day. Indeed he did not belie his reputation,' wrote Goronwy Rees, a fellow of All Souls, Oxford, who under Burgess's influence had a brief flirtation with Communism:

> His conversation had the more charm because he was very good looking in a boyish, athletic, very English way; it seemed incongruous that

almost everything he said made it quite clear that he was a homosexual and a communist. Among the multitude of his diverse activities, social and political, he spoke most freely of his success in helping to organize a recent strike of busmen in the town of Cambridge.[7]

Blunt was the eldest of the four and, by the time Burgess persuaded him to join the Comintern, already a fellow of Trinity. His father was a clergyman who had served as chaplain to the British Embassy in Paris, where Blunt acquired a passion for French art. He went to Marlborough before going up to Trinity on a scholarship in mathematics, later switching to modern languages. He was elected a fellow in 1932 on the basis of his work on *The History and Theory of Paintings with Special Reference to Poussin.*

Anthony Blunt

It was Blunt who got Burgess elected to the Apostles, an exclusive dining-club centred on King's College but including a number of Trinity scholars. Its values, based in part on the teaching of the philosopher G. E. Moore, included a belief in freedom of thought and expression and a denial of all moral restraints other than loyalty to one's friends. A significant number of its members were, like both Burgess and Blunt, homosexual.[8] John Cairncross, the Fifth Man, was recruited later and was never part of the group formed by the other four, who remained closely and unwisely linked through their continued mutual friendship with Burgess.[9]

On arriving back in Britain, Philby had attempted to join the Civil Service, but it soon became clear that his referees felt obliged to suggest that his political loyalties might be questioned. Rather than have that negative assessment placed on the official record, he withdrew his application and settled for a job in journalism with the *Review of Reviews*.

Blunt remained at Trinity. But Burgess and Maclean were now also seeking employment, and they and Philby carefully set about creating political personae that would expunge all memory of their 'youthful dalliances' with Communism. Burgess and Philby joined the Anglo-German Fellowship, a pro-German organization with close links to the German Ministry of Propaganda.

This was not just an attempt to create what one former colleague described as their 'unbreakable cover'; it was also a valuable source of intelligence for their Soviet masters. 'No one has so far suggested that I had switched from Communism to Nazism,' Philby later wrote. 'The simpler, and true, explanation is that overt and covert links between Britain and Germany at that time were of serious concern to the Soviet Government.'[10]

Burgess made a trip to the Soviet Union and a number to Germany, which allowed him to announce to those friends who were baffled by his membership of the Anglo-German Fellowship and his acceptance of the post of personal assistant to the far-right Conservative MP Jack Macnamara that, having seen both countries for himself, he now realized that his student infatuation with Communism had been misguided.[11]

Meanwhile Maclean was telling his mother that he intended to take the Foreign Office entry examination. When she asked whether this might not conflict with his Communist beliefs, Maclean replied, 'You must think I turn like a weathercock, but the fact is I've rather gone off all that lately.' He passed the entry exams with flying colours and had a good final interview, only stumbling momentarily at the end.

'I thought they'd finished when one of them suddenly said: "By the way, Mr Maclean. We understand that you, like other young men, held strong Communist views while you were at Cambridge. Do you still hold those views?"' Maclean later told his mother. 'I'm afraid I did a double-take: Shall I deny the truth, or shall I brazen it out? I decided to brazen it out. "Yes," I said. "I did have such views – and I haven't entirely shaken them off." I think they must have liked my honesty because they nodded, looked at each other and smiled. Then the chairman said: "Thank you, that will be all, Mr Maclean."'[12]

Maclean thus became the first of the Ring of Five to fulfil his mission, entering the Diplomatic Service in October 1935.

Burgess had more difficulty finding employment, but he was eventually accepted by the BBC, where he worked himself into a role as producer on *The Week in Westminster*, which gave him access to a wealth of political gossip. He also developed widespread contacts through the so-called 'Homintern', his network of well-placed homosexual friends, passing on what he could to friends in MI6. This and his BBC experience made him an ideal candidate when the service decided to create a special-operations organization which, among other things, would set up radio stations broadcasting black propaganda into Germany.[13]

Philby meanwhile had gone to Spain, ostensibly as a freelance journalist but in fact on the instructions of Maly, who in early 1936 had been sent to London to take overall charge of the NKVD networks. Maly had been ordered by Moscow Centre to send one of his British agents to Spain under journalistic cover. Once there his task was to help to assassinate General Franco. Philby acquired a letter of accreditation from a London news agency and arrived in Spain in early 1937. Reporting from the areas controlled by Franco's forces, he bombarded *The Times* with unsolicited dispatches until the newspaper agreed to take him on.

He swiftly became one of the best-informed correspondents on Franco's side, with a detailed knowledge of the involvement of German and Italian forces which he communicated to Moscow through regular meetings with Soviet contacts across the border in France. An incident in which a shell landed on a car in which Philby was travelling, fatally wounding the three other occupants, led to his acceptance by Franco's forces as a hero and the award from the General himself of the Red Cross of Military Merit. But by now the plan to assassinate Franco had been aborted.

On the outbreak of the Second World War *The Times* sent Philby to France. But he was soon back in London with little to occupy his time. He attempted to get into the Government Code and Cypher School at Bletchley Park, but was turned down. Burgess manoeuvred a position for him in SIS as his assistant. When Section D was swallowed up by the newly formed Special Operations Executive in June 1940, Burgess was pronounced surplus to requirements. But Philby retained his position, becoming an instructor at SOE's Beaulieu training school. When SIS was looking around for someone who would beef up the Iberian operations of Section V, its counter-espionage section, Philby's experience in Spain earned him the job.

'My new job would require personal contacts with the rest of SIS and MI5,' Philby wrote in an assessment of its usefulness to his Soviet masters. 'There was also a suggestion of Foreign Office interest, not to mention the service departments. By accident, I discovered that the archives of SIS were next door to Section V.'

Shortly after his arrival in Section V, Philby persuaded the archivist to allow him to look at the files on the Soviet Union and was able to provide his new controller, Anatoly Gorsky, code-named 'Henry', with details of the pre-war SIS agents there.[14]

Maclean had rapidly become a rising star within the Foreign Office and by 1938 was third secretary in the Paris embassy, where, according to Robert Cecil, he would have seen 'virtually all' the correspondence of Sir Eric Phipps, the ambassador and a staunch advocate of appeasement. It has to be assumed that he was passing the ambassador's views on to his Soviet control, Cecil said:

> Such reports can scarcely have failed to influence Stalin during the critical period in the summer of 1939 when he was making up his mind to ditch the democracies and throw in his lot with Hitler, as he finally did in August. After the war broke out, it would have been possible for Maclean to report the existence of Anglo-French military plans to support Finland in her winter war against the USSR, and to attack Soviet oil wells in Baku, in order to reduce the volume of oil flowing into the Nazi war machine.[15]

After leaving MI6, Burgess had gone back to the BBC, where he had responsibility for liaison with SIS and SOE and the organization of propaganda. His contacts within the political world were invaluable to him in collecting information from indiscreet friends, and ensured that news of the proposed D-Day landings reached Stalin 'well before either of his two allies saw fit to inform him'.[16]

Burgess spent much of the war living with Blunt in the Bentinck Street flat of Lord Rothschild. Blunt had resigned his Cambridge fellowship in 1936 and joined the Warburg Institute to continue his art studies, before applying for a job with the Field Security Police, the fledgling Intelligence Corps, the role of which was to hunt down suspected enemy agents behind allied lines and interrogate them. He received two replies, one rejecting him, the other accepting him, and ripping up the former he reported for training. Halfway through his course, MI5, which was vetting all applicants for such posts, ordered him to be recalled, since he had visited Russia and had once sent a contribution to a left-wing journal. But military intelligence, with its inbuilt mistrust of MI5, sent him back again to continue his course.[17]

Following the fall of France, Blunt was taken in by his friend Rothschild, who was himself working for MI5, and despite that organization's previous ruling that he was not to be employed in any sort of intelligence work he was soon recruited by Guy Liddell, one of its most senior officers. He spent much of the war collecting intelligence by intercepting the diplomatic bags of neutral missions based in London, and on occasion towards the end of the war, when the preparations for 'the next war' with the Soviet Union were being made, stood in as MI5's representative on the JIC. Blunt passed on to Gorsky full details of the Security Service's organization and operations and any intelligence that might be of interest to the Russians.[18]

Shortly before the evacuation of Paris, Maclean had met and married Melinda Marling, the eldest daughter of a Chicago businessman. They returned to London together, where he was promoted to second secretary and posted to the General Department, which liaised with the Ministries of Shipping and Economic Warfare – the latter being in charge of the SOE. How much high-grade information he was able to pass to his Soviet control is not clear. But Moscow Centre apparently regarded him as a valued agent, since he alone among the five was never seriously considered to be a double agent and when he was transferred to the Washington embassy in April 1944 his London case officer was also sent to the American capital to handle him.[19]

John Cairncross had joined the Foreign Office in 1936, topping the entrance examination, and at one point he shared an office with Maclean, unaware that he too was a Soviet spy. At the outbreak of the war, following a spell in the Treasury, he was made private secretary to Lord Hankey, who had a wide range of responsibilities including the intelligence services. According to Yuri Modin, Cairncross was the first Soviet agent to obtain details of Tube Alloys, the Anglo-American project to create the atomic bomb, known to the Americans as the Manhattan Project. Cairncross, ever anxious to play down his own role among the five, has denied this. But, since the Tube Alloys project fell within Hankey's responsibilities, Modin's claim holds the more credence.[20]

Cairncross was later transferred to Bletchley Park, where he passed the decrypt 'flimsies' directly to his Soviet control. It is possible to accept his argument that when he handed over details of the German Tiger tank and the complete plans for the Wehrmacht's 1943 offensive Operation Citadel he was helping the war effort in a way the British authorities seemed reluctant to do. His information was invaluable in the Soviet victory at the Battle of Kursk, the turning-point on the eastern front. But the Red Army and the KGB had been widely infiltrated by German agents during the period before June 1941 when Berlin and Moscow were working in tandem, and he could easily have compromised the whole of the Ultra operation.[21]

Philby's new job in Section V of MI6 was mainly concerned with following the trail of Abwehr agents arriving in Spain and Portugal as a prelude to infiltrating Britain. As such he was a key recipient of the Abwehr's radio traffic decyphered by GC&CS. One of the items that passed his desk was a decrypt revealing that Admiral Canaris, the head

John
Cairncross

of the Abwehr, was planning to go to Spain. Philby, unaware of the links
with Madame Szymanska, sketched out a plan to assassinate him, which
to his chagrin was swiftly vetoed by Menzies.[22]

Philby also volunteered for regular stints as duty officer in Broadway
Buildings, which gave him access to much more information. 'It was an
instructive occupation,' he wrote. 'In the course of a single night, telegrams would come in from all parts of the world, throwing new light on
the operations of the service. One file available to night-duty officers in
Broadway was especially valuable to me. It contained telegrams from the
War Office to the British Military Mission in Moscow, sent over SIS
channels.'[23]

But when Philby told Gorsky that British intelligence was not operating
any agents in Moscow, having been ordered to stop all operations against
the Soviet Union following the German invasion, Moscow Centre apparently found it impossible to believe. For two years Philby was suspected
by the KGB of being an SIS plant. 'He is lying to us in a most insolent
manner,' one report concluded. When Blunt confirmed what Philby said,
that only led Moscow Centre to conclude that he too must be a plant.
Burgess and Cairncross appear to have been similarly damned. Only
Maclean seems to have escaped suspicion.[24]

But in 1944, following a reshuffle in Moscow Centre, they were all
rehabilitated. It was to be a good year for the Cambridge Five. Maclean
was posted as a First Secretary to Washington, where he had access to
a wealth of information on Anglo-American relations and their secret

post-war agreements, including the exchanges of intelligence and atomic secrets. Philby took charge of Section IX, the SIS department handling the Soviet Union. Blunt began attending JIC meetings which increasingly discussed ways of countering the future Soviet threat. Even Burgess succeeded in getting a job with the Foreign Office, albeit in the News Department. Cairncross had been transferred to Section V of SIS at his own request. But his was a minor position, and he was not in a position to supply anything that Philby was not already giving to the Russians.[25]

In early 1945 Philby presented Robert Cecil, then personal assistant to 'C', with his proposals for the organizational structure of Section IX. 'It included a substantial number of overseas stations to be held by officers under diplomatic cover, who would be directly responsible to the Head of IX,' Cecil wrote:

> With hindsight, it is easy to see why Philby pitched his demands so high and why he aimed to create his own empire within SIS. Quite apart from his covert aims, it is also clear that he foresaw more plainly than I the onset of the Cold War, bringing with it more menacing surveillance and making necessary more permanent use of diplomatic cover.
>
> My vision of the future was more opaque and optimistic; I sent the memorandum back to Philby, suggesting that he might scale down his demands. Within hours, Vivian and Philby had descended upon me, upholding their requirements and insisting that these be transmitted to the FO. I gave way. But I have since reflected with a certain wry amusement on the hypocrisy of Philby who, supposedly working in the cause of 'peace' (as Soviet propaganda always insists), demanded a larger Cold War apparatus, when he could have settled for a smaller one.[26]

Philby's new job as head of the Soviet section of British foreign intelligence boosted his reputation to 'almost God-like proportions', according to Modin, who by now was routinely handling his product and that of the other members of the Cambridge Five in his role as a translator on the British desk at Moscow Centre.

But in the late summer of 1945 two defectors claimed that the Soviet Union had infiltrated British intelligence. Igor Gouzenko, a cypher clerk at the Soviet Embassy in Ottawa, exposed the British atom spy Alan Nunn May, a contemporary of Maclean's at Trinity Hall, and provided evidence of a Russian mole in British intelligence.[27]

While nothing Gouzenko said pointed directly to Philby, the other defector was far more dangerous. Konstantin Volkov, a KGB officer working under consular cover in Turkey, contacted the British Embassy, saying he wanted to defect. Volkov, who had served on the British desk at Moscow Centre, sought asylum and a large sum of money in return for a wide variety of intelligence, including information on a number of unnamed Soviet agents in Britain: two inside the Foreign Office (Burgess and Maclean) and seven who had served in wartime intelligence, one of whom was 'fulfilling the function of head of a section of British counter-espionage in London'.[28]

For security reasons, Volkov insisted that the offer be relayed to London in a handwritten communication addressed to a high-ranking official, but this could not prevent it landing on Philby's desk.

'Two Soviet agents in the Foreign Office, one head of a counter-espionage organization in London!' Philby wrote. 'I stared at the papers rather longer than necessary to compose my thoughts. The only course was to put a brave face on it.' Volkov had put a three-week time limit on his offer. Eight days had already elapsed. Philby needed to play for time. He also needed to warn Moscow. 'That evening I worked late,' he wrote. 'The situation seemed to call for urgent action of an extra-curricular nature.'[29]

Philby suggested to Menzies that an experienced officer be dispatched to Istanbul to deal with Volkov direct, hoping that he himself would be sent. He was disappointed when Menzies suggested that Brigadier Douglas Roberts, head of Security Intelligence (Middle East), be sent instead. But, since Roberts was scared of flying and would travel only by land or sea, this added a useful delay. Menzies then agreed that Philby should go himself, but the flight was delayed by weather and when he finally arrived in Istanbul the deadline was nearly up. All attempts to contact Volkov failed.[30]

'The exact details of what happened to the wretched Volkov in Moscow are unknown to me,' said Modin. 'Suffice it to say that he was summarily tried and shot. The official line was that he had fallen ill in Turkey. I imagine he was simply given an injection to put him to sleep and then sent home on grounds of ill-health. It was the usual practice.'

In his role in overall charge of operations against the Soviet Union, Philby was able to provide the KGB with details of the agents the British were sending into the Baltic republics. 'We knew in advance about every operation that took place by air, land or sea, even in mountainous and inaccessible regions,' Modin said. 'We knew who was coming, and when, and we neutralized these spies and saboteurs; most were arrested and imprisoned. The KGB let some of the agents go free temporarily, to avoid jeopardizing Philby, while others were turned and became our double agents.'[31]

Philby was himself posted to Istanbul, as head of the SIS station, in early 1947. His main job was recruiting agents to send into the southern

Soviet Union. It was a difficult task, Robert Cecil would later recall – not least because Stalin had ordered large numbers of the ethnic minorities who might be persuaded to side against Moscow to be deported to central Asia. 'Some Armenians were found, however, who would be induced to venture into the Soviet part of their homeland, and these were pitilessly sacrificed to the vengeance of the KGB.'

Maclean's Washington posting appeared to be going well, both for his Foreign Office career and for the KGB. The amount of information he was able to supply was phenomenal. He was appointed as one of the joint secretaries of the Anglo-American Combined Policy Committee, which was responsible for liaison on atomic matters. Despite the restrictions imposed by the McMahon Act, which prevented British involvement in the production of nuclear weapons, Maclean was able to tell Moscow how much uranium the Americans were acquiring, allowing the Russians to make a remarkably accurate assessment of the US nuclear arsenal.

He was also able to provide his control with details of the British-led plans for a West German state, comprising the French, American and British zones; the blueprint for the new North Atlantic alliance; and vital information on the allied reaction to the Soviet blockade of Berlin. Secure in the knowledge that, despite the American sabre-rattling, Truman had decided not to resort to force unless the Russians fired first, Stalin held the whip hand throughout the 1948 Berlin crisis.[32]

Melinda Maclean was living with her mother in New York, so 'Homer', as the KGB had now code-named her husband, had the perfect excuse to leave Washington each weekend, meeting Gorsky to pass on the week's take away from the routine surveillance of Soviet diplomats in the federal capital. The information he produced also included the content of Top-Secret exchanges, in March 1945, between Churchill and Truman over the fate of the leaders of the Polish Home Army who, while *en route* to London, had been 'diverted' to Moscow and incarcerated in the Lubyanka. Although this was by no means the most important information he was reporting to Moscow, it would ultimately prove to be among the most significant.[33]

Burgess was also becoming extremely useful to Moscow. Unproductive in his role in the Foreign Office News Department, he managed in 1946 to get himself a job as private secretary to Hector McNeil, Foreign Office Minister under Ernest Bevin, the British Foreign Secretary and a key figure in the negotiations over the future of Europe and the creation of NATO. Burgess also acted as a postbox for information from Philby in Istanbul.

Blunt had left MI5 at the end of the war to become Surveyor of the King's Pictures, but he continued to act as a go-between for Burgess and later for Philby and Maclean. Cairncross had also quit intelligence work and was at the Treasury, where his contribution had faded into insignificance. But Modin, who in mid-1947 had arrived in London to take control of the Cambridge Five, claims to have reactivated Cairncross, who he discovered had access to the defence estimates and was able to provide detailed information on Britain's defences and contribution to the fledgling NATO.[34]

Although Cairncross admitted having been in contact with Modin during this period, he always denied giving him any classified information. But he does appear to have used a meeting with a former colleague at Bletchley Park in an attempt to gather intelligence. 'He invited me to lunch at the Travellers Club in February 1949, when he was back at the Treasury,' Henry Dryden said. 'In the middle of the meal, he disconcertingly asked: "Are we still reading Russian cyphers?" I had no first-hand knowledge of any current work on Russian and the only off-putting response I could think of, on the spur of the moment, was to shake my head and mutter "one-time".* He did not pursue this.'[35]

But, despite the success of the network, things were about to unravel. In late 1949 Philby was sent to Washington as SIS liaison officer. Before his departure he was briefed in London on a major American-led counter-espionage operation. A mistake four years earlier by Soviet cypher clerks operating Moscow Centre's communications links with its officers in the field had led to a break into their one-time pad system. In January 1949 American cryptanalysts working on what had become known as the Venona material had succeeded in decyphering a message which showed that in mid-1945 Soviet intelligence had an agent in Washington code-named Homer who had access to the secret messages between Truman and Churchill on the fate of the leaders of the Polish Home Army.

Philby's later delight in ridiculing the Western intelligence agencies had a great deal to do with KGB propaganda. But since Harold Macmillan, the future British Foreign Secretary, would tell a House of Commons debate on the affair that 'there were 6000 people each of whom might have been the man', Philby's description of the FBI investigation into Homer at the time of his arrival in Washington appears to have been not far off the truth.

'Characteristically, they had put in an immense amount of work resulting in an immense amount of waste paper,' he said:

It had so far occurred neither to them nor the British that a diplomat was involved, let alone a fairly senior diplomat. Instead, the investigation had concentrated on non-diplomatic employees of the embassy,

---

* A reference to the supposedly unbreakable one-time pad cypher system.

and particularly on those locally recruited, the sweepers, cleaners, bottle-washers and the rest. A charlady with a Latvian grandmother, for instance, would rate a 15-page report, crowded with insignificant detail of herself, her family and friends. It was testimony to the enormous resources of the FBI, and to the pitiful extent to which those resources were squandered.[36]

The Homer investigation led both Maclean and Burgess to lose their nerve. Maclean, who was in the middle of a tour as Head of Chancery in Cairo when Philby learned of Venona, descended into an orgy of drunkenness and homosexuality, culminating in a rampage through the flat of a secretary at the American Embassy in May 1950 which led to his being recalled to London.

The Foreign Office blamed overwork and gave him time off before promoting him to be head of the American Department in the Foreign Office, a post that Harold Macmillan later attempted to play down. 'This department in the Foreign Office principally deals with Latin American affairs,' the then Foreign Minister told the House of Commons after Maclean's defection. 'The United States questions which are dealt with by the American Department are largely routine.'[37]

In fact the post was an extremely important one, and, in view of the tensions between America and Britain over the Korean War, almost certainly a highly profitable one for Moscow. 'Donald would have had access to almost any kind of information he wanted to see,' said Robert Cecil, Maclean's deputy in the American department. Among documents known to have crossed Maclean's desk was a detailed briefing-paper on a visit to Washington by Clement Attlee, the British Prime Minister, in order to dissuade the Americans from extending the war into China. 'Assuming that he succeeded even in getting a condensed version to the Russians, and assuming they believed it, it would have been of inestimable value in advising the Chinese and North Koreans on strategy and negotiating positions.'[38]

Perhaps predictably, Burgess was more of a problem for Modin, his Russian control. McNeil, apparently embarrassed by Burgess's 'insanitary habits', had sought to 'promote' him to a post in the newly formed Information Research Department. Christopher Mayhew, its head, very quickly decided that he was not suitable, although not before a Soviet Bloc newspaper had carried a remarkably accurate article on the secret organization. Burgess was moved in November 1948 to the Far East department, where, despite a relatively junior position, he too would have seen a number of important documents relating to the Korean War.[39]

By now he was declining into alcoholism, and in autumn 1949 a visit to

Gibraltar and Tangiers saw him loudly pointing out British and American intelligence officers in public. In what was seen in the Foreign Office as a last chance, he was posted to Washington, where, to the dismay of Philby's second wife, Aileen, he decided to lodge with his old friend. His role as a second secretary handling the Far East gave him a continued insight into the transatlantic tensions over the Korean War. But he soon fell out with his boss and was moved to deal with Middle Eastern affairs.[40]

Then in April 1951 US cryptanalysts working on the Venona material found the vital clue to Homer's identity. For part of 1944 he had regular contacts with his Soviet control in New York, using the fact that his wife was pregnant and staying there as an excuse. The 6000 names had been narrowed down to one – Maclean.

Philby had no way of warning him. But by chance Burgess had been suspended and ordered home after a series of complaints about his behaviour which culminated in his being booked for speeding on three separate occasions in one day. The two decided that when Burgess got to London he should warn Maclean that he must flee to Moscow. If he were interrogated, there was no doubt that the whole network would be exposed.[41]

Burgess crossed the Atlantic on the *Queen Mary* with Philby's warning 'Don't you go too' ringing in his ears. He went straight to Blunt, who passed the news on to Modin. Burgess had dinner with Maclean at the Reform Club and told him that he had no choice but to defect. Maclean was reluctant. But the Centre ordered him to go to Moscow, and, to make sure he did, Burgess was persuaded to go with him.[42]

The MI5 report on the Homer affair was due to be sent to London by Wednesday 23 May, which meant that Maclean's interrogation could be expected to begin the following Monday. Blunt suggested using one of the ships making mini-cruises across the English Channel. They sailed on Fridays, put in at several French ports, and returned on Sunday night or Monday morning. Passenger papers were not checked on the cruises. Maclean could disembark at the first French port and fail to return to the boat, and no one would be any the wiser until the ship returned to England.

On Friday 25 May the two men drove from Maclean's house at Tatsfield, in Kent, to Southampton and boarded a ship bound for Saint Malo. Once on mainland Europe they were given false documents by Soviet intelligence officers and made their way to Moscow.[43]

The realization that Burgess was also a Soviet spy came as a shock to British intelligence and, combined with the fact that their defection came just as Maclean was about to be interrogated, threw immediate suspicion on Philby. MI5 was convinced that Philby was the so-called 'Third Man'

<u>Reissue</u>(T83)

From: NEW YORK

To: MOSCOW

No: 915

28 June 1944

To VIKTOR[i].

    Your No. 2712[a].

    SERGEJ's[ii] meeting with GOMMER[iii] took place on 25 June. GOMMER did not hand anything over. The next meeting will take place on 30 July in TYRE[TIR][iv]. It has been made possible for G. to summon SERGEJ in case of need. SIDON's[v] original instructions having been altered,

                [34 groups unrecoverable]

travel to TYRE where his wife is living with her mother while awaiting confinement. [C% From there] [2 groups unrecovered] [C% with STEPAN[vi]]

                [11 groups unrecovered]

on the question of the post-war [C% relations] of the ISLAND [OSTROV][vii] with the COUNTRY[STRANA][viii], France and Spain

                [16 groups unrecovered]

on the ISLAND and material

                [8 groups unrecovered]

on several questions touching the ISLAND's interests

The decrypt of a message from the NKVD's New York *Rezidentura* to Moscow Centre which confirmed that Donald Maclean was a Soviet agent and led to the demise of the Cambridge spy ring. Although much of the message was indecypherable, the second paragraph was enough. At the time of its transmission only Maclean of those under suspicion had a pregnant wife living in New York, described here by its NKVD covername TYRE. Maclean's own covername HOMER is rendered as GOMMER since there is no H in the Russian Cyrillic alphabet (the double M appears to be a spelling error). VIKTOR was the head of Moscow Centre; SERGEI was the NKVD's deputy *Resident* in New York; SIDON was Washington; ISLAND was Britain; and COUNTRY was America.

Kim Philby hosts an impromptu press conference after his 'exoneration'
by Macmillan

who was assumed to have tipped Maclean off. He was recalled to London
and questioned by Dick White, then head of MI5.

Menzies then summoned him to Broadway and told him that the
Americans had insisted that he could not return to Washington. The
service had no choice but to ask for his resignation – much to the dis-
appointment of some of his fellow officers. A further interrogation by
MI5 followed six months later, but with no evidence forthcoming the
matter was dropped.[44]

Then in April 1954 Vladimir Petrov, the KGB *Rezident* in Australia defected, and confirmed that Burgess and Maclean were Soviet spies. The resultant publicity forced the government to issue a White Paper on the affair, and during a subsequent House of Commons debate Sir Marcus Lipton, the MP for Brixton, named Philby as 'the Third Man'. Macmillan was forced into a position where he appeared to exonerate Philby. 'I have no reason to conclude that Mr Philby has at any time betrayed the interests of this country, or to identify him with the so-called "Third Man", if indeed there was one,' he told parliament.[45]

Lipton's intervention had backfired, and Nicholas Elliott, a sympathetic former SIS colleague, was now able to get Philby a post as Beirut correspondent for the *Observer* and *The Economist*. Philby was used by MI6 in Beirut in what appears to have been an attempt to persuade the Russians that he was in fact a triple agent. But this failed to fool the KGB and only convinced the CIA that the British were being stupidly loyal to one of their own.[46]

The KGB defector Anatoly Golitsyn confirmed early in 1962 that there was a 'Ring of Five'. But it was not until later that year – when Flora Solomon, who had known Philby since university, told MI5 of his attempts to recruit her – that the evidence against Philby became incontrovertible.

Elliott was sent to Beirut in January 1963 to try to get a confession out of him in return for a guarantee of immunity. His remarks summed up the sense of betrayal felt by those SIS officers who had stood by Philby. 'You took me in for years,' he told him. 'Now I'll get the truth out of you even if I have to drag it out. I once looked up to you. My God how I despise you now.' But Elliott failed to get a confession, and, five days after he left Beirut, Philby boarded a Soviet tramp steamer and sailed for the USSR.[47]

Burgess and Maclean were kept out of view by the Soviet authorities until a 1956 press conference. Burgess fared badly. Although he did acquire a Russian boyfriend, he missed London, never learned Russian, and did not become a Soviet citizen. He drank to excess and was reportedly deeply upset that Philby did not seek him out once he had defected. Six months after Philby arrived in Moscow, Burgess died there of heart and liver problems. He is buried in the churchyard at West Meon, Hampshire.[48]

Maclean initially also drank heavily. But in 1953 his wife and children joined him and he built a new life for himself, teaching graduate courses at Moscow's prestigious Institute of World Economics and International Relations and publishing a highly praised study of British foreign policy. His wife and children left him by 1979, and he died in Moscow in March

1983. His ashes were brought back to England and buried in the family plot in Penn, Buckinghamshire.[49]

Blunt's treachery apparently went unconfirmed until 1963, when Michael Straight, an American whom he had attempted to recruit at Trinity, recounted the incident to the FBI. Blunt, who following the defections of Burgess and Maclean had been used by the Russians only once, as an intermediary to Philby, then made a full confession in return for immunity from prosecution. It was not until 1979 and the publication of a book pointing to him as the Fourth Man that his espionage activities became public. On 15 November 1979 Margaret Thatcher told the House of Commons that he had been an agent for Soviet intelligence. His knighthood was subsequently annulled, as was his honorary fellowship of Trinity College. He died in 1983.[50]

After the disappearance of Burgess and Maclean, MI5 searched Burgess's flat and, among a collection of classified documents, found one with an accompanying note written in Cairncross's handwriting. He was followed to a meeting with Modin, but the Russian spotted the MI5 watchers and aborted the meeting. 'As soon as I got back to the embassy, I dispatched a report to Moscow, expressing my personal view that the British Secret Service would continue to hound Cairncross in the foreseeable future,' Modin later wrote. 'The answer came back promptly. I was to cease working with him altogether.'

Cairncross was interrogated by MI5 but, on Modin's instructions, maintained that, although he had Communist sympathies, his relationship with Burgess was entirely innocent and he had no connection with espionage. He admitted innocently passing a secret document to Burgess and, damned as a security risk, resigned from the Civil Service. But in the absence of any convincing evidence against him a prosecution was impossible. He became an academic, working at Northwestern University, Chicago.

In 1964, in the wake of the Philby defection, MI5 reopened its molehunt and Cairncross was questioned again. This time he made a partial confession. But his identity as the Fifth Man was confirmed, by the Soviet defector Oleg Gordievsky, only in 1990. By this time Cairncross was living in the south of France. He wrote his memoirs and moved back to Britain in 1995, shortly before his death.[51]

None of the five had a more successful 'retirement' than Philby. Apart from a brief period in the late 1960s and early 1970s when the KGB appears to have ignored him, the legend of Kim Philby, Superspy, was used to extol the allegedly superior skills of the KGB at the expense of the reputations of the Western intelligence services, and in particular MI5 and MI6. Philby portrayed himself as a retired KGB general, con-

Guy Burgess playing the piano in a friend's house in Moscow

ducting lone inquiries for his former colleagues into operations that had
gone wrong – much in the manner of John le Carré's George Smiley. In
reality, by the 1980s his knowledge would have been of only limited use
to Moscow Centre and he was never a KGB officer. The legend was
simply Philby plying his old trade of black propaganda – this time on
behalf of the KGB, which had realized that the high level of public
interest in his activities could be harnessed as a continuing, nagging
embarrassment to the West.[52]

It is not clear which of the five actually was the superspy. For all his
undoubted value, it was certainly not Blunt. By the end of the Second
World War his intelligence-gathering days had come to an end, although
he continued to play a useful role, acting as an intermediary for Burgess,
Maclean and Philby and a reliable contact point for Modin.[53] The position
of Cairncross is more difficult to judge, the waters having been muddied
by his claims that he did not betray atomic secrets, never did anything
that might damage British interests, and stopped producing useful intelligence at the end of the Second World War.

The first claim is difficult to believe, given his role as private secretary
to Hankey, who was in charge of the British end of the atomic-weapons

project. The second does not hold water even if his claim not to have handed over atomic intelligence is believed. He certainly passed the Ultra secret to Moscow, and, with the Soviet armed forces riddled by German agents, it can only have been by good fortune that it was not subsequently passed to the Germans, thereby prolonging the war and costing many British lives. The third claim, that he did not produce any useful intelligence after the end of the war, is the most credible claim, although the evidence from both Modin and Dryden seems to suggest that he was at the very least still attempting to do so when the hounds closed in and Moscow stood him down.[54]

What is clear is that the information supplied by both Maclean and Burgess in the immediate post-war years, on Anglo-American relations and the plans for Germany and NATO, would have been of inestimable value to the Russians. While much, although by no means all, of what Burgess had to offer was gossip garnered from within the Homintern, Maclean's product was based on irrefutable evidence: high-level classified documents. He also provided vital information on the atomic-weapons programme. Assuming that his product was both trusted and used by Moscow in the formulation of policy – and all the evidence suggests that it was – he must have been the most valuable intelligence-gatherer.[55]

Nevertheless, Philby – a Soviet agent who rose to a senior post within MI6, at one point even heading the department tasked with countering Soviet espionage abroad – inevitably attracts the most attention. His main service to Moscow as an intelligence-gatherer was in betraying the countless allied agents sent to certain death behind the Iron Curtain in the early years of the Cold War.

Yet it is arguable that in the end the intelligence produced by the Ring of Five was not as useful to Moscow as the damage done to Western intelligence by the loss of trust between the British and the Americans. While Burgess and Maclean caused the initial damage, it was Philby in his role as the elusive Third Man and then as the alleged KGB superspy mocking the 'inept' Western intelligence services from Moscow who ensured the wounds within Western intelligence remained open. The attempts to heal them and regain American trust only caused more damage through the Fluency Committee's endless mole-hunts, the damaging allegations against Roger Hollis, and ultimately the *Spycatcher* affair.[56]

On the evidence of the intelligence he produced, Maclean was the real KGB superspy. But it was surely Philby who did the most damage, dominating people's perceptions of British intelligence until long after his death, his ghost exorcised only by the discovery of Aldrich Ames, a Soviet agent within the CIA who arguably passed on more intelligence to the Russians than the whole of the Ring of Five put together.

# CHAPTER 10

# Procurement, Persuasion and Charm

> Defectors probably play the largest role on the counter-
> espionage stage. One works hard to procure, persuade, charm
> and bribe key individuals to defect. Sometimes that hard work
> succeeds.
>
> John Bruce-Lockhart, former Deputy Chief of SIS, 1987[1]

The existence of yet another KGB mole within SIS was discovered
from information disclosed by Michal Goleniewski, a Polish intelligence officer who defected in 1960 and whose revelations to the CIA
also led to the exposure of the Portland spy ring. Goleniewski identified
fourteen SIS files which he had seen. The only common name on the
various distribution lists was that of George Blake.

Born in Rotterdam, Blake had inherited British citizenship from his
father, who had served with the British Army during the First World
War. He made his way to Britain during the Second World War and
enlisted in the Royal Navy. He was subsequently seconded to MI6, and
in 1947 he was taken on the permanent staff and sent to Cambridge to
study Russian. Posted to South Korea, he was captured during the 1950
Communist invasion, and it was during his three years captivity that he
was 'turned' – he became a Soviet agent.

In the light of Goleniewski's evidence, he was interrogated and eventually confessed. The damage to the service was horrendous. Blake, now
stationed in Berlin, had not only worked on both the Vienna and Berlin
tunnels, he had access to the file index housing the names of all SIS
contacts in Germany and he had almost certainly been responsible for
the deaths of forty agents. On 3 May 1961, at the Old Bailey, he was
jailed for forty-two years – the longest sentence ever imposed by a British
court.[2]

If the damage caused to internal morale was enormous, the means of
repairing it was already in place. Oleg Penkovsky was an ambitious officer
in the GRU, Russian military intelligence, who had cultivated influential
friends and married a general's daughter to ease his way through the
system. But when his career began to hit problems he became disgruntled
and began making approaches to the CIA, offering himself as an 'agent

in place'. All his approaches were rebuffed, vetoed by James Angleton, the agency's head of counter-intelligence, who reasoned that a career officer with a good record and an apparently bright future was an unlikely traitor. Penkovsky was clearly a plant, designed to draw the agency into an elaborate GRU provocation.

By November 1960 Penkovsky had become convinced that drastic measures were needed to convince the West that he was genuine. During a routine reception at the Canadian Embassy in Moscow, he handed a bundle of top-secret documents to an astonished diplomat. The Canadians passed them on to the MI6 head of station, who decided they were too technical to be evaluated in Moscow: they would have to be sent back to MI6 headquarters in London, Century House. The reaction within R4, the requirements section dealing with military matters, was incredulous. The documents were not just genuine, they were pure gold. Dick White decided that, whatever else Penkovsky was, he was not a plant. The Russians would not have risked handing over such valuable material simply for a provocation.

The CIA was inevitably brought into the operation. Many of the agency's old hands remained highly sceptical. But a combination of John Maury, the CIA's Chief of Soviet Operations, and Maurice Oldfield, head of SIS liaison in Washington, ensured that wiser counsels held sway.

Penkovsky's own knowledge was of minimal use, but he was an incorrigible collector of top-secret documents who seemed to have no fear of being caught. During the eighteen months he was run by MI6, he handed over 110 cassette films, including photographs of thousands of documents taken with a Minox mini-camera supplied by Century House. Among his many revelations was the fact that Soviet military strategy was based on the principle of a massive first strike using tactical surface-to-surface missiles making extensive use of chemical weapons – a revelation that led to a drastic revamp of Nato war plans.

The key intelligence he provided related to the 1962 Cuban Missile Crisis. One of the Penkovsky documents was a manual entitled *Methods of Protecting and Defending Strategic Rocket Sites*. Analysis of the information it contained allowed the CIA's photographic interpreters to identify the various 'footprints' of Soviet missile launch sites. It was the comparison of a U-2 photograph of a missile site under construction at San Cristóbal, 100 miles west of the Cuban capital of Havana, which led to the realization that the Soviet Union was planning to place medium-range ballistic missiles there, threatening the United States and breaking Khrushchev's pledge to Kennedy that Soviet military aid for Castro would be purely defensive.

It was this information that sparked the crisis, leading to a US blockade aimed at preventing the missiles arriving and a stand-off between Kennedy and Khrushchev that arguably brought the world closer to a nuclear holocaust than at any other time.

Colonel Oleg Penkovsky, the Soviet military intelligence officer whose information to MI6 was 'absolutely crucial' during the Cuban Missile Crisis

But the most important intelligence Penkovsky had to offer was what ensured that the crisis came to a peaceful end. The hawks in Washington had long argued that there was a missile gap to the Soviet Union's advantage. Their advice to Kennedy as he sought to prevent the Soviet missiles arriving in Cuba was that, if Khrushchev refused to back down, America would have no choice but to launch a pre-emptive nuclear strike. Penkovsky revealed beyond a shadow of a doubt that, while a missile gap existed, it was massively to America's advantage.

On 22 October 1962, with the Cuban Missile Crisis at its height, Penkovsky was arrested. He confessed almost immediately. From then on Khrushchev knew that Kennedy was aware that all the talk of Soviet missiles and their capabilities was just a bluff. A week later the Soviet ships turned around and the world was hauled back from oblivion. Greville Wynne, the British businessman and MI6 courier who had been Penkovsky's go-between, was arrested in Hungary a few weeks later. He and Penkovsky were put on trial. Wynne was sentenced to eight years' imprisonment but was exchanged a year later for Gordon Lonsdale, the Soviet intelligence officer who ran the Portland spy ring. Penkovsky was sentenced to death, and was shot shortly afterwards.

At the end of the crisis, White called his staff together in the cinema at Century House. 'I have been asked by the CIA to let you know of the absolutely crucial value of the Penkovsky intelligence we have been passing to them,' he said:

I am given to understand that this intelligence was largely instrumental in deciding that the United States should not make a pre-emptive nuclear strike against the Soviet Union, as a substantial body of important opinion in the States has been in favour of doing. In making known this appreciation of our contribution, I would stress to all of you that, if proof were needed, this operation has demonstrated beyond all doubt the prime importance of the human intelligence source, handled with professional skill and expertise.[3]

As British possessions across Africa gained their independence, SIS took over from MI5, which under the Attlee demarcation directive had responsibility for the colonies. White got rid of the last of the Robber Barons in a 1966 reorganization that created a new post of Controller (Africa), the other controllers taking charge of the Soviet Bloc, the Middle East, the Western Hemisphere and the Far East. The main reason for the new Africa 'controllerate' was to ward off attempts by France and Russia – or its surrogate, East Germany – to supplant British influence across the continent. Despite the British attitude towards South Africa and Rhodesia, which even under Labour administrations was at best ambivalent, many close relationships were formed with the intelligence services of the newly independent states.

By the late 1960s, with White retiring to be replaced by John Rennie, a career diplomat, and with the likelihood of British military intervention around the world diminishing, SIS acted increasingly as an arm of the Foreign Office. Notwithstanding a poor performance in Rhodesia, where SIS failed either to warn of Ian Smith's Unilateral Declaration of Independence or to point out the ease with which sanctions would be broken, good work had been done across Africa throughout the 1960s, cementing Britain's relationships with the new governments. This was particularly so during the Nigerian Civil War – when France unfortunately backed the wrong side but Britain did not – and in the Congo, where Daphne Park and some 'robust' SIS operations, carried out in tandem with the CIA and Mossad, ensured that Moscow was thwarted in its attempts to supplant Western interests. 'Quite frankly, I must have been arrested and condemned to be shot several times,' Baroness Park said of her experiences with MI6. 'It was a hazard that I got used to.'[4]

Rennie's appointment had not been popular within SIS, where it was generally assumed that Maurice Oldfield, White's highly able deputy, would get the job. It was seen as the result of a misapprehension within

Whitehall that 'putting an outside man in charge of the Secret Services will bring them under better control and curb the "wild men"', George Kennedy Young said. 'In fact, the opposite happens. The outsider knows neither the qualities of the individuals in the Service nor how in their daily routine work the events arise which determine their decisions. There was general relief when Maurice Oldfield took over as "C" in 1973.'[5]

Maurice Oldfield, whose appointment as 'C' brought 'general relief' to MI6

Under Oldfield's leadership, the reputation of SIS improved considerably. Widely seen as the inspiration for John le Carré's George Smiley, Oldfield – known within the service as 'Moulders' – had made his reputation in south-east Asia in the 1950s at the height of Britain's problems with its Far East colonies. He was subsequently posted to Washington, where he succeeded in re-establishing the service's good name with the Americans despite Philby's flight to Moscow. 'He and Young were the service's two great brains,' a former MI6 officer said. 'With them you always felt you had to be on your toes, whereas with other people you felt quite relaxed. I think George Smiley is as good a caricature of Oldfield as you could get. He was very bookish, devoted to work, had a flat very near to the office and, one always imagined, took work home with him every night.'[6]

It was also under Oldfield that the service acquired a second senior agent inside Soviet intelligence. Oleg Gordievsky was brought up within the intelligence establishment, his father having been a member of the NKVD, and in the early 1960s he joined the KGB. The decisive moment in his career apparently came with the 1968 invasion of Czechoslovakia. Posted to Copenhagen in 1972, he began looking for Western intelligence contacts, and by 1974 he was working for SIS.

As a unique high-level source within the KGB, working first in Denmark, then at Moscow Centre, and finally in London, Gordievsky provided the British with a great deal of valuable information. He tipped them off to Michael Bettaney's attempts at treachery, provided an assessment of the damage caused by Geoffrey Prime, a Soviet agent inside GCHQ, and confirmed that Roger Hollis was not, as repeatedly alleged, a KGB mole. But the most important intelligence he provided concerned the Soviet leadership's paranoia over Western intentions and Operation Ryan, set up to provide advance warning of the Nato first strike which the Russians had become convinced was a distinct possibility.

This had been sparked by a number of factors, mainly the development of the MX and Cruise missiles and by American anti-Soviet rhetoric, particularly Ronald Reagan's denunciation of Russia as 'the Evil Empire'. The most dangerous period came in late 1983, in the wake of the shooting down by Soviet MiG fighters of a Korean airliner over the Russian Far East. Amid an increase in international tension, Nato forces conducted a command-post exercise, Able Archer, involving widespread troop movements inside West Germany. The Russians had used such exercises as cover for preparations for the 1956 invasion of Hungary, the 1968 attack on Czechoslovakia, and a similar operation against Poland in 1981 which in the end was not given the go-ahead. When the Nato units changed their procedures halfway through the exercise in a simple communications security measure, Soviet signals intelligence temporarily lost track of what was going on, sparking panic in Moscow.

Oleg
Gordievsky

When Gordievsky told MI6 that Warsaw Pact commanders had been concerned the West might be about to launch a nuclear attack under the guise of Able Archer and that Operation Ryan derived from very real fears within the Soviet leadership, both Reagan and Margaret Thatcher began to scale down their anti-Communist rhetoric, leading to their wooing of Mikhail Gorbachev – who was seen as the coming man of Soviet politics – and the successful arms-reductions talks of the 1980s.

In January 1985 Gordievsky was summoned to Moscow to be told he was to be the next KGB *Rezident* in London. It was a stunning success for both him and his MI6 handlers, promising untold intelligence riches. But by May, while he was still only acting *Rezident*, he had been recalled to Moscow in disgrace, his role as a British agent apparently blown. His escape was the stuff of fiction. Avoiding his KGB watchers, he followed instructions hidden inside the cover of a book to warn MI6 that he needed to be 'exfiltrated'. The signal was to stand on a designated street corner, holding a Safeway carrier bag. Once this had been acknowledged by someone 'chewing something as he passed' – in this case a man with a Harrods bag eating a Mars bar – he was to follow the pre-set instructions and make his way to a rendezvous (RV) on the Finnish border, where he met up with the MI6 team that was to smuggle him across to the West in the boot of a car.

Gordievsky, who had never asked for money from SIS, had spent eleven years as an agent-in-place, risking his life to pass intelligence to the West. Nigel Clive, who retired from SIS while Gordievsky was still in place, has described him as 'the most successful British agent'. Lord Armstrong, who was Cabinet Secretary during much of Gordievsky's period as a British agent, said he was 'one of the most important sources we ever had'.[7]

The handling of Penkovsky and Gordievsky did more to restore the reputation of SIS than all its other operations put together. The service came under fire over the apparent lack of any warning of either the Falklands conflict or the Gulf War. But insiders said there was no lack of such intelligence – merely poor use of it by government.

In early 1982, with the British government in the process of negotiating the Falkland Islands away, SIS warned that there were clear signs of the Argentinians' willingness to invade. The fact that this was ignored was attributed by Young to the dislike within Whitehall of 'hard facts which would conflict with its preference for soothing description'. He said, 'The Falklands War is an example of where the latter prevailed at a high price. We had a very good assessment of the situation before it happened. Even our embassy was getting reports of the Argentinians' plans. But Carrington [the British Foreign Secretary] played them down.'[8]

Once the conflict had begun, the service played a key role in stopping Argentina's supply of the Exocet air-to-surface missiles which were proving so effective against the British warships. Anthony Divall, a former Royal Marine who had done a number of jobs for the service, persuaded Captain Alfredo Corti, the head of an Argentinian arms-procurement team, that he was in a position to provide thirty Exocets, at a cost of £1 million each, from Iraq and Libya. By committing Corti to the sale and then stringing it out, Divall ensured that the Argentinian Air Force's supply of Exocets dried up and undoubtedly saved the lives of numerous British servicemen.[9]

Despite the lessons of the Falklands conflict, the Scott Inquiry into the Matrix-Churchill affair – during which MI6 used the Iraqi-owned firm's British managing director, Paul Henderson, as an agent to discover details of Baghdad's weapons development – heard how the service's reports were still frequently ignored by other government departments.[10]

In the wake of the Cold War, Sir Colin McColl, Chief of SIS, ordered a review of the agency's operations. The result was a reorganization designed to leave it more flexible and more able to cope with a less predictable world where the main dangers would come from maverick states; nuclear, biological and chemical proliferation; terrorism; and the growth in international crime.

The basic structure has not been radically changed. There are a total of four directors in charge of Personnel and Administration, Support Services, Security and Public Affairs, and the main operational director-ate, Requirements and Production, which contains a number of regional 'controllerates' and one covering global issues, including serious crime and proliferation. Requirements and Production liaises direct with cus-tomer departments, while a secretariat attached to 'C''s office includes a number of liaison departments from other agencies to ensure smooth co-ordination of joint operations.[11]

By the time the service moved into its new £230 million Vauxhall Cross headquarters in 1994, its role was very different from that first envisaged for it in 1909. Some traditions remain. Those who work for MI6 still call it the Firm, while the Foreign Office refers to it 'politely, but not very sincerely', as the Friends. 'C' still sees the Prime Minister each Tuesday, and the service's reports still carry a CX serial number. But the discussions and reports cover areas that would never have been targets for MI6 in the old world.

The 1994 Intelligence Services Act made it clear that, as well as the traditional role of collecting foreign political, economic and military intel-ligence – particularly in the area of nuclear proliferation – the service had an additional task: 'the prevention or detection of serious crime'. This was an official mandate for operations that had already been going on for some time against terrorism, drug smuggling and money-

## Organization of MI6

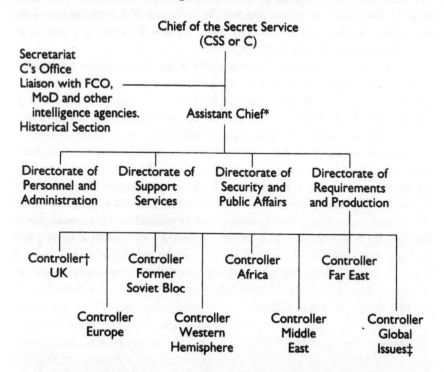

Chief of the Secret Service
(CSS or C)

Secretariat
C's Office
Liaison with FCO,
    MoD and other
    intelligence agencies.
Historical Section

Assistant Chief*

Directorate of Personnel and Administration

Directorate of Support Services

Directorate of Security and Public Affairs

Directorate of Requirements and Production

Controller† UK

Controller Former Soviet Bloc

Controller Africa

Controller Far East

Controller Europe

Controller Western Hemisphere

Controller Middle East

Controller Global Issues‡

\*This post exists only intermittently and in the recent past has tended to be used when C felt a need to anoint his successor.
†The number of controllers and controllerates fluctuates according to resources and requirements.
‡Includes specialist units dealing with crime and proliferation.

laundering aimed at Britain but carried out overseas, where the police, HM Customs and the Security Service would not normally be able to operate.[12]

'Individual law-enforcement agencies can sometimes benefit from the wider look and the further reach that a foreign intelligence service has when it comes to uncovering illegal networks which operate across frontiers,' Sir Colin McColl said. 'There is a tendency, I think, for bad men to operate where they think they are safe, and if we can help to reach out into some of those places, we can help the law-enforcement agencies in not only this country, but in other countries as well.'

But crime constitutes only a small part of MI6 operations with the main targets being proliferation and the old enemy in Moscow. While the operational effort against the Russians and the other former Soviet republics has reduced by about two-thirds since the end of the Cold War, the core element working in the Former Soviet Bloc controllerate is broadly the same as it was before the collapse of Communism. The reduction in effort reflects the dramatic decline in Moscow's influence and interference elsewhere in the world.

The service has contracted, a result of the cuts made within the intelligence community as a whole as the politicians demanded their 'peace dividend', but by introducing information technology and cutting bureaucracy in London, it has succeeded in maintaining the overseas stations at the 'sharp end' of its operations.

The new world order has also brought new links to other intelligence agencies. There had always been good liaison with the CIA and the other secret services of the UKUSA countries – in particular the Australian Secret Intelligence Service. ASIS was set up in 1952 as a direct result of the British need for a covert-operations organization that could cover the Far East. Its charter was based on that of its British counterpart, and the two services had shared stations and training facilities. Indeed the link was so close that until 1994, when there was a great deal of adverse publicity over its relationship with MI6, ASIS still referred to its senior partner as 'Head Office'.[13]

The current MI6 building at Vauxhall Cross

But SIS links with its foreign counterparts were not limited to the services of the UKUSA countries, as indicated by the Intelligence Services Act, which authorizes 'liaison with a wide range of foreign intelligence and security services'. Even before the European Union, there were close relations with the German Bundesnachrichtendienst and the French SDECE, now known as the DGSE. Links with Mossad and the South African intelligence services transcended the occasional difficulties in Britain's formal relations with Tel Aviv and Pretoria. Now new partnerships have been formed with old enemies in the former Soviet Bloc, in particular the Czechs, the Poles and the Hungarians.[14]

The 1993 reorganization was accompanied by a separate review of Britain's foreign intelligence requirements and capability. Although the report backed the present system, it has not been published. But Britain's foreign intelligence requirements are still dominated by the former Soviet Union – an area which, apart from the two world wars, has been seen as a major threat ever since the Great Game was first played out in central Asia in the early part of the nineteenth century.

Baroness Park, who herself served in Moscow as a young MI6 officer, said:

We are looking at a country which still has the largest army in Europe, which has got a lot of new research and development, and which, although it is destroying obsolete weapons, is replacing them by new ones all the time. What we have to find out are the intentions of the Russians. They have still got all those missiles pointing straight at this country. That hasn't been changed yet.[15]

One of the service's most important areas of interest in the former Soviet Union is nuclear, biological and chemical weaponry. MI6 was able to provide crucial evidence of Russia's biological-weapons programme in 1989 when a Soviet 'walk-in' turned up at Britain's Paris embassy, claiming to be the director of the Leningrad institute of Biopreparat – the agency which runs Russia's programme for 'weaponry of special designation' – on a research trip to the West.

Vladimir Pasechnik told MI6 that, although Biopreparat was allegedly a medical research organization, this was only a cover for its real role. 'Officially we had been told that 85 per cent of the resources of the institute should be directly connected with biological warfare problems and 15 per cent towards concealing our activity,' Pasechnik said:

There was zero support for real scientific and technological projects on behalf of the National Health.

Being the director of one of the institutes, I was involved in all sorts of discussions and was able to see top-secret classified documents which described the aims of these developments. I came eventually to the conclusion that it would be most advantageous if I brought this information to the attention of the West.

His description of Biopreparat's operations included details of a strain of bubonic plague resistant to twenty-six different types of antibiotic and the fact that Biopreparat had at least twenty separate research facilities capable of producing large quantities of biological weapons – only five of which were disclosed by President Yeltsin in a 1993 declaration on Russia's biological and chemical weapons.[16]

In July 1992, MI6 had an even more startling success. Col Viktor Oshchenko, the 52-year-old head of Russian intelligence in Paris, was spirited out of France and into Britain. Like Gordievsky, he had been recalled to Moscow where, according to the Russian foreign intelligence service, the SVR, 'certain aspects of his work had given cause for suspicion'. He had 'decided to defect to the West, fearing that his "double game" might be exposed.'

He told his colleagues at the Russian embassy, where he operated under cover as an economics counsellor, that he was spending the weekend travelling in the Loire valley with his wife and 14-year-old daughter Olga. Staff at the embassy first suspected that the weekend away might not be all it seemed when Oshchenko's elder daughter rang to ask what she was supposed to do with a new car her father had had delivered to her St Petersburg home. The next day when he did not return to work, a search was set in place.

Oshchenko's car was found abandoned at Orly airport in Paris. The British Home Office announced that he was in Britain where he had asked for political asylum. Oshchenko's defection led to the expulsion from France of four of his former colleagues, including his deputy Sergei Smirov, who controlled a ring of spies at the heart of the French nuclear weapons programme. Oschenko was also responsible for the arrest of Michael Smith, a British electronics engineer who had passed military secrets to the Russians, after being recruited by Oshchenko in the early 1970s.[17]

Despite the end of the Cold War, Russia and Britain still regularly report the discovery of each others' spies. One MI6 agent, arrested by Russia's Federal Counter-Espionage Service, the FSK, confessed on Russian television to having been paid £8000 for details of Russian arms sales to the Middle East and to other parts of the former Soviet Union. The FSK claimed the MI6 head of station was expelled as a result of Vadim Sintsov's arrest. In fact, his visa was withdrawn in retaliation for the

British refusal to allow a senior SVR officer to come to London. 'It was all handled in a gentlemanly fashion,' the FSK said.

Sintsov, an export manager for a Russian weapons company specializing in armour and artillery systems, was apparently filmed during his interrogation in the Lubyanka. 'I started working with a certain Mr James Self and after a while he introduced me to his successor, a liaison officer,' he said. 'We met at first in other countries, that is outside Russia. But later they made arrangements for communicating here. They were interested mainly in two areas where I could offer information because of my job. The first was Russian arms deliveries to Middle Eastern countries and the second was general details about arms deliveries in Russia.'[18]

The defence links between the former Soviet republics are a major intelligence priority for the West, as is the fate of the Soviet military-industrial complex. Are weapons factories really being converted to civilian uses or are their products still being produced for export to potential world trouble-spots like the Middle East and the Balkans?

The resurgence of Communism has also intensified the British intelligence agencies' interest in the political situation in Russia, as shown by a somewhat less gentlemanly spy row between Moscow and London in May 1996. The Russian Security Service, or FSB, as it was now known, announced that it had arrested a young Russian diplomat who had been caught handing over information on 'the internal situation, disarmament and the behaviour of Russian leaders' to MI6 officers. Under interrogation, 28-year-old Platon Obukhov described his recruitment: 'They told me they would pay me $2000 a month and give me $1000 extra for really good information.' The FSB announced that nine British diplomats were to be expelled from Moscow because there was 'irrefutable evidence of activities incompatible with their diplomatic status'. After lengthy negotiations, that figure was reduced to four and, in a tit-for-tat reaction, four Russian diplomats were expelled from London.[19]

The political stability of all the other former members of the Soviet Union – particularly those in central Asia and the Transcaucasus – is also a major concern, as is the growth in organized crime in the old Soviet Bloc, primarily in Russia itself, Poland and the Czech Republic.

As early as 1988, MI6 had begun to help the police uncover attempts to smuggle drugs into Britain via Poland and Czechoslovakia. One such operation began after detectives in London arrested two Czechs, Miroslav Vrana and his son Roman, with five kilograms of cocaine. The detectives found they had stumbled across a drugs route leading from Colombia via Poland, Czechoslovakia, Germany, The Netherlands and into Britain. Working with members of the old Czech secret service, the StB, a member of the Colombian Cali drugs cartel had set up a front company in Prague and was using it to smuggle 500 kilograms of cocaine into Europe a month.

Alonso Delgado Martinez had studied in Prague in the 1960s and returned twenty years later to set up the Yaros trading company, ostensibly to import Colombian food to the Soviet Bloc. But that was not all Yaros was importing. In every cargo, a number of the pallets carrying the containers of beans, rice and sugar had been specially hollowed out to provide space for plastic bags full of cocaine. In what turned out to be a major smuggling operation, the company was bringing in millions of pounds worth of pure cocaine every year. MI6 tracked the shipments, which came in via the Polish port of Gdynia and were then transported by road to a warehouse in the Czech town of Hradec Králové, where they were recontainered, given fresh documentation indicating that they had originated in Czechoslovakia, and sent on to destinations in Germany, The Netherlands and Britain.

In September 1991 a joint operation was put in place to track a shipment along the route, picking up each member of the ring as the containers passed. The operation faltered at the Czech border post in Nachod, where an alert border guard, unaware that the shipment was already under surveillance, became suspicious. A closer examination revealed the hollows containing 100 kilograms of cocaine. Delgado and two Czech associates were arrested, and a second shipment of 116 kilograms of cocaine was seized in Gdynia. Delgado denied any involvement, but was sentenced to ten years' imprisonment, increased to thirteen years on appeal.[20]

Douglas Hurd, then Foreign Secretary, described another MI6 anti-drugs operation during the Commons debate on the Intelligence Services Bill in 1994:

A British law-enforcement agency recently asked the SIS to monitor a large consignment of drugs from a developing country believed to be destined for the UK. The service could not rely on the co-operation of the authorities in the country concerned, so it sent an officer there under an assumed identity.

Soon after his arrival, in difficult and dangerous circumstances, the officer was able to identify and enlist the support of an employee of the transport organization which was innocently handling the movement of the consignment. With the help of that employee, the consignment was monitored to a point outside that country, where it was seized through international action, and the gang of traffickers involved were arrested.[21]

The more traditional targets, such as monitoring potential enemies and world flashpoints, remain – with lack of stability making the former Yugoslavia and the Middle East clear priorities. South Africa is perhaps a less obvious problem in this regard, but, given the country's strategic importance and the new republic's dependence on an ageing Nelson Mandela, there is a great deal of interest in internal ANC politics and in the activities of groups from both the extreme right and the extreme left.

China unsurprisingly dominates intelligence priorities in the Far East – particularly as regards the situation in Hong Kong – but Afghanistan, Vietnam, North Korea and Cambodia are also important targets, as are relations between Pakistan and India, notably with regard to the disputed territory of Kashmir.

In Latin America, Argentina and the continuing problems over the Falkland Islands are the main areas of interest, followed closely by cocaine and heroin trafficking from Colombia, the Caribbean and the Andean region of South America. Brazil, as one of the world's major weapons producers, is also high on the list of priorities.

But, potential flashpoints aside, the main areas of interest are weapons proliferation, terrorism and transnational crime.[22] Specific operations in any of these areas have to be officially cleared by the Foreign Office, or in the most 'politically sensitive' cases by the Foreign Secretary himself. A written proposal is prepared within the service outlining the planned operation and what it is intended to achieve together with an assessment of the risks involved. There is also a detailed internal rule-book laying down what officers may and may not do.

Sir Gerry Warner, a former MI6 officer who as Intelligence Co-ordinator had responsibility for determining how Britain's intelligence requirements are met, claimed that SIS officers did not carry arms and that it would be 'unthinkable' for them to be authorized to use violence in peacetime. Perhaps. But given the nature of the people they are operating against, both in the serious-crime role and in the more traditional espionage role, this would seem to put individual officers at unacceptable personal risk.[23]

This is particularly so in the wake of the McColl reorganization, which cut posts abroad with the intention of inserting officers into various areas as and when intelligence requirements developed. These operations, and the exfiltration of agents or defectors, have traditionally been carried out with the assistance of the armed forces – usually members of the British special forces, the Special Air Service and its Royal Navy counterpart, the Special Boat Service, which specializes in the classic spy-thriller-style insertion and exfiltration of agents by inflatable dinghy launched from a submarine waiting offshore.

The decision to use the SAS in such operations appears to have been made during the late 1960s, following a confidential report by Colonel John Waddy, then Colonel of the SAS, which called for closer co-operation between the SAS and both the Secret Intelligence Service and MI5 in 'tasks of a more delicate nature'. These would involve members of the regiment in covert operations abroad, some of them anti-terrorist, others Cold War-related. David Stirling, the founder of the SAS, later wrote, 'Certain delicate operational roles require the Secret Service to invest in the SAS command highly classified intelligence necessary for the effective planning of these operations and, just as importantly, for special training.' To co-ordinate such operations, an SAS officer, with the rank of lieutenant-colonel, acts as permanent liaison with MI6. Servicemen employed on such jobs are temporarily transferred to the reserves to ensure that where necessary the regiment's active involvement can be denied.

For operations where there is a real risk of compromise, such as the Gordievsky exfiltration, MI6 has a select list of specialists, mostly former SAS/SBS members, who are taken on for specific contracts. Some of these contract officers are still on 'the Circuit' as it is called, working as bodyguards for Middle Eastern diplomats and businessmen, providing training for foreign governments in anything from basic security to special operations, and sometimes carrying out specific mercenary operations abroad. Others, having left the services, have made new careers for themselves, totally unrelated to the security world, and only become involved 'when someone from Six goes through the list and calls them up'.

'Teams' are put together as and when they are required. Each member is allocated a cover-name and told not to reveal his true identity to any other members of the team, which, given the exclusivity of 'the Circuit', frequently makes for strange situations with close friends working alongside each other as if they have never met. The need-to-know principle is strictly adhered to, and individual contract officers will not be briefed on anything other than their own role in the affair.

One operation for which SIS claimed the credit, although it was actually carried out completely by contract 'labourers', was the retrieval of a Soviet Hind helicopter gunship which had been brought down by Afghan rebels. A team of rebels led by three contract men brought it back across the border into Pakistan. The men were apparently paid a basic wage with bonuses for retrieving particular items – the Hind's control panel and the lightweight armour-plating on its underbody being among the most highly priced.[24]

'The Hind helicopter went down in Afghanistan, and of course the collectors of Soviet equipment and methodology were grasping for different ways of getting a recovery team into the country to retrieve the helicopter,' said Ed Juchniewicz, former CIA Assistant Deputy Director, Operations:

> And of course the Soviets, I believe, suspected that many of these services were out there trying to retrieve their equipment. So they were sending teams to try and retrieve their own helicopter and take it back to their own lines. My understanding is that a British team – and I don't know what the composition of the British team was – succeeded in getting in and retrieving and bringing the Hind out in pieces.

Baroness Park said the Afghanistan War was:

> the most wonderful opportunity for acquiring knowledge of, and in some cases possession of, a large range of the most up-to-date Soviet equipment, including helicopters. And when our forces came to fight the Iraqis in the Gulf War, the Iraqis were of course armed with those very Soviet weapons, and because of that activity in Afghanistan – which is one of the arguments for being global: you never know when things are going to turn up that are going to be very useful – they knew roughly what they were up against. In fact they knew in great detail what they were up against.[25]

Part of the recent campaign of 'openness', which led to McColl and his GCHQ counterpart, Sir John Adye, appearing in person at a 1993 press conference on the government's plans to create a parliamentary oversight committee, has been an attempt to play down the special-operations side of MI6. The word has been carefully put about that the service's reputation for covert operations and clashes with MI5 has been 'overplayed'.

But the rivalry with the Security Service remains, and since the McColl changes swept away the older officers and promoted the 'young Turks' the fascination with covert action that marked the 1950s appears to have returned. Under David Spedding, McColl's successor, there has been an increasing tendency among the younger officers to model themselves on what one contract officer described as 'a cross between James Bond and the SAS'. These officers train in the 'killing houses' of the SAS and SBS at Hereford and Poole and have apparently acquired a penchant for the black overalls they wear on exercises that rivals the Circuit's predilection for Army-style 'green kit'.

Under the 1994 Intelligence Services Act, the Secret Intelligence Service is allowed 'to obtain and provide information relating to the actions or intentions of persons outside the British Islands; and to perform other tasks relating to the actions or intentions of such persons'. If covert action is no longer on the agenda, what are the 'other tasks' that SIS is supposed to carry out, and why is it thought necessary to grant officers immunity under the Act from prosecution for criminal activities undertaken abroad if the Foreign Secretary deems them to be necessary for the proper discharge of those 'other tasks'?

The reality is that most major countries have some form of organization to carry out human intelligence and covert action abroad. It does not cause the same level of public concern as for example the anti-subversion activities of MI5 did during the early 1980s, and the attempt to play down the SIS covert action role seems little more than a legacy of the previous position – discarded only in 1993 with the introduction of the Intelligence Services Bill – that Britain had no such organization except in times of war.

'Secrecy is our absolute stock in trade, our most precious asset,' said Sir Colin McColl, explaining his refusal to give all but the barest details of his organization. 'People risk their lives, often their jobs, because they believe SIS is a secret service. I am very anxious that I should be able to send some sort of signal to these people that we're not going to be undressed in public.'

Sir Gerry Warner's suggestion that MI6 officers do not carry arms seems to be just another part of the attempts to draw a discreet veil over the service's operations. One source who had worked alongside MI6 in Beirut in the mid-1980s described them as being 'armed to the teeth', while an MI6 contract officer gave a much stronger response: 'What he says may be the official line, but frankly it's just cobblers. Of course they carry weapons. They use them on exercise and they use them on jobs. Would you seriously expect them not to?'[26]

SIS officers certainly do not routinely carry weapons. But there is a difference between for instance an officer working under diplomatic cover, who would not be armed, and one employed on a particular operation which may or may not involve an element of risk. 'Just because you were taking part in an operation you wouldn't necessarily say, "Oh, I must go to the safe and get out a gat,"' one officer said. 'But where there is some likelihood of weapons being needed, given the proper authorization, they can be carried.'[27]

# CHAPTER 11

# *Ultra Special Intelligence*

The decyphered telegrams of foreign governments are without
doubt the most valuable source of our secret information
respecting their policy and actions.
Lord Curzon, Foreign Secretary, at the time of the
creation of the Government Code and Cypher School,
1919

The British began intercepting foreign communications in earnest at
the beginning of the fourteenth century, when King Edward II
ordered that 'all letters coming from or going to parts beyond the seas
... be seized'. A royal writ dated 18 December 1324 reminded ports
officials that it was part of their duties to 'make diligent scrutiny of all
persons passing from parts beyond the seas to England ... to stop all
letters concerning which sinister suspicions might arise'.[1]

Cardinal Wolsey's open seizure of diplomatic correspondence during
the reign of Henry VIII sparked strong protests. Reporting back to the
Doge in Venice, Signor Giustiniani, the Venetian ambassador in London,
complained, 'The letters received by me from your Sublimity had been
taken out of the hands of the courier at Canterbury by the royal officials
and opened and read: the like being done by private letters from the
most noble, the ambassador Badoer of France and others.'[2]

Under Oliver Cromwell, British intelligence was centred on the postal
system, with John Thurloe, Cromwell's spymaster, taking the role of
Postmaster-General and installing a 'Secret Man' in the Post Office to
open letters. The process was enshrined in an act of Parliament which
declared openly that the postal system was the best means 'to discover
and prevent many dangerous and wicked designs ... the intelligence
whereof cannot well be communicated but by letter of escript'.

By the eighteenth century, Thurloe's 'Secret Man' had become a Secret
Department, charged with monitoring correspondence between foreign
embassies and their governments, and in 1703 it was further strengthened
by the creation of a Secret Decyphering Branch, which was soon taken
over by the Revd Edward Willes, an Oxford don who later became the
Bishop of Bath and Wells.

The Bishop and his sons ran the decyphering branch as if it were a family concern, and, in 1844, when it was finally abolished, his grandson Francis Willes and great-grandson John Lovell, who carried out the decyphering at their home in Wiltshire, were pensioned off with Secret Service money, still protesting loudly at the great financial loss to their family. The Foreign Office dismissed their complaints, pointing out that, since taking over from his uncle, Willes had cracked 'scarcely any' codes. According to one official, there were great suspicions that he was merely 'a fraudulent trickster who leads a life of pleasure and relaxation out of sight of the office'.[3]

The Secret Department itself was housed in the Post Office head-quarters but was similarly manned largely by members of one family. John Ernest Bode, 'Chief Clerk in the Secret Service of Hanover', was brought to England in 1732 to forge new seals for the intercepted letters 'which was then badly done'. Two of Bode's brothers and two of his sons joined the Secret Department. It appears to have been a fairly efficient operation, surviving a parliamentary inquiry in 1742. John Barbutt, then Secretary to the Post Office, explained to the MPs why the Secret Department had been set up.

'The projectors of a General System of Postal Communication seem to have perceived the necessity for the public welfare of subjecting it to some control,' Barbutt said. 'They did not consider it to be the duty of Government to facilitate and protect the conveyance of treason from one end of the country to the other.'[4]

The vast majority of material intercepted was Russian, Swedish or French, reflecting Britain's main enemies at the time. But, amid repeated calls for the department to be abolished to save money, it was persuaded by the Home Office to step outside its foreign intelligence brief and open the letters of private individuals who were seen for some reason as a threat to the state, starting in 1838 with the Chartists and continuing with the ringleaders of the industrial unrest of 1842–3. The move was to be its undoing.[5]

When it was revealed in the House of Commons in June 1844 that Sir James Graham, the Home Secretary, had ordered the opening of letters addressed to the Italian nationalist Giuseppe Mazzini, a political refugee in Britain, another parliamentary inquiry was ordered into the activities of the Post Office. It proved to be one inquiry too many.

William Bode mounted a courageous defence of the Secret Depart-ment, insisting that on 'only very few' occasions had it interfered with the domestic mail, where 'there was room to believe that it contained political matters'. His testimony also revealed the existence of another part of the Post Office which did open private correspondence: the Secret Department had examined the Mazzini letters only at the request of 'the

Private Office under the Home Department', he said. Colonel William Maberley, the Secretary of the Post Office, who was in charge of the Private Office, had asked Bode to look at them because they were written in Italian and he could not understand them.[6]

In an impassioned plea on behalf of his own department, Bode told the inquiry:

> Whatever opinions may be entertained in the country, Foreign Governments will not desist from a practice which they all follow, nor will they believe that the English Government has abandoned all control over the Post Office. The motive of state necessity which can alone justify the practice will accordingly still exist. In my humble opinion it is expedient for the service of Government.

The inquiry was effectively a whitewash, defending the opening of private letters. 'The information which has been derived from this source has been regarded as valuable and may have given better information upon dangers apprehended in particular districts than could be derived from local observation,' the inquiry's report said. 'To leave it a mystery whether or no this power is ever exercised is the way best calculated to deter the evil-minded from applying the Post to improper uses.'

The Private Office, which had been responsible for the furore in the first place, was saved. But the Secret Department was already doomed, condemned not by the inquiry but by the Foreign Office's reluctance to continue to fund its operations. It was soon suspended on the orders of the Postmaster-General, and its Secret Decyphering Branch was closed – to the chagrin of the Willes family. Just over two years later, on 1 January 1847, the Secret Department itself was abolished and Bode too was pensioned off.[7]

Following the abolition of Bode's Secret Department, British intelligence ignored the potential of intercepting foreign communications – apparently believing it to be ungentlemanly. The French had no such scruples. In 1902 the British ambassador in Paris warned a shocked Lord Lansdowne, the Foreign Secretary, that their official correspondence was insecure, saying, 'Your recent letters by post have been palpably opened by the *Bureau Noir*.'[8]

It was not until shortly before the First World War that Britain again began full-scale interception of the communications of foreign governments. MO5 started 'censoring' foreign telegraph cables on 2 August 1914. The results were enhanced by the Royal Navy's success in cutting Germany's submarine cables, forcing it to use those controlled by the British.[9]

The severing of the German cables also led to greater use of naval radio signals, assisting the Admiralty's own codebreaking section, NID25, which set up its office in Room 40 of the Old Admiralty Buildings under Sir Alfred Ewing, the Director of Naval Education.[10]

MO5 had set up its own cryptography department shortly before the war, to examine the possibilities of exploiting enemy wireless traffic. Building on pre-war links with the French Bureau des Chiffres, it set about decrypting German radio messages with rapid success. 'Nobody could desire more admirable opponents than the Germans for this class of work,' said E. W. B. Gill, one of the academics employed to unravel the German codes and cyphers. 'The orderly Teutonic mind was especially suited for devising schemes which any child could unravel.'[11]

One of the more notable successes for the British cryptographers came in December 1916, when the commander of the German Middle East signals organization sent a drunken Christmas greeting to all his operators. During the Christmas inactivity, the same isolated and clearly identical message went out in six different codes, only one of which, up until that point, the British had managed to break.[12]

When the Directorate of Military Intelligence was formed in 1916, the cable censorship section became known as MI8. The codebreaking section was renamed MI1(b) and moved to 5 Cork Street, in London's West End. With the assistance of Major Malcolm Hay, a noted historian, a large number of academics were drafted in to help and, by the Armistice, there were forty-five codebreakers, supported by forty ancilliary 'ladies'.[13]

They worked closely with MI1(e), which was responsible for all wireless monitoring. It also carried out direction-finding from stations at Leiston in Suffolk, Devizes in Wiltshire, and on top of the War Office building, allowing it to chart the course of the Zeppelins as they approached London.[14]

A number of radio masts were set up in a circle linked to a receiver. The mast which received the strongest signal was assumed to be closest to the source of the transmission. A line drawn from the centre of the circle through that mast would produce a bearing to the transmitter that could be plotted on the map. By carrying out the same operation at other 'DF' sites, a number of different bearings could be plotted and the transmitter would be located somewhere in the area where the lines met.[15]

The British SIGINT effort was not helped by the great rivalry between MI1(b) and Room 40. A. G. Denniston, the first head of GC&CS, later expressed his regret at this. 'Looking back over the work of those years, the loss of efficiency to both departments caused originally by mere official jealousy is the most regrettable fact in the development of intelligence based on cryptography.'

Isolated from each other, the two sections went their separate ways, with Room 40, which recruited a number of distinguished members of the future staff of Bletchley Park, including Denniston and the 'most brilliant' Dilly Knox, enjoying the greater success. Following the 1915 capture of a German diplomatic code-book, Captain 'Blinker' Hall, the controversial Director of Naval Intelligence, expanded Room 40's operations to include diplomatic traffic. The result was the interception of the so-called Zimmermann Telegram.

Alastair Denniston
Head of GC&CS
from 1919 to 1942

The encyphered message from Arthur Zimmermann, the German Foreign Minister, to the German Minister in Mexico City suggested an alliance with Mexico against the United States, offering in return 'generous financial support and an undertaking on our part that Mexico is to reconquer the lost territory in Texas, New Mexico and Arizona'. Its publication in the American newspapers in March 1917 brought the United States into the war, ending American isolationism and ensuring Germany's defeat.[16]

The future President Franklin D. Roosevelt, visiting London as Assistant Secretary of the Navy in 1918, was much impressed by Hall's explanation that the intelligence from the intercepts had been obtained by spies who slipped across the German–Danish border each night to be brought back to Britain by flying-boat. Roosevelt's impression of Hall's 'wonderful intelligence service' may well have influenced his support for the close intelligence relationship between Britain and America during the Second World War.[17]

After the war, Room 40, now run by Denniston, and MI1(b) were amalgamated to become the Government Code and Cypher School, the forerunner of GCHQ. The cable censorship department was disbanded around the same time, despite the fact that 'every government department was strongly opposed to this because they all wished still to get the information derived from the censorship'.

The simple solution was for GC&CS to take over the monitoring of the cables. So the cable companies were told to continue handing over their traffic to GC&CS, which copied it and returned it to them within twenty-four hours. 'Secrecy is essential,' wrote Lord Curzon, the then Foreign Secretary. 'It must be remembered that the companies who still supply the original messages to us regard the intervention of the Government with much suspicion and some ill-will. It is important to leave this part of our activity to the deepest possible obscurity.'[18]

The official brief for GC&CS was 'to advise as to the security of codes and cyphers used by foreign powers'. A secret charter added the main role of studying 'the methods of cypher communications used by foreign powers'. GC&CS initially came under the Admiralty, but since most of the work now concerned diplomatic traffic it was quickly transferred to the Foreign Office and in 1923 it came under the direct command of Admiral Hugh Sinclair, the head of MI6, subsequently moving to a joint SIS/GC&CS headquarters in Broadway Buildings.[19]

During the inter-war period, GC&CS intercepted Russian, French, American and Japanese diplomatic telegrams and radio communications. Germany, having been taught a hard lesson by the Zimmermann Telegram, began using the so-called 'one-time pad', thereby making its messages unreadable for the British cryptographers.

'The decyphered telegrams of foreign governments are without doubt the most valuable source of our secret information respecting their policy and actions,' wrote Lord Curzon in 1919. 'They proved the most accurate and, withal, intrinsically the cheapest means of obtaining secret information that exist.'[20]

Diplomatic radio communications were intercepted by a Metropolitan Police intercept station, originally set up by Sir Basil Thomson as part of his Directorate of Intelligence, which together with its staff was 'loaned' to the codebreakers. 'These constables (10 to 12) had a small station at Denmark Hill,' Denniston wrote. 'The admiral undertook to pay for these men and the upkeep of the station while the police commissioner agreed to ask no questions about their work.'

The War Office, the RAF and the Admiralty all set up their own stations to carry out wireless interception, known for security reasons as 'procedure Y'. An Army station at Fort Bridgewoods, Chatham, Kent, and an RAF station, initially Waddington in Lincolnshire, but later at Cheadle, in Staffordshire, passed any high-grade encyphered traffic they intercepted direct to GC&CS.

There was useful intelligence from the American – and presumably also the Japanese – cables during the 1921–2 Washington Naval Conference. But the most productive source was Russian diplomatic traffic, which provided endless material on Anglo-Soviet trade talks and Communist subversion of Britain and the empire.[21]

By 1927 the Conservative government had determined to break off relations with Moscow. In an abortive attempt to find documentary evidence against the Russians that would justify such a move, Special Branch officers raided the London offices of ARCOS, the All-Russia Co-operative Society, and the Soviet trade delegation. When they failed to find any usable evidence against the Soviet mission, the government decided to use the intercepted evidence to justify its decision in the House of Commons.

Baldwin took the opportunity of a House of Commons statement on the ARCOS raid to read out four Russian telegrams 'which have come into the possession of His Majesty's government'. The debate turned into what one commentator has described as 'an orgy of governmental indiscretion about secret intelligence'.

For GC&CS it was a disaster. The Russians introduced their own one-time pads, seriously cutting the amount of accessible Soviet material and leaving the codebreakers with an obsession about secrecy that was to last through to the present day. Denniston, lamenting that the government had 'found it necessary to compromise our work', impressed the need for absolute secrecy on all his employees.[22]

As the Second World War approached, GC&CS was able to read Italy's diplomatic cables and Tokyo's communications with its embassy in Berlin, from where the ambassador, General Hiroshi Oshima, was passing detailed information on German plans back to Japan. Under an arrangement with Cable & Wireless, copies of all encyphered telegrams passing through its Malta relay station were sent back to London, 'ostensibly for accounting purposes' but in fact to be handed over to Denniston, giving British intelligence a useful overview of the build-up of the Axis alliance.[23]

Shortly after the outbreak of the war, GC&CS moved to the specially prepared 'Station X' at Bletchley Park in Bedfordshire. Sinclair had lobbied hard for a wartime station for MI6 but had failed to obtain any funds from official sources, so he bought Bletchley out of his own pocket. 'We know he paid for it, we're not even sure if he was ever repaid,' one former MI6 officer said. 'He died soon afterwards so he probably wasn't.'

Denniston had been busy talent-spotting 'men of the professor type' to expand his organization. They were mainly approached through the universities. Selected by their tutors or the university appointments board, the new recruits were invited to interviews with Denniston for what was

Bletchley Park, wartime headquarters of the Government Code and
Cypher School

described as 'highly interesting work in the Foreign Office'. They were
puzzled to be asked if they played chess, did crosswords or could read
an orchestral score – three good indicators of the mental agility required
for codebreaking and intelligence analysis.[24]

With secrecy paramount, the authorities often went to bizarre lengths
in order to identify potential candidates. At the end of 1941, in response
to a number of letters to the *Daily Telegraph* from readers claiming never
to have missed one of its crosswords, a 'Mr Gavin of the Eccentrics Club'
put up a £100 prize for anyone who could solve a *Telegraph* puzzle in
less than twelve minutes and a speed competition was arranged at the
newspaper's Fleet Street offices.

'We sat at individual tables in front of a platform of invigilators, including the editor,' recalled Stanley Sedgewick, then a City accountant:

> I was one word short when the twelve-minute bell rang, which was
> disappointing as I had completed that day's puzzle in the train to
> Waterloo in under twelve minutes. Imagine my surprise when, several
> weeks later, I received a letter marked 'Confidential', inviting me, as
> a consequence of taking part in the '*Daily Telegraph* Crossword Time
> Test', to make an appointment to see a Colonel Nicholls of the General
> Staff who 'would very much like to get in touch with you on a confi-
> dential matter of national importance'.

Thus it was that I reported to the Inter-Service Special Intelligence
School at No. 1 Albany Rd, Bedford – known locally as The Spy

School – for a 'special course in connection with a certain type of intelligence work'. On completion of the course, I received a letter from the Air Ministry AI4(f) offering me an appointment as a Temporary Junior Assistant at the Government Communications Centre at Bletchley Park.

Because of the secretive nature of the work, Sedgewick was unaware until fifty years later that the German weather codes he worked on throughout the war were a valuable means of entry into some of the Enigma cyphers.[25]

The Enigma machine had been developed by Arthur Scherbius, a German engineer, from a Dutch invention patented in 1919 in the wake of the signals intelligence successes of the First World War. Similar in appearance to a typewriter, the machine itself could neither produce a typewritten version of the encyphered message nor transmit it. Electrical impulses generated by keying in each letter of the clear text translated it into another letter which lit up on a 'lampboard' on top of the machine. These were taken down by hand to produce the encyphered message, which then had to be sent in the normal manner. By typing each letter he received into his own identically set machine, the operator at the other end was able to see each letter of the original message light up on his own lampboard.

Although the Bletchley Park cryptographers are renowned for breaking the Enigma cypher, the first steps in solving it were made early in 1933 by Marian Rejewski of the Polish Cypher Bureau, using stolen instructions provided by French intelligence. The British did not manage to break the Enigma cyphers until after they had been given access to Rejewski's work at a meeting with the Poles and the French in the Pyry Forest, near Warsaw, in July 1939.[26] Thereafter, they began to make significant progress, recording their first breaks within six months, although the decrypts of the Enigma traffic did not begin to flow in a useful form until June 1941, at which point they were allocated the now famous code-word Ultra. From having only limited impact on the war effort, they began to make a significant contribution.[27]

By breaking the German Navy's Enigma cyphers, Bletchley Park allowed the Royal Navy's Operational Intelligence Centre to track German naval movements and re-route the Atlantic convoys that provided Britain's lifeline with America safely away from the areas patrolled by the U-boats. But it was probably in North Africa, as a result of Bletchley Park's ability to read numerous Axis cyphers, that the codebreakers' major success came. The cracking of an Italian shipping cypher created havoc for Rommel as the Royal Navy picked off many of his supply ships at ease. It also had the added bonus of leading to twenty-one U-boats being diverted from the Battle of the Atlantic to the Mediterranean.

This and decrypts of the Wehrmacht's Enigma keys, which gave access to radio links between Rommel and Berlin and provided intelligence on what the Desert Fox was planning, allowed the Eighth Army to turn the tide in North Africa. 'Ultra was quite decisive in both the first Battle of the Atlantic and the north-African campaign,' said Sir Harry Hinsley, the former codebreaker who became the official historian of wartime intelligence. 'The other great turning-point was the second defeat of the U-boats in 1942, to which it made a great contribution, although there were a number of other decisive contributions.'[28]

Stringent security measures were imposed on the distribution of the deciphered material to ensure that the Ultra secret was not disclosed. 'Any action based upon Ultra must be so camouflaged that the action itself cannot lead the enemy to suspect that his communications are being read,' one document outlining the need for secrecy said:

> Momentary tactical advantage is not sufficient ground for taking any risk or compromising the source. No action may be taken against specific sea or land targets revealed by Ultra unless appropriate air reconnaissance or other suitable camouflage measures have also been undertaken.
>
> If from any document which might fall into his hands, from any message he might intercept, from any word revealed by a prisoner of war, or from any ill-considered action taken upon the basis of such intelligence, the enemy were given cause to believe that his communications are not adequately safe-guarded against interception, he would effect changes which would deprive us of knowledge of his operations on all fronts.[29]

Bletchley Park's contribution did not lie solely in codebreaking. It was perhaps inevitable that a collection of Britain's most brilliant intellects – men of the calibre of the Cambridge mathematicians Alan Turing and Gordon Welchman – would produce some remarkable achievements. Not the least was the development, by Turing, Max Newman, Donald Michie and Thomas Flowers, of Colossus, the world's first programmable electronic digital computer, built to help in deciphering 'Tunny', automatically enciphered transmissions from the German Schlüsselzusatz teleprinter. The development of the modern computer was given a massive head start by these men.[30]

Welchman, along with Turing, was to be credited with most of the important work on Enigma. But initially he was asked to look after more mundane material. 'As I studied that first collection of decodes, I began to see somewhat dimly that I was involved in something very different. The callsigns came alive as representing elements of those forces whose comrades at various echelons would have to send messages to each other.'

He realized that by studying the interrelationship between the various radio stations in conjunction with the use of direction-finding and radio-fingerprinting – a technique which identified radio transmitters by their individual idiosyncrasies – it would be possible to piece together the complete order of battle of the German army or air force. The process, which came to be known as traffic analysis, was to prove as useful an intelligence tool as cryptography, transforming GC&CS from an organization which concentrated almost entirely on breaking codes and cyphers into a global body capable of making use of all the resources at its disposal, including service-interception stations across the world, to exploit the raw traffic to its fullest potential. As such, the structure of Britain's post-war signals intelligence organization owes much to Welchman's vision.[31]

In mid-1940 the BBC agreed to set up a 'special unit to monitor enemy broadcasts' after British intelligence found 'definite substantial evidence' that the Abwehr was using German radio stations to send coded messages to its agents abroad. Initially split between Wood Norton, near Evesham, and Broadcasting House, but from 1943 based at Caversham Park, north of Reading, the BBC Monitoring Service operated a 'Flash' service direct to the JIC and the Prime Minister's office, where it was regarded as an

Alan Turing, widely seen as the most brilliant of the GC&CS codebreakers

'indispensable source of intelligence'. During speeches by Hitler, Churchill frequently rang Caversham direct to ask, 'What's that fellow been saying?'[32]

The bulk of the material coming into Bletchley Park 'Control' was from RAF intercept stations at Chicksands Priory and Cheadle; War Office Y Group sites at Beaumanor in Leicestershire and Fort Bridgelands, Kent; and Admiralty stations at Flowerdown, near Winchester, and Irton Moor, Scarborough, which also controlled the navy's network of direction-finding stations locating enemy shipping. The RAF monitored Luftwaffe attacks on Britain from West Kingsdown in Kent.

There were also a number of service-intercept sites around the world, notably OIC Malta; Combined Bureau (Middle East) based at the former Flora and Fauna Museum in Heliopolis, near Cairo; pre-war military stations in Palestine and India; and an Admiralty station at the Far East Combined Bureau which was set up in Hong Kong in 1934 but moved first to Singapore, in September 1939, and then, as the fortunes of war fluctuated, to Colombo, Mombasa and back to Colombo. The overseas stations tended to be more self-contained than their UK counterparts – it was the FECB which did most of the British work on Japanese military and naval cyphers, breaking the main naval code JN25 in 1939, two years before the start of the Pacific War.[33]

Bletchley Park 'Control', based in Hut 6, ensured that all target radio networks were adequately covered. 'We received hourly reports from the intercepting stations, of which those I most clearly remember were War Office Y Group at Beaumanor, RAF Chicksands, and – most surprisingly – the police station at Denmark Hill in south London, where there were machines for intercepting and recording high-speed transmissions,' recalled one GC&CS officer. 'Part of our job was to ensure that important frequencies were double-banked [taken by more than one station at any one time], both to avoid messages being missed and to provide confirmation of texts. A single false letter could wreck a crib or the accurate placement of the recyphered text.'

Neither GC&CS nor military intelligence officers in the field would have been able to operate as well as they did without the help of the Y Service – the military and RAF intercept units based both at home in the United Kingdom and in various theatres around the world. Tactical intelligence has a limited shelf-life. If it is not delivered quickly, the moment, and in many cases the battle, is lost. Information from Bletchley Park took an average of six hours to reach commanders. Even with much more limited resources, a mobile Y unit on the spot was able to deliver far faster.[34]

One other little-publicized success by GC&CS was the solving of an allegedly unbreakable one-time-pad system by the Diplomatic Section. This had moved to Berkeley Street, Mayfair, in 1942 under Denniston in a reshuffle which saw GC&CS placed under the control of Commander Edward Travis.

The one-time-pad system uses a book of keys in which each is torn off and destroyed once it has been used. By limiting usage, 'depth' of encyphered material is not built up and therefore, in theory, no recognizable pattern emerges to allow decryption. As a result, Bletchley Park had ignored all such messages. But when Berkeley Street put in a sustained effort against a German diplomatic version they found they were in fact able to break it.[35]

Although the first Battle of the Atlantic and the war in North Africa are clear examples of how Ultra had a tangible effect on the war, it is difficult to quantify the overall difference it made. But Sir Harry Hinsley believes that it cut the length of the war by about three years. It would, for instance, have been impossible without Ultra to launch the D-Day landings in 1944, he said. 'Operation Overlord would certainly not have been launched at that time without Ultra. Or at least, if it had been launched, it would probably not have been successful.'

It was still possible that the Russians might have gone on to capture Berlin in 1945 or that Britain might have been so badly hit by Hitler's V-bombs that the allies responded by using the atomic bomb, he added. 'But my own belief is that the war, instead of finishing in 1945, would have ended in 1948 had GC&CS not been able to read the Enigma cyphers and produce the Ultra intelligence.'[36]

# CHAPTER 12

## *Post-War Signals Intelligence*

GCHQ has been by far the most valuable source of intelligence
for the British Government ever since it began operating.
Denis Healey, House of Commons debate on the
GCHQ unions, 1984

At the end of the war, the JIC agreed that all intelligence on German
scientific advances gained from Ultra could be handed over to British
scientists under the pretext that it had been obtained from captured
documents. War historians were also to be allowed to use some of
the material, since otherwise 'these men would be forced to write history
which they knew did not correspond with the facts as known'.[1] But in
general the work of GC&CS remained surrounded by stringent security,
since it was to form an important part of the post-war intelligence
machinery.

Interception of Soviet signals had ended in June 1941 after the start
of Operation Barbarossa, the German invasion of the Soviet Union. But,
with the end of the war, Russia was again a principal target. One of the
earliest potential flashpoints of the Cold War was in Iran, where British
intelligence again found itself opposing the Russians in central Asia, the
scene of the Great Game.[2]

'I spent almost a year at a tiny outpost at Abbottabad, in North-West
Frontier Province, after a one-man crash course in that elegant language
Farsi,' wrote Alan Stripp, an Intelligence Corps officer who was monitoring Iranian diplomatic traffic. The Indian Intelligence Branch had
been using the Abbottabad station to monitor Russian diplomatic and
military traffic since before the First World War. Having dropped Soviet
coverage in 1941, it was now back in business. 'By October 1946, I was in
Singapore halfway-through yet another crash course, in Russian,' Stripp
said. 'The Cold War was already beginning to concentrate everybody's
minds.'[3]

The Government Communications Headquarters was officially established in June 1946 as the successor to GC&CS, although Bletchley Park
appears to have been using this name and a number of other similar titles
since very early on in the war, almost certainly as cover. GC&CS had

transferred to Eastcote in north-west London in 1945. It moved to its present location in Cheltenham in 1952.[4]

Until the 1946 official establishment of GCHQ, GC&CS still came under MI6 and shared its top priority: determining Soviet atomic capabilities. This appears to have remained the most important target at least until September 1949, when the Soviet Union tested a nuclear device.[5]

Although no Russian radio traffic was monitored after June 1941, Bletchley Park had been able from early 1943 to read the cypher of the Luftwaffe signals intelligence organization, which was listening to Soviet communications and passing them back to Berlin. This material was used by the JIC to build up a picture of Soviet capabilities. It also seems likely that further German signals intelligence on the Soviet Union was obtained after the war from captured documents and, possibly, from intelligence officials themselves. In February 1946 British intelligence officers based in occupied Germany asked the JIC for 'authority to release at their discretion, certain categories of interned individuals connected with the German Intelligence Service'.[6]

Soviet encyphered communications used the theoretically unbreakable one-time pad. But messages passed between the KGB's Moscow Centre and its stations in the West were decyphered by the Americans after shortages led to identical pads being used for different links. The resultant intelligence, code-named Venona, was passed to the British under the terms of the wartime co-operation agreement between the two countries. One of the first decrypts proved that Donald Maclean was a spy. Other Venona transcripts revealed the identities of the British atom spy Klaus Fuchs and his American counterparts, Ted Hall and Julius and Ethel Rosenberg.[7]

Britain's post-war signals interception was carried out by all three services and by civilians working initially under cover of the Admiralty Civilian Shore Wireless Service, the Government Civilian Radio Organization and the Air Ministry and War Office wireless services. These organizations were later absorbed into the GCHQ-controlled Composite Signals Organization. The main UK intercept sites were at the wartime bases of Chicksands, Cheadle, Winchester, Beaumanor and Scarborough. Overseas bases were in Germany, the Middle East, Ceylon, Singapore and Hong Kong.[8]

Understandably, there was considerable interest in Russian military communications throughout eastern Europe and the Soviet Union itself, in an effort to determine both short- and long-term Soviet objectives. JIC reports on Soviet intentions in the Middle East for the immediate post-war years show detailed knowledge of military dispositions and troop levels in southern Europe. This may well have been gleaned from signals intelligence gathered by the main Middle East site at Sarafand in Palestine, which had targeted Soviet communications before the German attack on the Russians.[9]

The War Office had intercept stations in Constantinople and Iraq during the First World War, and these were kept on in the inter-war years. In 1923 they were moved to Sarafand, where they monitored both Arabic and Russian communications. A. G. Denniston, in a 1944 history of GC&CS, wrote that for twenty years 'a close liaison between GC&CS and Sarafand has always been a satisfactory factor'. At the end of the war the Palestine-based unit became No. 2 Special Wireless Regiment and a detachment was set up in Habbaniya in Iraq, at least in part as a result of the concern over Russian activity in Iran.[10]

With the 1947 decision to withdraw from Palestine, plans were put in place to build a new intercept site for No. 2 Special Wireless Regiment at Ayios Nikólaos, near Famagusta in Cyprus. It eventually became 9 Signal Regiment, which remains GCHQ's main Middle East base, with a relationship that if anything appears to be far closer than in Denniston's time.

The Ayios Nikólaos base has a remote site at Troodos, 1800 feet up on Mount Olympus, and is manned by members of all three armed services together with 'a large civilian contingent'. It monitors a wide range of communications and electronic transmissions throughout the Middle East and southern Russia – a brief that appears to have changed very little from that allocated to Sarafand in the period between the wars.[11]

Soviet military activity in eastern Europe was most easily monitored from the British zones of Germany and Berlin. The main Army Y organisation in Europe, No. 1 Special Wireless Group, was a direct descendant of No. 1 Wireless Regiment, formed in Aldershot in 1934. It ended the war at Bad Oeynhausen, before becoming No. 1 Special Wireless Regiment and moving to a permanent intercept site at Münster. By the late 1950s it had been renamed 13 Signal Regiment and was based at Birgelen, close to the Dutch border town of Roermond. It had remote sites at Dannenberg and Jever on the East German border, and at Teufelsberg in Berlin. But in late 1994, following the end of the Cold War and the unification of Germany, the regiment was disbanded and its staff were dispersed to other units.[12]

It is not clear what happened to the Y Service concept of mobile ground-based signals intelligence units in the immediate aftermath of the Second World War, although amid fears over the existence of Nazi 'Werwolf' stay-behind units some troops based in Germany were involved in the monitoring of telephone communications. It seems likely, with Soviet 'agents' seen as posing a more realistic threat than ex-Nazis, that it was not just the right-wing whose conversations were monitored. Certainly the Intelligence Corps in Germany was still tracking down suspected Nazi war criminals and carrying out surveillance of left-wing trade unionists in the early 1950s.[13]

In the immediate post-war period, GCHQ expressed interest in the RAF's mobile monitoring vehicles, which had facilities both for intercepting VHF and HF voice transmissions and for direction-finding. The Admiralty, however, noted that, while mobile units had more than proved their worth during the war, there was currently 'little effort in this direction'.[14]

The Army would seem to be the most obvious user of such systems, although since the first of its many post-war confrontations was in Palestine, which was also the location of the main Middle East intercept site, it may not initially have seen any grounds for retaining the mobile units. In the short term at least, the main priority – establishing Soviet atomic and military capabilities – was best pursued from static sites. The reaction to the various emergencies and counter-insurgency campaigns in which British troops became involved appears to have been similar to the response to the 1946 Azerbaijan Crisis: the dispatch of a small static detachment following a crash-course in the local language.[15]

Mobile Y Service-style operations appear to have come back into vogue in the late 1970s, when an Army signals intelligence detachment was sent to Rhodesia as part of Operation Agila, the mobile Commonwealth force monitoring the ceasefire between Rhodesian government forces and the rebel Patriotic Front in the run-up to the 1980 elections.[16]

A few years earlier a mobile electronic warfare unit, 14 Signal Regiment (EW), had been formed in West Germany to carry out both ELINT and COMINT tasks. Following the end of the Cold War, it moved to a former US Navy intercept site at Brawdy in South Wales, from where it appears well placed to provide small detachments for the Bosnia-type operations which are seen as the most likely confrontations of the 'Hot Peace' that military planners believe has succeeded the Cold War.[17]

In 1982, a detachment from Communications and Security Group (UK) – a signals intelligence training unit then based at the old Beaumanor site – went to the Falklands with the Task Force together with elements of 14 Signal Regiment. Since then a tri-service SIGINT unit, Joint Service Signals Unit (Falklands), has been based on the islands. A similar unit was located in British Honduras/Belize from 1972 to 1994, helping to ensure a secure transition to independence which had been threatened by Guatemalan territorial claims.[18] Signals intelligence operators also took an active part in the Gulf War, and in 1994 elements from

9 Signal Regiment were still serving in the area, in Jordan and Kuwait.[19]

During the early days of the Cold War, considerable research was undertaken into the use of aerial interception platforms, or 'ferrets', for gathering both communications and electronic intelligence. The first RAF ELINT flights had been flown during the Second World War, using specially equipped Anson reconnaissance aircraft to jam the Knick-ebein beam navigation system that guided German bombers to their targets, while a radio receiver had been fitted into a Hudson aircraft during the 1944 Italian campaign to intercept E-boat communications in the Ligurian Sea.[20]

There were attempts to build on this early use of aerial platforms during 1947 and 1948, when the RAF's 192 Squadron flew a series of experimental SIGINT missions using specially adapted aircraft – initially Ansons, then later converted Lancaster and Lincoln bombers – over the Middle East, the Baltic and the border with East Germany.

In September 1948 a Lancaster and a Lincoln equipped with both photo-reconnaissance and SIGINT equipment flew to Habbaniya in Iraq, from where they undertook a number of eight-hour missions, almost certainly along the Soviet border. Further experimental sorties were flown using Lincoln, Washington and Canberra aircraft. At the end of 1951 a dedicated communications intelligence Lincoln was 'urgently required for useful work', most likely related to the decision to beef up the intelligence operation in Malaya following the assassination in October 1951 of the British High Commissioner. But there were also problems in Egypt and a continual need for more intelligence from the Soviet Bloc countries. An RAF Lincoln shot down over East Germany by a MiG-15 fighter aircraft in 1953 with the loss of six crew appears to have been carrying out both photographic and signals reconnaissance.[21]

There were a number of such 'crashes' during the Cold War. The most famous came in 1960, when the American pilot Gary Powers bailed out after his U-2 spyplane came under attack. Although the publicity surrounding the affair stressed the photo-reconnaissance aspect of his flight, the Russians put signals intelligence equipment recovered from the crashed aircraft on show in Moscow. They also produced a communications expert who described the aircraft's role as being 'the collection of information on the structure of the radio-technical service of the anti-aircraft defence system of the Soviet Union'. The Pentagon estimates that as many as 138 American airmen and technicians may have died in such missions.[22]

RAF electronic reconnaissance flights continued through the 1950s with 192 Squadron being re-formed at Watton in Norfolk in August 1958 as 51 Squadron. It initially flew modified Canberras, but later acquired

Comet R2 dedicated aircraft, carrying up to twenty signals operators. The squadron moved to Wyton, in Cambridgeshire, in 1963, and in 1971 it received the first of its three Nimrod R1 aircraft. By the early 1980s the Nimrods had been repeatedly spotted overflying the Baltic. Modifications had been made to the three aircraft which appeared to indicate that much of the equipment was being operated by remote control.[23]

The squadron is now based at RAF Waddington, in Lincolnshire. Its three Nimrod R1s, which are expected to remain in service until 2003, are equipped with the computerized Star Window system. This has two high-speed-search radio sets to locate active frequencies, twenty-two intercept receivers to which those frequencies can then be transferred – allowing further search operations – and a wide-band digital direction-finding system to locate target transmitters. The ground analysis station can access the data directly via satellite.[24]

Royal Navy vessels have been used as signals intelligence platforms since 1924, when Lieutenant Eric Nave was appointed to the flagship of the China Squadron to monitor Japanese radio traffic, sending it back to GC&CS in London by diplomatic bag. During the war a number of Royal Navy warships were fitted out to intercept radio communications, but only in support of particular operations, such as the amphibious landings at Anzio and Salerno.

The Royal Navy's main wartime interest was in locating enemy shipping, and this was done via a series of direction-finding stations around the coast, controlled from Irton Moor. A number of Royal Navy vessels, both surface vessels and submarines, had intercept capability during the Cold War – among them HMS *Endurance*, which monitored Argentinian communications in defence of the Falklands – and the early 1980s saw an expansion of the Royal Navy's SIGINT capability, with some vessels being fitted with a system which, according to one GCHQ official, would 'provide a major contribution to NATO's tactical planning'.[25]

But by far the biggest advance in aerial platforms has been in the use of satellites. In the mid-1960s Goonhilly Downs near Falmouth, in Cornwall, one of the first satellite earth stations, became an important staging post for the new Intelsat international satellite communications system. Both GCHQ and its American counterpart, the National Security Agency (NSA), were anxious to ensure they could tap into the new systems, and in early 1967 GCHQ announced plans to set up its own satellite station near Bude, sixty miles north of Goonhilly.

Officially, the two satellite dishes were to be used to provide a secure communications link between Britain's embassies abroad and London. GCHQ officials even visited the GPO site at Goonhilly 'to study the methods used there for handling telephone traffic'. In reality, the dishes were designed to scoop up all the communications passing through the Intelsat system.

The close ties with the Americans forged during the Second World War and formalized under the UKUSA Accord had allowed GCHQ to punch above its weight ever since. But if Britain did not get into satellite monitoring from the start its contribution to the alliance would drop dramatically, raising questions on the other side of the Atlantic as to whether it should continue to receive the fruits of the massive American effort.

Leonard Hooper, the then GCHQ Director, was determined to prevent this happening, and later admitted to having shamelessly exploited the need to keep the UKUSA relationship intact in order to persuade the government that the move into satellite monitoring was justified.[26]

Around the same time, the NSA took over the RAF base at Menwith Hill, near Harrogate, North Yorkshire, installing a number of satellite dishes. The Menwith Hill site acts as a ground station for signals intelligence 'ferret' satellites targeting Europe and the former Soviet Union.[27]

The first US signals intelligence satellite, code-named Rhyolite, was launched in June 1970, and there have been at least ten more since, with later models code-named Vortex and Orion. All are in a so-called geostationary orbit, 22,300 miles directly above the Equator, which allows them to remain in the same location in relation to the ground at all times.

Despite their distance from the earth, they have a remarkable ability to pick up communications across the frequency range. During the Chernobyl nuclear disaster, a Vortex satellite stationed above Africa was able to monitor all the communications of the various Soviet organizations involved, from the short-range VHF radios of the police, to the military's command links back to Moscow and the telephone conversations of party officials.[28]

By the early 1980s, with satellites reducing the need for the bases around the world that had made the UKUSA deal with Britain so attractive to the Americans, it became clear that the special relationship was waning. One GCHQ official noted that the Americans were taking a tougher stance on exchanges of information under the UKUSA Accord. 'This hard-nosed attitude was becoming apparent during the mid-70s as overseas bases became less and less efficient and useful because of technical advances,' he said. 'In the past, allied operational policy was based upon close ties with, and a begrudging respect for and reliance on, GCHQ. Time alone has severed many of the close personal ties as Hot and Cold War colleagues retired, died or otherwise passed on.'[29]

The Falklands conflict made it clear that Britain had become too dependent on US satellite intelligence. The government authorized a 'Top

Secret' project to place Britain's own SIGINT satellite above the Indian Ocean under cover of Britain's Skynet military satellite system. The £500 million project, code-named Zircon, caused a major row in 1987 when its existence was revealed in the left-wing journal *New Statesman*. It was subsequently abandoned.[30]

Instead, the British agreed to pay for one of the NSA's three new Orion satellites in return for control of a third of the network. In August 1990 – around the time Zircon was to have been launched – a satellite was placed into the Skynet system. Although that particular Skynet satellite had been due to be placed one degree west, above the Atlantic, it took the precise spot fifty-three degrees east above the Indian Ocean that had been planned for Zircon.[31]

GCHQ's stated role is to monitor all forms of radio, electronic and acoustic transmissions to gain political, military and economic intelligence. It also provides advice on the security of communications and computer systems for government departments, the armed forces and the police, through its Communications Electronics Security Group.

As with SIS, it is required to act 'in the interests of national security, with particular reference to the defence and foreign policies of Her Majesty's Government in the United Kingdom; or in the interests of the economic well-being of the United Kingdom in relation to the actions or intentions of persons outside the British Islands; or in support of the prevention or detection of serious crime'. The most noteworthy point of this brief is that only in respect of 'economic well-being' does the act specify that the monitored activity must be taking place abroad.[32]

GCHQ is based at two separate sites in Cheltenham – Oakley and Benhall – and is divided into a number of directorates, the most important of which is the Directorate of SIGINT Operations and Requirements. This has been the main area of reorganization since the Cold War, when its eight divisions included:

**Z: Requirements and Liaison** – the department that co-ordinates coverage according to the requirements of the domestic customers, of which the foremost are likely to be the Foreign Office, the Ministry of Defence, the Department of Trade and Industry, the Treasury, the Bank of England, and GCHQ's sister organizations MI5 and MI6, as well as the police – in particular the National Criminal Intelligence Service. It also performs the same role with similar foreign organizations with which exchange deals exist or could be negotiated, not just those from the main UKUSA countries but also including Germany's Bundesnachrichtendienst.

**X: Computer Services** – in charge of the agency's highly developed supercomputers that are capable of decyphering the most sophisticated

The GCHQ headquarters in Cheltenham

of encryption systems, picking out keywords from a mass of transmissions or detecting suspicious financial transactions passing through the international banking system.

**H: Cryptanalysis** – still Britain's most important bargaining chip in terms of the UKUSA Accord. One GCHQ official, speaking in 1982, described H Division's contribution as 'the major factor in GCHQ's case'. At that time it was estimated that the division constituted 75 per cent of GCHQ's practical worth to the Americans. US officials frequently based their foreign policy on reports derived from signals intelligence collected by both the British and the Americans which only the British had been able to decypher. 'The time difference alone means that material can be on desks first thing in the morning.'

**J and K: SIGINT Production.** These are almost certainly the main areas of reorganization. J Division was formerly Special SIGINT, the analysis and reporting of signals intelligence from the Soviet Bloc. K was General SIGINT, covering the rest of the world and economic intelligence. Clearly J's role has changed, with total SIGINT effort against the former Soviet Union cut by a half since the end of the Cold War, although it remains the highest foreign intelligence priority. GCHQ says the reorganization is not along geographical lines, so it may simply affect internal sections, reflecting the increased importance of such targets as nuclear proliferation, terrorism, organized crime and economic intelligence. Alternatively, these topics may have been allocated specific divisions of their own.[33]

In the late 1950s the group of Baltic émigrés originally employed in Regent's Park to process SIS's Berlin-tunnel material were transferred to GCHQ's control, working from a building in the City of London as the London Processing Group and transcribing Russian language intercepts. But by the late 1960s many of the émigrés were reaching retirement age and their replacements were mainly language graduates or former servicemen who had carried out similar work with the armed forces. The group, which became known as the Joint Technical Language Service, was moved to Cheltenham in the mid-1970s.

The Composite Signals organization still exists, although advances in satellite monitoring and computer automation have left it bearing the brunt of the cuts in staffing levels. For similar reasons many of the post-war monitoring sites have gone. GCHQ maintains two offices in London: at 8–9 Palmer Street, only yards from New Scotland Yard, the headquarters of the Metropolitan Police, and at Empress State Buildings in Earls Court, west London, from where international commercial telexes and cables are monitored.

Chicksands was handed over to the Americans in 1948. The US facility closed in 1994 and by mid-1997 the base will house the Defence Intelligence and Security Centre, which will include the Defence Special Signals School formed from the Army signals intelligence training unit Communications and Security Group (UK) and its RAF counterpart the Communications Analysis Training School. Cheadle was closed following the end of the Cold War. Irton Moor, the site near Scarborough, is still in existence, and there are satellite-monitoring stations at Bude and Taunton. There is also a large joint-services site at RAF Digby in Lincolnshire.

The foreign monitoring stations at Colombo and Singapore all went in the retreat from empire. Hong Kong will go in 1997 with the hand-over of the colony to China, leaving bases on Ascension Island, Gibraltar and Cyprus, together with a number of small detachments at embassies and High Commissions around the world.[34]

Radio and television broadcasts are monitored by the BBC in conjunction with the CIA's Foreign Broadcast Information Service (FBIS) under a 1948 arrangement similar to the UKUSA Accord which also divides the world up between traditional areas of influence and interest. The 1948–49 *BBC Handbook* said there was 'close cooperation between the BBC's Monitoring Service and its American counterpart the Foreign

Broadcast Information Branch of the Central Intelligence Agency, and each of the two services maintained liaison units at each other's stations for the purposes of a full exchange of information'.

BBC Monitoring is still based at Caversham Park, Reading, in Berkshire, and is funded in part by a grant-in-aid from the Foreign Office. While FBIS is wholly geared to overt intelligence-gathering, BBC Monitoring is a news-based organization staffed by journalists. But the main British customers include the Foreign Office, the Cabinet Office and the Ministry of Defence, who provide an annual list of target priorities that reflect the intelligence requirements laid down by the JIC. In addition, under the terms of its exchange agreement with FBIS, it is bound to monitor whatever the Americans want from within its coverage area.

GCHQ retains the obsessive secrecy inherited from Denniston and the 1927 ARCOS affair. But in the early 1980s it was thrust into the public limelight first by the discovery that Geoffrey Prime, a former GCHQ linguist, had been a major Soviet spy, and then by the government's 1984 ban on trade unions, a misguided and crassly handled move that served only to draw attention to the organization and what it did, thereby chipping away at the very security the government claimed to want to protect.

Since the end of the Cold War, GCHQ has undergone a drastic 'redirection of effort' following two separate inquiries ordered into its work as the politicians sought to reap their peace dividend.

A specific review of GCHQ's operations, carried out in 1995 by a committee chaired by Roger Hurn, chairman and chief executive of Smiths Industries, and including representatives of MI5, MI6 and the Ministry of Defence, suggested that, with the main threat perceived to have decreased, and with the expansion of satellite and computer technology making it possible for fewer operators to perform more tasks, GCHQ's £500 million share of the £800 million intelligence budget was ripe for the axe. Civilian staff levels, which in 1993 stood at 6500, are expected to fall to at least 5000 under David Omand, the new Director.[35]

Any cuts in staff will have to have been passed by the Americans if the UKUSA Accord is not to be badly damaged with a corresponding effect on Britain's intelligence network that would be potentially far more costly than keeping the organization as it is. GCHQ staff were reassured during the reorganization that its contribution to the UKUSA collection effort had to remain 'of sufficient scale and of the right kind to make a continuation of the SIGINT alliance worthwhile to our partners'. UK resources would still have to be available to meet US requirements, and the budget would have to remain at such a level that GCHQ did not reach 'a point of overdependence' on America.[36]

# CHAPTER 13

# A Contradiction in Terms

Military intelligence is a contradiction in terms.
Old army adage

David Henderson, the head of British intelligence in the Boer War, had a lasting influence on British military intelligence, repeatedly lobbying the War Office to set up an Intelligence Corps 'to enable the General Staff to deal with the large and varied staff of subordinates required for Field Intelligence work'. In response to Henderson's sustained offensive, Colonel George M. W. Macdonogh, who in 1910 had succeeded Edmonds as head of MO5, began to compile a list of likely members.[1]

Macdonogh selected his candidates on the basis that they would need a mixture of intellect, linguistic ability and an unorthodox approach. On the outbreak of war, an odd assortment of academics, businessmen, artists, schoolteachers, musicians and adventurers were surprised to receive a telegram inviting them to join the new Intelligence Corps. They were to report to Southampton, where they were graded as Second Lieutenants (Interpreters) or Agents (1st Class).

The commandant of the new corps was Major T. G. J. Torrie of the Indian Army – appointed because he was back on leave when war broke out and, not wanting to miss the action, badgered Macdonogh into giving him a posting to France.[2] But within weeks of arriving in France Torrie had moved on, having found himself a posting to an infantry regiment where he was assured of front-line action. He was replaced by Major A. P. later Field Marshal Lord, Wavell, who had been working as a Russian linguist in the Directorate of Military Operations but was also eager for action.

Wavell was unimpressed by his subordinates – 'an odd crowd of thirty to forty officers with a smattering of languages' – and, like Torrie, had no commitment to intelligence work. 'Once I had got a grip on the purpose of the Intelligence Corps, got it organized, cleared up one or two minor scandals and dismissed one or two unsuitable types, I found there was only one or two hours work a day.' After three and a half weeks as corps commandant – even less time than Torrie – Wavell had found himself a more active post.[3]

Most regular officers took a somewhat dim view of their new colleagues. 'The green-tabbed official of the Intelligence Corps was at first regarded with the utmost suspicion,' wrote one:

His reserve was very marked and he had an insatiable curiosity, a combination of characteristics which the average Britisher resents, and this rather led the soldier to imagine that his efforts were not so much directed towards gleaning information about the enemy as about the state of the unit that he visited, and he was consequently looked upon at first as suspect.[4]

The corps had not got off to a good start and, given the hostility of many of the Army's senior officers, might have completely fallen apart were it not for the presence in France of two of its main architects within the Directorate of Military Operations, Major Walter Kirke and Colonel Macdonogh, who had been posted to the British Expeditionary Force's GHQ as Head of Intelligence. While working in MO5 with Macdonogh, Kirke had laid down the role of the Intelligence Corps as being to provide linguists, to carry out secret service work and to form the nucleus of a counter-espionage network.[5]

Henderson had stressed that counter-espionage was just as important as intelligence-gathering, and his recommendations had been fully reflected in the regulations. 'Preventing the enemy from obtaining information is, in European warfare, almost as of great importance as securing information for one's own side,' he wrote. 'With civilian inhabitants, foreign military attachés and newspaper correspondents about, it will be impossible to obtain complete concealment, but measures must be taken to secure that they see as little as possible and hear nothing.'[6]

But it was inevitably the secret service work, which was to play a minimal role in military intelligence, that captivated the minds of those recruited into the corps. Sigismund Payne-Best, who was later to become better known for his role in the Venlo incident, recalled how he and a number of other potential 'I' Corps officers had been recruited. Best, who was not on Macdonogh's original list, was told to report to the War Office:

Men were being ushered in, one by one to this room. Some of them came out very promptly, others stayed there some time, and gradually it was rumoured that it was intelligence. They were recruiting men for intelligence work in France. A lot of talk then went on about intelligence service. Spying. You get shot if you get caught spying in France.

When the last man had been interviewed, we were told to follow a sergeant and he led us out and we marched, or rather we straggled, behind the sergeant to Burlington House. Well, the sergeant walked in front. I think if he'd walked at the back, perhaps more of us would have reached Burlington House, for I certainly noticed that quite a number of people seemed to disappear. I think they had got cold feet. They'd got the idea that we were to spy and that spying was a dangerous job.

Best was one of the few corps officers who did find themselves involved in secret service work. Two separate sections were set up – one based in London, the other in Folkestone – to collect intelligence from refugees coming into Britain from the Lowlands. Best, working under Major Ernest Wallinger, from a headquarters in Basil Street, Kensington, was successful not only in obtaining information from the refugees but in setting up networks of agents and train-watchers in Belgium to report on German troop movements. The train-watchers included housewives living in houses overlooking railway lines who knitted encoded reports of the German movements: a plain stitch for a carriage containing men, purl for those carrying horses. Wallinger controlled agents throughout Belgium, Holland, Switzerland and Germany, competing with MI6 operations – much to Cumming's chagrin.[7]

But spying was to play only a peripheral part in the new corps' work. Intelligence was being transformed by new technology in the shape of the radio and the aircraft. Aerial reconnaissance and the interception of wireless signals were to be two of the three main methods of intelligence collection employed by the new corps. The other, with the scope for forward reconnaissance limited by trench warfare, was the interrogation of enemy prisoners and deserters.

Henderson had advocated the classic 'nice guy, nasty guy' method of interrogation. 'Skill in eliciting information grows rapidly with practice,' he wrote:

Sympathy with inhabitants, camaraderie with prisoners, affected suspicion of deserters, are often successful. Gentleness will sometimes melt reserve, harshness may break it down ... A bottle of brandy is a powerful weapon against a physically exhausted man. A method frequently found effective in important cases is to bring an unwilling witness first before an officer who will question him harshly and threaten him, and then hand him over to the care of a sympathetic underling.[8]

Aerial reconnaissance had begun with a balloon flown over the battle-field at the Battle of Fleurus in July 1794. During the American Civil War, Union troops used a balloon to take photographs of Confederate positions at Richmond. Similar methods were used in the Franco-Prussian War, and in 1884 the British Army set up its own balloon reconnaissance unit. By the turn of the century the War Office was being urged to carry out 'special and early experiments in connection with a dirigible balloon, man-lifting kite and photographic equipment for the balloon sections'.[9] As a result, the main military advantage of the fixed-wing aircraft was at first seen in its use as a vehicle for aerial reconnaissance. The first recorded use of an airplane for such purposes was by Captain Piazza of the Italian Army in October 1911, during the Italo-Turkish war. He was also the first to take aerial pictures, photographing Turkish positions on 24 and 25 February 1912.[10]

David Henderson – who had been appointed to head the newly formed Royal Flying Corps – set up an experimental photographic section which developed an aerial camera that could be fitted on to the fuselage of an aircraft. During the 1916 Battle of the Somme alone, the RFC took more than 19,000 air photographs. Intelligence sections were attached to any squadron carrying out aerial reconnaissance. The amount of intelligence provided was beyond the belief of many officers.[11]

The British Army was very slow to realize the potential of radio. The British Expeditionary Force had some wagon-mounted wireless transmitters intended for the use of the cavalry, but by the end of 1914 they were being used almost exclusively to intercept German radio communications – 'a task that was carried out with considerable success'.[12]

At the end of the war, the Intelligence Corps continued in operation in occupied Germany, monitoring German compliance with the Armistice and carrying out counter-espionage. But there were few who saw any need for military intelligence in peacetime, and by December 1929 the corps had disappeared.[13]

This created predictable difficulties in 1939, with the corps being hurriedly pulled together now under cover of the Corps of Military Police. Yet again the Army targeted intellectuals who, while undoubtedly suited to the work, were unlikely to have the respect of the professional soldier. Malcolm Muggeridge, one of those arriving at the training centre at Mytchett in Surrey, recalled, 'The Red Caps looked with ill-concealed distaste and disdain at we Field Security men, mostly schoolmasters, journalists, encyclopaedia salesmen, unfrocked clergymen and other displaced *New Statesman* readers'.[14]

As in 1914, they had similar problems getting field commanders to take their work, and perhaps more importantly their product, seriously.

Under persistent lobbying from Major W. F. Jeffries, the officer responsible for military intelligence personnel, the War Office finally agreed to the creation of an independent Intelligence Corps, approved by King George VI on 15 July 1940. Jeffries was appointed as its first commandant.

'Intelligence, with all its ramifications and duties, became so vast and grew up so rapidly that I felt it was impossible to control properly or obtain that *esprit de corps* which was essential,' Jeffries said.

I had numerous talks with the late Brigadier Martin (the DDMI) and with General Beaumont-Nesbitt (the DMI) pleading for a Corps. Both agreed on the necessity, but masses of difficulties arose, chiefly as to where a proper and large enough building and training ground could be obtained. I asked for Holloway College, Virginia Water, which would have been ideal, but was told that the education of women could not be interfered with![15]

Nevertheless, using private connections, Jeffries succeeded in acquiring two Oxford colleges, Oriel and Pembroke, as a corps headquarters and officer training centre, while other ranks were trained at King Alfred's College, Winchester, where their experiences were similar to those of Muggeridge.

'Having been brought up on Buchan's Richard Hannay novels, there was a certain romance in answering an advertisement in the personal column of *The Daily Telegraph* in 1940 inviting one to apply to a box number if one spoke foreign languages and wished to serve one's country,' recalled David Engleheart, one of those joining the new corps:

Spice was added on discovering that the address for the subsequent assignation was the legendary shop at the Trafalgar Square end of Northumberland Avenue.

Upstairs to a door opened by a bespectacled corporal and into an untidy room presided over by an unmistakably schoolmasterly captain, who, without ceremony, proceeded to give a few chaps and me a French dictée which was taken away to be corrected by the corporal. He then told us to confess to any pink, red or other political rashes into which we might have broken out during adolescence ('We will find out anyway'), said that we had volunteered for the Intelligence Corps and would be inducted at an undisclosed date.

Engleheart, who was transferring from the Royal Signals, was told to report to Winchester:

Having slept for weeks on a palliasse on the floor of a shoddy mill in a rundown Yorkshire town called Ossett, I thought there was little new King Alfred's could teach me. This was a mistake. Instead of the heterogeneous intake up north from every walk of life, welded together by homesickness, compulsory fitness, a better diet than most civilians, and Vera Lynn, I found a sophisticated mixture of intellectuals, world travellers, artists, journalists, film directors, jockeys, MPs – you name it they were there.[16]

The Directorate of Military Intelligence had expanded with the start of the war and a number of new sections had been created, including MI8, controlling signals intelligence; MI9, prisoner-of-war intelligence; and MI14, a special section concentrating on building up a complete picture of German military formations from all available sources.[17]

The main roles of the new Intelligence Corps were the collection of strategic intelligence from aerial photography and signals intelligence; the assimilation of tactical intelligence from a variety of sources – including both of the above plus forward reconnaissance, captured documents and the interrogation or debriefing of prisoners of war, agents and refugees – and counter-intelligence and security, of everything from documents to military bases, airfields, ports and even brothels.

Debriefing one soldier who had reported information being freely circulated in a Middle East 'knocking shop', Maurice Oldfield, then just an Intelligence Corps lieutenant, asked, 'Couldn't you have stayed with the girl just a bit longer, until breakfast time, say? I'm sure she could have told you a lot more.'[18]

Interrogation of enemy prisoners was controlled by MI9 and carried out in theatre by the Combined Services Detailed Interrogation Centres. The headquarters organization and main interrogation centre for PoWs brought to Britain was based initially at Cockfosters in London, before moving to Chesham and then finally to Wilton Park, Beaconsfield.[19]

The Second World War established signals intelligence and air photography as the two most valuable methods of gathering information on enemy military activity. Before the war, the RAF's reluctance to undertake aerial intelligence missions over Europe had led the Air section of MI6 to create its own photo-reconnaissance organization.

Sydney Cotton, an Australian pilot, carried out a number of missions, some in co-operation with the French, to photograph border areas of Germany and Italian-occupied territory in the Mediterranean and East Africa. In July and August 1939 Cotton flew his Lockheed 12A deep into German territory, under cover as a businessman and amateur pilot, photographing a number of locations of interest to British intelligence, including Berlin and the German naval base at Wilhelmshafen.

One former colleague recalled how, before war broke out, Cotton flew to Berlin:

Goering and his lieutenants were there. Seeing the aircraft, they made enquiries as to whom it belonged. On finding out, they approached Cotton for a flight and asked where he would take them. Cotton said: 'I have a dear old aunt who lives in such an area and if you have no objections we could fly over there.' It was agreed and off they set. But what they did not know was that dear old Sydney was pressing the tit the whole time, taking photographs.

Cotton offered his services to the RAF in August 1939 but was turned down, the RAF being 'unsympathetic to irregular operations in general, and Cotton in particular'. But when it became clear that Cotton was providing MI6 with valuable intelligence the RAF insisted on taking his operation over. Cotton was commissioned as a wing commander in charge of the Photographic Development Unit at Heston, just west of London. Initially the RAF tried to use Blenheim and Lysander aircraft, but they could not fly high or fast enough to evade the German fighters and eventually 'Cottonized' Spitfires were used.

Cotton himself continued to rub the RAF top brass up the wrong way. 'He obtained what he wanted where he could get it; he was impatient of "the usual channels"; he applied business methods to government officials and, instead of filling in forms, put them in the waste-paper basket,' one officer said. 'Nor did he hesitate to tell senior air officers who obstructed him precisely what he thought of them. The air staff loathed him. Their opinion was that he was "a line-shooter, racketeer and salesman who does not deliver the goods".' But the other services had an entirely different view of him. Admiral John Godfrey, the Director of Naval Intelligence, said, 'He has delivered the goods most loyally as far as we are concerned and has been the driving force in the development of air intelligence from photography.'

By mid-1940, demand for aerial photography had grown to such an extent that the services of 'Cotton's Crooks' were no longer sufficient. The RAF gratefully used this as an excuse to dispense with his services. The unit was rechristened 1 Photographic Reconnaissance Unit and a separate Photographic Interpretation Unit was set up in the north-London suburb of Wembley.[20]

Within a year the success of aerial reconnaissance – which was in marked contrast to the lack of human intelligence from MI6 and the early difficulties in both acquisition and dissemination of signals intelligence – led all three services to clamour for more, and the number of photo-reconnaissance aircraft was more than doubled, from thirty-three to seventy-eight. 'Intelligence information from other sources has proved most difficult to obtain on account of the stringent German security precautions and other reasons,' one JIC report said. 'Moreover, we have practical proof of the value of air photographs as they enabled the front of the German attack on 10 May 1940 to be predicted with accuracy more than one month before the attack took place.'[21]

Shortly afterwards, the Wembley PIU moved to Danesfield House on the banks of the Thames at Medmenham in Buckinghamshire, where it was renamed the Central Interpretation Unit to reflect the fact that Intelligence Corps and Royal Navy photographic interpreters had joined the original RAF contingent. From then on Medmenham was involved in the planning stages of virtually every wartime operation.[22]

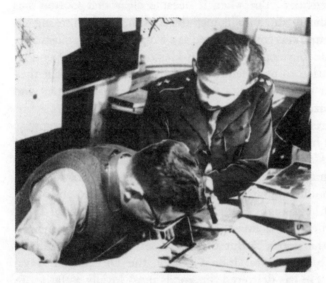

Two Intelligence Corps officers from the *Bodyline* team, which specialized in the German V-bombs, studying aerial photographs at the Central Interpretation Unit in Medmenham

At the end of the First World War, naval intelligence rested on the laurels earned by Room 40 – with disastrous results. For most of the inter-war period it virtually ignored signals intelligence, relying largely on the pre-war naval agreements for its knowledge of enemy shipping. As a result, the Naval Intelligence Division took a far too optimistic view of German intentions and it was not until Godfrey took over as Director of Naval Intelligence, in January 1939, that it began seriously to prepare for war.

The central focus of naval intelligence during the Second World War was NID8, the Operational Intelligence Centre, which tracked the passage of enemy shipping and in particular the U-boats. Its sources were initially limited. Attempts to place intelligence officers on merchant ships to gather evidence from ports and passing ships were largely unproductive. Godfrey recalled how one officer sent to the Black Sea, apparently to observe Russian naval movements, 'ended up in a Braila nightclub defying the Romanian Gestapo with a pistol in each hand. It was only by the personal intervention of the British minister that he was smuggled out.' At one point the NID even devised a scheme to predict what Hitler might do next by having astrological charts drawn up for him, since 'it had been known for some time that Hitler attached importance to astrological advice'.

But by mid-1941 the breaking of the German navy's Enigma cyphers at Bletchley and the use of direction-finding and radio-fingerprinting co-ordinated from the Admiralty Y station near Scarborough were providing more reliable methods of charting the movement of enemy shipping. Signals intelligence was supplemented by human intelligence from MI6's agents and coastal watchers in Scandinavia and France, but by the latter stages of the war nearly 90 per cent of the intelligence handled by NID8 was signals intelligence, with human intelligence used in the main for confirmation.[23]

At the end of the war the Intelligence Corps was run down but not disbanded, playing an important security role in the occupied zones of Germany and Austria and in the areas liberated from Japanese control. One of the primary roles in Germany and Austria was tracking down war criminals and prominent members of the Nazi Party. Intelligence Corps field security sections captured Heinrich Himmler, the SS leader, Joachim von Ribbentrop, the Nazi foreign minister, and the entire government of Hitler's successor, Admiral Dönitz. They also worked alongside their colleagues from MI5 and MI6, many of whom wore the corps uniform as cover, preventing the spread of Communist influence to the British zones and ensuring the return of a democratic political system.[24]

With anxiety over Russian intentions high, demands for both SIGINT and PHOTINT continued. For much of the war the Medmenham photographic intelligence centre had effectively been a joint British/US organization, known as Allied Central Interpretation Unit, and approaches were made to Washington as early as August 1944 to continue these close links in peacetime. The Americans were very keen – not least because Britain provided an ideal location for photo-reconnaissance flights across eastern Europe and the Soviet Union, as well as a number of strategic airfields elsewhere, in the Middle East, the Indian subcontinent and south-east Asia.[25]

At the end of 1945 the RAF had begun a large-scale aerial reconnaissance operation, taking stock photographs first of the whole of western Europe, then of the Middle East, and later of north Africa. The USAF meanwhile was covering south-east Asia and the Americas. Neither side was prepared to overfly eastern Europe or the Soviet Union, for fear of offending the Russians.[26]

But in August 1946 the RAF began making a limited number of flights over Russian-occupied Europe, 'in order that the present shortage of factual intelligence should, in some measure, be remedied'. The risk of detection was slight, the JIC was told. The Russians had only a few captured German radar installations, and the British aircraft – camouflaged pale blue – were invisible from the ground. Even if they were spotted, there was no Soviet aircraft capable of intercepting them.[27]

The Central Interpretation Unit moved to Nuneham Park, Oxfordshire, in April 1946 and was renamed the Joint Air Photographic Intelligence Centre. It was heavily involved in evaluating intelligence from the Korean War and from joint US/British reconnaissance flights over the Warsaw Pact countries. When President Truman banned such operations by US crews in May 1950, following the shooting down of a US Navy Privateer caught in Latvian airspace, RAF crews flew the US RB-45 Tornado aircraft, repainted with RAF insignia, in a number of missions over eastern Europe and the Soviet Union.[28]

'There were three routes,' said Wing Commander Rex Sanders, the navigator on one of the flights:

One was through Germany to the Baltic states. The second was south of that, through Germany towards Moscow, and the third was south of that, going down through the centre of Russia and then arcing down south on the way out. There was a fear, of course, that they might think this was something more serious than just reconnaissance. It did cross our minds that the Soviets might think we were attacking.[29]

An RAF Canberra – a new aircraft capable of flying higher than the Soviet fighters – flew an aerial reconnaissance mission over a new Soviet missile test site for the Americans in late 1953, overpassing the Volgograd site and then landing in Iran. The Canberras made a number of such flights over the Soviet Union and were so effective that the latest variant remains the main RAF photo-reconnaissance aircraft. The successor to Cotton's Crooks – 39(1 PRU) Photographic Reconnaissance Unit at Marham in Norfolk – is equipped with three Canberra PR9s and one PR7. There are also two Tornado reconnaissance squadrons, also based at Marham, and a Jaguar squadron at RAF Coltishall.[30]

Meanwhile, the Nuneham Park interpretation unit had undergone a further name change, to the present Joint Air Reconnaissance Intelligence Centre (JARIC), and in July 1957 it moved to Brampton, just outside Huntingdon, where it remains. Photographic Interpretation has become Imagery Analysis, reflecting the growing importance of stand-off radar and infra-red imagery which can see in the dark through poor weather conditions and through camouflage. Advances in communications and computer technology have transformed aerial reconnaissance. Imagery can now be 'remotely sensed' and transmitted direct to JARIC's computers, which can produce enhanced three-dimensional pictures of the target area and even identify standard pieces of equipment.[31]

The close links with the Americans fostered in the early years of the Cold War paid dividends even at the most unlikely of times. During the Suez Crisis, with America violently opposed to the Anglo-French/Israeli invasion, a USAF U-2 on a routine reconnaissance flight over the Mediterranean flew over an Egyptian military airport the RAF was about to bomb. Normal procedure was to make one overpass, turn, and make a second overpass before continuing on the mission. Between the two overpasses, the attack had taken place. The CIA, intelligence links, unfazed by the inter-governmental friction, wired the 'before and after' photographs to the British, receiving the response: 'Warm thanks for the pix. It's the quickest bomb damage assessment we ever had.'

That co-operation continued in the Falklands in 1982, when the lack of usable air photographs led to successful British requests for a flight over the South Atlantic by an American SR-71 Blackbird aerial reconnaissance aircraft and access to the product of a US Keyhole satellite. Until its retirement, the SR-71 flew out of British bases in the UK and Cyprus. USAF U-2R spy aircraft continue this tradition. The quid pro quo appears to have been access to photographic, infra-red and radar imagery from the American Keyhole and Lacrosse satellites.[32]

There is an inevitable rivalry between imagery analysts – the eyes of the strategic intelligence world – and their signals intelligence counterparts – the ears – as to who is the more effective. The end of the Cold War has produced more rather than less work for both as they track the locations of old Soviet units, particularly those equipped with nuclear weaponry, and build up fresh pictures of potential enemies around the world. The Russians have complained that, although there has been some let-up in the number of reconnaissance aircraft breaching their airspace, there have still been 2600 such incursions each year, most of them carried out by Nato aircraft.[33]

# CHAPTER 14

# *Setting the House in Order*

> He who knows his adversary as well as he knows himself will
> never suffer defeat.
>> Sun Tzu, Chinese military tactician in *The Art of War*,
>> sixth century BC

The pre-war attempts to improve intelligence co-ordination between the Navy, Army and Air Force through the 1936 Inter-Service Intelligence Committee and its successor the JIC were not a great success. There was a marked tendency for each to go its own way without consulting the others, epitomized by the Royal Navy's refusal to accept the inevitability of war with Hitler until shortly before it began.[1]

As VE Day approached, the JIC worked on ways to improve the situation. 'Intelligence before the war was starved of resources, especially in trained personnel,' it said in a report on the *Post-War Organization of Intelligence*:

> It was not then realized that the less money we have to spend on preparations for war, the more important it is to have a first-class intelligence system in peacetime. An equally important shortcoming was the lack of a sufficiently authoritative means of putting forward considered views based upon the results of the intelligence produced.
>
> This failure to maintain an adequate intelligence organization in peacetime led to the need for rapid and largely improvised expansion under the imminent threat of war and to the development of a complicated and uneconomical organization. We now have an opportunity to set our house in order.

The solution was to be the creation of the Joint Intelligence Bureau, a tri-service organization that would 'collect, assess and, where appropriate, appreciate intelligence material of inter-departmental significance'. Although the JIB was headed by the influential General Sir Kenneth Strong, formerly Eisenhower's chief intelligence officer, it never quite fulfilled these lofty ambitions. 'The Bureau had a considerable battle for existence,' Strong wrote later. 'The armed services never really liked it and many of their senior men regarded it as a threat to the traditional forms of service intelligence.'

The JIB never acted as the co-ordinating body that the JIC had envisaged but was primarily concerned with the collation of topographical, logistical, scientific, technical and economic intelligence. This last task, taken over from the Ministry of Economic Warfare, was seen as an important indicator of potential trouble spots. 'The economic contribution in assessing the strength of potential enemies is bound to be considerably more important than in wartime,' the JIC noted. 'Since in peace a country's capacity for war-making must chiefly lie in its war potential which is predominantly an economic factor.'

The JIB was a relatively large body, with 220 staff. It had four separate divisions: one General division – which acted as a link with the service intelligence bodies and SIS – and three geographical divisions: Western, covering western Europe; Central, covering the Soviet Union, eastern Europe, the Balkans and the Middle East; and Eastern, for Asia, the Pacific and the Americas.[2]

A 1963 reform of the Ministry of Defence carried out by Lord Mountbatten led to an amalgamation of the three service intelligence organizations with the JIB to form the Defence Intelligence Staff, 'to provide objective all-source integrated intelligence assessments of defence matters in peace, crisis and war'. As that implies, the information is collected from a variety of sources, including openly available material published or broadcast in the media and the more covert material collected by GCHQ, JARIC, SIS and defence attachés posted to Britain's embassies abroad.[3]

The intelligence role of the attaché is often played down but remains important, both in gauging intentions and in the collection of overt and covert intelligence. The appointment of military attachés to embassies abroad as intelligence officers was begun by the French in the early part of the nineteenth century, but it was not until 1854 that Britain took up the practice, appointing 'commissars of the Queen' to Britain's allies in Paris, Turin and Constantinople and to the French headquarters in the Crimea.[4]

During the Cold War, the British and the Russians set up official missions to each other's zones of occupation, ostensibly as a liaison and confidence-building measure, although in fact they were little more than defacto human intelligence organizations. The British mission, BRIXMIS, was formed in mid-1946 with a staff of around thirty, including interpreters, drivers, radio operators and 'four fairly high-ranking intelligence officers representing all three services plus a technical expert to collect technical intelligence, scientific intelligence and economic intelligence'.

The missions were given qualified freedom of travel. There were a number of permanent restricted areas, and on occasions temporary restricted areas were imposed, to cover an exercise or a secret deployment. BRIXMIS spent much of its time making covert expeditions into the restricted areas to gather intelligence on military installations and equipment or to monitor military exercises. As a result, its staff were frequently attacked by the Russians or the East Germans. Their vehicles were forced off the road, they were beaten up, and on occasion they were even shot at.[5]

The Defence Intelligence Staff is headed by the Chief of Defence Intelligence, a three-star general, admiral or air marshal, who also acts as Deputy Chairman of the JIC. His deputy, a civilian who is also a member of the JIC, is responsible for the DIS analytical wing and its assessments. A two-star officer controls intelligence collection and is responsible for defence attachés, the Joint Air Reconnaissance Intelligence Centre, the Directorate-General of Military Survey, and the Defence Intelligence Centre.

The DIS had a staff of around 800 in the immediate aftermath of the Cold War when the politicians came looking for their 'peace dividend'. 'The target for reductions in the DIS was about 25 per cent,' said Admiral Sir John Kerr, former Chief of Defence Intelligence. 'But I argued that in a more uncertain world with smaller forces, some at lower states of readiness, and with a wider involvement geographically, there was a need for better intelligence not less. I succeeded in constraining the cuts to about half of those sought.' The budget was cut from £70 million to just over £50 million, forcing a reduction in staff to around 600.[6]

DIS analysts – a mixture of members of all three services and civilians – examine traditional military intelligence topics such as the tactics, orders of battle, weapons, capabilities, personalities, loyalty and morale of the armed forces of around 100 countries around the world. But this provides only a part of the defence intelligence picture. Other areas of interest include economic, political and scientific information relevant to defence capabilities or intentions; defence industries; technology transfer; and arms sales. DIS is responsible for collating the information needed to verify arms control, working with the teams of inspectors who check weapons stockpiles, and, as with MI6 and GCHQ, one of its biggest areas of interest is the proliferation of nuclear, chemical and biological weapons.[7]

'It is self-evident that five years ago when there was a Warsaw Pact, there was a huge concentration on the Warsaw Pact,' a senior defence intelligence official has said:

> As the world has developed, our organization changed to reflect the fact that we no longer expect Russia to invade the UK in the immediate future.
>
> The analytical wing has three main branches. One looks at the world geographically, another covers functional areas – things like proliferation – and there is a third very important branch which looks after science and technology. Now within that third element you have a distinction between technologies and, if you like, technologies incorporating weapons systems. So we have some people who are looking at tanks but we'll have other people who look at the technology that we reckon in years to come could be critical on the battlefield.

DIS intelligence assessments are disseminated in a variety of forms: in contributions to JIC and MOD papers, in separate DIS reports and minutes, and in various briefings, including a weekly closed-circuit television briefing for MOD customers that can be extended to include other government departments in times of crisis.

The Defence Intelligence and Security Centre, a tri-service intelligence organization which by mid-1997 will be based at Chicksands, Bedfordshire, will include the Defence Intelligence and Security School – which also provides training in psychological operations – and the Joint Services Intelligence Organization, which trains military interrogators and those who may need to resist interrogation measures – among them members of MI6, the SAS and its naval equivalent, the Special Boat Service. It also supports the Defence Debriefing Team, which gathers intelligence by interviewing people returning from war zones, typically mercenaries who have been operating in Bosnia.

The Chicksands base will also include the Intelligence Corps training depot, previously based at Ashford, Kent; the Defence Special Signals School formed from the RAF's Communications Analysis Training School and its Army equivalent, Communications and Security Group (UK); and the Joint School of Photographic Interpretation.[8]

In the retreat from empire that marked the decades following the Second World War, the British Army found itself involved in a series of conflicts in which intelligence was to play a major role. The most influential of these was the Malayan Emergency of 1948–60, which saw the first use of the 'hearts and minds' policy that lay at the heart of the British post-war counter-insurgency successes. It was linked to an intensive intelligence campaign, closely integrating military intelligence (both the

# Organization of Defence Intelligence Staff

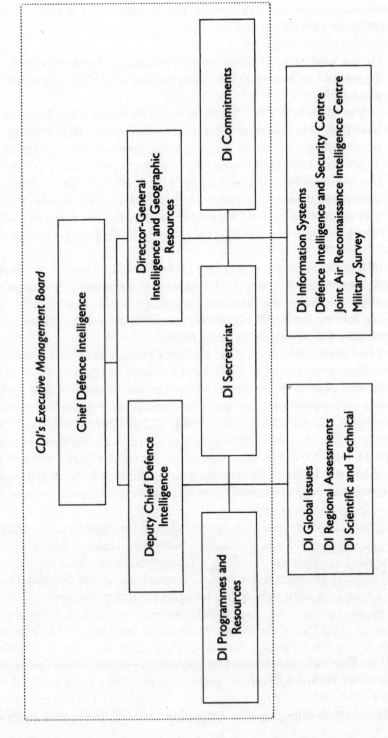

CDI's Executive Management Board

Chief Defence Intelligence

Director-General Intelligence and Geographic Resources

Deputy Chief Defence Intelligence

DI Commitments

DI Secretariat

DI Information Systems
Defence Intelligence and Security Centre
Joint Air Reconnaissance Intelligence Centre
Military Survey

DI Global Issues
DI Regional Assessments
DI Scientific and Technical

DI Programmes and Resources

Intelligence Corps and the Special Air Service) with MI5, the Malayan Security Service (an inferior local equivalent of MI5) and the Malay Police Special Branch.

The SAS, formed to fight in north Africa in 1941, had been disbanded at the end of the Second World War. But the regiment's senior officers fought a rearguard action to keep it alive, and in 1947 a territorial regiment was created. One of its squadrons was subsequently sent to Malaya and merged with the Malayan Scouts – a special forces unit set up by Mike Calvert, a veteran SAS officer. The result was a regular British Army unit, 22 SAS – The Regiment.

The 'hearts and minds' policy – known early on as political pacification – was devised by General Sir Harold Briggs, taking advice from Calvert. The intelligence plan was implemented by General Gerald Templer. Formerly the post-war Director of Military Intelligence, Templer was dispatched to the colony in early 1952, following the assassination by Chin Peng's Communist insurgents of Sir Henry Gurney, the British High Commissioner. He brought with him MI5 officers intended to revitalize the inefficient Malayan Security Service.[9]

The SAS set about denying local support for the Communist guerrillas, identifying and eliminating causes for discontent with the British to win over the 'hearts and minds' of the local population. In a carefully staggered operation, more than 400 villages were moved to specially constructed kampongs away from the insurgents as area after area was declared 'white' – clean of Communist influence. The intelligence contribution, in a context where British troops had problems simply identifying the enemy, was to build up a comprehensive picture of Communist activity and support in each area – a job that had to be started practically from scratch.

'What was lacking was information about the terrorist organization and order of battle and their supplies,' one officer said:

> Our main task was to track them down by means of every kind of intelligence – informers from the towns and villages where supplies were obtained, captured documents from camps overrun by our patrols, prisoners and aerial photographs. At the start of the year, we knew where Chin Peng had been four months before and when I left we knew where he had been six weeks before. Eventually, some time later, they got so close on his tail that he fled over the border into Thailand.[10]

The combination of extensive highly integrated intelligence and a minimum-force 'hearts and minds' operation was to work throughout the retreat from empire in Borneo, Aden, Kenya, Cyprus and Oman. Critics have pointed out that it would not have worked closer to home, where the ubiquitous intelligence operations would have been seen as something akin to a secret police. Nor would it have been successful without a willingness to retreat from empire and hand over the reins of power to local government. Northern Ireland is frequently cited as the proof of both puddings. But the Templer method was created for a particular situation, not as a general counter-insurgency panacea, and it worked.[11]

The requirement for tactical or combat intelligence can vary considerably from campaign to campaign. The Gulf War has been described as the first Space War, with commanders having access before the battle to considerable signals and imagery intelligence on the Iraqi forces, their deployments and tactics – much of it provided by satellite.[12]

During the 1982 Falklands conflict, on the other hand, at least one area of strategic intelligence appears to have been lacking. 'Not until the very end of the campaign were there any air photographs showing enemy dispositions, defence positions, strong positions, gun positions and so forth,' wrote Brigadier Julian Thompson, commander of the 3rd Commando Brigade. 'Even they arrived late and were so poor that they had no influence on planning. Detailed intelligence would have to be gleaned by the "mark one eyeball".'

Teams of SAS and SBS were landed on the islands by helicopter or from submarine from early May, a month after the Argentinian invasion, to survey potential landing-sites and to collect information on enemy positions, strengths and morale. Thompson said, 'So important was the acquisition of intelligence that Special Forces, and particularly the assets to insert them, could be spared for only one direct-action raid in the run-up to D-Day.'[13]

By the time the British troops landed on the Falklands three weeks later, considerable intelligence had been collected. Much of this would have been provided from signals intelligence, which is believed to have produced the complete order of battle of the Argentinian forces. The British had a number of SIGINT collection methods available.

There was a GCHQ station on Ascension monitoring the area, and HMS *Endurance* was also intercepting Argentinian communications. An Army SIGINT detachment from Communications and Security Group (UK) sailed with the task force, and a number of other vessels would have had Royal Navy electronic-warfare operators on board. As the task force assembled, one GCHQ official noted that Royal Navy surface vessels had recently been fitted with signals intelligence equipment that would 'provide a major contribution to NATO's tactical planning'. RAF Nimrod aerial SIGINT platforms also overflew the area from Ascension, monitoring Argentinian communications.

'We are evidently able to intercept much if not all of the enemy's signal traffic,' wrote one British officer. The intelligence available from military radio and even international radio-telephone communications was 'impressive indeed', he wrote. 'Without it, we would never have achieved what we have.'[14]

Although the official American stance was that of a neutral intermediary, this did not affect the close links between GCHQ and its US counterpart, the National Security Agency, which monitored the build-up to the conflict from its station in Panama, passing raw take on to GCHQ. The American SR-71 which overflew the Falklands at the request of the British may also have been used in a SIGINT mode. But, as with Ultra during the Second World War, the battle tended to have moved on before the process of interception, decryption, analysis and reporting could be concluded. The DIS subsequently ordered that in some circumstances raw intelligence could be passed direct to commanders.

Other information was being collected by an Intelligence Corps unit which debriefed the Royal Marine detachment repatriated from Port Stanley and interrogated Argentinian soldiers captured in South Georgia. Once the land battle was in place, joint forward interrogation teams obtained considerable intelligence from the large numbers of Argentinian prisoners. All operational intelligence was collated by the intelligence cells of 5 Infantry Brigade and 3 Commando and the intelligence section of Major-General Jeremy Moore's headquarters organization Land Forces Falkland Islands. There was also a nine-man reporting team with analytical back-up at the Joint Services HQ in Northwood, north-west London.

Despite his complaints over the lack of useable imagery, Thompson later said he had been impressed by 'the quality of the intelligence assessments that were produced from quite early on and right through the campaign by the intelligence staffs in my own headquarters. The "pièce de résistance" was the identification of positions occupied by the Argentine regiments, before we landed, which proved to be amazingly accurate.'[15]

The long run-up to the Gulf War allowed the allies to collect a great deal of intelligence from strategic assets. A comprehensive knowledge of the Iraqi order of battle, weaponry and tactics was already on file, built up during the Iran–Iraq War, largely from signals and imagery intelligence. By the time the air war began, intelligence reports available to divisional commanders were providing extensive details of the dispositions of Iraqi forces in Kuwait and southern Iraq, although a number of enemy formations remained unidentified or on the move.[16]

A great deal of this information could also be ascertained from signals and imagery intelligence collected by satellites, static monitoring stations in the region – among them the British Army's Cyprus-based 9 Signal Regiment – and aerial platforms like the American RC-135 Rivet Joint aircraft, the high-altitude U-2Rs and the E-8A Joint-STARS aircraft. Air activity was monitored and controlled by the E-3B Sentry AWACs aircraft.

The E-8A's Joint-STARS stand-off battlefield surveillance radar, still in the development stage, reported direct to the allied headquarters in Riyadh, providing invaluable 'real time' intelligence throughout the war. Patrolling along the Saudi side of the border and tied in to the Navstar satellite global positioning system, it was able to produce detailed imagery of the situation deep inside Iraq, pinpointing the position of a vehicle the size of a small jeep and even determining whether it was tracked or wheeled. A British version known as ASTOR is not scheduled for operational testing until 2003.

The most forward elements of the intelligence machine were the special forces from the SAS and the SBS; the US Army Rangers; the Green Berets; Delta Force; the US Marines; and the SEALs, the American equivalent of the SBS, operating behind Iraqi lines. Although the location of the Iraqi Scud missiles was their highest priority, they also relayed back intelligence on the positions of Iraqi troops in central and western Iraq and a wide variety of information vital to divisional commanders.[17]

This did not just include the location and strengths of enemy defences. Major-General Rupert Smith, commander of the British 1st Armoured Division, will also have required details of any artillery in a position to bring down fire on the division, and of all enemy armoured and mechanized infantry formations within twenty-four hours of divisional positions. He needed to know the types of terrain and obstacles, both natural and man-made, his troops would have to face; details of any roads capable of supporting heavy, wheeled fuel-tankers and the locations of alternative sources of fuel; the predicted weather conditions; the times of sunrise and sunset; and the likely extent of any civilian resistance.

Once the ground war began, information would have started coming into the divisional int. cell from a variety of tactical intelligence assets. At the forward edge of the battle area, army advanced posts (APs) and observation posts (OPs) typically scan the skyline for enemy activity, reporting back to their units. Infantry and armoured reconnaissance patrols probe the enemy defences to obtain information about the numbers of troops and the types of equipment. Sound-ranging and mortar-locating units act as self-contained intelligence for the artillery, bringing down fire on any enemy guns or mortars they detect, but also constantly feeding information back to the divisional headquarters.

Forward interrogation teams question PoWs, deserters and refugees to determine enemy dispositions, the state of morale, and how supply lines have been affected by the air war. Mobile signals intelligence units locate and identify enemy positions ahead of the advance, gathering a wealth of information from low-level encoded traffic. Communications security would have been an early casualty as enemy units came under pressure from the advancing allies, providing easy pickings from 'clear' radio messages that ought to have been encyphered.

Tactical imagery intelligence (Imint) is provided by 'drones' – remote-controlled aircraft – or unmanned aerial vehicles (UAVs), the most modern of which are equipped with electro-optical sensors and fly over enemy positions providing the analyst with 'real-time' imagery via a video terminal.[18]

The remarkable combination of strategic and tactical intelligence assets available to the Gulf War allies should have produced a comprehensive picture of the battlefield. Yet so much information was being collected that dissemination became a major problem. General Norman Schwarz-kopf, the allied commander, later complained of receiving inadequate intelligence. Satellite intelligence in particular rarely reached the war zone in anything like 'real time'. The Pentagon's official history pointed a finger at the CIA and NSA, who were simply unable to cope with the speed of the allied advance. 'National intelligence co-ordinated by the CIA proved to be of limited value to the military. Most military com-manders wanted up-to-date imagery from reconnaissance satellites, over-the-horizon radars and infra-red sensors, but they often could not get it.'[19]

Clearly, a satisfactory method of co-ordinating strategic and tactical intelligence was one of the main challenges facing the Defence Intelli-gence Staff in the wake of the Gulf War. 'Probably more effort has gone into the study of how the intelligence world supports operations over the past two or three years than into any other area,' one senior DIS official said:

> But I think we genuinely have learned the lessons of the Falklands and the Gulf War on the need to ensure that we have the 'architecture' which makes sure that whoever he is, wherever he is on the battlefield, there are mechanisms whereby he can ask for information and a national system which can either say we've got the information or we need to get the information and, whatever the case may be, will then get it to him.

Military intelligence units have been used in a variety of situations since the Gulf War, including Kuwait and Jordan, Angola, Rwanda and Bosnia.

The four-man Intelligence Corps detachment sent to Rwanda was tasked with gathering information on anything that might affect the UN relief operation, including movement of refugees, the orders of battle of the warring factions, details of any atrocities, and assessments of the political or military intentions and capabilities of the new and previous governments.[20]

There were a number of initial difficulties in the former Yugoslavia, with one intelligence officer claiming that the UN Protection Force, UNPROFOR, 'lost ownership of the picture of the battlefield to the point where it was irrecoverable'. The UN has traditionally had a poor reputation in the intelligence field, preferring to use the term 'military information', which is seen as avoiding the subterfuge and secrecy inherent in intelligence-gathering operations.[21]

Intelligence Corps personnel working with the UN in Bosnia were initially attached informally to various units and to the multinational military information staff in Zagreb. But in April 1995 they were grouped together in a single Force Military Information Unit which not only monitors the military situation but also collects intelligence on political, economic and humanitarian issues. Aerial reconnaissance is provided by RAF Nimrod, Jaguar and Sentry AWACs aircraft, and signals intelligence by a small tactical unit set up in late 1992. There is also a small Joint Services Interrogation Organization which doubles as the Defence Debriefing Team.[22]

It is a standing joke among members of the Force Military Information Unit that 'if you understand the situation in the former Yugoslavia, you must have been poorly briefed'. Yet, despite the early problems, the recent British intelligence record is said to be excellent. 'I think history will actually show that we have a good story to tell about Yugoslavia,' the senior defence official said:

> I don't think we're going to have anything to be embarrassed about. We have a very high degree of confidence that, if it is available, our forces can get the intelligence they need in a timely fashion.
>
> But ultimately while the Chief of Defence Intelligence has a role in determining co-ordination of defence intelligence, he is not in command of the intelligence assets on the battlefield. There is no way that a man commanding forces in Bosnia is going to delegate command of his intelligence assets to a man sitting in London.[23]

# CHAPTER 15

# *Talking to Terrorists*

A line of contact has existed between Sinn Fein and London
for over twenty years.
Gerry Adams, *Free Ireland: Towards a Lasting Peace*, 1995

One of the least discussed uses of the intelligence services is in 'parallel diplomacy' – establishing channels of communication with the enemy that would be too dangerous, both physically and politically, for ministers or ordinary civil servants to contemplate. Such links have the political advantage of being totally deniable, and in the early 1990s they were used to bring a number of long-running conflicts to an end.[1]

Despite their public refusal to talk to the IRA, British governments have made use of parallel diplomacy to do just that from the time of Lloyd George right up to the present day.

During the early part of the twentieth century, intelligence operations in Ireland were dominated by the assumption that first the French and then the Germans would seek to foment rebellion there as a means of attacking Britain. There were a number of organizations collecting intelligence on the militant advocates of independence, though none of these organizations was particularly efficient and all of them were caught off guard by the growth in support for the republican movement that followed the First World War. 'Our Secret Service is simply non-existent,' complained Field Marshal Sir John French, the Lord Lieutenant of Ireland, in 1920. 'What masquerades for such a service is nothing but delusion and a snare.'[2]

Police intelligence was split between the Dublin Metropolitan Police Detective Department's G Division and the Royal Irish Constabulary Special Branch, most information being collected by sending officers to public meetings, reading the newspapers or by 'discreet inquiry'. It suffered badly from lack of funds, and what intelligence it did produce was 'meagre and patchy'.[3]

A 1916 report on intelligence operations in Ireland, compiled by Basil Thomson, the head of Scotland Yard's Special Branch, noted that the budget for paying informers was so small that 'it cannot be said that any system of secret information has been developed'.

The British Army had an Intelligence Branch with an intelligence officer in each of the military districts to supply reports of what was going on. This and the 'meagre' intelligence gleaned from the police was passed on to MI5, which in turn provided information derived from the interception of mail and communications, and reports from mainland police and the Naval Intelligence Division.

In Thomson's view there was 'much overlapping' and not enough liaison. 'Although all the material reports may reach the Irish executive,' he noted, 'there is certainly a danger that from lack of co-ordination, the Irish Government may be the last Department to receive information of grave moment to the peace of Ireland.'

The lack of funds left police intelligence overstretched and its officers underpaid. Both the civil administration and the police were riddled with republican sympathizers. A rare British informant code-named Chalk estimated that 'the Sinn Feiners obtain a considerable amount of official information and that as far as can be ascertained it comes from the Chief Secretary's Office'. A number of the British secret agents, fearing that they might be betrayed at any minute to the IRA, 'refused to work under the police' and offered their services to the Army.[4] An urgent inquiry into the state of police intelligence operations remained written in hand because the committee could not be sure that whoever was tasked to type it was not an IRA informer.

To add to the low morale, Sinn Fein swiftly realized that it could seriously disrupt the British intelligence system by assassinating the more efficient officers. 'The compilation of complete and up-to-date records was very difficult owing to the inadequate staffs available and as time went on and the Sinn Fein movement spread, it became impossible,' an internal Army history of the conflict noted:

> Each crimes special sergeant or man was compelled to rely more and more on his memory and less and less on records. Sinn Fein were not long in recognizing that these men and the best and most energetic of the RIC who had accurate local knowledge were the most dangerous of their opponents.
>
> From 1919 they carried out a systematic murder campaign, with the result that many of the best of the RIC were killed. Consequently the police source of information, at the time the only one on which the authorities could rely, was dried up and the intelligence service paralysed.[5]

The IRA, which had previously been easy for British intelligence to infiltrate, developed a very effective method of deterring informants. 'Contacts with my so-called agents had to be personal and this could be an extremely dangerous undertaking for the informant,' one intelligence officer recalled. 'A few shots in the night and next morning a corpse and pinned to it a label "Traitor. Shot by orders of the IRA."' The army history noted that 'Secret Service was on the whole a failure in Ireland. For many reasons it was practically impossible to place a man in any inner circle. Consistent, regular and unsuspected informers, such as had been employed on other occasions were almost unobtainable at any price.'

The inquiry into police intelligence concurred with that view. 'Owing to the terrorism of Sinn Fein and kindred organizations, even respectable and loyal people are afraid of speaking to a policeman.' It was scathing about the ineffectiveness of the RIC Special Branch, and its view was shared by the Army. When the authorities decided to deport several hundred leading Sinn Feiners in the hope that this would break the back of the movement, the Army was dismayed to discover that 'the local RIC could give little reliable information about such persons beyond a statement that so and so was "a bad boy" or "a bad article"'.[6]

The inability of the Dublin administration to deal effectively with 'the Troubles' and the recommendations of a highly critical report by Sir Warren Fisher, the head of the Civil Service, led in May 1920 to a drastic reorganization. Within weeks, a new administration was in place headed by Sir Hamar Greenwood as Chief Secretary and Sir John Anderson as Under-Secretary.

From the start, the new government's public brief was to instigate a tough crackdown on Sinn Fein. This was epitomized by the activities of police reinforcements and auxiliaries – the so-called Black and Tans – who committed a series of outrages that served only to increase support for the republican cause.[7] But its secret brief – a result of Fisher's call for 'an exploration or settlement of problems' that acknowledged the fact that the majority of Irishmen now supported Sinn Fein – was completely different.

Alfred 'Andy' Cope, a member of Fisher's inquiry team, was given a key role within the new regime 'ostensibly as assistant under-secretary but actually as the Prime Minister's personal and secret envoy for the purpose of establishing contact with the Sinn Fein leaders with a view to negotiating peace'.

Cope, a 43-year-old former customs officer, had spent ten years investigating the smugglers and illicit distillers of London's Dockland – 'a calling which taught him the intricacies of undercover work and the technique of dealing on terms of intimacy with gunmen and lawbreakers'. He was sent 'on Special Service in Northern Ireland' and was told by Lloyd George to find someone in Sinn Fein who could 'deliver the goods'.[8]

One of the most vital prerequisites for both the public and secret

Sir Alfred 'Andy' Cope (seated, second from left), the British official
who initiated the 1920 talks between the British Government and the IRA,
pictured with other members of the British administration in front of
Dublin Castle. Seated on his left are John Anderson and Mark Sturgis

briefs was to improve intelligence. 'The police forces were in a critical
condition,' Anderson wrote later. 'The all important matter of intelligence and secret service had been entirely neglected.'

A short-lived attempt to take civilian intelligence out of the hands of
the DMP and the RIC, placing it under Thomson's control, had enjoyed
little success, and a decision was taken to appoint an intelligence co-

ordinator based in Dublin Castle, the headquarters of the British administration, 'to collate information and form by degrees a secret service or
detective branch for the police force in Ireland, which is non-existent'.[9]
The man chosen, the bemonocled Brigadier-General Ormonde de l'Epée
Winter, or 'O', was described by one member of the administration as
'a most amazing individual. He looks like a wicked little white snake, is
clever as paint, probably entirely non-moral, a first-class horseman, a
card genius, knows several languages.'[10]

Distrustful of the police, the Army formed its own Special Branch in
Dublin and, with the assistance of MI5, set up a 'spy school' in the relative
safety of London. One of those recruited into the so-called Cairo Gang,
was Captain R. D. Jeune. 'After a short course of instruction at Hounslow,
we were sent over to Dublin in the early summer of 1920,' he recalled.
'The first batch were instructed to pose, initially, as Royal Engineer
officers, but this rather futile procedure was soon dropped and the work
consisted of getting to know the town thoroughly, tailing "Shinners" and
carrying out small raids.'[11]

Much of the Cairo Gang's material came from informers, the interrogation of suspects, and captured documents. Women made the best informants, 'but their employment sometimes involved relations that were more
than friendly. This was occasionally inconvenient.'

Then on Sunday 21 November 1920 – the original 'Bloody Sunday' –
the IRA shot dead thirteen men and wounded a number of others. 'The
object of this exercise on the part of the IRA was to eliminate Intelligence
and Courts Martial officers because the gunmen felt that the net was
closing round them,' Jeune wrote. 'Men were brought up to Dublin from
other parts of the country, particularly Tipperary, in order to catch as
many as possible of us unawares.' The cream of the Army's Special Branch
died in the attacks, leaving it 'temporarily paralysed'. Shortly afterwards
its work was handed over to the police.[12]

If the authorities hoped that Winter's appointment would improve the
flow of intelligence, they were to be disappointed. 'The double system
of police and military intelligence continued to involve loss of efficiency,
duplication of work and complications in almost every way,' the Army
history concluded. If all the intelligence had been controlled from one
office, 'better results might have been achieved and a great deal of friction
and irritation would certainly have been avoided'.[13]

When Sir John Anderson complained about the poor supply of intelligence, General Nevil Macready, the Army commander, testily blamed
Winter. 'Everything seems to point to the view that he has not got the
right method, and we here very much doubt whether he will ever get
it,' Macready wrote. 'He is, I fancy, a "born sleuth", but I doubt his

organizing power, and that, so far as I can see, is what is holding up the machine.'[14]

But the military's opinion of the police was as nothing to its view of those within the administration who appeared to be willing to 'conspire' with the enemy. Cope made contact with Eamonn Duggan, a Dublin solicitor who was the IRA's Director of Intelligence, and 'at considerable danger to himself' began a series of exploratory talks including visits to Dublin's Mountjoy Prison to see Arthur Griffith, the Sinn Fein founder and a key Republican leader who had been interned after the Bloody Sunday killings.

'Taking his career in his hands, he abandoned the traditional methods of the Castle peace parleyings and got into direct and personal contact with the leaders of the Irish people,' one contemporary recorded. 'He had first to convince the powers of Sinn Fein that he meant to play straight with them, and then to persuade the powers residing in Dublin Castle and elsewhere that the leaders of "the murder gang" desired an honourable settlement.'[15]

Cope's activities were so secret that very few people knew about them, and he soon came under suspicion of being an IRA informer. 'In September 1920, it was decided to raid several houses in Drumcondra,' Jeune wrote. 'Particular attention was attached to the house of a man called O'Connor, known to us as an active Sinn Feiner.'

During the search, the soldiers found a letter from Cope, Jeune said:

> It was on official Dublin Castle paper and was in these words:
> Dear Mr O'Connor,
>     I am having the papers you require
> sent up to you.
>                 Yours sincerely
>                 A. W. Cope

This was distinctly interesting. Here was the Assistant Under-Secretary writing to a notorious Sinn Feiner with whom he had obviously already been in contact.

After this, I made a point of trying to find out more about this individual's doings and found that he had done some rather strange things, such as arranging for some electricians of known Sinn Fein views to come into the Castle at unusual times. Also he was one of the very few Castle officials who could safely walk about the streets of Dublin. But it was decided that no drastic action could be taken against him, as it turned out that he was a protégé of Lloyd George who had picked him out . . . and sent him over to Ireland in order to get a foot in the Sinn Fein camp.[16]

Cope's years in the East End of London meant that he was used to 'irregular negotiations, unavowable activities and unconventional approaches'. He was also a very unorthodox character, extremely persistent, 'as brave as he was quick witted', and willing to try anything to secure peace.

There were several false starts, but eventually Cope managed to build up a relationship of trust with the rebels. The military clampdown was having its effect on them, creating 'divided counsels' among the republican leadership. Although many were quite prepared to fight the British to a standstill to create a united, independent Ireland, a growing minority was willing to contemplate negotiations.[17]

On 26 September 1920, Arthur Griffith and Sir John Anderson met in a solicitor's offices in St Andrew's Street, Dublin, for preliminary talks. It is not clear how far these went, and leading members of Anderson's administration were later divided over whether the two men even sat down in the same room. But by early November optimism in Dublin and London over the potential of the peace feelers was such that Lloyd George declared, 'We have murder by the throat.' Less than two weeks later came Bloody Sunday. 'It has been a day of black murder,' Mark Sturgis, Cope's fellow under-secretary, wrote in his diary that night. 'What they hope to gain by it, God alone knows.'[18]

But Cope kept his lines of communication to the IRA leadership open, constantly probing for a possibility of peace. 'Again and again all Mr Cope's laboriously worked-out schemes must have seemed to everybody but himself completely wrecked,' a contemporary wrote. 'But besides inexhaustible optimism and belief in himself, he had extraordinary powers of work and during the Terror would frequently sandwich an all-night excursion into the country between two long days at his desk.'[19]

A few weeks after Bloody Sunday, the Most Revd Dr Patrick Joseph Clune, Roman Catholic Archbishop of Perth in Australia, stepped in as a mediator, arriving in Dublin in early December with proposals from Lloyd George for an armistice and a peace conference. At the same time the British Prime Minister increased the military pressure, imposing martial law on Cork, Kerry, Tipperary and Limerick and hinting that it could be extended to the whole of Ireland.

With Cope's assistance, Clune saw Griffith and Michael Collins, the IRA leader, who was still on the run. They agreed a cease-fire, but it was vetoed by the military. 'They have convinced themselves that they have the boys in the hills beaten and they want no talk of truce to interfere with them now,' Cope said. The Cabinet, a coalition of the Liberals and the staunchly unionist Conservative Party, insisted that the IRA must surrender its arms as a precondition of any truce. Anderson, Cope and Sturgis all warned that this would wreck the talks, but to no avail.[20]

'There is no evidence of sincerity on the other side,' Eamon de Valera, the Sinn Fein president, told the volunteers. 'The British Premier was but manœuvring for an opportunity to put the attitude of the representatives of this nation in a false light.'[21]

Cope was living on his nerves by now – 'a victim alike to ebullient optimism and devastating despair' – and the failure of the Clune talks left him despondent. But by the spring of 1921 pressure on both sides for some form of agreement was intense.[22] Lloyd George's coalition government had lost public confidence, with the failure to resolve the Irish situation one of the most frequent criticisms, while the military campaign had brought the IRA close to defeat.

Slowly, Cope's efforts began to bear fruit. Lord Derby, a former ambassador to France, went to Ireland in April for secret talks with the IRA, wearing horn-rimmed glasses in an attempt at disguise and booking into a Dublin hotel under an assumed name.[23]

On 21 April 1921 Lloyd George went public with an offer of peace talks, telling the House of Commons that he was ready to meet representatives of the Irish people 'for the purpose of discussing any proposals which offer the prospect of reconciliation and settlement'.

Cope persuaded Sir James Craig, the leader of the Ulster Unionists, to meet de Valera at a secret location just outside Dublin. Since Cope had brought the two together by telling each of them that it was the other who wanted the meeting, it broke up without any tangible results, but the mere fact that they had met was enough to give the peace process fresh impetus in London.[24]

One of Cope's colleagues said, 'He had the power of bending people to his will. He cared not how or where he had to seek his information provided that it led him a step nearer to his goal.' He had contacts at the highest levels within the IRA, with volunteers swapping stories of how after one boozy night Collins had 'carried him to bed'.[25]

The military, having got the IRA on the run, saw little need for peace talks and regarded Cope as very close to a traitor. 'By the early summer, the IRA were driven into the south-west corner of Ireland and would have been quickly finished,' wrote Captain Jeune. 'But certain influences were to save them as I learned in London later from Jeffries, who had been in our show in Dublin and had set up, from London, a proper secret service in Ireland.'

On 22 June an Army search party arrested a suspected member of Sinn Fein at a house in Mount Merrion, just outside Dublin. A few days earlier one of their officers had been ambushed by the IRA, taken from his car, and shot dead in front of his three female companions. The soldiers were therefore understandably cock-a-hoop when they realized that the 'Shinner' they had arrested was de Valera. Their elation turned to bewilderment when Cope ordered his release.

'Army GHQ at Kilmainham wired to his London Office: "De Valera captured. Cope suggests release,"' Jeune wrote. 'Jeffries took it to Lloyd George who rubbed his hands together and said: "Well done the military. He must on no account be released." But as soon as he had gone Lloyd George sent orders for de Valera to be released, which was done.'

The incident has been portrayed as a simple case of lack of communication between the Army and the civilian authorities. But the raid produced invaluable intelligence on the rebels' negotiating stance and may well have been deliberately engineered for that purpose. Two days after the raid the British made a formal offer of a truce. The Troubles were effectively over.[26]

The bitterness of many in the military and the Conservative Party over what was seen as a betrayal orchestrated by Cope continued well after the creation of the Irish Free State. 'Negotiations with the murder organization began long before the Army or the Police knew that a truce was being arranged,' the *Morning Post* complained. 'While they were still fighting in the illusion that the Government was behind them, Mr Cope was establishing friendly relations with their would-be murderers.'[27]

When the conflict resurfaced in Northern Ireland in the late 1960s, the Army was again horrified at the dearth of police intelligence. 'Financial constraints and lack of foresight led, in Ulster, to insufficient attention being paid to the activities of the Special Branch and other intelligence-gathering agencies,' one senior Army officer recalled.[28]

The Royal Ulster Constabulary was totally dominated by Protestants, and the Special Branch suspect files included no one but Catholics. With the help of Metropolitan Police Special Branch officers and a small team of MI5 officers, the Army and the RUC began to build up the intelligence picture. Local censuses were carried out to create a street-by-street record of the local population, Army patrols reported whatever information they could, and details of suspected terrorists were placed in a card index which recorded their families, friends, known contacts and lifestyles.[29]

Although the principle of police primacy remained paramount, the paucity of RUC intelligence led to pressure from above to obtain information through other means, and Brigadier Frank Kitson, the Army's counter-insurgency expert, set up a covert intelligence operation based on his Kenyan 'counter-gangs', groups of Mau Mau terrorists who were turned and used against their former colleagues.

A small group of IRA terrorists were rounded up and told they had two options: either face the prospect of very long terms of imprisonment or work under cover for the Army. They all opted for the latter, and under the command of a British Army officer became known unofficially as 'the Freds', or more formally as the Special Detachment of the Mobile Reconnaissance Force.[30]

The military sought to obtain covert information by virtually any means it could, but it remained distrustful of the RUC and there was little intelligence co-ordination. The politicians talked tough, backing the role of the Army in public, but behind the scenes looking for a political solution.

The post of UK Representative in Northern Ireland was created in August 1969 with a brief to build up contacts with all sections of the community and to encourage moderate Catholic political activity. The formation, a year later, of the Social Democratic and Labour Party (SDLP) provided representatives of nationalist opinion with whom the government could talk without giving the impression of bowing to terrorist pressure.[31]

The problems with intelligence in the province were demonstrated most vividly by the government's decision – against the advice of some, although not all, of the experts – that internment of all known IRA suspects would end the violence. The only intelligence on which a round-up could be based was that of the RUC, which varied across the province from weak to practically non-existent and still did not include details of Protestant extremists. The Army set up a joint internment working-party with the RUC and MI5 in an attempt to improve the picture, but to no avail.

Operation Demetrius, implemented in the early hours of 10 August 1971, was a shambles. On the basis of the largely inadequate RUC list (some of those apparently seen as a threat to law and order were already long dead), the Army picked up 342 men across the province. As interrogations got under way, it became clear that the numbers of active terrorists did not reach beyond double figures. Within forty-eight hours the security forces had been forced to release 115 of the detainees. They included middle-class civil-rights activists, trade unionists and a drunk arrested as he waited for a bus.[32]

The débâcle of internment forced the generals and the politicians to realize that things had to change. 'The Army's frustration led to gradual and increasing pressure that it should rely less on Special Branch and do more to obtain its own intelligence,' wrote Michael Carver, Chief of the General Staff at the time:

> It was a tendency which I was initially reluctant to accept, all experience in colonial fields having been against this and in favour of the total integration of police and military intelligence. However, the inefficiency of the RUC Special Branch, its reluctance to burn its fingers again, and the suspicion, more than once proved, that some of its members had close links with Protestant extremists, led me finally to the conclusion that there was no alternative.[33]

The intelligence picture had to be improved. In early 1971 Edward Heath, the British Prime Minister, decided to send in the Secret Intelligence Service. Within weeks, the UK Representative had a new deputy. Frank Steele was a large man, rarely seen without his pipe, who, according to his entry in *Who's Who*, had held a number of diplomatic posts, mainly in the Middle East. He was also a senior MI6 officer.

Frank Steele, the MI6 officer who set up the 1974 talks between the British Government and the IRA

SIS began its own covert operations in the province while Steele used the UK Representative's office at Laneside, a large surburban house on the shores of Belfast Lough, as a base for contact with the 'street communities' – a euphemism that allowed contact between a senior government official and extremists on both sides of the political divide. The dangers involved in operating in the no-go areas of Belfast and Londonderry were obvious. At one point Steele had to warn his contacts, 'If the IRA were to shoot me now there would be rather a row.'[34]

The Army was opposed to MI6 involvement. It saw Northern Ireland as a classic counter-insurgency situation. Collecting intelligence was its role and, in Kitson's words, 'We beat the terrorists before we negotiate with them.' But William Whitelaw, Secretary of State for Northern Ireland, overruled the objections.

At the same time, the SDLP was making its own contacts with PIRA/ Sinn Fein, through Austin Currie, Paddy Devlin and John Hume, who had links with David O'Connell, one of the IRA's most senior leaders, that dated back to his involvement in the Irish Credit Union movement.[35]

The extent of the difficulties were explained by Merlyn Rees, the Opposition spokesman on Northern Ireland, following a meeting with leading republicans, including O'Connell, in Dublin in March 1972. 'O'Connell was reputed to have acute political judgement,' Rees wrote. 'But at this meeting none of the three men seemed to me to show much sign of it. These were hard men who talked and looked like soldiers. They thought solely in terms of military victory; there was no sign of compromise.'[36]

But the imperative for talking peace was strong. Northern Ireland appeared to be on the verge of civil war. With the death toll mounting rapidly and the eyes of the world focused on the province, the government was anxious to find some way of defusing the situation. SIS covert intelligence indicated that there was potential for splits within the IRA, with some volunteers becoming disillusioned with its lack of success.

In June 1972 Martin McGuinness, commander of the Derry Brigade, suggested to Sean MacStiofain, the IRA Chief of Staff, that they offer Whitelaw a seven-day truce if he agreed to meet them. MacStiofain saw it as a clever idea that would ease the pressure on the IRA to respond to the imposition of direct rule and would put the British on the defensive. 'If Whitelaw made a public refusal, Britain's stock would go down,' he said. 'The onus of rejecting a reasonable offer would be on London and we would be none the worse off.'

The offer was publicly rejected by Whitelaw. But behind the scenes his advisers persuaded him that the time was right for secret talks with the IRA. 'Within hours of publicly refusing to treat with terrorists, the British were secretly agreeing to discuss a truce with us,' MacStiofain said.[37]

Working through Hume and Devlin, the two sides agreed to talks, with the IRA laying down two preconditions: that the prisoners be granted political status and that Gerry Adams, a leading member of the IRA's Belfast Brigade, should be released from internment in Long Kesh prison to take part in the talks.[38]

The first preliminary meeting – between Steele and Phillip Woodfield, a deputy secretary in the Northern Ireland Office, and O'Connell and Adams – took place in a pub across the border from Derry in County

Donegal. A series of meetings followed, mainly held in IRA safe houses in Derry. Despite the enmity of their two sides, a cautious relationship grew up between them. Steele was pleasantly surprised to find that, instead of the aggressive young tough the briefings had led him to expect, Adams was 'a very personable, likeable, intelligent, articulate and persuasive young man'.[39]

The talks were fixed for London on 7 July. The IRA representatives met up with Steele at a prearranged location in the Derry countryside and were taken by helicopter to Belfast's Aldergrove airport, a nervous flight in which McGuinness was somewhat concerned that they might prove to be too tempting a target for some of his unsuspecting colleagues on the ground. From there they were flown by RAF Andover to RAF Benson in Oxfordshire, and two cars driven by Special Branch officers then took them to London, to the Chelsea home of Whitelaw's junior minister Paul Channon.[40]

The IRA delegation comprised O'Connell; MacStiofain; McGuinness; Adams; Ivor Bell, the commander of the Belfast Brigade; and Seamus Twomey, the hard man and firmest opponent of any deal with the British. He was there to keep an eye on O'Connell, a realist who was the most committed to the talks. On the British side were Whitelaw; Channon; Woodfield; and Steele. The meeting was, in Whitelaw's words, 'a non-event'. He attempted to dispense bonhomie. They were distrustful – anxious to ensure that the British were treating them seriously.

MacStiofain demanded the British withdrawal from Northern Ireland by 1 January 1975, a general amnesty for political prisoners, and an end to internment. London's interest in talks appears to have misled the IRA into believing that it was close to achieving its objectives. Why else would the British want to negotiate unless they were defeated? But it had badly misjudged the situation. Whitelaw's view of the talks shows how far apart the two sides remained. 'The IRA's leaders simply made impossible demands which I told them the British Government would never concede,' he said. 'They were in fact still in a mood of defiance and determination to carry on until their absurd ultimatums were met.'[41]

Despite the failure of the talks, the two sides agreed to keep up the unofficial channel of communication via Steele. On the flight back to Belfast, the MI6 man tried to impress the realities of the political situation on the Provisional leaders. As he began to talk, MacStiofain whispered to Twomey, 'Listen very carefully to this guy. What we are getting off the cuff is as valuable as anything at the meeting.'

They were listening but they did not hear. 'I hope you're not going to start your bloody stupid campaign of violence again,' Steele said. If the IRA really wanted a united Ireland, it was wasting its time shooting

British soldiers and bombing Northern Ireland into an industrial and social slum, he said. It would be better employed persuading the Protestants that they could have a good life in some sort of union with the South. They dismissed his arguments. There was only one way to get a united Ireland – by forcing the Brits out – and the only way to do that was through 'physical force' which included 'economic warfare'.[42]

To the IRA, the British appeared to be engaging in 'doublespeak and jargon'. The hard men took control. Two weeks later, on Friday 21 July, the campaign resumed. More than twenty bombs exploded across Belfast in the worst violence the city had seen. Nine civilians died. More than 100 were injured.

Designed to teach the British a lesson, Bloody Friday backfired badly. Whitelaw's political initiatives had caused problems for the Army's intelligence effort, by cutting back on patrols and interrogations. Now the Army was given the go-ahead to move into the 'no-go areas' of Free Derry. Ten days after Bloody Friday, armoured cars and bulldozers moved into the Creggan and the Bogside. Operation Motorman brought a wealth of intelligence from ordinary Catholics disgusted by the resumption of the killings.[43]

The failure of the old leadership's tactics, both during the talks and in the bloody response, led to the establishment of a younger, more political, leadership able to develop the policy of 'the Armalite and the ballot box', boosting the role of Sinn Fein and ensuring a more sophisticated approach to any future dealings with the British.[44]

The inability of the various agencies to get on with each other, the Littlejohn fiasco (in which a Dublin bank was allegedly robbed on behalf of MI6) and the spread of IRA violence to the mainland led in 1973 to an increase in MI5 activities at the expense of SIS. The Security Service was seen as being better able to liaise with both the Army and the RUC than MI6. The senior MI5 officer was given the title of Director and Co-ordinator of Intelligence.[45]

But the SIS political role continued. The Whitelaw talks had established the principle of a secret channel of communication to the IRA. When Rees became Northern Ireland Secretary in March 1974, he authorized Woodfield's and Steele's successors, James Allan and Michael Oatley, to continue with what he described as 'explanatory talks'.

While refusing to speak specifically about the Northern Ireland situation, one senior intelligence officer said such contacts serve a dual purpose:

> Firstly, if you have an undeclared back channel, which carries with it the kind of trust which a front channel of politicians meeting openly

in order to move one step forward in negotiations can't possibly carry – because each knows the other has his own agenda – it is easy to develop that to the point where you can have some basis for trusting what the other person's telling you. Because they're not completely committed to it. If they say, 'Look, this is the way it's going to be as far as our party's concerned. I'm telling you this off the record. There is no comeback on me if it doesn't turn out as well,' then it's much easier to develop a concept of both sides going a little further than it is possible to go in an open negotiation.

Secondly, you can verify what is being said because you have got the intelligence. So when you are in quasi-negotiation with the other side in fact you are also running intelligence sources into them and penetrating them, and when they say, 'This is the situation,' you also have some means of judging whether or not they're telling you something that isn't a lie. It makes it a little more solid foundation to help to resolve conflicts.

Following the Birmingham pub bombings which killed nineteen people in November 1974, concerted attempts were made to bring an end to the violence. Within weeks, a group of Protestant clergy met O'Connell and Twomey in the Republic with the full backing of the British government. The IRA declared a temporary cease-fire and asked for 'an indication of the British government's attitude' towards their calls for withdrawal and an amnesty for all political prisoners.

Encouraged by a clear sign that the IRA leadership wanted to talk, attempts were again made to raise the status of the behind-the-scenes talks, Rees said. 'I laid down the basis for meetings between staff and Provisional Sinn Fein which I now decided to put on a more formal basis than the sort of explanatory meeting I had already sanctioned.'[46]

A series of low-level talks followed. But in mid-January 1975 they broke down and the cease-fire came to an end. 'It was evident that despite all our efforts the Provisional IRA had not understood what we were saying,' Rees commented. 'We were convinced that our basic problem lay with the Provisional Sinn Fein representatives in Belfast, who were inexperienced and not up to their task. I authorized that in future contact with the Provisional Sinn Fein should be at a higher level and away from Belfast and its incestuous gossip.'

Allan and Oatley met two senior PIRA/Sinn Fein officials, Proinsias MacAirt and Jimmy Drumm. The first meeting was difficult but led to further talks and eventually to a new cease-fire in return for the phasing out of detention without trial. Numerous meetings with the IRA took place at 'incident centres' set up across the province, at Laneside, and through the 'back channel' run by Allan and Oatley to the Provisionals' leadership in Dublin.[47]

The political moves caused widespread disquiet within military intelligence and MI5. General Sir Frank King, the Army commander in Northern Ireland, openly attacked the Northern Ireland Office 'interference', claiming it was merely giving the IRA time to regroup. 'The Army was making such good progress that in another two or three months we would have brought the IRA to the point where they would have had enough,' he said. The phasing out of detention without trial was giving the IRA back its best men. 'About 200 have been freed from detention and nearly all the remainder – perhaps another 300 or 400 – will probably be out by October. Then they will be in a position to start all over again.'[48]

The Army began to engage in 'dirty tricks' in an attempt to discredit Rees. 'On one occasion, I spent three weeks discussing with senior soldiers how we could carry out an operation that would put no one's life at risk,' Rees said. 'The following day in the newspapers, briefed by the Army Department, was a report that I had put the lives of soldiers at risk – a deliberate policy of double briefing.'[49]

The IRA also felt it gained nothing from the cease-fire, and by the end of 1975 this had petered out amid widespread internal feuding. Meaningful discussions on the 'back channel' to the Dublin leadership ended around the same time, after Oatley was posted to MI6's Hong Kong station. But he remained the British government's most trusted contact with the IRA.[50]

The turf battles between the various agencies continued, and the decision, in January 1977, to put the RUC in charge of intelligence collection did nothing to help. The Army still marked many of its documents, 'UK Eyes Only: Not for RUC' – particularly when they referred to future operations. In October 1979, following the murder of Lord Mountbatten and the Warrenpoint massacre of eighteen members of the Parachute Regiment, Sir Maurice Oldfield, the former chief of SIS, was sent to Belfast as Security Co-ordinator with a brief to end the rivalries.[51]

The Army's early covert intelligence activites had been regarded as amateurish by MI5 and MI6. The operations run by the Mobile Reconnaissance Force included the Four Square Laundry, which collected dirty clothes and tested them for traces of explosives or blood before washing; a massage parlour which provided ample opportunity for blackmail; and door-to-door cosmetics sales run by female soldiers. But in October 1972 they were blown when the IRA succeeded in turning one of the Freds. The IRA ambushed a Four Square van in West Belfast, killing the driver. A few months later the MRF was disbanded.[52]

Within a year the Army was mounting new covert operations. This time they were developed with the aid of the SAS and were a great deal more professional. Like the Cairo Gang before them, the soldiers involved were recruited from a variety of units and originally operated under cover as Royal Engineers. A variety of cover-names followed – most famously 14 Int. – but within the limited circle of soldiers familiar with the unit's activities it became known as 'the Det'.

The Det's role was Close Target Reconnaissance (CTR): undercover work in among the civilians, observing the terrorist at close quarters, carrying out covert searches of offices and houses for information and weapons. These were left where they were found but were 'jarked' with tiny transmitters placed inside them that would provide warning should they be moved. The unit had three sub-units in Northern Ireland – one in Derry, one in Belfast and one in Newry – and, in the words of one former member, its operations were 'invariably hairy'.[53]

On 28 May 1981 the officer commanding the Derry 'North Det', having completed a job earlier than expected, decided to carry out a recce for the next. It was a stupid thing to do without backup, and a clear breach of standing operating procedures. He was driving an unmarked Opel Ascona car but was 'tagged' by four members of an IRA active service unit who followed him and then drove their car in front of him, blocking his path. Two of the terrorists, each carrying an Armalite rifle, approached the Opel – one of them standing at the front, one at the rear.

This was not an easy situation. But the man at the front made the mistake of turning to signal to the two men left in the car. The British officer took his chance, firing a series of pistol shots into the IRA man's back, followed by an over-the-shoulder shot at the man at the rear. The two other terrorists fled, firing at the Opel but missing the British officer, who returned to the North Det HQ to be given a thorough dressing-down by the duty ops officer – a lowly corporal – for venturing into a republican area without backup.[54]

The RUC Special Branch, which co-ordinates all intelligence and covert operations through the Tasking and Co-ordinating Groups, is split into a number of sections, of which the most important are E3, Intelligence, and E4, Operations. The latter has its own surveillance unit, similar to the Det, known as E4A. The RUC Special Support Unit and Headquarters Mobile Support Units have a backup role similar to that of the SAS. Members of these units were involved in the Lurgan hayshed killings that led to the Shoot-to-Kill inquiry.[55]

The SAS was deployed officially to Northern Ireland in 1976. Although it was heavily involved in the Det in the early stages and small teams had been sent to the Province for special jobs on a number of earlier occasions, it was not until 1976 that it could deploy there in strength. It has two main roles: covert reconnaissance, often spending weeks in hides dug into the ground in the South Armagh 'bandit country' to report on IRA activity, and ambushing terrorists. This latter role has caused controversy, with allegations that the SAS carries out 'assassinations'.

If an SAS team mounts a successful ambush, the terrorist is unlikely to come out of it alive. But, while many of the wilder claims about SAS assassinations can be discounted as IRA propaganda or conspiracy theory, there is no doubt that in the early days a number of killings did take place – at least one of them in the Irish Republic. In addition, a number of wanted IRA men were lifted from across the border and brought into Northern Ireland where they could be arrested by the security forces.[56]

Military intelligence comes under the control of the Force Intelligence Unit and includes the Special Military Intelligence Unit, which liaises with the RUC; the Intelligence Database Management Company, which operates the joint Army/RUC intelligence computer; the Reconnaissance Intelligence Centre, which interprets air imagery, looking for bombs, arms caches and evidence of IRA activity; and the Incident Investigation Company, which attends the scene of every bombing, shooting or weapons find, to help establish terrorist *modi operandi* and forensically to identify the weapons and try to pinpoint the terrorists involved.[57]

The Security Service has always had the lead role in countering Irish terrorist activities outside of Britain, primarily in preventing groups from both sides of the divide from acquiring weapons and supplies. It took over the lead role on the mainland from the Metropolitan Police Special Branch in October 1992. Within Northern Ireland itself, where the RUC has the lead role, MI5's operations are controlled by the Director and Co-ordinator of Intelligence. The section responsible for countering Irish terrorism on the mainland and in the rest of the world is now known as T Branch.[58]

The worst blow to the British intelligence organization in Northern Ireland came not from the IRA or the turf wars but with the June 1994 crash of a Chinook helicopter near the Mull of Kintyre, in Scotland. The twenty-five senior officials who died included John Deverell, MI5's Director and Co-ordinator of Intelligence Northern Ireland, and Assistant Chief Constable Brian Fitzsimmons, the head of RUC Special Branch. The Chinook passengers – senior RUC and Army officers and civil servants on 'special duties' with the Northern Ireland Office, including at least one GCHQ official – had been flying to a conference in Scotland to consider what action to take if the peace process broke down.[59]

Despite the initial problems, the odd fiasco and the turf wars, the record of British intelligence operations in Northern Ireland is good, said Assistant Chief Constable Ronnie Flanagan, head of RUC Special

Branch. 'Together my officers – with the help of other agencies and the public – have been responsible for saving countless lives, and for averting atrocity after atrocity. I know on the basis of firm intelligence that four out of every five planned terrorist attacks were thwarted.'[60]

The MI6 'back channel' to the IRA resurfaced during the 1980–81 hunger strikes, when Oatley, now back in London, negotiated directly with the IRA in an attempt to end the protests. Known to the IRA by the code-name Mountain Climber, he remained its main point of contact with the British government, sometimes passing messages through an intermediary – a Catholic businessman living in the North – sometimes meeting face to face. In October 1990, after a long period of silence, Oatley got in touch with Martin McGuinness to tell him that he was about to retire and would like to see him. Intelligence from inside the PIRA/Sinn Fein leadership indicated that some members were looking for ways to end the violence.

'The meeting was in a quiet residential area somewhere in the north of Ireland,' McGuinness said. 'I arrived by car; he arrived by car. There was absolutely no security whatsoever and everybody was at ease. He intimated to me that after his retirement a new British Government Representative would be appointed and there would be an effort to reactivate the line of communication.'[61]

There was then a break in communication until April 1991, when Mountain Climber again got in touch, to tell McGuinness that the loyalist paramilitaries were about to call a cease-fire. Two months later, the new British Government Representative, or BGR, introduced himself, with a letter of confirmation from Peter Brooke, the then Northern Ireland Secretary.

According to Gerry Adams, Mountain Climber's meeting with McGuinness and a subsequent statement a few weeks later by Brooke that the British government had 'no selfish strategic or economic interest in Northern Ireland' led to a period of 'protracted dialogue' between the two sides. 'Over three years, outlines of Sinn Fein and British Government policies were exchanged and discussed.'[62]

There are differences between the two sides over the precise chronology and extent of the talks, with the British government – anxious to keep the Unionists on board – denying that individual contacts occurred or describing them as 'unauthorized'. While not every meeting may have been authorized beforehand, the overall policy was, and it should be remembered that part of the value of parallel diplomacy is its deniability.

An indication of the true position was given to Parliament by Douglas Hurd, the former Foreign Secretary, when asked by David Trimble, the Ulster Unionist MP, about claims that the SIS talks were unauthorized.

'The SIS and GCHQ do not work to their own agenda, invent their own requirements for information or act independently without the prior knowledge and clearance of ministers,' he said. 'They do not invent adventures of their own; they carry out tasks in support of specific policies.'[63]

According to the British Government, the first official contacts followed an unsolicited oral message from the Provisionals in February 1993 which allegedly said, 'The conflict is over but we need your advice on how to bring it to a close. We wish to have an unannounced cease-fire in order to hold dialogue leading to peace.' The IRA denies that this message was ever sent. But, with their need to keep the hard-liners on board, those within the PIRA/Sinn Fein leadership who are looking for peace have as much reason to deny such conciliatory messages as does the British government in claiming that this was the first contact.

This does appear to have been an important point in the ongoing talks. The British government responded with a conciliatory position paper which indicated that, in exchange for a cease-fire, it was prepared to engage in 'dialogue', with nothing – neither a united Ireland nor a continuation of partition – ruled out. According to McGuinness, the BGR subsequently said, 'Eventually, the island of Ireland will be one. It is going to happen anyway. Unionists will have to change.'[64]

The talks continued throughout 1993, despite the IRA's Warrington, Bishopsgate and Shankhill bomb attacks and the Loyalist Greysteel massacre, and into 1994 as part of a twin-track process that was fronted by the Hume–Adams talks and the Anglo-Irish agreement. Sir Patrick Mayhew, Brooke's successor, emphasized the importance of this process when he finally conceded the existence of the secret back channel to the IRA.

'There has been a channel of communication open for something like twenty years – a secret channel by which messages have been able to be passed,' he said. 'I think that if you have an established channel of communication which has proved its value it is not only very sensible but it is your duty to maintain its secrecy. If that chain of communication had been destroyed, I think there would be a lot to be answered for.'[65]

# CHAPTER 16

# *A Very Dirty Game*

The Cold War is over: the most dangerous threat to a nation's security comes from organised crime. Europe is now one vast criminal space, from the Atlantic to the Urals. What matters is using intelligence to crack the criminal at source.
Raymond Kendall, British General-Secretary of Interpol, May 1996[1]

The creation of the Secret Service Bureau in October 1909 brought substantial changes to the role of the Special Branch. Previously it had never had more than thirty-eight officers and its main targets had been Irish and anarchist bombers. Now it expanded to help the domestic counter-espionage section of the SSB, under Vernan Kell, in the hunt for German spies, with the odd diversion against that other great threat to the empire – the suffragettes.

The greatest increase in its activities came under Basil Thomson, who was appointed Assistant Metropolitan Police Commissioner with responsibility for the Special Branch in June 1913. Thomson was the son of an Archbishop of York and had at various times been the governor of Wormwood Scrubs prison and the Prime Minister of Tonga. He was an inveterate empire-builder, and the First World War gave him ample opportunity. In the summer of 1914 the Branch had just seventy officers. By the time of the Armistice there were 700, and German spies were the least of their concerns. Thomson set them loose on anyone who might disrupt the war effort, from pacifists to trade unionists.

He was far more politically adept than Kell, whom he repeatedly out-manoeuvred. It mattered not that MI5, as Kell's section became in 1916, was uncovering the spies and subversives: since the Branch arrested them and he personally interrogated them, Thomson was able to exploit the secrecy of Kell's role to take full credit for any successes himself. But, despite his expertise at political infighting, Thomson's interrogation technique bore all the hallmarks of Inspector Clouseau. He began his questioning of Roger Casement, the Irish nationalist, by asking, 'What is your name?' When a puzzled Casement, replied, 'But you know it', Thomson's response was, 'Ah yes, but I have to guard against impersonators.'

It was Thomson, and not Kell, whom the government chose in March 1919 to head its new civilian Directorate of Intelligence, with a role 'to foresee and prevent political agitators from committing crime in order to terrorize the community into granting them what they want'. Thomson sought to have MI5 brought under his control, but Field Marshal Sir Douglas Haig was reluctant to allow a branch of military intelligence to involve itself in civil matters and Kell was restricted to maintaining internal military security.

'I would not authorize any men being used as spies,' said Haig. 'Officers must act straightforwardly and as Englishmen. "Espionage" among our men was hateful to us Army men. Thomson's machinery for getting information of sedition must work independently of the Army and its leaders.'

Thomson produced a weekly 'Report on Revolutionary Organizations in the UK' which was circulated to Cabinet ministers and senior officials. But by 1921 both the politicians and the new Metropolitan Police Commissioner, Sir William Horwood, had had enough of his reluctance to let them know what was going on. Thomson's obsession with the scourge of Bolshevism had led him to carry out intelligence operations against the Labour Party and had produced only 'misleading and inaccurate' reports, Horwood complained. The Directorate of Intelligence was 'approaching the continental system of domestic espionage' and offensive to a large proportion of working people.

In what bears all the hallmarks of a sting operation, Thomson was finally forced to resign after being arrested in Hyde Park for indecency with a known prostitute called Thelma de Lava.

Special Branch, then reduced to around 120 officers, was absorbed back into Scotland Yard under Sir Wyndham Childs, whose reputation for subservience had earned him the nickname of Fido. Unlike Thomson, Childs could be relied on to do what he was told, although virtually his first act was to refuse the Labour Prime Minister Ramsay MacDonald access to his secret file. The Branch retained control of the fight against Bolshevik subversion and espionage, taking charge of the 1927 raid on the Soviet ARCOS trade mission, but in 1931 that role was handed back to MI5. Special Branch responsibilities were cut and its intelligence staff were absorbed into the Security Service.

From then on, Special Branch's role in Britain's security, apart from the threat of Irish republicanism and the protection of VIPs, was strictly as a subordinate of MI5, gathering intelligence on Bolshevik subversion and foreign espionage and making arrests as directed by Kell. The Branch became MI5's link with the judicial process. Security Service officers could not make arrests, nor did they have the expertise needed to gather evidence that would pass muster in the courts. That work was performed by Special Branch officers.[2]

From the mid-1930s the size of the Special Branch remained constant at around 200 officers, apart from an increase during the Second World War to cope with the threat of German spies. But in the early 1960s there was another expansion, with the number of officers in the Metropolitan Police Special Branch jumping to 300 and a series of small Branches being set up in provincial forces. There are now around 500 officers in the Metropolitan Police Special Branch and several hundred in the provincial Branches.[3]

The main role of the modern-day Special Branches is to gather and analyse intelligence in relation primarily to terrorism, but also with regard to public order, espionage, proliferation and subversion – the last three in support of MI5. They are directly accountable to their chief constable, and officers have no powers additional to those of any other police officer. Special Branch officers are stationed at each major port and airport in Britain, where their main role is to monitor the entry of 'persons of interest', be they foreign agents or terrorists. Officers based at points of entry to Britain assist in some immigration and child-abduction cases and in the arrest of wanted criminals attempting to flee the country or return surreptitiously.[4]

The Branches also gather intelligence on animal-rights extremists, and the Metropolitan Police Special Branch oversees the Animal Rights National Index, a database on all animal-rights activity to which all police forces have access.[5]

The relationship between Scotland Yard's Special Branch, SO12, and its Anti-Terrorist Branch, SO13, is often misunderstood. Essentially, Special Branch mounts intelligence-gathering operations, often covertly, while the Anti-Terrorist Branch is restricted to investigating the circumstances surrounding specific bombings and shootings. Although the two work closely together, arrests and compilation of evidence would normally be carried out by anti-terrorist detectives, allowing the Special Branch to keep its own role out of the public eye.[6]

A number of officers work in A Squad of the Metropolitan Police Special Branch, providing specialist personal protection for ministers, former ministers, and those thought to be under threat mainly from terrorists – one prime example being Salman Rushdie. Foreign dignitaries are also given Special Branch bodyguards. Heads of foreign missions who are thought to be at particular risk from terrorist attacks, as in the case of the American and Israeli ambassadors, are allocated a team of A Squad officers.

B Squad of Scotland Yard's Special Branch has responsibility for collecting intelligence on Irish terrorism in London. The main covert collection operations are carried out through B Squad's Intelligence Source Unit, which recruits and handles agents. Analysis is undertaken by the Research Unit, which acts as a clearing-house for all incoming intelligence reports. A number of Special Branch officers are routinely attached to MI5, which has its own liaison cell within B Squad.

International terrorism is the responsibility of the Met Branch's CE Squad, which also has responsibility for countering subversion and the activities of extremist groups on both the left and the right. Special Branches still retain their responsibility for collecting intelligence on threats to public order, advising chief constables on the likely implications of marches and demonstrations where there is a threat of subversion or politically motivated violence. Under the 1984 guidelines for Special Branches, this was regarded as paramount, reflecting a traditional fear among successive governments from the 1920s onwards that the left-wing would seek to use demonstrations and industrial unrest to overthrow or undermine parliamentary democracy. But with the end of the Cold War, and despite the Northern Ireland peace process, the counter-terror role has become the most important single function.[7]

Many Special Branches outside the metropolitan areas are very small, and there tends to be a lot of co-operation within regions, either informally or through the Regional Special Branch Conference, allowing the exchange of information and experience and the sharing of specialist technical resources.

Representatives of the various Special Branches man the National Joint Unit at New Scotland Yard, which helps to prevent embarrassing incidents such as the 1991 escape from Brixton prison of two leading IRA terrorists. Staffordshire Special Branch had conducted 'a long-range operation' inside Brixton employing an informant to get close to Nessan Quinlivan and Pearse McAuley. The three discussed an escape plan under which Quinlivan and McAuley would smuggle in a gun and shoot their way out of the prison after Sunday mass. Their subsequent escape followed that plan to the letter.[8]

All Special Branch officers are trained by the Metropolitan Police Special Branch and the Security Service. The Met Branch also provides a great deal of technical and operational assistance to the provincial forces and acts as the link on Irish terrorism with MI5.

'The Metropolitan Police Special Branch and the Security Service act in a close partnership to ensure that intelligence is exploited to the maximum to counter terrorist activity,' the 1994 Special Branch guidelines state. 'This also enables the Metropolitan Police Special Branch to add the police perspective and to provide advice for provincial forces on assessed intelligence where police action may be necessary.'[9]

The Special Branch responsibilities of terrorism, subversion and espionage are no longer the only areas of policing that require sophisticated intelligence operations. Police officers generally use the term 'intelligence' to mean any information collected from a covert source, such as a 'snout' or informer, that will help in a specific investigation – what might be called tactical intelligence.

Scotland Yard had its own Criminal Intelligence Branch, which traditionally took on a defacto nationwide criminal intelligence role, although the collection of long-term intelligence was fairly limited. But from the 1970s onwards, the easy-profits, low-risk potential of drug trafficking brought a new type of criminal to the streets of Britain.

Although gangs such as the Krays and the Richardsons had long had an organized structure, they tended to operate only within their own territories and were relatively easy to keep track of. Those criminals involved in drug-related crime acted very much like international corporations: they operated across national borders, developed links with numerous domestic criminal groups in order to market the drugs, and had long-term strategic goals. The need to track the patterns of activity of such groups, and where possible to anticipate their next move, created a requirement for strategic rather than tactical intelligence. But operational police forces rarely had the time or resources to undertake long-term intelligence operations.

A series of reports in the 1970s and early 1980s on Britain's relative lack of any such strategic criminal intelligence capability gave rise first to the Central Drugs and Illegal Immigrants Intelligence Unit. This was subsequently split into two, to become the National Drugs Intelligence Unit and the Illegal Immigrants Intelligence Unit. A number of other intelligence units were also set up during this period, among them the National Football Intelligence Unit, to keep track of the central core of hooligans causing soccer violence.

But the explosion in organized crime – and in particular drug-related crime – that occurred in the 1980s and was exacerbated by the relaxation of the strict controls over eastern Europe following the fall of Communism revealed how inadequate this system was, and in 1992 a new National Criminal Intelligence Service (NCIS) was created. It brought together the various national police and customs intelligence units, with a brief 'to develop and assess information and intelligence on serious crime and major criminals and to disseminate that intelligence to the police, other law-enforcement agencies and government departments'.

At the same time, Scotland Yard also re-examined its use of intelligence, employing outside consultants to conduct an eighteen-month study which concluded that its Criminal Intelligence Branch, SO11, should become a Directorate of Intelligence run on similar lines to a military intelligence operation. A central intelligence unit at Scotland Yard would control a network of intelligence officers at the various stations around London whose main role was to be long-term targeting of organized crime groups.[10]

The threat from organized crime was seen as so great that even national security might be at risk. MI5 had recognized this danger as early as 1991, when Stella Rimington flew to Moscow for talks with Russian officials on 'co-operation in the fight against international terrorism and drug trafficking'. The JIC ordered the foreign intelligence services, GCHQ and MI6, to look at the problem, and a role in the fight against 'serious crime' was included in the 1993 Intelligence Services Bill. Senior SIS officers were initially highly sceptical that they had a role to play in this area, but the agency's success in a number of major operations against drug smugglers persuaded them otherwise. It does not take up a large proportion of the service's resources. There is no organized crime directorate, merely a small section within the Global Issues controllerate, but MI6 does have a number of officers working on organized crime, mainly international financial fraud and international criminal organizations.

The Treasury had been a key player behind the call for the intelligence services to investigate organized crime. With the annual figure for the laundering of drug money alone exceeding £500 billion worldwide, the process of laundering the profits could easily cause considerable damage even to a strong domestic economy. There was particular concern that the transfer of illicit funds out of Asia, South Africa and eastern Europe through 'underground' banking systems operated by organized crime groups could be used to manipulate the currency markets and might destabilize the British economy.[11]

The chaos caused in the old Soviet Bloc by the collapse of the Soviet system had led to widespread fears over the threat from transnational organized crime. Even before the collapse of the Communist regime, the level of crime in the Soviet Union was rocketing, encouraged by Mikhail Gorbachev's market reforms. By mid-1995 the anti-*Mafiya* department of the Russian interior ministry estimated that there were more than 8000 criminal gangs in the country, with around 35,000 members. An estimated 80 per cent of Russian businesses were said to pay protection money to the gangs, who controlled close to half the country's turnover in goods and services. Many 'owned' corrupt government officials and operated behind legitimate 'front' companies whose only role was to launder money. The number of gangs that had diversified into overseas operations was growing.[12]

'There has been an astronomical growth of organized crime in eastern Europe as they try and move towards democracy – particularly decentralized banking systems,' said Commander John Grieve, former Director of Intelligence at Scotland Yard. East-European organized crime has a relationship with drug-related violence. The Directorate of Intelligence and NCIS have built up the links with their counterparts in the former Soviet Bloc to track senior crime figures from the Balkans, the Baltic, Russia and Ukraine, he said. 'We have a good working relationship with all those places – some better than others. Some of them we have a very tight working relationship with. They are good people to work with.'

Russian gangs are involved in drug trafficking, widespread protection rackets which have forced many of the Western firms that originally bought into Russian companies to withdraw, illegal immigration, organized prostitution, and large-scale car theft, with high-value vehicles being targeted in western Europe for resale within eastern Europe and the former Soviet Union.[13]

The former Soviet Union has always been a major drug producer. The economies of the central-Asian republics of Kirghizstan, Tajikistan and Uzbekistan depend to a large extent on drugs and are therefore accorded a high priority by British intelligence. Even before the 1917 revolution, Kirghizstan accounted for a fifth of the world's opium supply. An Uzbekistani farmer can earn between 15,000 and 20,000 roubles a year from a hectare of fruit orchards. The same area planted with poppy would produce five kilograms of raw opium worth an estimated 2.5 million roubles.

The drug routes start out in the southern Tajik town of Khorog, heading either up through Osh in Kirghizstan on the border with Uzbekistan or west through Dushanbe, the Tajik capital. Underpaid police and customs officials are bribed to turn a blind eye to the trade, and once through the borders the drugs are moved on to Europe, mostly via rail.

The Russian drug smugglers are so adept at using these routes that the Colombian cartels are even moving cocaine into western Europe via Moscow, exporting it in containers labelled as food products and repackaging it as Russian exports to the West.[14]

The former Soviet Bloc has also become a major source of synthetic drugs produced in the old state laboratories of Poland, the Czech Republic, Latvia, Lithuania and Estonia. Poland is Europe's largest producer of amphetamine sulphate and is a significant source of heroin, made from poppies grown in the Polish Triangle between the south-west cities of Kraków, Miechów and Proszowice. The gangs move the drugs west and easily disposable consumer products such as high-prestige cars east, while the authorities look on helplessly.[15]

The growth in Russian and east-European organized crime led in 1994 to a joint British intelligence study of the potential threat, under the direction of NCIS but also including MI5, MI6, GCHQ and Scotland Yard's Directorate of Intelligence. This led to increased operations against Russian criminals, said Albert Pacey, NCIS Director. 'There is a significant threat posed by gangs organized in, or centred on, that geographic area,' he said. 'Our assessment is that the greatest threat to the UK in the long term is from the money-launderer.'[16]

There is a false perception that Britain has remained relatively untouched by the growth in international organized crime. 'You have to understand that organized crime does not work on the strict hierarchical model of the Mafia and the Triads here in London,' said Commander Grieve:

It is very attractive to impose a hierarchy on these things, and the Mafia, the Triads, they do have a hierarchy and they are here. But most of what goes on under the heading of organized crime is loosely organized. Yes, it is project crime. Yes, it nets them vast profits. But it is not hierarchical like people want it to be. It is much more like a patchwork quilt. It is like a webwork of old relationships, hatreds, alliances, blood relationships.

A number of the more recognized organized-crime groupings are active in Britain. There has been a noticeable increase in Italian criminal activities in the UK since 1990, especially in the London area, where the Sicilian Mafia, the Neapolitan Camorra and the Calabrian Ndrangheta are all known to have set up front companies and been mainly involved in money-laundering, drug trafficking and fraud. Paradoxically, Britain's reputation as a reasonably violence-free country has led some Italian gang members to use it as a safe haven from vendettas at home.

Drugs are imported by a number of groups. The Colombian cartels, which have diversified into growing poppy to produce heroin because of a glut of cocaine on the American market, have been active in the UK, linking up with the Jamaican Yardies and Posses which dominate the UK drug market.

The Jamaican gangs are mainly involved in pushing cannabis and crack cocaine. The hallmark of both Yardies and Posses is an extravagant use of weaponry to enforce territory and status that is largely responsible for the increasing pressure within the Metropolitan Police Force for officers to be armed. Both Posse members and Yardies base their respect for other gang members on the firepower of their weapons and their willingness to resort to extreme violence. They are largely restricted to the inner-city areas of London, Manchester, Bristol, Birmingham and Leicester, and they tend to rely on loose, often family-based, links between Britain, the

Caribbean and the eastern seaboard of the United States and Canada.

But the Jamaicans are not the only groups active in the drug market. Indian and Pakistani gangs specialize in heroin, which is reasonably easy to import as a result of the close links between Britain and the sub-continent, and they have easy opportunities to launder money within the British-Asian business community. Turkish and Kurdish immigrant groups have been particularly active in north London in drug trafficking and extortion, and the increasing importance of Nigeria as a trans-shipment point for drugs from the Caribbean and Latin America has led West African gangs based in London to graduate from organized illegal immigration and benefit fraud to drug trafficking. The Hells Angels, with twelve chapters in the United Kingdom, have also become increasingly involved in organized crime, largely trafficking in cannabis, LSD and amphetamines.

Triad groups, mainly from Hong Kong and working almost exclusively within the Chinese communities, are involved across a wide spectrum of organized crime, including drug trafficking, prostitution, illegal immi-gration from both mainland China and Hong Kong, illegal gambling, extortion and fraud. Murder is frequently used to enforce obedience, with the most favoured 'muscle' being Vietnamese associates, whose willing-ness to resort to extreme violence makes them an extremely potent threat.

Despite a good deal of media hype, senior police officers express doubt that the number of Triad gangs in Britain will increase significantly in the wake of the 1997 hand-over of Hong Kong to China. This is at least in part because those who wished to transfer their operations to Britain have already done so in anticipation of the hand-over, or have at least made precautions to do so if it should go badly. In addition, it is by no means certain that the Chinese authorities will attempt to clamp down on Triad activities. A number of leading Communist officials have spoken of being able to work with 'patriotic Triads' in what appears to be recog-nition of the power the societies have over their *Sey Kow Jai*, or ordinary members.

Another group which has had a great deal of publicity is the Japanese Yakuza, who have a far stronger influence within Japan itself than the Mafia has in America for instance. As Japanese companies diversified their operations and set up factories abroad, the Yakuza followed. They traditionally follow the tenets of *giri*, the obligation to repay favours, and *ninjo*, compassion for the weak. Their main activities in Britain so far have been confined to that of the financial crime specialists, the *Sokaiya*, who have been involved in commodity futures fraud and money-laundering.[17]

The main NCIS unit tracking those groups is the Strategic and Specialist Intelligence Branch, which is split into a dedicated organized-crime unit; a drugs unit; a football-violence unit; a specialist crimes unit, covering kidnapping and extortion, paedophilia, and organized vehicle crime; and an economic crimes unit, which covers fraud, counterfeiting and money-laundering and has direct links to the major clearing banks. There are also regional offices in Manchester, Birmingham, Wakefield, Bristol and Scotland.[18]

The Directorate of Intelligence is organized around its Drugs and Violence Intelligence Unit. The DRVIU co-ordinates all intelligence-led operations against organized crime in the capital. There are five devolved Force Intelligence Bureaux (FIB) – one in each of the Metropolitan Police areas – and a network of sixty-three intelligence cells – one in every police station in London.

'Each of the sixty-three cells has its own analytical capability, and some to a greater or lesser extent have some surveillance capability – though mostly this is static surveillance as opposed to mobile,' said Commander Grieve:

> You really don't get mobile surveillance until you get to the area force intelligence bureaux, each one of which has a mobile surveillance team and an analytical capability.
>
> Our focus is always on London. But on a daily basis, at this very moment, there will be somebody on the phone in some part of both SO11 at the centre and the FIBs and the divisions talking to the rest of the country. There is nothing in London that doesn't touch on something somebody else is doing. Coming the other way, 70 per cent of serious crime has its focus in the South-East, and the bulk of that will be something to do with London, so they're talking to us all the time. It is never-ending, and we probably have the biggest intelligence database – massive.

The directorate's Memex computer is linked to forty different databases from all over the world, including the New York District Attorney's records of all known Jamaican drug dealers.

> We do a lot of work on what we call thematic crime, of which drug-related violence is probably the most noteworthy – very dangerous people. Sometimes the threat is so great that you have to act before you might want to and just hope that you are going to generate the evidence that you want. We do a lot of strategic analysis, and NCIS do a lot of strategic analysis. We also run some of the most dangerous live sources of information, and we run a lot of technical kit to go with that.

There is clear demarcation between the roles of SO11 and NCIS, with the former now very much restricted to the London area. 'My boundaries are the M25,' said Commander Grieve. 'But I am also tasked with liaising with all the other criminal intelligence agencies in the country and in fact worldwide on behalf of London, whereas NCIS has got the whole country.'

Liaison between the two organizations is very close, Grieve said. 'It is unlikely that we are running a major intelligence development plan and we haven't got NCIS in. It is very unusual not to find NCIS in it. It is very unusual not to find the South-East Regional Crime Squad in it, and not to find some local team in it as well. It is generally a task unit put together from all those people, trying to take out the main quarry.'[19]

The strong co-ordination developed not just because it made sense to pool intelligence but as a result of limitations imposed on NCIS from its conception. Because of fears over lack of accountability, there were severe restrictions both on the extent to which it could collect intelligence and on what it could do with it once it had been collected. It had no operational arm and was not allowed to carry out mobile surveillance. All it could do was produce intelligence packages which it then attempted to 'sell' to the relevant provincial forces, with no control over how or even whether they would be acted on.

A confidential 1994 Home Office report found that NCIS was 'under-funded, under-used and ineffective'.[20] 'If there is anything that we need at the moment it is a development arm,' Albert Pacey said. 'We have some regional intelligence officers, one per police force and more than that in the South-East because of London. It is just not enough. They are allowed to carry out only static intelligence-gathering on the ground. If someone goes out of his house and round the corner and gets into a car, strictly speaking my officer cannot turn that corner to take the number of the car.'

As a result, NCIS had to ask the regional crime squads or individual police forces to carry out surveillance operations, but often they would be called off the operation midway through to deal with operationally urgent matters such as an armed robbery, Pacey said. 'Frequently we find that when they are able to get back to it the intelligence lead has gone dead. It is not enough. Ultimately, I need the facility to be able to direct the development of intelligence. You can do so much analytical work from behind a computer and a desk, but in the end you have to be on the ground to do some checking and make enquiries.'[21]

In October 1995 the government announced a national crime squad based on NCIS supplemented by other agencies – mainly the regional crime squads, but also including elements of MI5 and GCHQ. Michael

Howard, the Home Secretary, stressed that it was not intended to be a British FBI:

> We are going to develop the role of our National Criminal Intelligence Service, allowing their staff to undertake mobile surveillance of targets. We are going to build on the work of the regional crime squads to ensure that national problems are met with national solutions. The Security Service has a part to play in support of the law-enforcement agencies. The government will legislate shortly to enable the service itself to work in this area.[22]

While this would provide NCIS with a dedicated operational arm, it was in fact little more than a formalization of procedures that had been in force for some time. Despite Mr Howard's admission that the Security Service Act needed to be changed to allow MI5 to operate in this area, it was already taking part in operations against organized crime led by NCIS and co-ordinated through the Joint Intelligence Committee, as were SIS and GCHQ, whose remits allowed for such activities.

Detective Superintendent Larry Covington, head of the NCIS International Unit, said he had been working very closely with MI5 and MI6 for some time:

> I deal with them and work with them on a daily basis. Because it's all about sources of intelligence. They've got some fantastic sources of intelligence, and at the end of the day I would be naïve in the extreme if I didn't work with them. But in all our dealings with the Security Service and the Secret Intelligence Service it is made abundantly clear to everyone that it is in support of law enforcement, and in fact we task them in our field.[23]

The most common source in criminal intelligence operations is the informer. According to Commander Grieve:

> Paying informants is very cost-effective, providing that you manage all the risks – all the moral risks, all the physical risks, and all the legal risks. Economically it is a very, very cost-effective way of doing it if you compare the price of one of my mobile surveillance teams, an eight-hour day for them, and then you compare that with how much you pay informers. With an informer, we have got somebody inside the tent looking out. With a surveillance team, you are outside the tent looking in. There are very few jobs with the category of people that I deal with that two or three days work by a surveillance team will get a result. Very usually you will barely be off first base.[24]

However, the handling of informers presents a difficult balance

between ensuring that they do enough within their group to gain acceptance without ever crossing the very thin line between being an informant
and acting as an *agent provocateur*. The Directorate of Intelligence was
widely criticized in 1995 over its recruitment of a member of a Jamaican
Posse as the inside man on a major international operation against drug
trafficking. While still working as a Scotland Yard informer, Eaton Green
took part in an armed robbery in Nottingham, shooting one man in the
leg. He was subsequently jailed for six years. But Nottinghamshire police
were irate to discover not only that he was an informer but that his
handlers were apparently very anxious that he be allowed to remain free
so that he could continue in that role.

'We were involved in an international intelligence operation,' Grieve
said. 'We took a view that it is better to know where some of these people
are if you have no grounds to bar them from your country at the time.'
He conceded that his officers were operating in 'morally difficult territory'
but was unrepentant about the fact that Green had continued to sell crack
cocaine, carry arms and commit robberies during his time as an informer:

Criminals involved in some parts of drug-related violence are paranoid,
treacherous, violent and unstable. It is an unstructured and chaotic
environment. They operate in a culture which is different from other
cultures and which is more difficult to penetrate. It's impossible to
tackle serious crime of this nature without the use of informants who
turn out – surprise, surprise – to be criminals who are still committing
crimes. If they didn't have that sort of background, they wouldn't be
accepted. Green was an extremely successful informant. He was well
worth the investment and it is extremely unfortunate that we no longer
have him available to us.[25]

International co-operation is co-ordinated through the NCIS International Intelligence Branch, which controls links with Interpol and with
the drug liaison officers, police or customs officers who are posted to
Britain's embassies abroad and whose role is being expanded to cover all
aspects of organized crime. Interpol – set up in 1956 – was until recently
little more than an international conduit for police communication. But,
following widespread criticism, it has now been revamped with the
creation of a European Liaison Bureau to help national forces to mount
joint operations and an Analytical Criminal Intelligence Unit to exploit
the information stored on the agency's computer database.[26]

Both NCIS and the Directorate of Intelligence also liaise with Europol,
the European police organization based in The Hague. First proposed
by Germany in 1991 as the European equivalent of the FBI, it was
formally set up as part of the Maastricht Treaty but its role was limited

to that of a co-ordinating body for the exchange and analysis of criminal intelligence and it had no operational powers. Its responsibilities are being increased on a step-by-step basis, starting with countering drug trafficking and gradually adding money-laundering; the international trade in stolen cars, illegal immigrants and nuclear materials; enforced prostitution; and finally terrorism.[27]

There are inevitable security worries for any intelligence organization sharing the product of covert operations with foreign organizations over which it has no control. Stella Rimington has pointed to the need for Europe's security services and law-enforcement agencies to be sure that any information they exchange is kept secure:

> They must have confidence in each other's ability to keep the most sensitive information secret. Because there is no doubt at all that those people who risk their lives to give us intelligence from within the hearts of those organizations which threaten our security will not do so unless they are confident that we will not compromise their safety.[28]

But Commander Grieve says such worries have not hampered SO11's links with Europol. 'We have a very close relationship with Europol,' he said:

> Most of the work we do with them is on east-European organized crime and banking systems. I would be surprised if there was a single solitary country in Europe that we haven't run an operation with. Of course there is intelligence that is UK Eyes Only. There are things that are my eyes only. But you do not want to have a major row running with one of your allies, so there is a need for diplomacy and tact, and on operational issues we share everything. We have no problems with that.

Chasing drug money through the banking system represents an increasing part of the work of the Directorate of Intelligence. 'Our actual activity in this area is skyrocketing,' Commander Grieve said:

> We learn some stuff from it by serendipity. Things come in that are very obviously drug trafficking. Things crop up that are really good intelligence coups for us, really good sources of intelligence.
>
> The problem is that you have to get into the world banking system, and different countries have a very different set of regulations. You need an organized banking structure with its own self-regulation as well as external regulations before you can make that work. There are countries in the world that just don't play that game, and once the money reaches them it is very hard to track it – very, very hard.[29]

Money-laundering – the process by which illicit funds are given the appearance of legally owned income – can take many forms. The money, which normally begins as cash, will be passed through a series of stages to disguise its origins and make it difficult to trace. In its most basic form, a luxury item like a car or a piece of jewellery is bought and then resold. But in more complex cases this will be only the first stage – the so-called 'placement' of the funds. The next stage is 'layering', in which the funds are normally split up and passed through a complex trail of financial transactions. This has become particularly easy for the international criminal since the introduction of electronic payment systems which allow the money to be transferred easily around the world to a variety of different bank accounts. Finally comes 'integration', the point at which the money has all the semblance of legitimate funds and is regarded as safe to use.[30]

Frequently, 'shell' companies are used as fronts through which to launder the money. Totally innocent companies become drawn into the web. Investigators in the United States discovered that Colombia's Cali drug cartel had used hundreds of American companies – including General Electric, General Motors, Apple Computer and Microsoft – to launder the money earned from the sale of drugs. One of Scotland Yard's joint operations with the New York District Attorney's office found that the Cali drug cartel was laundering the proceeds of its drug operations by buying and selling pictures in the art galleries of Mayfair and Manhattan.[31]

In Britain, financial organizations are obliged under the 1988 Drug Trafficking Offences Act and the 1993 Criminal Justice Act to report any transactions which they suspect of being part of a money-laundering operation to the police, who have extensive powers to trace the so-called 'money trail' through the banking system and to freeze or confiscate funds acquired through criminal means.

'It is often said that the way to tackle organized crime is through the money trail,' said Albert Pacey. 'If publicity is the oxygen of the terrorist, then money is the oxygen of organized crime. If we can remove the illegally acquired assets from the criminal then we can remove their motivation, their *raison d'être*.'

The banks made 15,000 so-called 'suspicious transaction reports' in 1994 – a figure that Pacey expected to rise to 20,000 as the system improved. 'Whilst we do not claim that these disclosures by themselves lead to the conviction of gangsters, it is true to say that they have in many cases supplied the missing piece of the jigsaw that has led to the completion of a fuller picture of criminality.'[32]

One of the biggest problems facing the intelligence services as they tackle organized crime is disclosure. Under the British legal system, the defence must have access to any evidence collected against its client that might help its case. Police reluctance to disclose evidence that will reveal intelligence sources leads to an average of one court case a week being aborted.[33]

Disclosing the identity of an informer has to be avoided at all costs, and numerous prosecutions have had to be aborted because the judge backed up demands from the defence for an informer to be identified. Even the act of aborting such a case is risky, said Simon Crawshaw of NCIS. 'It tips off the defendants that they had an informer in their midst and they will try to find him by a process of elimination. With the increased use of violence, that could well cost him his life.'[34]

But it is not only informers that need to be protected. Methods of detection can be just as vulnerable. 'The constant see-saw is the counter-intelligence from their side,' said John Grieve. 'They are constantly trying to find out how we did it.' Even where a case proceeds and the defendant is convicted, other members of the gang frequently learn enough about police methods from disclosure of evidence to allow them to develop their own counter-measures and render sources useless.

The German urban terrorist group the Red Army Faction developed into a highly professional organization, always ensuring that no finger-prints were left behind in safe houses. But the Bundeskriminalamt (BKA), the German federal police, discovered the terrorists were neglecting to check the underneath of toilet seats. When fingerprints were produced as evidence in open court, the terrorists' defence lawyers insisted on being told exactly where in a safe house the fingerprints were discovered. Although that prosecution was successful, the BKA never found finger-prints under a toilet seat again.

For security reasons, the Red Army Faction would pay the rent and power bills for its safe houses in cash. But since Germany has become a relatively cashless society BKA investigators were able to search through the power company's computers for customers who moved out of addresses close to where attacks took place at roughly the same time and who paid their bills in cash. After the Red Army Faction's lawyers forced disclosure of this technique in open court, the terrorists stopped paying in cash.[35]

John Grieve said defence lawyers constantly mount 'fishing expeditions' to find out what they can about police intelligence techniques. 'The big issue for us is how to do these things without showing all our secret toys,' he said:

Intelligence is anathema to the lawyers. They want their hands on absolutely everything. They are not just content with the product.

They want the process as well, including some of our tricks of generating live sources of information. 'Where was the microphone? What was the frequency? Where was it positioned in the room?' All those kind of issues. 'Where were the surveillance teams? What technical kit did you use? What colour vehicle were you in? Tell us everything about everything. Or drop the case.' If we get a weak judge, we get ordered to disclose all kinds of things, and no lawyer in this day and age will say, 'I won't tell my client.' So a massive amount of material gets released. It's a big issue for us – a really big issue.[36]

MI5 has already come across these problems in open court. 'Sometimes this acts as a constraint on our investigations,' Stella Rimington said.

There is an inherent uncertainty in judging in advance how the courts may view individual operations and methods which we regard as sensitive. Many such sensitive techniques have to be protected at all costs, because they cannot be replaced. This sometimes means that we are unable to use the most effective investigative methods in cases which may result in prosecution. In some cases, rulings by the judge may cause the prosecution to be discontinued because the material information is so sensitive that it is not possible to disclose it in any form.[37]

While many police officers have expressed disquiet about the use of MI5 to counter organized crime, those involved in criminal intelligence are less dismissive. 'We have a very good relationship with the Security Service,' said Commander Grieve:

They have been very supportive. We aren't doing well enough to reject help from anybody quite frankly. We're awash with drugs in London – and violence and everything else. If they want to help, they want to get a bit of the action, fine – come and help us. But be ready for rolling about in the gutter and getting yourself smeared in excrement, because this is a very dirty game out there with the people we're dealing with.[38]

# CHAPTER 17

# *Milk and Honey*

Commercial intelligence may very largely supplement political
intelligence, if it be properly used.
War Office report dated 9 December 1893

As the Cold War came to an end and the intelligence services cast around for new roles, one of the most commonly suggested was economic espionage. Frequently it was put forward as if it was something new that spies had not considered before. Its significance was by turns either overstated or discounted. Depending on who was asked, it was the most important target for the intelligence services in the new world or it was just something the spies were inventing to keep themselves busy and their budgets intact – a straightforward case of jobs for the boys.

In fact economic espionage has been carried out since Moses – obeying God's orders to send spies into Canaan – laid down the first list of intelligence priorities. Caleb and his men were to find out 'whether the land is rich or poor' – a directive that was reflected in the main thrust of their report on 'a land flowing with milk and honey'.[1]

But, new role or not, by the early 1990s, with the old world order falling apart, it had become clear that economic intelligence had to be a high priority. In the short term at least, the new superpower system would be based on economic strength. The new 'geo-economic' power blocs would be the United States, the European Union and a Pacific Rim dominated by Japan but also including other commercially powerful newly industrialized countries (NICs) such as South Korea and Singapore.[2]

Economic intelligence has long been a useful tool in evaluating the strategic threat, and has continued to be so with the collapse of Communism. The stability of the countries of the former Soviet Union and eastern Europe is heavily dependent on the success of economic reforms, and British intelligence has carefully tracked their progress, looking for signs of industrial unrest and the social problems associated with high unemployment.[3]

For the same reasons, the economies of post-apartheid South Africa and the countries involved in the Middle East peace process are kept under close surveillance for any problems that might bring renewed tensions, while those of the West's main *bêtes noires* – China, North Korea, Libya, Iran and Iraq – are monitored for any sign that sanctions or restrictions on technology imports are being breached and for economic problems that might lead to instability or to the weakening or strengthening of anti-Western policies.[4]

The state of trade and economic links between the various countries of the former Soviet Bloc is also a very high priority, as are the financial activities of various Central and South American governments which are monitored closely to determine their ability to repay international debt. Intelligence on Argentinian fishing and oil exploration activities around the Falklands is also a natural priority for the British agencies.[5]

Britain, buoyed by its position as the world's leading trading nation, took what one official described as a '*laissez-faire* approach' to the collection of commercial intelligence until the later part of the nineteenth century, when a 'revival of economic nationalism' and the widespread belief that war in Europe was inevitable led to a growing interest in such matters. Not only would commercial information help Britain's exporters to ward off the increasing competition in trade – particularly from Germany – but an army fighting abroad would need to know where supplies might be found.[6]

By 1893, General E. F. Chapman, the British Director of Military Intelligence, was pointing out that the ability of a potential enemy to wage war would depend on the strength of its economy, and that its preparations for war could be detected by studying government contracts. 'Commercial intelligence may very largely supplement political intelligence, if it be properly used,' Chapman wrote. 'Whenever warlike operations are about to be undertaken, it is clear that the issue of contracts, and other steps affecting the commercial world must precede the actual start of any expedition,' he explained. 'The subject requires study, but the great advantage we possess over other nations, in possessing the closest commercial relations with every port, and every large town in Europe, should gain us in the matter of obtaining information, which I believe to be one of the main reasons for success in every operation of war.'

Chapman suggested that Britain's commercial attachés abroad be asked to monitor any new contracts for supplies of war *matériel*, food, horses or medicine and to relay the information back to England 'with the utmost expedition, consistent with secrecy'.

While the recipient of his report found his ideas 'excessively obscure', they were taken up within the Foreign Office, where one official called for 'a separate intelligence organization' to be set up within the Commercial

Department 'for obtaining early information of all contracts made by foreign governments for the supply of such stores as may be required in the active operations for war, and of the collection of such stores in such places, or under such circumstances as may indicate their intended application in premeditated active operations'.[7]

In 1900 the Board of Trade formed a Commercial Intelligence Branch which collated economic intelligence sent home by British diplomats around the world. But the Foreign Office did not like the idea of another government department having control over what went on in its embassies, and the two sides 'squabbled like kids' over who should control the new branch.

By 1917, with the First World War creating a large demand for commercial intelligence, military intelligence was collecting economic information on foreign countries, and in particular 'questions of military policy connected with the economic and financial resources of the enemy'. Meanwhile, the turf battle between the Board of Trade and the Foreign Office over the Commercial Intelligence Branch showed no signs of abating, and it was agreed that it would be resolved only by creating 'a single department charged with the compilation and distribution of intelligence, from whatever source it is obtained'.

That new ministry was called the Department of Overseas Trade, and by the mid-1930s it was not only sending out routine reports on Britain's trading partners to exporters and to other government departments but had also set up a 'Special Register' of companies who, for a nominal fee, received 'some information . . . particularly that which is of a confidential character'.[8]

The Committee of Imperial Defence had meanwhile set up its own subcommittee specifically to look at the potential of economic intelligence. This was not just a question of detecting preparations for war. Destroying the enemy's means of production would severely limit his ability to wage war, and economic intelligence would be vital in determining which targets would cause most damage. The subcommittee built up its own research staff, known as the Industrial Intelligence Centre and led by Major Desmond Morton, a former MI6 officer.

The centre, which was initially controlled by the War Office and based at MI6 headquarters, became part of the Department of Overseas Trade in 1935. Its role was 'to collate, study and interpret existing industrial and other civilian information in relation to the war potential of foreign countries'. There were six sections, whose main targets were Germany, the Soviet Union, the Americas, the Far East, France, and the Mediterranean and Middle East. Its reports were sent to the War Office, the Treasury, the Foreign Office and the Board of Trade.

The IIC was very successful, warning that Hitler was preparing for war long before the War Office or the Air Ministry. But at the outbreak of the Second World War it was subsumed into the Intelligence Department of the Ministry of Economic Warfare, where its role was 'to collect, collate, appreciate and present to the Service and other departments . . . all information about the enemy's economic strength, dispositions and intentions, which may be of use in attacking him'. At the same time, a special commercial circulating section (Section VI) was set up within MI6 to pass on any economic intelligence collected by SIS agents or the Government Code and Cypher School.[9]

At the end of the war, when MI6 was reorganized and the circulating sections became the Directorate of Requirements, the commercial section was retained as R6, with a brief to disseminate economic intelligence, which was then seen as one of the main post-war roles. 'The economic contribution in assessing the strength of potential enemies is bound to be considerably more important than in wartime,' a secret Foreign Office report said. 'In peace a country's capacity for war-making must chiefly lie in its war potential, which is predominantly an economic factor.'

There was particular interest in acquiring German 'trade secrets' and passing them on to British companies. The JIC decreed that economic intelligence gathered in occupied Germany 'should be pooled between the US and British Governments on the understanding that they were free to make such use of it as they thought fit, including its release to civil industry'.

Ian Fleming, then a naval intelligence officer, told the JIC that the British Overseas Airways Corporation was among a number of companies being given intelligence by the British authorities, and another Admiralty representative said there was no reason why other British companies would not be willing to work with British intelligence on a reciprocal basis. 'Business firms had been keen to co-operate before the war and he saw no reason why the Joint Intelligence Bureau should not have the same co-operation from business firms at the present time.'[10]

The collection of economic data has provided a key role for the British intelligence services ever since – a fact which was tacitly acknowledged when both the 1989 Security Service Act and the 1994 Intelligence Services Act authorized operations in the interests of Britain's 'economic well-being' and by the identification of the Department of Trade and Industry as one of 'two key "customer" departments for intelligence' in the first interim report of the recently formed House of Commons Select Committee on Intelligence and Security – the other 'key customer' being the Foreign Office.

The intelligence is analysed by the JIC's assessments staffs, and their conclusions are overseen by the Economic Current Intelligence Group, a JIC subcommittee which issues intelligence reports to a number of customers, including the Department of Trade and Industry, the Export Credit Guarantee Department, the Treasury and the Bank of England.[11]

Although such intelligence is intended for use by government departments, the extent of informal relationships with British companies who have been given useful information in exchange for allowing their executives to be used to collect intelligence was confirmed with surprising alacrity by Baroness Park, a former SIS officer. Asked what businessmen and women might expect from MI6 in return for risking their lives on its behalf, Baroness Park said:

I think that is an entirely individual thing. With some people, it may be money; with others a little bit of help, a little bit of influence, a little bit of knowledge. For instance, if you knew a British company was coming out to try and get the order for helicopters in a particular country and you knew from other sources that the Italians and the French were both bidding, you would certainly tell the man you wanted to help that so that he was forearmed and knew that he had competition.[12]

A former GCHQ official who worked for the agency in the early 1970s described monitoring what she said were 'random pick-ups' of commercial telexes. But GCHQ's role in collecting economic intelligence was well-entrenched long before that. GC&CS, its predecessor, set up a specialized section to monitor foreign commercial traffic, mainly on behalf of the Industrial Intelligence Centre, in 1938, and even this was not the first time it had involved itself in such matters. 'Once or twice perhaps we may have looked out for individuals,' said A. G. Denniston, the then Director of GC&CS, in an internal history of the inter-war years. 'Once most certainly we did investigate the telegrams of certain oil companies.'

GCHQ's interest in this area appears to have increased. Recent advertisements for linguists have asked for graduates with a specialist knowledge of Japanese, Portuguese, Dutch, Italian and German – languages more likely to be used by our commercial competitors than by our military or political enemies.

Dennis Mitchell, a former GCHQ cryptanalyst, gave evidence to the Scott Inquiry on how the communications of foreign companies were monitored. Sir Robin Butler, the Cabinet Secretary, intervened to ensure that Mr Mitchell's evidence remained secret. But Robin Robison, a former administrative officer for the Joint Intelligence Committee in the

1980s, claimed that the communications of leading British and foreign companies were routinely intercepted. The companies under surveillance included GEC Marconi, Rolls Royce, Lonrho, and a large number of foreign companies, among them General Motors, he said. 'Sackfuls' of commercial information were collected.[13]

Lord Mackay, the Lord Chancellor, told Parliament in 1994 that preserving Britain's role as the world's fifth largest trading nation was essential for its economic well-being and that the intelligence agencies kept 'a particular eye on Britain's accesss to key commodities like oil or metals'. Justifying this, he pointed out that 'the profits of Britain's myriad of international business interests . . . and the jobs of a great many British people are dependent on the ability to plan, to invest, and to trade effectively without worry or danger'.[14]

American Congressional hearings examining what the post-Cold War intelligence targets should be were told that the British were among a number of 'friendly countries' carrying out espionage against US companies. 'The British almost never get caught and they fully exploit the access provided by a long history of colonial alliances,' said Gerard Burke, a former CIA official who now heads one of America's leading commercial security companies.[15] They would certainly not be alone among America's allies in doing so. Former CIA Director James Woolsey told the Senate that a number of so-called friendly countries – including France, Japan, South Korea, Israel, Sweden and Switzerland – were spying on US companies. 'Not everyone around the world plays the game the way we do,' he said. 'Some of our friends and allies are involved in economic intelligence operations against our corporations.'[16]

Perhaps the most aggressive of America's 'friends' in the search for commercial secrets have been the French. Count Alexandre de Marenches, former head of the SDECE, Service de Documentation Extérieure et de Contre-Espionage, the French equivalent of MI6, revealed in his memoirs that it had an Economic Intelligence Service which gathered 'not only financial and economic intelligence but industrial espionage as well'. De Marenches claimed that in 1971 the SDECE learned in advance of American plans to devalue the dollar, allowing the French treasury to make enormous profits on the currency markets. The coup 'financed the service for years', he claimed.[17]

After François Mitterrand came to power in 1981 the SDECE was renamed the Direction Générale de la Sécurité Extérieure (DGSE). The new President appointed Pierre Marion, a former head of Air France, to head the agency, ordering him to improve its ability to gather economic, financial, industrial and scientific intelligence. Marion set up a section for global economic intelligence, assigning twenty agents to collect such information from America alone. Marion later claimed that his men placed bugs in the seats of Air France aircraft to pick up the conversations of foreign businessmen, and that, among other things, the intelligence obtained by the section had secured a billion-dollar sale of French Mirage warplanes to India in the face of stiff competition from the United States and the Soviet Union. 'It would not be normal that we spy on these states. In political or military matters, we are allied,' Marion said. 'But in the economic competition, in the technological competition, we are competitors.'[18]

Despite a 1988 agreement between the DGSE and the CIA not to steal each other's commercial secrets, the French made repeated efforts to recruit employees of IBM and Texas Instruments to acquire technological and marketing information that would help prop up the ailing Compagnie des Machines Bull, a partly state-owned French computer company. These operations culminated in a botched attempt at garbology – spy tradecraft in which the contents of rubbish bins are examined in an attempt to find information that might help build up the pieces of the intelligence jigsaw.[19]

The incident in question took place in the early hours of 18 February 1991. America and France were ostensibly staunch allies, preparing for the ground offensive against Iraq in the Gulf. But in an affluent suburb of Houston, Texas, a very different relationship between the two countries was being played out. A van stopped outside the executive mansion of a senior official of Texas Instruments, and two men jumped out, rummaged through the refuse bins, and threw some sacks in the back of the van. As it drove off, the licence-plate number was noted by an off-duty policeman. It was later traced to the French Consulate in Houston, and the FBI were called in. The French diplomats claimed they were collecting grass cuttings to fill in an unfinished swimming-pool in the consulate gardens. 'Spy on people's garbage?' said Bernard Guillet, the French Consul-General, when questioned about the affair by FBI agents. 'That's ridiculous.'[20]

Then in April 1993 the CIA obtained a secret 21-page French file listing the types of technologies the DGSE was interested in, together with a total of seventy-three business and financial organizations that had been or were to be the subject of French economic espionage. Most were American, such as aircraft manufacturer Boeing and the computer giants IBM and Texas Instruments. But others were British, including Ferranti, Vickers, Westland and British Aerospace, the subject of a DGSE operation to discover the full specifications and performance details of the European Fighter Aircraft, a direct competitor of the French-produced Rafale.[21]

A number of American aerospace companies subsequently pulled out of the Paris Air Show after being warned that the DGSE planned to use it to conduct covert operations against them. Two French agents discovered working at the Bell Helicopter plant in Fort Worth, Texas, and identified as a result of the DGSE file, were recalled to Paris and, amid intense embarrassment, Claude Silberzahn, the new head of the DGSE, was fired after admitting that the organization now concentrated on economic intelligence and that much of the information it acquired was passed on direct to French companies.[22]

The simmering row between the two countries over French economic espionage erupted into a major diplomatic incident in February 1995, when France ordered five CIA agents – four of them diplomats – out of the country on the grounds that they had engaged in 'activities incompatible with their status'. Privately, French officials briefed journalists that they had been gathering economic intelligence. The Americans conceded that that was true, but said it was nothing to what the French had done to them. Robert Gates, the CIA's Director, said, 'France is among a certain number of countries who have planted moles inside American firms, stolen American businessmen's briefcases and who carry out classic spying operations to obtain industrial and economic information.'[23]

The diplomatic row with America had little if any effect on the amount of economic espionage conducted by France. A few weeks later the French government set up a new body, the Committee for Economic Competitiveness and Security, to 'research, analyse, process and distribute information in order to help industrialists and to carry out prospective and strategic research for the government'.[24]

The only country to rival France in its willingness to spy on its allies' commercial secrets is Japan. A 1987 classified CIA survey estimated that 80 per cent of Tokyo's intelligence assets were directed against America and western Europe. The Ministry of International Trade and Industry (MITI) and the Japanese foreign ministry's Information Analysis, Research and Planning Bureau trawl any publicly available commercial documents, translating and analysing them before passing the resulting data on to Japanese companies.

Japanese businessmen and academics travelling abroad routinely collect documents and take photographs or video-recordings of equipment. The bigger Japanese corporations such as Hitachi, Mitsubishi and Mitsui run their own intelligence departments, many of whose employees were trained at the Institute for Industrial Protection, a school for commercial spies set up in 1962 with MITI backing.[25]

But even Japan is not as voracious in its efforts to uncover Western technology as the Chinese. With Beijing's record on human rights severely limiting its access to Western technology, around a half of all illegal technology-transfer cases investigated by the FBI in the Silicon Valley area of California are the result of covert economic intelligence operations by the Chinese intelligence services. One senior FBI official has described China as 'the most active foreign power engaged in illegal acquisition of American technology'.[26]

Chinese students and businessmen travelling abroad are routinely briefed to acquire targeted technologies. French military investigators recently spotted members of a Chinese scientific delegation to a Paris trade show discreetly dipping their ties into a new photographic processing fluid developed by the German company Agfa. One British university which introduced photocopier access cards to keep track of the use of its facilities found that the vast bulk of its annual usage was taken up by a visiting Chinese academic who was copying virtually every scientific paper and sending it home. Some restricted technology is purchased direct by Hong Kong-based front companies, and where this is not possible the Chinese have attempted to buy foreign companies with access to the desired technology.[27]

The Soviet intelligence services have stolen Western commercial and technical secrets since the New Economic Policy of the early 1920s. The Tcheka, the early predecessor of the KGB, acquired an economic intelligence role in 1920. By the mid-1970s 'Line X', as the operation to acquire Western technology became known, was worth an estimated $50 million a year, leading Leonid Zaitsev, the head of Directorate T, the KGB department responsible for economic espionage, to claim that it was funding the KGB's entire foreign operating costs.[28]

The full scale of the Soviet economic espionage effort was revealed to the West in the early 1980s by a French 'agent in place' code-named Farewell. By 1983 Western intelligence was reporting that 'technology procurement' was now the KGB's primary foreign role. Several thousand economic spies, armed with precise shopping lists, were using a variety of different methods to bypass the COCOM regulations which restricted exports to Communist countries, mainly in America, Japan, France, Britain and Germany. As well as straightforward theft of economic secrets, the KGB was setting up phoney front companies to buy Western technology.[29]

This activity is reported to have increased during Mikhail Gorbachev's presidency, with a major drive to acquire the latest Western developments in advanced electronics. Oleg Gordievsky, the KGB's former deputy *Rezident* in London, recalls that in a speech to staff at the Soviet Embassy during a 1984 visit to Britain the former Soviet leader singled out the 'Line X' work for special praise. 'It was already clear that he regarded

covert acquisition of Western technology as an important part of economic *perestroika*.'[30]

Farewell is believed to have been executed by the KGB in 1983, but
the French expelled more than fifty Soviet diplomats and journalists as
a direct result of the information he supplied. A 1985 Pentagon report
based on analysis of the Farewell material said, 'The magnitude of the
Soviets' collection effort and their ability to assimilate collected equipment and technology are far greater than was previously believed.' Soviet
intelligence obtained 6000 to 10,000 pieces of equipment and 100,000
documents every year, the report said.[31]

Before the collapse of Communism, east-European intelligence agencies, like Hungary's AVH, Czechoslovakia's StB and in particular the
East German Stasi, made a major contribution to Soviet accumulation
of Western technology. Robbed of their assistance, the Russian foreign
intelligence services, the SVR and the GRU, have increased their espionage activity, with economic intelligence accorded an even higher priority
than it already had.[32]

'Of course one of our emphases will shift to the commercial sphere, that
is quite natural,' said Yevgeny Primakov, shortly after he was appointed as
SVR director. With numerous restrictions on the export of high-tech
equipment still in place, Russia had no choice. 'Many secrets are still
kept from us. If this information were openly available then there would
be no need to engage in such intelligence.'[33]

In America, the post-Cold War debate was dominated by calls, particularly from Congress, for the intelligence agencies to use some of the
resources previously aimed at the Soviet Bloc in order to collect economic
intelligence that would help America compete with the other 'geo-
economic' superpowers.[34]

William Webster, CIA Director at the time of the collapse of eastern
Europe – anxious to keep the agency's resources and show that it was
still relevant to the new world – formed an Office of Resources, Trade
and Technology to produce economic intelligence that would allow
America to keep track of 'what our competition is doing' and remain in
a position to 'confront it or confound it'.[35]

The FBI drew up a new National Security Threat List, adding 'issue-
oriented' guidelines to its traditional list of countries carrying out espionage in America. The adapted guidelines were intended to allow FBI
agents to act against countries, like Britain and other allies, which would
not necessarily appear on the previous list but which might still be
involved in the theft of 'industrial, proprietary, economic information
and technology, the loss of which would undermine the US strategic
position'. William Sessions, the then FBI Director, said the new issues

were being added to the list 'to preserve the economic vitality of this country and to ensure the continued competitiveness of the United States in the international market-place'.[36]

The new threat list led to a dramatic increase in the detection of foreign economic espionage against American companies, with the number of cases jumping from 10 to 500 in the space of nine months. Robert Gates told Congress that nearly twenty countries regularly spy on American companies. Although the resultant damage to US industry is hard to quantify, one estimate put it as high as $100 billion a year.[37]

Few people bothered to point out that America, like all those nasty so-called allies who were stealing US secrets, had a long history of economic espionage of its own. During the 1950s the CIA carried out economic espionage only against the Soviet Bloc and Communist China – responsibility for the rest of the world fell to the State Department's Office of Intelligence and Research. Co-ordinated economic reports were produced by the Economic Intelligence Committee, a subcommittee of the Intelligence Advisory Committee – an early American equivalent of Britain's JIC.

But in the mid-1960s the CIA expanded its economic intelligence effort worldwide, setting up an Office of Economic Research within the Directorate of Intelligence. The National Security Agency – America's equivalent of GCHQ – also carried out commercial intelligence. One former US Air Force signals specialist who worked at a US SIGINT base in Britain in the 1960s described how he had to watch printouts of commercial telexes, picking out those that referred to specific companies or commodities. 'I was provided with a list of about a hundred words I had to look out for. I had to keep a watch for commercial traffic, details of commodities that big companies were selling like iron and steel and gas. Some weeks the list of words to watch for contained dozens of names of big companies.'[38]

In the 1970s and '80s both the NSA and the CIA expanded their operations against foreign governments and companies. One of the CIA's eleven national intelligence officers was given specific responsibility for economic intelligence. The agency began to make more use of open-source economic databases, and NSA computers took over the role of searching international telexes for key companies, commodities and trans-actions.[39]

Under Admiral Stansfield Turner, CIA Director in the late 1970s and early 1980s, a secret programme was set up to brief selected companies on industrial and economic intelligence from countries with which they did business. The quid pro quo was that the companies were to allow the CIA to debrief their executives on return from foreign trips. Under a separate programme operated through the Commerce Department, American companies were provided with declassified economic intelligence.[40]

Howard Teicher, the National Security Council's Middle East Director in the mid-1980s, alleged that the NSA used its base at Menwith Hill in Yorkshire, England, to monitor the al-Yamamah deal under which Saudi Arabia agreed to buy £20 billion worth of British military equipment, including the Tornado fighter.[41]

In 1993 James Woolsey said economic intelligence was 'the hottest current topic in intelligence policy'. But the CIA would not 'engage in industrial espionage to help American firms get a leg up on the competition'.[42]

Nevertheless, there are areas, like the al-Yamamah contract, where corporate and national priorities merge. Contracts worth £20 billion will involve large numbers of jobs and sustain industries that are vital to the economy but which might otherwise go to the wall. This produces a grey area into which the CIA has certainly strayed on a number of occasions. French Prime Minister Éduard Balladur's decision in early 1995 to expel five CIA agents was not merely, as was widely believed, an attempt to divert attention from a domestic phone-tapping scandal that threatened his ambitions for the presidency, but the result of pent-up frustration over a year-long period during which American economic intelligence had succeeded in blocking at least two major French contracts, one of them remarkably similar to al-Yamamah.

Balladur had flown to Jeddah a year earlier to sign a £6 billion contract under which Saudi Arabia would buy French warships and missiles as well as replacing the Saudi state airline's fleet of American aircraft with the French-led Airbus. The deal was never signed. The NSA and the CIA had found out the details, and a high-pressure campaign by the US government, including a telephone call from President Clinton to King Fahd, had persuaded the Saudis to buy airliners from the American companies Boeing and McDonnell Douglas and to put the rest of the contract on hold. US intelligence could justify its intervention by pointing to the 'sweeteners' that are inevitable in such contracts and saying that it was only 'levelling out the playing field'. But the French were not impressed.

They were even less happy when a few months later the CIA discovered that bribes had been paid to Brazilian officials to gain a £1.4 billion contract for a satellite surveillance system that would measure the health of the Amazon rainforest and detect drug trafficking. Washington put pressure on the Brazilian government, and the American corporation Raytheon walked away with a contract that had been due to go to the French electronics company Thomson CSF.

Woolsey rubbed salt into the wounds by bragging, during a visit by President Clinton to the CIA headquarters at Langley, that the agency had already saved 'several billion dollars worth of US contracts'. 'We make it possible for the Secretary of State or Secretary of Commerce to go to his counterpart in that country, or to the ruler, and say: "Your telecommunications minister is on the take and the US doesn't favour business done this way,"' he said. 'Quite frequently this results in at least some part of the contract, sometimes all of it, being dealt with in a fairer fashion for American corporations. We are doing that sort of thing all over.'

But the French pointed out, convincingly, that in order to have alternative, acceptable contracts ready for the Saudi and Brazilian deals, the Americans must have given Boeing, McDonnell Douglas and Raytheon the secret financing terms of the original contracts. There was at least prima facie evidence that the CIA had been indulging in straightforward commercial espionage.

The DGSE took its revenge by revealing that America was quite as ready to indulge in such devious activities as anyone else. The French press was briefed that a CIA 'Mata Hari' had been caught red-handed offering cash bribes to an official who knew France's secret negotiating position in the GATT world-trade talks. One of the five CIA agents expelled by France was a woman working with non-diplomatic cover who chatted up an adviser to Balladur at a cocktail party. She became his mistress, and subsequently offered him money for details of the French negotiating position. American officials admitted that the French allegations were true. One CIA analyst said, 'We have been involved in GATT and every trade negotiation I know of. We take tasks from the US negotiators to find out the positions. We usually have someone who is right there. We tell our negotiators: "Here's what the other side left out or is holding back."'[43]

John Deutch, Woolsey's successor as CIA Director, has confirmed the agency's more aggressive stance on economic espionage, which was placed 'near the middle' of a list of intelligence priorities set out by President Clinton in early 1995. 'The collection and analysis of intelligence related to economic development can help level the economic playing field by identifying threats to US companies from foreign intelligence services and unfair trading practices,' he said.[44]

But the ethical and practical problems remain unresolved. There is a clear need to include economic factors in strategic intelligence reports. Indeed, one of the key criticisms of the CIA during the post-Cold War debate was that it had failed to pick up on the parlous state of the Soviet economy that led Mikhail Gorbachev, initially with the support of the

KGB, to introduce the *perestroika* that would lead eventually to the collapse of the Soviet system. There can be no arguments against the collection of this sort of economic intelligence.[45]

The real ethical and moral concerns centre around commercial espionage. In America, where the debate over such issues has been most pronounced, there has been widespread support for the FBI's new role in countering commercial espionage by foreign intelligence services against American companies.[46]

Moves by both Congress and the White House to force the intelligence agencies to take reciprocal action have met with less support. 'The agency's new-found enthusiasm for analysis of certain economic issues is disturbing,' said Jay Young, a former senior CIA analyst. The agency's obsession with 'economic competitiveness' analysis and the creation of the Office of Resources, Trade and Technology represented 'an almost desperate bid' by the CIA to demonstrate its relevance in the post-Cold War era, Young said.[47]

Nor is it clear to what use the agency can legally or ethically put such information once it has acquired it. It can scarcely give it to one US company without risking accusations of favouritism from rival firms. Many big multinational companies provide jobs in a number of countries. Should the CIA, for example, give commercial secrets to foreign multinationals that provide American jobs? Stansfield Turner has suggested making the information public, to avoid worrying about who the intelligence should be given to. But declassifying any information collected by the intelligence agencies can compromise the individual sources or methods used to collect it, and to do so on such a grand scale seems certain to cause damage.[48]

And what of the much vaunted special relationship in intelligence, the UKUSA Accord? How would that stand up to a situation where, as they did with the French projects, the CIA and the NSA scuppered a deal like al-Yamamah? The Cold War may have ended, but UKUSA's division of the world into intelligence fiefdoms has left both the American and British agencies dependent on each other – albeit the British more heavily so than the Americans. The relationship between the US and French intelligence agencies was always less close than the UKUSA arrangement, but it was useful to both sides. The highly public row over the CIA's clumsy attempts to uncover the French GATT negotiating position threatened to damage it almost beyond repair. If such a row were to erupt between America and Britain, how could UKUSA survive?

Commercial espionage is likely to create other headaches as well. The intervention of the intelligence agencies in the market verges on the sort of protectionism that America and Britain spend much of their time attacking. Uncompetitive businesses would gain while efficient companies suffered. The end effect of levelling the international playing field would be to create an uneven one at home.[49]

Economic intelligence will continue to be needed, as it has been continuously throughout the past century, for assessment of the strategic threat and for the shaping of government economic policy. But commercial intelligence – spying on foreign companies in order to help your own keep ahead of the game – is a waste of resources that would be better spent on other new roles such as countering international organized crime, fighting terrorism, or, what is perhaps the most dangerous of the new roles, preventing maverick states from acquiring the technology to produce nuclear, chemical or biological weapons.

# CHAPTER 18

# *Poisonous Snakes*

We have slain a large dragon, but we live now in a jungle filled
with a bewildering variety of poisonous snakes, and in many
ways the dragon was easier to keep track of.
    James Woolsey, former CIA Director, hearing on the
    Select Committee on Intelligence, 2 February 1993

When the Soviet Union began to break up, it caused immense
problems for those seeking to keep track of the more than 30,000
nuclear warheads scattered across its territory. Strategic missiles based in
Belarus, Ukraine and Kazakhstan left these newly independent states as
nuclear powers in their own right. There were suggestions that, with
financial problems widespread and crime soaring across the former Soviet
Union, scientists or servicemen with access to the weapons might be
prepared to sell them off to the highest bidder: to the Russian *Mafiya*,
to terrorists, or to rogue states like Iraq, Iran or North Korea.[1]

Three things happened to reduce this threat: in a major clandestine
operation, the Russian armed forces managed to remove all the tactical
nuclear weapons back to Russian soil; the US Congress passed the 1991
Threat Reduction Act – the so-called Nunn–Lugar programme – pumping more than a billion dollars into the former Soviet Union to help
dismantle nuclear weapons and ensure their security and safety; and
Belarus, Kazakhstan and Ukraine were persuaded to sign up to the
Nuclear Non-Proliferation Treaty and, in exchange for financial compensation, to return the strategic missiles based on their soil to Russia.

But the problems of security were immense. 'US government officials
and support contractors who have visited some of these facilities can
give you hair-raising accounts of the lack of adequate physical security,'
Thomas Cochran, senior scientist for the National Resources Defense
Council, told the US Senate. At some Russian sites, the first thing US
inspectors had to do was install locks.[2]

Intercontinental ballistic missiles were on static sites well protected
by minefields, electric fences and highly trained armed guards. Tactical
weapons, being mobile, were far less secure. Some were guarded only by
civilians and passive defences. The country's financial problems meant

that the real value of wages was plummeting – by 40 per cent in 1990, 30 per cent in 1991, and 60 per cent in 1992. Government workers were not being paid on time. Rations supplies were erratic. Theft from military bases reached epidemic proportions as servicemen sold off anything they could – including weapons – to make money. Scientists at Russia's leading military nuclear establishment complained directly to President Yeltsin over the government's repeated failure to pay them.

Low morale and lack of funds also led to poor levels of maintenance, and in some cases electricity supplies to nuclear reactors were cut off because the authorities had not paid the bills. This culminated in a series of incidents including a decision by the Moscow regional electricity authority to switch off power to the country's strategic nuclear-missile command centre and a near-meltdown of nuclear reactors on board four submarines when the Murmansk naval base was cut off for non-payment of bills. In the latter case, a catastrophe was averted only when armed servicemen forced the electricity company to restore power at gunpoint.[3]

The potential for trafficking in nuclear materials led Bernd Schmidbauer, the junior minister in charge of Germany's foreign intelligence service, the Bundesnachrichtendienst (BND), to call in June 1994 for a change in the law to allow his agency 'to study nuclear material or bring it back to Germany for investigation'. The German cabinet ruled this out.

But, from that point on, a number of cases of nuclear smuggling began to emerge. Most involved radioactive material that could not have been used to make nuclear weapons. In August 1994 Schmidbauer appeared to have been vindicated when two Spaniards and a Colombian were arrested at Munich airport with a briefcase containing 363 grams of 87.7 per cent enriched plutonium-239. But it swiftly emerged that the arrests were part of a sting, code-named Operation Hades, in which BND agents had approached the three men and offered them $276 million to procure weapons-grade nuclear material.[4]

Four months later police in Prague made a more worrying discovery. Three men, all of whom had connections with the nuclear industry, were arrested with 2.73 kilograms of 87 per cent enriched uranium-235 – the largest amount of stolen weapons-grade material seized, and approximately half of that required to make a crude nuclear device. But this turned out to be linked to a separate German sting, involving the Bavarian police. The two operations had shown that such material could be procured but not that there was a market for it other than among intelligence agencies eager to show their political masters that they still had a worthwhile role to play.[5]

A subsequent BND report concluded that of the 182 nuclear smuggling cases recorded between June 1994 and May 1995, none had produced any pointers to potential purchasers. 'There is no new information about demand,' the report said. 'The market still seems to have only a supply side, if one disregards the appearance of investigating authorities as potential buyers. For the most part, it is still valid to say that weapons-grade fissionable material or nuclear weapons have not yet appeared on the market and there is as yet no nuclear terrorism.'

What the Prague and Munich cases had shown, the report said, was that, if you wanted weapons-grade material, there was no shortage of well-placed Russian officials willing to supply it. 'There are credible intelligence reports that individual high-ranking persons from ministries, embassies, industrial concerns and research facilities are involved.'[6]

Perhaps the clearest indication that the market was at best limited was the apparent lack of interest from Russian organized crime. The potential for bribery, blackmail or straightforward theft among such officials is high, and if the *Mafiya* perceived the market to be a worthwhile risk it would no doubt take part in it.

The suggestion that terrorists might be interested in acquiring a nuclear bomb is highly questionable. There are, of course, other uses to which they might put radioactive material – the poisoning of water supplies to a major city for example – but the production of a nuclear weapon requires a level of technology and the ability to hide extensive scientific facilities to which terrorists would not normally have access. Although there is a possibility that terrorists might be in the market for a pre-built nuclear weapon – millenarian groups looking to hasten the Apocalypse, for example – the more likely purchasers for weapons-grade material would be maverick states such as Iran, Iraq or North Korea.[7]

'A few countries whose interests are inimical to the US are attempting to acquire nuclear weapons – Iran and Iraq being two of our greatest concerns,' David Osias, CIA National Intelligence Officer for Strategic Programs, told the Senate. 'Knowledge of weapon designs is sufficiently widespread that the former weapon secrecy no longer offers adequate protection. Today, there is basically only one obstacle to a committed nation: acquisition of fissile material.'[8]

The most likely starting-point for any nuclear war appears to be in one of three main flashpoints: the Middle East, where both Iran and Iraq are working on nuclear weapons programmes which could be targeted either at each other or at Israel, itself a nuclear power; the Korean peninsula, where concerns over Pyongyang's nuclear capabilities have led to protracted negotiations with Washington; and the Indian subcontinent, where there has been a series of confrontations between India and Pakistan over the border area of Kashmir.

In early 1990, amid an Indian crackdown on Kashmiri separatists, the Research and Analysis Wing, India's equivalent of MI6, reported that Pakistan was reinforcing its troops along the border and appeared to be preparing for war. The RAW reports were inaccurate – allegedly deliberately so, in order to strengthen the resolve of the Indian government. If that was the case, it worked with a vengeance. Indian Prime Minister Vishwanath Pratap Singh warned the country to be ready for war. 'While nuclear stockpiles are being destroyed in the world, Pakistan is close to producing its own nuclear weapons and means for their delivery,' he said. 'Confronted by a nuclear challenge, we have no choice but to accept and worthily rebuff it. Indian scientists are able to do it.'

As both sides built up their troops along the border, Western intelligence began reporting increasing signs that Delhi and Islamabad were preparing for all-out war. Robert Gates, then US Deputy National Security Adviser, said the two sides appeared to be 'bumbling and fumbling' towards a conflict:

> We began receiving intelligence that the Indians and the Pakistanis were both engaged in a cycle of escalating military tensions and the analysts and our intelligence community became persuaded that there was a growing chance of an accidental war, of a miscalculation that would lead to first a conventional war and then, if such a war started, a very high likelihood that it would at some point go nuclear. The analogy used most often in the White House situation room was that these two countries reminded people of Europe in the months before World War I broke out. Where nobody really wanted a war but it happened anyway.

At that point an American spy satellite picked out a heavily guarded convoy leaving the Pakistani nuclear research facility at Kahuta and heading for an air-force base together with what appeared to be the equipment used to fit nuclear bombs to American-made F-16 fighter-bombers.

Gates was sent to Islamabad and Delhi to try to prevent the situation escalating into full-scale nuclear war. Brent Scowcroft, President Bush's National Security Adviser, said:

> We had a fairly accurate assessment of where India was and where Pakistan was in the nuclear business and fairly good intelligence about what was going on in Kashmir, which is the reason we were worried and which led us to send Gates to say: 'Come on both of you. Come off it.' If Kashmir got out of hand, then the preoccupation, certainly on the Indian side, would be to destroy the Pakistan facilities. Each

one, in case of a conflict, would go after the nuclear facilities of the other.

Gates briefed both sides on the 'extraordinarily detailed' US intelligence on their troop movements and nuclear activities – much of it from satellites, but also from human sources. He also suggested a number of confidence-building measures to try to cool things down. 'Among other things, we offered to provide the kind of information we have provided to the Egyptians and the Israelis since 1973 over the Sinai,' Gates said. 'That is provide exactly the same information to both sides on one another's military moves in an effort to prevent a miscalculation.' Following the Gates mission, India and Pakistan finally ratified a 1988 agreement that neither side would attack the other's nuclear facilities. In July 1996 an official at the Pakistani High Commission in London was deported after an investigation by the counter-proliferation units of both MI5 and GCHQ found that since 1991 he had run a network of Pakistani students studying nuclear technology at British universities to acquire expertise useful to Islamabad's nuclear weapons programme.[9]

Despite the fears over the possible use of nuclear weapons by rogue states or terrorists, chemical and biological proliferation is probably a more likely threat. North Korea, Iran, Iraq and Libya all have active chemical and biological weapons programmes, and, while the traditional terrorist methods are the gun and the bomb, there have been signs of a growing willingness among some modern groups to resort to more unconventional means.[10]

The use of Sarin nerve gas by the Japanese Aum Shinru Kyo sect to attack commuters on the Tokyo underground in March 1995 and the uncovering of similar plans by Fundamentalist Christian/White Supremacist groups in the United States have forced the security authorities to reappraise their view of the main terrorist threats.

'The clarity which the Cold War brought has gone,' said Stella Rimington, the former MI5 Director-General:

We must now look through a much more complex prism, which blurs the focus and the depth of the security picture.

As is all too evident, the collapse of centralized controls in parts of the former Soviet Union as well as in the Balkans has provoked regional instability. From that may come new sources of terrorism and heightened risks from the spread of chemical, nuclear and biological weapons. New types and sources of terrorist violence have emerged. They work in relatively unstructured groups, make no claim for their attacks, and appear to have as their aim the creation of maximum alarm and insecurity.[11]

The new terrorist threat is far less easy to quantify than the relatively straightforward behaviour of, for instance, the Provisional IRA or the Palestinian hijackers of the 1970s. While few in the West agreed with their violent methods, the use of 'spectaculars' in order to draw attention to their aspirations was easy to understand and even to identify with. These terrorists were unhappy with specific aspects of the society in which they lived and were using violence to force the changes they required. The aim was not to kill *per se*, but to extract the maximum publicity, to publicize the cause, and to wear down resistance to their demands. Excessive violence was regarded as counter-productive. When it occurred – often because the cellular structure adopted by such groups had led to a temporary loss of control over maverick individuals – it tended to alienate their supporters and even many within the groups themselves.

But religious terrorists do not operate under the same set of assumptions. They do not see themselves as part of society, and they have no regard for anyone other than members of their own sect. Anyone who is not a believer is seen as expendable, making mass indiscriminate violence not only morally acceptable but in fact compulsory – a divine duty incumbent on any true believer. Since the early 1980s, when they first came to prominence, Islamic fundamentalist groups have committed only 8 per cent of all terrorist acts, yet they have been responsible for nearly 30 per cent of all those killed.[12] A further problem for the security and intelligence services is that the lack of any identification with society makes religious terrorism far less easy to understand and predict.

The 1994 hijacking by Algerian fundamentalists of an Air France A300 Airbus provided a good example of both these phenomena. The initial assumption was that this was an attempt by the terrorists to draw attention to the civil war taking place in their homeland, much in the manner of the spate of Palestinian hijackings of the late 1960s and early 1970s, the main value coming from the worldwide publicity achieved during long-drawn-out negotiations for the release of the hostages. In fact the terrorists planned to blow the aircraft up over the centre of Paris, killing as many people as possible, and would have done so had the French authorities not discovered the plan and carried out a successful assault on the aircraft as it stood on the ground at Marseilles airport.

But as the Tokyo attacks and the bombings of a government building in Oklahoma and the Atlanta Olympics showed, religious terrorism is not the sole prerogative of Middle Eastern groups: the same characteristics and attitudes are displayed by radical members of the Aum Shinru Kyo and the fringes of the American White Supremacists. The late 1980s and early 1990s saw a large rise in such groups across America.

More than 50,000 Americans are thought to belong to various branches of the Christian White Supremacist movement, which is based on a shared belief that Anglo-Saxons are the chosen race and America is the promised land. Non-whites are regarded as 'children of Satan'. The Jews are impostors who control the banks, the media and the government, which is derided as ZOG: the Zionist Occupation Government. This usefully allows any action taken by the authorities against the movement, any bad publicity it attracts, and even the mortgage foreclosures suffered by many of its members in the American Mid-West to be depicted as part of a widespread Jewish conspiracy.

One self-styled terrorist group, calling itself the Confederate Hammer Skins, decided in 1987 to place cyanide crystals in the air-conditioning unit of a Dallas synagogue, hoping to kill not only the worshippers but also a group of children in the synagogue crèche. A Los Angeles group calling itself the Fourth Reich Skinheads was forced to postpone a series of bombings of Jewish targets, culminating in a machine-gun and hand-grenade attack on a synagogue, only when the parents of the getaway driver refused him permission to borrow the family car.

It took the Oklahoma bombing in April 1995, when 169 people were killed by a fertilizer bomb allegedly put together by ultra-right amateurs using easily acquired materials, to bring home the realization that the problem could not just be laughed off. Those concerned might be amateurs compared to the likes of the IRA, the Red Army Faction or the Palestinians, but they had the potential to be far more dangerous.[13]

As the year 2000 approaches, a combination of the proliferation of nuclear, biological and chemical weapons, resulting from the break-up of the Soviet Union, and the possibility that religious terrorists might attempt to seek the redemption associated with the new millenium by creating their own apocalypse has led to more attention being given to millenarian groups. The British Cabinet Civil Contingency Unit first carried out a full-scale rehearsal of the steps to be taken in the event of a nuclear terrorist attack, with an exercise involving the police, the SAS and the civilian emergency services, in spring 1994.

The Security Service and the Special Branch have stepped up their monitoring of so-called 'Doomsday cults'. The lack of a gun culture in Britain is thought to limit the likelihood of anything as widespread as the American Christian militia, but senior anti-terrorist officers have pointed to the heavy British presence in the Branch Davidian movement involved in the 1993 Waco siege and the unpredictability of such sects as shown by the Tokyo chemical attacks.[14]

For the intelligence services, countering terrorism has always presented a major problem. 'Politically motivated violence meant that Western security services needed a new approach,' said Stella Rimington:

The tried and tested techniques used in the often long-term process of catching spies and monitoring Soviet intelligence officers had to be adapted to these very different problems.

Classic long-term intelligence investigations into terrorist groups, their activities and methods were essential. But there were – and still are – real difficulties in trying to penetrate small and secretive cells of terrorists, many of whom are based far away in inaccessible and sometimes hostile territory, not infrequently under the wing of regimes whose purposes they also serve. Even when knowledge of an impending attack can be obtained, the intelligence is rarely precise enough for us to be certain that it can be prevented.[15]

The problems of penetrating terrorist groups were most amply illustrated by the Brian Nelson case. Nelson, a former member of the Black Watch, was an Army agent inside the Ulster Defence Association, the largest of the Protestant paramilitary groups in Northern Ireland. As the UDA's senior intelligence officer, he was given the key role of identifying Catholic targets. This allowed him to provide the security forces with superb intelligence from within the heart of the UDA. But it also meant that the Army's agent was involved in conspiracy to murder.

As a result of a 1990 inquiry into how loyalist terrorists had acquired British intelligence reports, Nelson was arrested and charged with two counts of murder and five of conspiracy to murder. The murder charges were dropped at the last minute amid suggestions of a deal to ensure that Nelson pleaded guilty, preventing details of the affair from coming out. Belfast Crown Court nevertheless heard how he had repeatedly given the security forces warning of planned terrorist attacks, among them the attempted assassination of Gerry Adams. While that attack had been thwarted as a direct result of Nelson's information, not all attacks had – his handlers arguing that to do so would have risked compromising him.

One former intelligence officer expressed dismay at the willingness of the authorities to prosecute Nelson for doing his job. Long-term penetration agents had no choice but to act like other members of the organization they were infiltrating, he argued:

Any lack of enthusiasm would be an instant pointer for men already alert for infiltration. The agent must, if discovery is to be avoided, join enthusiastically in the activities of the organization, even if they are seriously criminal. What would have happened if Nelson had said: 'Sorry, I can't carry that machine-gun, it is illegal'? Subversive organizations will always be on the look-out for agents. In Ireland, the consequences of discovery are final and very painful.

Despite those arguments, the Nelson case led to a ban on the use of informers within the Northern Irish terrorist groups that caused immense problems for the security services. While signals intelligence can often have a role in building up a picture of terrorist groups, and photographic reconnaissance can pick up individual operations and arms caches, the only really effective method of keeping track of the terrorist group as a whole is human intelligence. Penetration of the organization itself ensures that the security services can keep ahead of the game rather than constantly being forced on to the back foot by terrorist attacks.[16]

The responses of Western governments to terrorism has varied widely. The British response was typified by the uncompromising public stance of Margaret Thatcher – 'We do not negotiate with terrorists' – and her support for the similarly tough stance taken by the Reagan government against countries seen as aiding terrorism, as in the 1986 attack on Libya. The British Prime Minister made much of the contrast between Britain's resolute stance and the more pragmatic policies of some of its 'woolly-minded' European allies.

But it is questionable whether the 'no compromise' talk was useful for anything other than electoral posturing. The tough British stance came under particular fire during the Beirut hostages crisis, when an apparently more pragmatic approach by other countries was effective in gaining the release of their citizens, in direct contrast to the continued incarceration of Brian Keenan, John McCarthy and Terry Waite. The British government's lack of pragmatism simply cut down the number of options open to those tasked with countering terrorism, while at the same time making their actions more predictable to the terrorists.

Nor did the attack on Libya provide any evidence that such actions are an effective method of countering terrorism. Colonel Gaddafi's response was to order a number of attempted retaliatory attacks in the United States itself and to provide the IRA with larger quantities of more sophisticated weaponry. When Libya finally began to cut back on its support for terrorism, it was as a result of a more flexible stance which, instead of attacking other countries for their 'woolly-minded' approach, sought to reach a level of consensus with them on how the problem might be tackled, realizing that the splits among the international community over how to deal with terrorism only served the interests of the terrorists themselves.

The turning-point appears to have been reached following the 1990 Iraqi invasion of Kuwait, when fears of a terrorist campaign to create disunity within the anti-Saddam alliance led to a strongly co-ordinated international counter-terrorist operation. This co-operation led to the creation of a 'special information exchange' between the world's security services and intelligence agencies which drastically reduced the terrorist threat worldwide.[17]

'The success that there has been against this international or transnational terrorism has only been achieved through co-ordinated and collective effort,' said Stella Rimington:

> This involves security and intelligence agencies worldwide; police forces, and government departments working to ministers who are responsible for setting national security policies and also for the law which governs all our activities.
>
> During the Gulf War, it was international co-operation which prevented the Iraqi regime from carrying out acts of terrorism designed to undermine the allies. This multi-faceted co-operation ranged from the exchange of information between security agencies, to the co-ordination of policies between governments.
>
> We in this country have particular cause to know the value and importance of such international co-operation: it has been vital to the UK in countering terrorism arising from the troubles in Northern Ireland. We have not always been successful. But often we have, and those successes – rarely visible to the general public – can be put down to the enormous support and co-operation freely given by more than 100 security, intelligence and police services with whom we are in contact around the world. In many cases, deeper or more extensive co-operation would be hard to envisage.[18]

That co-operation is now being utilized in the fight against organized crime as part of the national crime squad announced in October 1995, with NCIS taking the lead role, supported by the regional crime squads. This announcement was in fact not much more than official confirmation of a system that had been in place for some time. But, although MI5 is operating solely under direction from NCIS, a number of police officers remain unhappy about the use of the Security Service, citing its lack of both accountability and experience in gathering evidence. Yet, paradoxically, the courts may bring a degree of accountability to the service that Parliament has so far failed to deliver.

Under Britain's disclosure rules, which allow the defence access to any evidence collected during an investigation that might help its case, MI5's intelligence operations are likely to be examined in great detail in open court, with any irregularities resulting in the case being thrown out by the trial judge.[19]

MI5 has already experienced such problems, but ventures into organized crime will make them an everyday occurrence. Nor in a simple drugs case is the service likely to receive the special treatment its officers have been used to in terrorism cases: the ability to testify anonymously from behind screens, and judges sympathetic to the use of such weapons as public-interest immunity certificates to protect sources and intelligence methods.

The rules of disclosure have been changed to ensure that defence lawyers cannot 'ambush' the prosecution in mid-trial by asking for sensitive details like intelligence sources or methods, forcing it into a position where it has either to produce details of secret sources of intelligence or to drop the case. But this will not stop the defence from demanding the information beforehand. Nor is it likely that any effective way of getting around this difficulty can be found that will not seriously jeopardize the possibility of a fair trial.[20]

The problem is unlikely to go away. The fact that organized crime poses a substantial threat to Britain's security means that not just MI5 but the foreign intelligence agencies, MI6 and GCHQ, have been tasked with fighting it. They will be just as reluctant as MI5, if not more, to allow their sources to be disclosed as evidence.[21]

Although organized crime, economic intelligence, proliferation and terrorism have grabbed the headlines as the new threats, the Gulf War, the volatile situation in the former Soviet Union and the desirability at least to contain if not to prevent regional conflicts such as in Bosnia, Chechnya and Kashmir have all highlighted the fact that the traditional requirements for political and defence intelligence tasks cannot be ignored.

While MI6, GCHQ and the Defence Intelligence Staff have all had long experience in such tasks, disseminating the material collected remains a problem. In the case of political intelligence, the main difficulty appears to be getting politicians to accept the validity of the information that is being placed on their desks. The appalling lack of regard for intelligence displayed by a number of politicians during the Scott Inquiry clearly has to be addressed.[22]

Defence intelligence presents an entirely different dissemination problem: how to get the information collected by strategic assets such as satellites and static SIGINT stations far from the battle area to commanders in time for it to be of any use. The problems suffered in the Falklands, where signals and imagery intelligence were not reaching commanders in 'real time', were repeated in the Gulf War. Since similar difficulties occurred in getting the Ultra product to field commanders during the Second World War, it might reasonably be expected that, fifty years on, they would have been solved.

Following criticism by General Schwarzkopf of the way the American intelligence system functioned during the Gulf War, John Deutch, the

CIA Director, announced a five-year study to find a better method of disseminating intelligence collected by strategic assets for use by tactical commanders. 'Battlefield awareness requires a collector-to-user link that is immediate, within seconds,' he said. 'There is a lot of work that has to be done to make that happen.'

The difficulties encountered in the Gulf War also caused much debate in Britain, leading the Defence Intelligence Staff to introduce a new system of disseminating intelligence to the battlefield. But in a fast-flowing situation like the land war in southern Iraq the time-gap between collection and dissemination, caused largely by the analysis process, is always too long for the commander in the field.[23]

'We are now looking much harder at how to support military operations,' a senior defence intelligence official said:

> I am not going to pretend we have always got it right. In the past it is arguable that we made too big a separation between strategic up here, tactical on the battlefield, and we have put a lot of effort into working out how best the defence intelligence organization in its various facets can support commanders on the battlefield.
>
> The old distinction between strategic and tactical is largely redundant. In recent years we have had forces deployed in Bosnia, Rwanda, Angola, and each one of those produces its own unique set of requirements. There is a very important educational process on both sides. We have to understand the operational process, and the operators have to understand us better, and that is what we have spent a great deal of time and effort on.
>
> One of the other important things to do is to make sure that intelligence is usable. You can produce the best intelligence in the world, but if it's so damn secret you cannot give it to anyone there is no point in having it. So another thing we are looking at – as are our friends – is how can we actually get intelligence into the field in a form in which it can be used. Not simple – particularly when that intelligence needs to be timely.[24]

The links with 'the Friends' have also been the subject of some debate following the demise of the Warsaw Pact, with suggestions that the UKUSA Accord will be replaced by new agreements with Britain's European allies. But both of Britain's foreign intelligence collection agencies – MI6 and GCHQ – have made it clear that membership of the European Union will not affect the exchange arrangements with their American counterparts.

'In modern times, relations with the French and German services have always been good, and I don't think they have been much affected by our membership of the EU,' a senior intelligence officer said. 'For us, the Americans are still the most important partner, just because their capacity is so much greater than for example the Germans' capacity. If you said, "Let's substitute the relationship with the Germans for the Americans," you would lose quite a lot. The Americans are just better at it.'

The need for a continuing close intelligence relationship with the USA was stressed by Michael Portillo, the British Defence Secretary:

> Resources will be limited and intelligence will be expensive. This means that the assets can only be developed collaboratively with allies. That underlines the importance of keeping the United States engaged with her allies; and, as intelligence will be the critical factor in predicting a threat, fighting it, and winning, British policy will need to remain focused on maintaining a particularly close relationship with the United States.[25]

The other major problems for the intelligence and security services arising out of the end of the Cold War are coping with the rationalization demanded by politicians anxious for their 'peace dividend' and handling moves towards more openness and parliamentary oversight.

The members of the parliamentary Intelligence and Security Committee, set up under the 1994 Intelligence Services Act, cannot be serving ministers, but it has been placed under the chairmanship of Tom King, who as a former Defence Secretary and Northern Ireland Minister will already have had a fair degree of experience in dealing with the intelligence community. Although Mr King is no doubt seen within Whitehall as 'a safe pair of hands', it is far too early to dismiss the committee as a 'toothless' sop to those calling for more openness. In his utterances thus far, King seems well aware of the potential pitfalls. 'This committee can either be a whitewash or it can be extremely effective in discharging a remit that I think the nation expects of us,' he said. 'Let's wait and see.'

In its first annual report, the committee highlighted the dangers posed by the fact that MI5 is self-tasking, and criticized the agencies for 'serious lapses' in not keeping ministers well enough informed of their activities. It also examined whether the resources available were being used in a cost-effective way, and warned agency heads that they might have to be prepared to make compulsory redundancies.[26]

Few would question the need for financial prudence. But, while the Warsaw Pact has gone, there are arguably far more threats that now need to be monitored or countered. Both the agencies and their political masters should be wary of the traps that befell MI5 and MI6 in the wake of the First World War, when the axing of experienced staff led to a marked decline in the quality of intelligence.

In America, where the debate over the future of intelligence has been conducted far more publicly, and with the aid of a series of inquiries, there are clear signs that those in charge realize the danger. 'Because the Cold War is over, some say that we should and can step back from the world and that we don't need intelligence as much as we used to,' President Clinton told CIA staff worried over their futures. 'I think these views are profoundly wrong. I believe making deep cuts in intelligence during peacetime is comparable to cancelling your health insurance when you are feeling fine.'[27]

Despite the British government's reticence to discuss intelligence, it is clear that at least some within government appreciate that argument. 'Since conflict can arise anywhere and for any number of reasons, intelligence will be a critical tool of defence,' said Michael Portillo. 'We shall need to predict crises, and if the unexpected happens we will need to know speedily who did what. Weapon technology will transfer quickly even to poor countries, but the intelligence advantage is likely to remain with developed countries for a long time yet. We need to make the most of it.'[28]

There is no doubt that the intelligence agencies have a continuing role to play in the new world. The glib calls for radical pruning, or even disbandment, as some kind of peace dividend, are at best misguided, at worst highly damaging. Today's threats are more numerous, just as dangerous and far less easy to recognize than in the past, and without good intelligence those charged with our defence will not be properly equipped to make the right decisions.

But that is not to say that everything can remain as it is. The Scott Inquiry provided clear evidence that the intelligence services need to improve their reputation, even at the highest levels of government. Erskine May's old adage that 'nothing is more revolting to the Englishman than espionage' remains substantially true.

The use of the intelligence services in the fight against organized crime will bring them far more into the public eye than the new parliamentary oversight committee. It will be how they perform in the courts, where their activities will be probed by defence lawyers looking for any hint that something is not right, that will determine their future reputation, providing some with a useful opportunity to put dubious pasts behind them, but with the risk that any error of judgement will merely reinforce public distrust.

There is a heavy onus upon them to ensure that the inevitably more open nature of their new roles improves rather than tarnishes their reputations. The latter would almost certainly lead to renewed calls for a reduction in their activities that neither they nor the country can afford.

# References

## Chapter 1

1. 'Senate Freezes Cost of Fairfax Spy Satellite Facility', *Washington Post*, 13 August 1994
2. *Central Intelligence Machinery* (HMSO, London, 1993)
3. *MI5: The Security Service*, 2nd edn (HMSO, London, 1996); 'What a Waste of Money', *New Statesman*, 12 April 1996. The Single Intelligence Vote is negotiated annually in a similar way to the budget of any other government department. GCHQ, MI6 and MI5 make their own expenditure forecasts which are then scrutinized by the Treasury and by the Permanent Secretaries' Committee on the Intelligence Services, comprising the permanent under-secretaries at the Home Office, the Foreign and Commonwealth Office, the Ministry of Defence and the Treasury. But the vote does not include the cost of criminal intelligence, which comes separately under the Home Office budget, nor that of military intelligence, which includes a large part of GCHQ's expensive technical costs together with those of imagery intelligence
4. Andy McNab, *Bravo Two Zero* (Corgi, London, 1994)
5. Press conference held at Foreign Office, 24 November 1993
6. Lord Denning, *Report into the Profumo Affair* (Cmnd 2152, HMSO, London, 1963)
7. Nicholas Eftimiades, *Chinese Intelligence Operations* (Frank Cass, London, 1994)
8. Denning, op. cit.
9. Glenn P. Hastedt (ed.), *Controlling Intelligence* (Frank Cass, London 1991)
10. Robert G. Angevine, 'Gentlemen Do Not Read Each Other's Mail: American Intelligence in the Interwar Era', *Intelligence and National Security*, Vol. 7, No. 2 (April 1992)
11. 'When They Took Bond's Licence Away', *The Times*, 24 August 1994
12. *Intelligence Services Act* (HMSO, London, 1994)
13. *Central Intelligence Machinery*; Laurence Lustgarten and Ian Leigh, *In From the Cold: National Security and Parliamentary Democracy* (OUP, Oxford, 1994)
14. Lustgarten and Leigh, op. cit.; Bernard Porter, *Plots and Paranoia: A History of Political Espionage in Britain 1790–1988* (Unwin Hyman, London, 1989)
15. Porter, op. cit.
16. Peter Wright, *Spycatcher: The Candid Autobiography of a Senior Intelligence Officer* (Viking, New York, 1987)
17. 'CND/Miners "Under MI5 Monitoring"', *Guardian*, 21 February 1985; The Right Honourable Sir Richard Scott, *Report of the Inquiry into the Export of Defence Equipment and Dual-Use Goods to Iraq and Related Prosecutions* (HMSO, London, 1996)
18. Walter Lacquer, *A World of Secrets: The Uses and Limits of Intelligence* (Basic, New York, 1985)

19. See Sir Harry Hinsley's spirited and highly convincing defence of Ultra from the attacks of the revisionist historians in F. H. Hinsley and Alan Stripp [eds.], *Codebreakers: The Inside Story of Bletchley Park* (OUP, Oxford, 1993)

## Chapter 2

1. 'CIA Plans to Close 15 Stations in Africa Pullback; Budget Cuts Cited, but Advocates of Human Intelligence Collection Think it's a Mistake', *Washington Post*, 23 June 1994
2. 'White House Labors to Redefine Role of Intelligence Community', *Washington Post*, 13 June 1994
3. Admiral Stansfield Turner, 'Intelligence for a New World Order', *Foreign Affairs*, Vol. 70, No. 4 (Fall 1991)
4. 'The Gulf Crisis: US Refrained From Warning Off Saddam', *Guardian*, 12 September 1990
5. Turner, op. cit.; 'For Smarter Intelligence: Separate Spies from Analysts', *Washington Post*, 24 July 1994
6. 'Congress Moving To Remap CIA's Direction', *Washington Post*, 2 July 1994
7. Allan E. Goodman and Bruce D. Berkowitz, 'Intelligence Without the Cold War', *Intelligence and National Security*, Vol. 9, No. 2 (April 1994)
8. Lord Franks, *Falkland Islands Review* (Cmnd 8787, HMSO, London, 1983)
9. 'The Ames Case: A Symptom of Crisis', *Washington Post*, 15 July 1994; *Intelligence Services Act 1994* (HMSO, London, 1994); *Interim Report of the Intelligence and Security Committee* (Cmnd 2873, HMSO, London, 1995); 'Security MPs In "Ring of Secrecy": Whitehall "Cell" For New Committee on Intelligence Service', *Guardian*, 16 January 1994; 'Tories Will Dominate "Toothless" Security Services Watchdogs', *Guardian*, 15 December 1994; 'Policy and Politics: MPs Unhappy at "Limited" Oversight of Spy Services', *Guardian*, 23 February 1994
10. Goodman and Berkowitz, op. cit.
11. 'US Intelligence Was Faulty on Iraq', *Washington Post*, 9 May 1992
12. *Intelligence Services Act, 1994*
13. 'US Demands for Economic Intelligence up sharply, Gates Says', *Washington Post*, 14 April 1992
14. 'Woolsey: Why the CIA is Still in Need of Human Touch', *Jane's Defence Weekly*, 6 August 1994
15. Laurence Lustgarten and Ian Leigh, *In From the Cold: National Security and Parliamentary Democracy* (OUP, Oxford, 1994)
16. Information made available to the author in confidence
17. Lustgarten and Leigh, op. cit.
18. *Washington Post*, 15 July 1994
19. Michael F. Hopkins, 'The Washington Embassy: The Role of an Institution in Anglo-American Relations, 1940–45' in Richard J. Aldrich and Michael F. Hopkins (eds.), *Intelligence, Defence and Diplomacy, British Policy in the Post-War World* (Frank Cass, London, 1994); James Bamford, *The Puzzle Palace* (Sidgwick & Jackson, London, 1982)
20. PRO CAB81/98; HW1/2; Thomas F. Troy, *Donovan and The CIA: A History of the Establishment of the CIA* (Alethia Books, Frederick, MD, 1981); Kathryn Brown, 'Intelligence and the Decision to Collect It: Churchill's Wartime Diplomatic Signals Intelligence', *Intelligence and National Security*, Vol. 10, No. 3 (July 1995); A. G. Denniston, 'The Government Code & Cipher School

Between The Wars', *Intelligence and National Security*, Vol. 1, No. 1 (January 1986)

21. Bamford, op. cit.
22. Donald Cameron Watt, Review of Bradley F. Smith, *The Ultra-Magic Deals and the Most Special Relationship 1940–1946* (Airline Press, Shrewsbury, 1993), *Intelligence and National Security*, Vol. 9, No. 1 (January 1994)
23. F. H. Hinsley and Alan Stripp [eds.], *Codebreakers: The Inside Story of Bletchley Park* (OUP, Oxford, 1993); Smith, op. cit.; Christopher Andrew, 'The Making of the Anglo-American SIGINT Alliance', in Hayden B. Peake and Samuel Halpern (eds.), *In the Name of Intelligence: Essays in Honor of Walter Pforzheim* (NIBC Press, Washington DC, 1994)
24. PRO CAB81/92; CAB81/93
25. PRO CAB81/92; CAB81/93
26. PRO CAB81/93; Smith, op. cit.; Richard J. Aldrich, 'Secret Intelligence for a Post-War World: Reshaping the British Intelligence Community, 1944–51', in Richard J. Aldrich (ed.), *British Intelligence. Strategy and the Cold War 1945–51* (Routledge, London, 1992); R. V. Jones, *Reflections on Intelligence* (Mandarin, London, 1990); Andrew, op. cit. The presidential edict was in response to a 'Top Secret' memorandum sent that same day by Henry Stimson (by then Secretary of War and an enthusiastic convert to reading the mail of other gentlemen), James Forrestal (Navy Secretary) and Dean Acheson (then acting Secretary of State), in which they said, 'In view of the disturbed conditions of the world and the necessity of keeping informed of technical developments and possible hostile intentions of foreign nations . . . it is recommended that you authorize continuation of collaboration between the United States and the United Kingdom in the field of communications intelligence.' It is to be found in the Harry S. Truman Library, Independence, Missouri, in Naval Aide files, Box 10, File 1
27. PRO CAB81/92; CAB81/93; CAB81/94; Jeffrey T. Richelson and Desmond Ball, *The Ties that Bind*, 2nd edn (Unwin Hyman, Boston, 1990); Andrew, op. cit. The date of the agreement is often given as 1947, but Dr Louis Tordella, a former NSA Deputy Director who was present at the final signing of the full text, says it did not take place until 1948. JIC proposals for post-war intelligence exchange with South Africa suggested that Pretoria provide information on South Africa itself, Portuguese East and West Africa, the Belgian Congo, Southern and Northern Rhodesia, Nyasaland and Madagascar
28. Memorandum from Directorate of Intelligence and Research for Dean Rusk, 'What Now for Britain? Wilson's Visit and Britain's Future', REU-11, 7 February 1968, Papers of Philip M. Kaiser, Box 8, Harry S. Truman Library, Independence, Missouri. See Richard J. Aldrich, ' "The Value of Residual Empire": Anglo-American Intelligence Co-operation in Asia after 1945', in Aldrich and Hopkins, op. cit.
29. Aldrich, 'Secret Intelligence for a Post-War World'
30. PRO CAB56/2; Edward Thomas, 'The Evolution of the JIC System up to and during World War II', in Christopher Andrew and Jeremy Noakes, *Intelligence and International Relations 1990–1945* (University of Exeter, 1987)
31. F. H. Hinsley et al., *British Intelligence in the Second World War Vol. 1* (HMSO, London, 1979)
32. PRO CAB84/2; CAB79/8
33. PRO CAB81/88; CAB81/132; Thomas, op. cit.
34. PRO CAB81/93; CAB81/94; CAB81/130; CAB81/131; Franks, op. cit.; Michael Herman, 'Assessment Machinery: British and American Models', *Intelligence and National Security*, Vol. 10, No. 4 (October 1995)
    Although the Franks report recommended that the JIC Chairman be made

a full-time post – something that had long been demanded by senior British intelligence officials – the post has now reverted to a part-time position

35. *Central Intelligence Machinery* (HMSO, London, 1993)
36. *New Spies for Old*, BBC Radio 4, 20 March 1995; *Central Intelligence Machinery*; The Right Honourable Sir Richard Scott, *Report of the Inquiry into the Export of Defence Equipment and Dual-Use Goods to Iraq and Related Prosecutions* (HMSO, London, 1996); *New Spies for Old*, BBC Radio 4, 4 April 1995; Richard Norton-Taylor with Mark Lloyd, *Truth is a Difficult Concept: Inside the Scott Inquiry* (Fourth Estate, London, 1995); Herman, op. cit.; 'Picking the Lock of Britain's Security', *Guardian*, 6 April 1988
37. *Central Intelligence Machinery*; *New Spies for Old*; *Guardian*, 6 April 1988
38. Ibid.; 'Woman Spy Chief to be Major's Fixer', *Sunday Telegraph*, 23 January 1994
39. Thomas, op. cit.
40. 'Inside Story: Truth and the Big Guns', *Guardian*, 18 February 1995
41. Walter Lacquer, *A World of Secrets, The Uses and Limits of Intelligence* (Basic, New York, 1985)
42. John A. Gentry, *Lost Promise: How CIA Analysis Misserves the Nation, an Intelligence Assessment* (University Press of America, Lanham, Maryland, 1993); 'US CIA Chief Nominee Gates Defends himself against Allegations of Intelligence-Tampering', Associated Press, 3 October 1991; 'CIA Chief Upset over "Politicization" Seen within Agency, *New York Times*, 28 March 1992
43. Numbers 13–14

## Chapter 3

1. Bernard Porter, *Plots and Paranoia: A History of Political Espionage in Britain 1790–1988* (Unwin Hyman, London, 1989); Erskine May, *Constitutional History of England Vol. II* (Longmans, London, 1863)
2. Patrick Bishop and Eamonn Mallie, *The Provisional IRA* (William Heinemann, London, 1987); Porter, op. cit.; Christopher Andrew, *Secret Service: The Making of the British Intelligence Community* (William Heinemann, London, 1985); J. A. Cole, *Prince of Spies: Henri le Caron* (Faber, London, 1984); Henri le Caron, *Twenty-Five Years in the Secret Service* (William Heinemann, London, 1892)
3. Porter, op. cit.
4. Ibid.
5. PRO HD3/91
6. Col. G. A. Furse, *Information in War* (W. Clowes & Sons, London, 1895)
7. Thomas G. Fergusson, *British Military Intelligence 1870–1914: The Development of a Modern Intelligence Organization* (Arms and Armour Press, London, 1984); Andrew, op. cit.; Robert Baden-Powell, *My Adventures as a Spy* (Methuen, London, 1915)
8. PRO HD3/111; Jock Haswell, *British Military Intelligence* (Weidenfeld & Nicolson, London, 1973); Andrew, op. cit.
9. Haswell, *op. cit.*
10. PRO HD3/124

The Secret Service Fund:

| | | | |
|---|---|---|---|
| 1854–55 | £32,000 | 1886–87 | £15,000 |
| 1855–56 | £32,000 | 1896–97 | £15,000 |
| 1856–57 | £32,000 | 1905–06 | £65,000 |
| 1866–67 | £25,000 | 1906–07 | £50,000 (FO £40,000) |
| 1876–77 | £15,000 | | |

Intelligence Division Budget:

| | | | |
|---|---|---|---|
| 1897–98 | £400 | 1902–3 | £4600 |
| 1898–99 | £1782 | 1903–4 | £2500 |
| 1899–1900 | £1325 | 1904–5 | £4600 |
| 1900–1 | £1800 | 1905–6 | £5000 |
| 1901–2 | £3300 | 1906–7 | £4000 |

11. PRO HD3/111
12. PRO HD3/125; HD3/128; HD3/132; HD3/133; information supplied to the author in confidence
13. PRO HD3/128; HD3/124; HD3/111
14. PRO HD3/111
15. PRO HD3/124; MEPO21/32 and documents in the Metropolitan Police Museum kindly supplied by the curator, Mr Ron Gilles
16. PRO HD3/124; MEPO21/32; Bernard Porter, *The Origins of the Vigilant State: The London Metropolitan Police Special Branch before the First World War* (Weidenfeld & Nicolson, London, 1987); documents in the Metropolitan Police Museum
17. PRO HD3/124; HD3/130; HD3/131; HD3/133; HD3/138; Bernard Porter, 'The Historiography of the Early Special Branch', *Intelligence and National Security*, Vol. 1, No. 3 (September 1986); Porter, *The Origins of the Vigilant State*
18. PRO HD3/130
19. Porter, *Plots and Paranoia*; PRO HD3/131; The Memoirs of Dr Jack Dancy (the author is grateful to Dr Dancy's son, Professor John Dancy, for permission to use these brief extracts from the memoirs which he is currently editing for publication)
20. Documents in the Metropolitan Police Museum
21. PRO HD3/111; Fergusson, op. cit.
22. PRO HD3/124, HD3/128, HD3/130, HD3/133
23. PRO HD3/111
24. PRO HD3/111; Charles à Court Repington, *Vestigia: Reminiscences of Peace and War* (Houghton Mifflin, Boston, 1919)
25. Fergusson, op. cit.; Lt-Col. B. A. H. Parritt, *The Intelligencers: The Story of British Military Intelligence up to 1914* (Templer Press, Ashford, 1971); F. H. Hinsley et. al., *British Intelligence in the Second World War Vol. 1* (HMSO, London, 1979); Andrew, op. cit.
26. PRO HD3/139
27. 'Work of the Secret Service, by a Former Member of the Service', *Daily Telegraph*, 24–9 September 1930
28. MO5 was known as the Special Duties Branch of the Directorate of Military Operations, which by 1907 had been expanded to six sections. The full DMO structure in 1907 was as follows:

MO1 Imperial Defence: Strategy and Operations
MO2 Foreign Intelligence: Europe and the Near East
MO3 Foreign Intelligence: Asia and the Americas
MO4 Topography of potential foreign theatres of operation
MO5 Special Duties (covert intelligence and counter-intelligence operations)
MO6 Medical information on foreign theatres of operation.

Of the three intelligence sections, MO5 took the lead in intelligence operations. The role of MO2 and MO3 was more analytical, and was defined as:

Collection, preparation and distribution of information concerning the military geography, resources and armed forces of all foreign countries. Supply of information regarding India and adjoining territories. Questions relating to the defence of India, other than those concerning coastal defences.

Correspondence with military attachés. Examination of foreign journals and literature generally.

(PRO HD3/139; HD3/138; *War Office List* (HMSO, London, 1905); Fergusson, op. cit.; Haswell, op. cit.

29. William le Queux, *The Invasion of 1910* (Hurst and Blackett, London, 1906); William le Queux, *Spies of the Kaiser: Plotting the Downfall of England* (Hurst and Blackett, London, 1909)

30. Andrew, op. cit.

31. Fergusson, op. cit.; *Daily Telegraph*, 24–9 September 1930

32. PRO HD3/128; HD3/131; Andrew, op. cit.

33. *MI5, The Security Service* (HMSO, London, 1993); PRO CAB/16/8

34. PRO CAB/16/8. Despite the 1988 reforms, the Official Secrets Act remains largely unchanged from the one recommended by the subcommittee and hustled through the House of Commons late on a Friday afternoon in 1911 when all but a handful of MPs had already left for their constituencies

35. Hinsley et al., op. cit.; *MI5, The Security Service* (HMSO, London, 1993)

## Chapter 4

1. Brig.-Gen., James Edmonds from his unpublished memoirs. Edmonds Papers III, Ch. 2, held in the Liddell Hart Centre for Military Archives, King's College, London

2. Sir Eric Holt-Wilson, 'Security Intelligence in War': Lecture Notes 1934, in the Private Papers of Sir Vernon Kell held in the Imperial War Museum, London

3. Holt-Wilson, op. cit.; Stella Rimington, 'National Security and International Understanding', Lecture to the English-Speaking Union, Skinners Hall, London, 4 October 1995

4. Richard Thurlow, *The Secret State: British Internal Security in the Twentieth Century* (Blackwell, Oxford, 1994); Bernard Porter, *Plots and Paranoia: A History of Political Espionage in Britain 1790–1988* (Unwin Hyman, London, 1989); The Memoirs of Dr Jack Dancy (the author is greatful to Dr Dancy's son, Professor John Dancy, for permission to use these brief extracts from the memoirs which he is currently editing for publication)

5. Christopher Andrew, *Secret Service: The Making of the British Intelligence Community* (William Heinemann, London, 1985); Porter, op. cit.; J. C. Bird, 'Control of Enemy Alien Civilians in Great Britain 1914–1918', University of London Ph.D. dissertation, 1981; F. H. Hinsley and C. A. G. Simkins, *British Intelligence in the Second World War, Vol. 4* (HMSO, London, 1990); P. Panayi, *The Enemy in our Midst* (Clarendon Press, Oxford, 1991); Thurlow, op. cit.

6. PRO WO32/10776; Nicholas Hiley, 'Internal Security in Wartime: The Rise and Fall of PMS-2 1915–1917', *Historical Journal*, Vol. 28, No. 4 (1985); Andrew, op. cit.; Porter, op. cit.; Thurlow, op. cit.

7. Thurlow, op. cit.; Hinsley and Simkins, op. cit.; PRO HO45/22901

8. Andrew, op. cit.; *Report of the Passport Control Sub-Committee*, PRO HO45/ 19966/31848; T161/501; FO371/10480

9. Andrew, op. cit.; Kell Papers; PRO WO33/1077; WO33/1025

10. Andrew, op. cit.; National Archives, Washington DC, RG 165 9944

11. John G. Hope, 'Surveillance or Collusion?: Maxwell Knight, MI5 and the British Fascisti', *Intelligence and National Security*, Vol. 9, No. 4 (October 1994); Thurlow, op. cit.

12. Andrew, op. cit.; Porter, op. cit; Thurlow, op. cit.; John Ferris and Uri

Bar-Joseph, 'Getting Marlowe to Hold his Tongue: The Conservative Party, the Intelligence Services and the Zinoviev Letter', *Intelligence and National Security*, Vol. 8, No. 4 (October 1993)

13. Hinsley and Simkins, op. cit. (according to Hinsley, 'It had been agreed that the designation MI5 should be retained for such official convenience as it could afford without prejudice to the appropriate internal organization of the Security Service'); Thurlow, op. cit.; Philip H. J. Davies, 'Organizational Politics and the Development of Britain's Intelligence Producer/Consumer Interface', *Intelligence and National Security*, Vol. 10, No. 4 (October 1995)

14. 'Sentences on Three Ex-Employees of Woolwich Arsenal', *Daily Telegraph*, 15 March 1938; Anthony Masters, *The Man Who Was M: The Life of Maxwell Knight* (Blackwell, Oxford, 1984). The classification 'Most Secret' changed to 'Top Secret' during the Second World War to conform with US practice

15. Thurlow, op. cit.; Hope, op. cit.

16. Robert Cecil, 'The Cambridge Comintern', in Christopher Andrew and David Dilks (eds.), *The Missing Dimension: Governments and Intelligence Communities in the Twentieth Century* (Macmillan, London, 1984); Nigel West, *The Faber Book of Espionage* (Faber, London, 1993); Andrew, op. cit.

17. Nigel West, *A Matter of Trust, MI5 1945–72* (Coronet, London, 1982); Tom Bower, *The Perfect English Spy: Sir Dick White and the Secret War 1935–90* (William Heinemann, London, 1995)

18. Joan Miller, *One Girl's War* (Brandon, Dingle (Eire), 1986); Richard Thurlow, *Fascism in Britain, A History 1918–85* (Blackwell, Oxford, 1987)

19. Thurlow, *The Secret State*; Andrew, op. cit.

20. *MI5: The Security Service* (HMSO, London, 1993); Hinsley and Simkins, op. cit.; West, *A Matter of Trust*
    The reorganisation left the service with six divisions: A, Administration; B, Counter-Espionage; C, Security; D, Military Liaison; E, Overseas; F, Political Parties

21. PRO CAB81/87; CAB81/96; FO371/25247; FO371/25210; Hinsley and Simkins, op. cit.; A. W. Brian Simpson, *In the Highest Degree Odious: Detention Without Trial in Wartime Britain* (Clarendon, Oxford, 1992); Thurlow, *The Secret State*; Richard C. Thurlow, 'Internment in the Second World War', *Intelligence and National Security*, Vol. 9, No. 1 (January 1994)

22. J. C. Masterman, *The Double-Cross System of the War of 1939–45* (Yale UP, New Haven and London, 1972); Kenneth Benton, 'The ISOS Years: Madrid 1941–3', *Journal of Contemporary History*, Vol. 30, No. 3 (July 1995); Obituary: 'Lt-Col. T. A. Robertson', *Daily Telegraph*, 12 May 1994; Hinsley and Simkins, op. cit. F. H. Hinsley, 'MI5' in I. C. B. Dear (ed.), *The Oxford Companion to the Second World War* (OUP, Oxford, 1995); Nigel West, *MI5: British Security Service Operations 1909–45* (Bodley Head, London, 1981); Andrew, op. cit.

23. Masterman, op. cit.; Benton, op. cit.; The Radio Security Service under Major E. W. B. Gill operated a network of Post Office stations and 'also a large band of most efficient voluntary interceptors' to monitor the Abwehr's communications with its agents. The intercepts were all sent to the RSS, which carried out traffic analysis and passed all encyphered material on to GC&CS. For a brief history of the Radio Security Service, see PRO ADM223/297

24. Dusko Popov, *Spy Counter-Spy* (Weidenfeld & Nicolson, London, 1974); Andrew, op. cit.; Porter, op. cit.

25. Jean Pujol and Nigel West, *Garbo* (Weidenfeld & Nicolson, London, 1985); Masterman, op. cit.; *Daily Telegraph*, 12 May 1994; West, *MI5*; Andrew, op. cit.

26. Masters, op. cit.

27. Derek Tangye, *The Road To Minack* (Michael Joseph, London, 1978); Richard J. Aldrich (ed.), *British Intelligence, Strategy and the Cold War 1945–51* (Routledge,

London, 1992); Alanbrooke Diary, Liddell Hart Centre for Military Archives, King's College, London

28. 'Prime Minister's Broadcast Attack on Socialism: Policy Abhorent to British Ideas of Freedom', *The Times*, 5 June 1945

29. Percy Sillitoe, *Cloak without Dagger* (Cassell, London, 1955); Aldrich, op. cit.; R. V. Jones, *Reflections on Intelligence* (Mandarin, London, 1990)

30. West, *A Matter of Trust*

31. 'MI5 Phone-tap Centre Goes Up For Sale', *Daily Telegraph*, 23 December 1994

32. Anthony Glees, 'War Crimes: The Security and Intelligence Dimension', *Intelligence and National Security*, Vol. 7, No. 3 (July 1992)

33. Aldrich, op. cit.; West, *A Matter of Trust*; Christopher Andrew and Oleg Gordievsky, *KGB: The Inside Story of its Foreign Operations from Lenin to Gorbachev* (Hodder & Stoughton, London, 1990)

34. P. Hennessy and G. Brownfield, 'Britain's Cold War Security Purge: The Origins of Positive Vetting', *The Historical Journal*, Vol. 25, No. 4 (1982); Porter, op. cit.

35. West, *A Matter of Trust*; Hinsley and Simkins, op. cit.

36. *The Security Service Act 1989* (HMSO, London, 1989)

37. Peter Wright, *Spycatcher: The Candid Autobiography of a Senior Intelligence Officer* (Viking, New York, 1987)

38. *Daily Telegraph*, 3 January 1994; West, *A Matter of Trust*. Documents relating to MI5's involvement which should under the thirty-year rule have been released on 1 January 1994, have been 'retained in department' indefinitely. But those documents on the Profumo affair that have been released make it clear that Harold Macmillan and his cabinet blamed MI5 for the scandal

39. Aldrich, op. cit.; Thurlow, *The Secret State*

40. Bower, op. cit.; West, *A Matter of Trust*

41. West, *A Matter of Trust*; Bower, op. cit.; information supplied to the author in confidence

42. Information supplied to the author in confidence; A. Glees, *The Secrets of the Service: British Intelligence and Communist Subversion 1939–1951* (Jonathan Cape, London, 1987); Thurlow, *The Secret State*; Bower, op. cit. (See also Sheila Kerr, 'Roger Hollis and the Dangers of the Anglo-Soviet Treaty of 1942', *Intelligence and National Security*, Vol. 5, No. 3 (July 1990))

43. Andrew and Gordievsky, op. cit.; West, *MI5*; West, *A Matter of Trust*

## Chapter 5

1. Richard Thurlow, *The Secret State: British Internal Security in the Twentieth Century* (Blackwell, Oxford, 1994)

2. Peter Hennessy and Keith Jeffries, *States of Emergency* (Routledge & Kegan Paul, London, 1983)

3. D Branch's counter-espionage responsibility had been taken over by the newly formed K Branch in 1968. Peter Wright, *Spycatcher: The Candid Autobiography of a Senior Intelligence Officer* (Viking, New York, 1987)

4. *Hansard*, House of Lords, 26 February 1975. For further details of what was regarded as subversion, see *Statement on the Recommendations of the Security Commission* (Cmnd 8540, HMSO, London, May 1982)

5. Articles by Miranda Ingram: 'Trouble with Security', *New Society*, 31 May 1984, and 'Living a Lie: The Inside Story of an MI5 Officer', *Observer*, 12 May 1985. Letter from Cathy Massiter published in *New Society*, 14 June 1984, and interview with Massiter in *MI5's Official Secrets*, produced by 20/20 Vision and broadcast by Channel 4 Television on 8 March 1985

6. Barrie Penrose and Roger Courtier, *The Pencourt File* (Secker, London, 1978); 'MI5 Bugged No 10', *Daily Express*, July 1977; 'Wilson Resignation Sparked Spy Plot Claim', *Daily Telegraph*, 30 April 1987

7. 'United Kingdom: Internal Security', *Keesing's Record of World Events*, 31 January 1986, article refs. 34115, 34116, 34117, 34118, 34119; 'Jury Told of MI5 Man and Midnight Offers to KGB', *Daily Telegraph*, 11 April 1985

8. 'Russian Ignored Bettaney "Letter Boxes", Jury Told', *The Times*, 11 April 1985

9. 'Testament of a Turncoat', *Daily Telegraph*, 16 April 1985

10. *Report of the Security Commissioner* (Cmnd 9514, HMSO, London, May 1985)

11. Ingram, 'Trouble with Security'

12. Ingram, 'Living a Lie'

13. Massiter letter in *New Society* and *MI5's Official Secrets*

14. *MI5's Official Secrets*

15. Thurlow, op. cit.; Laurence Lustgarten and Ian Leigh, *In From the Cold, National Security and Parliamentary Democracy* (OUP, Oxford, 1994)

16. *MI5's Official Secrets*. Until the passing of the 1985 Interception of Communication Act, all telephone taps and interception of mail were illegal. The Act was a direct result of a European Court ruling in 1984 that the UK had no law governing the authorization of telephone taps. To be within the law, the power to intercept must be defined with reasonable precision in rules that were accessible to all, the court ruled. (*Legal Executive Journal*, January 1995; Lustgarten and Leigh, op. cit.)

17. *Hansard*, House of Commons, 10 July 1984.

18. Wright, op. cit.; Tom Bower, *The Perfect English Spy: Sir Dick White and the Secret War 1935–90* (William Heinemann, London, 1995); 'United Kingdom-Australia: The "Spycatcher" Case', *Keesing's Record of World Events*, 30 November 1987, article refs. 35537A, 35538 and 35539; 'United Kingdom: Court Rulings in Spycatcher Affair', *Keesing's Record of World Events*, article refs. 36155A, 36155; *Panorama*, BBC Television, 13 October 1988.
*Spycatcher* was to be published in Australia where Wright lived and accordingly the British government obtained a temporary injunction in the New South Wales Supreme Court to prevent publication. But a subsequent, and ill-considered, court battle to make the injunction permanent on the grounds that the book was likely to cause 'unquantifiable damage' to British security failed ignominiously and the book was published first in America, then in Australia, and finally, after a further battle at the High Court in London, in Britain.
The British High Court judge, Mr Justice Scott, said he could accept neither the government's insistence on being able to censor all information on the intelligence services, nor the media's on being able to print what they liked. He also said it was puzzling that, while the government had taken strenuous steps to prevent British newspapers printing extracts from the book, it had taken no action to prevent copies being imported from America or to stop publication of any of the other books carrying similar allegations that had been previously published

19. *Hansard*, House of Commons, 3 December 1986; *Hansard*, House of Commons, 16 January 1989; *Hansard*, House of Commons, 17 January 1989

20. 'MI5 Proposals for Openness Praised by Former Officers', *Independent*, 6 September 1989; 'Letting a Little Light on a Murky World', *Guardian*, 7 September 1989

21. *MI5: The Security Service* (HMSO, London, 1993)

22. 'A Shy Spymaster Shepherding MI5 Towards the Light', *Sunday Times*, 10 September 1989; 'Inside Story: Scargill and the Spooks', *Guardian*, 19 November 1994

23. *Hansard*, House of Commons, 23 November 1988; *Hansard*, House of Commons, 16 January 1989
24. *The Security Service Act 1989* (HMSO, London, 1989). (Attempts by Conservative back-benchers to include a clause banning surveillance of 'legitimate and lawful dissent' were rejected by the government. The requirement to appoint a Commissioner to whom staff could complain merely legalized the existing situation: Sir Philip Woodfield, a former permanent under-secretary in the Northern Ireland Office had been appointed to the post in 1987)
25. *MI5: The Security Service*; Stephen Dorril, *The Silent Conspiracy: Inside the Intelligence Services in the 1990s* (Heinemann, London, 1993)
26. *MI5: The Security Service*
27. Lustgarten and Leigh, op. cit.
28. James Adams, *The New Spies: Exploring the Frontiers of Espionage* (Hutchinson, London, 1994); Dorril, op. cit.
29. 'Woman to be Head of MI5 Spycatchers', *Daily Telegraph*, 17 December 1991
30. *Hansard*, House of Commons, 8 May 1992; 'MI5 Given Lead Role in Fight Against IRA', *Daily Telegraph*, 9 May 1992; 'Major Gives MPs Clues to Solving Enigma of MI6', *Independent*, 12 May 1992; 'Law and Order will not escape Clarke's "Tough Guy" Approach', *Daily Telegraph*, 14 May 1992
31. *MI5: The Security Service*; *MI5: The Security Service*, 2nd edn (HMSO, London, 1996)
32. 'MI5 Proposals of Openness Praised by Former Officers', *Independent*, 6 September 1989; *Guardian*, 7 September 1989
33. 'Drug War Speculation over MI5 Head's Trip to Moscow', *Daily Telegraph*, 7 September 1992; 'New KGB Chief Meets Hurd', TASS, 1 September 1991
34. *MI5: The Security Service* (1993); *Hansard*, House of Lords, 9 December 1993; 'Police Chiefs Warned of Threat from MI6', *Independent*, 18 March 1994
35. *Intelligence Services Act 1994* (HMSO, London, 1994); Stella Rimington, The 1994 Richard Dimbleby Lecture, BBC Television, 12 June 1994
36. *Hansard*, House of Lords, 9 December 1993; *Hansard*, House of Commons, 1 September 1994
37. *Hansard*, House of Commons, 23 March 1994
38. Stella Rimington, The James Smart Lecture, City of London Police Headquarters, 3 November 1994
39. Correspondence between Michael Howard, Home Secretary, and Alan Milburn MP, dated 30 January 1995 and 13 March 1995; 'Secretive Police Role of MI5 Feared', *Observer*, 26 March 1995; 'Police Demand Their FBI to Fend Off MI5', *Observer*, 13 November 1994
40. *Regina* v. *Jack and Fryers*, Central Criminal Court, London, 5 December 1994 to 21 January 1995
41. Rimington, James Smart Lecture; information supplied to the author in confidence
42. *MI5: The Security Service* (1993); Correspondence between Michael Howard, Home Secretary, and Alan Milburn MP, dated 18 January 1995; 'Late MI5 Alert Leaves Government Exposed', *Computing*, 2 February 1995
43. 'Yard chief backs MI5 role in Fighting Crime', *Sunday Telegraph*, 12 March 1995
44. Lustgarten and Leigh, op. cit.; Adams, op. cit.; *MI5: The Security Service* (1993); Rimington, Dimbleby Lecture; Rimington, James Smart Lecture
45. Stella Rimington, 'National Security and International Understanding', Lecture to the English-Speaking Union, Skinners Hall, City of London, 4 October 1995; 'Counter-spy to be New Head of MI5 Crime War', *Daily Telegraph*, 24 November 1995
46. 'Police Want to Take Lead in MI5 Link-up', *Daily Telegraph*, 14 October 1995;

Detective Superintendent Larry Covington, NCIS, Lecture on Organized Crime, *Proceedings of the Security and Intelligence Studies Group Workshop on Intelligence Policy 1995, Reading, 23 September 1995*

47. The Commons Home Affairs Committee, in its report on organized crime, expressed concern over the lack of legislation governing new surveillance techniques, concluding, 'Legislation should be introduced to put on to a statutory footing new surveillance techniques which are not subject to the Interception of Communications Act 1985' (Home Affairs Committee, *Organized Crime* (HMSO, London, 1995). Rimington, Dimbleby Lecture. For MI5's budget see 'Spending on Security and Intelligence Totals £900m', *Guardian*, 1 December 1993, and 'First the Cold War Ended. Now the Ceasefire Spells Big Changes for MI5', *Observer*, 18 September 1994

48. Rimington, James Smart Lecture; Rimington, Dimbleby Lecture

49. Information provided to the author in confidence; *MI5: The Security Service* (1993); Rimington, Dimbleby Lecture; Rimington, James Smart Lecture; 'Spy Students Alert', *The Times*, 20 July 1994

50. For further discussion, see Peter Gill, *Policing Politics: Security Intelligence and the Liberal Democratic State* (Frank Cass, London, 1994) and Lustgarten and Leigh, op. cit.

51. Intelligence and Security Committee, *Annual Report 1995* (HMSO, London, 1996). For an extraordinarily candid description of the Home Office's lack of control over MI5, from the senior Home Office official responsible, see Lustgarten and Leigh, op. cit., pp. 426–7

52. Letter: 'Beware MI5 Replacing Police', *Observer*, 13 November 1994; 'Right-Wing "Secret Police" Threat', *Today*, 14 November 1994

## Chapter 6

1. Paul Dukes, *The Story of ST-25: Adventure and Romance in the Secret Intelligence Service* (Cassell, London, 1938)

2. Ibid.

3. 'Work of the Secret Service, by a Former Member of the Service', *Daily Telegraph*, 24–9 September 1930

4. PRO FO371/2163; *Daily Telegraph*, 24–9 September 1930

5. PRO WO32/10776; F. H. Hinsley et al., *British Intelligence in the Second World War Vol 1* (HMSO, London, 1979); Nicholas P. Hiley, 'The Failure of British Espionage Against Germany, 1907–1914', *The Historical Journal*, Vol. 26, No. 4 (1983)

6. Christopher Andrew, *Secret Service: The Making of the British Intelligence Community* (William Heinemann, London, 1985); W. Somerset Maugham, *Collected Short Stories* (Pan, London, 1976)

7. Hiley, op. cit.; *Daily Telegraph*, 24–9 September 1930

8. *Daily Telegraph*, 24–9 September 1930

9. John Bruce Lockhart, 'Intelligence: A British View', in Ken Robertson (ed.), *British and American Approaches to Intelligence* (Macmillan, London, 1987)

10. PRO WO32/10776; F. H. Hinsley et al., op. cit.

11. Dukes, op. cit.

12. PRO FO611/19; FO372/2756; Richard B. Spence, 'Sidney Reilly in America, 1914–1917', *Intelligence and National Security*, Vol. 10, No. 1 (January 1995)

13. Spence, op. cit.; Christopher Andrew and Oleg Gordievsky, *The KGB: The Inside Story of its Foreign Operations from Lenin to Gorbachev* (Hodder & Stoughton, London, 1990)

14. Sidney Reilly, *Britain's Master Spy: The Adventures of Sidney Reilly* (E. Matthews and Marrot, London, 1933)

15. Phillip Knightley, *The Second Oldest Profession: The Spy as Bureaucrat, Patriot, Fantasist and Whore* (André Deutsch, London, 1986)

16. Robert Bruce Lockhart, *Memoirs of a Secret Agent* (Putnam, London, 1934)

17. Ibid.

18. John W. Long, 'Plot and Counter-Plot in Revolutionary Russia: Chronicling the Bruce Lockhart Conspiracy', *Intelligence and National Security*, Vol. 10, No. 1 (January 1995); Andrew and Gordievsky, op. cit.; Richard K. Debo, 'Lockhart Plot or Dzerzhinsky Plot?', *Journal of Modern History*, XLIII, September 1971; George Leggett, *The Cheka: Lenin's Political Police* (Clarendon, Oxford, 1981)

19. R. B. Lockhart, op. cit.; PRO FO371/3348

20. R. B. Lockhart, op. cit.

21. Long, op. cit.

22. PRO FO371/3350; Andrew, op. cit.; George Hill, *Go Spy the Land* (Cassell, London, 1928)

23. Andrew and Gordievsky, op. cit.; Long, op. cit.; R. B. Lockhart, op. cit.

24. R. B. Lockhart, op. cit.; Information supplied to the author in confidence; Andrew and Gordievsky, op. cit. Under the rules governing the secret work of the passport control officers, they were banned from operating against the country in which they were based. Operations against the Soviet Union were conducted out of Scandinavia – principally Finland

25. Hinsley et al., op. cit.

26. Philip H. J. Davies, 'Organizational Politics and the Development of Britain's Intelligence Producer/Consumer Interface', *Intelligence and National Security*, Vol. 10, No. 4 (October 1995); Hinsley et al., op. cit.

27. Hinsley et al., op. cit. Between 1919 and 1922 the MI6 budget was reduced from £240,000 to £90,000

28. Hinsley et al., op. cit.; Davies, op. cit.; Andrew, op. cit.

29. Andrew, op. cit.; Hinsley et al., op. cit.; Kim Philby, *My Silent War* (MacGibbon & Kee, London, 1968); Davies, op. cit. The late Robert Cecil attempted to include Section N on an organizational chart which he produced for the 1995 *Oxford Companion to the Second World War*. But when he submitted the chart to the Foreign and Commonwealth Office for clearance he was strictly forbidden from mentioning the section, even though he offered to refer to it only as 'non-communication intercepts'. Given the vintage of the information and the fact that the existence of Section N and of a similar operation by MI5 have already been published in a number of accounts, it is difficult to see the reason for the FCO's concern, unless perhaps the practice is still continuing. (Conversation between Robert Cecil and Philip Davies, University of Reading, recalled in correspondence with the author; Robert Cecil, 'MI6', in I. C. B. Dear (ed.), *The Oxford Companion to the Second World War* (OUP, Oxford, 1995). See also Anthony Cave Brown, '*C*': *The Secret Life of Sir Stewart Graham Menzies, Spymaster to Sir Winston Churchill* (Macmillan, New York, 1987); Nigel West, *MI6: British Secret Intelligence Service Operations 1909–1945* (Weidenfeld & Nicolson, London, 1983); Philby, op. cit.; Robert Cecil, 'The Cambridge Comintern', in Christopher Andrew and David Dilks (eds.), *The Missing Dimension: Governments and Intelligence Communities in the Twentieth Century* (Macmillan, London, 1984)

30. Cecil, 'MI6'; Davies, op. cit.

31. Cecil, 'The Cambridge Comintern'; Andrew, op. cit.

32. John Whitwell, *Secret Agent* (William Kimber, London, 1966); Andrew, op. cit.

33. F. H. Hinsley et al., *British Intelligence in the Second World War Vol. 1* (HMSO, London, 1979)

# Chapter 7

1. F. H. Hinsley et al., *British Intelligence in the Second World War Vol. 1* (HMSO, London, 1979); Robert Cecil, 'MI6', in I. C. B. Dear (ed.), *The Oxford Companion to the Second World War* (OUP, Oxford, 1995)
2. Hinsley et al., op. cit.; PRO CAB4/24
3. PRO T160/787
4. Information supplied to the author in confidence; 'Jews Honour the British Schindler: Frank Foley', *Sunday Times*, 26 February 1995; Letter: 'Saved from the Nazis by British Schindler', *Sunday Times*, 5 March 1995; Letter: 'Foley's List', *Independent*, 25 March 1995; Anthony Read and David Fisher, *Colonel Z* (Hodder & Stoughton, London, 1984); Christopher Andrew, *Secret Service: The Making of the British Intelligence Community* (William Heinemann, London, 1985); Cecil, op. cit.; Philip H. J. Davies, 'Organizational Politics and the Development of Britain's Intelligence Producer/Consumer Interface', *Intelligence and National Security*, Vol. 10, No. 4 (October 1995)
5. Andrew, op. cit.; Hinsley et al., op. cit.; Davies, op. cit.; F. W. Winterbotham, *The Ultra Secret* (Weidenfeld & Nicolson, London, 1974)
6. PRO FO371/21659
7. Information supplied to the author in confidence; Hinsley et al., op. cit.; 'German Secret Police Arrest a British Officer', *Daily Telegraph and Morning Post*, 19 August 1938; 'Strong British Protest to Berlin: Serious View of Captain's Arrest', *Daily Telegraph and Morning Post*, 20 August 1938; 'Germany Asks for Withdrawal of Capt Kendrick', *Daily Telegraph and Morning Post*, 22 August 1938; Davies, op. cit.
8. PRO FO371/22965; Hinsley et al., op. cit. 'Menzies [head of MI6] this morning said that he had from the v best source, report that Germans had abandoned any idea of offensive,' Alexander Cadogan, the Permanent Under-Secretary at the Foreign Office, wrote in his diary for 29 November 1939. 'I believe all the stuff we get is put out by the Germans to puzzle us! After all that's what we do!' (David Dilks (ed.), *The Diaries of Sir Alexander Cadogan, 1938–1945* (Cassell, London, 1971))
9. PRO FO800/270
10. See Chapter 2 for more details of the creation of the JIC
11. Information supplied to the author in confidence; Imperial War Museum, Payne Best Manuscript 79/57/1; Andrew, op. cit.; Davies, op. cit.; Cecil, op. cit.; Hinsley et al., op. cit. Up until the Second World War, the highest British security classification was 'Most Secret'. It only became 'Top Secret', against Churchill's better judgement, after America entered the war, to bring it into line with US practice
12. Information supplied to the author in confidence; Hinsley et al., op. cit.; Cecil, op. cit.
13. Hinsley et al., op. cit.; Dilks, op. cit.
14. PRO CAB81/87
15. PRO CAB81/97
16. PRO CAB81/97; Philip Johns, *Within Two Cloaks: Missions with SIS and SOE* (William Kimber, London, 1979); M. R. D. Foot, *Resistance* (Paladin, London, 1976); Hinsley et al., op. cit.
17. Cecil, op. cit.; M. R. D. Foot, 'Sir Claude Dansey' and 'MI9', both in Dear, op. cit.; PRO ADM223/475; CAB81/92; Anthony Clayton, *Forearmed: A History of the Intelligence Corps* (Brasseys, London, 1993); Nigel West, *MI6: British Secret Service Operations 1909–45* (Weidenfeld & Nicolson, London, 1983)

18. Hinsley et al., op. cit.; Davies, op. cit.; Robert Cecil, 'Five of Six at War: Section V of MI6', *Intelligence and National Security*, Vol. 9, No. 2 (April 1994)

19. PRO CAB81/88; Timothy J. Naftali, 'Intrepid's Last Deception: Documenting the Career of Sir William Stephenson', *Intelligence and National Security*, Vol. 8, No. 3 (July 1993)

20. PRO CAB81/88; CAB81/102

21. PRO CAB81/99; CAB81/100

22. Hinsley et al., op. cit.; West, op. cit.; Davies, op. cit.; Cecil, 'The Cambridge Comintern', in Christopher Andrew and David Dilks (eds.), *The Missing Dimension: Governments and Intelligence Communities in the Twentieth Century* (Macmillan, London, 1984)

23. Robert Cecil, 'C's War', *Intelligence and National Security*, Vol. 1, No. 2 (May 1986); Davies, op. cit.; George Blake, *No Other Choice: An Autobiography* (Jonathan Cape, London, 1990)

24. Cecil, 'MI6'

25. R. V. Jones, 'A Sidelight on Bletchley, 1942', *Intelligence and National Security*, Vol. 9, No. 1 (January 1994); Cecil, 'MI6'; Nigel West, *GCHQ* (Weidenfeld & Nicolson, London, 1986); Andrew, op. cit. The first use of CX was in 1914, when an agent in Brussels was told, 'If you've got urgent material you want to get to us quickly you should put CX CX CX CX.' By 1917 it was routinely used as a prefix for the serial numbers on all intelligence reports (information made available to the author in confidence)

26. PRO HS4/39; Andrew, op. cit.

27. Hinsley et al., op. cit.; E. D. R. Harrison, 'More Thoughts on Kim Philby's *My Silent War*', *Intelligence and National Security*, Vol. 10, No. 3 (July 1995); C. G. McKay, 'The SIS Network in Norway, 1940–1945', Review of Bjorn Rorholt, *Usynliche Soldater: Nordmenn i Secret Service Forteller* (Aschehaug, Oslo, 1990), in *Intelligence and National Security*, Vol. 10, No. 3 (July 1995); Cecil, 'MI6'; I. C. B. Dear, 'Source K and Sussex Teams', in Dear, op. cit.; Foot, *Resistance*; West, *MI6*

28. C. G. McKay, *From Information to Intrigue: Studies in Secret Service Based on the Swedish Experience 1939–45* (Frank Cass, London, 1993); Cecil, 'MI6'; Conversation with Sir Harry Hinsley, 17 July 1995; R. V. Jones, *Reflections on Intelligence* (Mandarin, London, 1990). Sir George Warner, the recalcitrant British minister in Berne who had refused to allow a passport control officer into his mission, had by now been replaced by Clifford Norton, whose attitude to secret service work was in stark contrast to that of his predecessor. One former MI6 officer wrote, 'Members of the intelligence service on his staff later spoke warmly of his professional co-operation in their work' (Nigel Clive, Obituary: 'Sir Clifford Norton', *Guardian*, 21 December 1990)

29. C. G. McKay, *From Information to Intrigue*; PRO ADM223/475; '*Bismarck*, Sinking of', in Dear, *Oxford Companion*; information supplied to the author in confidence

30. Information supplied to the author in confidence; I. C. B. Dear, 'Admiral Wilhelm Canaris', in Dear, *Oxford Companion*; Hinsley conversation; McKay, *From Information to Intrigue*; Harrison, op. cit.; Winfried Heinemann, 'Abwehr', in Dear, *Oxford Companion*; West, *MI6*; Nigel West, *Unreliable Witness: Espionage Myths of the Second World War* (Weidenfeld & Nicolson, London, 1984). Canaris's fall from grace is generally believed to be related to the defection of an Abwehr officer stationed in Istanbul. Clearly without further evidence it is impossible to prove a link between Hitler's order that he should stay out of Berlin and R34's testimony. But it would not be incompatible with the Gestapo believing that Canaris might be the 'leading Nazi' but not having any evidence to prove it. Canaris was not arrested until after the July 1944 bomb attempt on Hitler's life, when his previous links to the conspirators came to light. He was

eventually hanged in April 1945.

With regard to the Szymanska affair generally, Hinsley's official history alludes merely to 'the formation of . . . new links with Berlin via Switzerland' as being part of the service's recovery from the dark days at the beginning of the war, but gives no greater detail (Hinsley et al., op. cit., p. 276)

31. Cecil, 'C's War'; 'Wartime Head of Secret Service Dies', *Daily Telegraph*, 30 May 1968

32. McKay, 'The SIS Network in Norway'; Cecil, 'MI6'. Despite the low regard in which MI6 was held by many within the services, a final verdict on its war will have to wait until the wartime files are released, since the Szymanska episode shows that the whole story was clearly not reflected in the official history

## Chapter 8

1. Robert Cecil, 'Five of Six at War', *Intelligence and National Security*, Vol. 9, No. 2 (April 1994); Robert Cecil, 'Philby's Spurious War', *Intelligence and National Security*, Vol. 9, No. 4 (October 1994); PRO CAB81/132; HS4/327; HS4/329

2. PRO CAB81/132

3. PRO HS4/144; HS4/327; HS4/329; HS4/334

4. Kim Philby, *My Silent War* (MacGibbon & Kee, London, 1968); Robert Cecil, 'The Cambridge Comintern', in Christopher Andrew and David Dilks (eds.), *The Missing Dimension: Governments and Intelligence Communities in the Twentieth Century* (Macmillan, London, 1984); Cecil, 'Five of Six at War'; Cecil, 'Philby's Spurious War'

5. PRO CAB81/124

6. PRO HS4/291; HS4/51; HS4/52; HS4/127

7. PRO CAB81/91; CAB 81/92; Tom Bower, *The Red Webb: MI6 and the KGB Master Coup* (Aurum Press, London, 1989)

8. PRO CAB81/128

9. PRO CAB81/93; CAB81/94; CAB81/125; CAB81/128; CAB81/130; Philip Johns, *Within Two Cloaks: Missions With SIS and SOE* (William Kimber, London, 1979)

10. PRO CAB81/93; CAB81/134; FO1032/1271A; FO1032/1231B; Anthony Glees, 'War Crimes: The Security and Intelligence Dimension', *Intelligence and National Security*, Vol. 7, No. 3 (July 1992)

11. PRO FO371/46604; WO193/637a

12. PRO CAB81/93; Richard Aldrich, 'Secret Intelligence for a Post-War World', in Richard J. Aldrich (ed.), *British Intelligence, Strategy and the Cold War 1945– 51* (Routledge, London, 1992); Anthony Verrier, *Through the Looking Glass: British Foreign Policy in the Age of Illusions* (Jonathan Cape, London, 1983)

13. PRO HS4/327; HS4/204; HS4/45. When the Russians complained that SOE radio networks in Poland supposedly closed down at the end of the war were still operating, the Foreign Office, anxious to recognize the new Moscow-controlled regime in Warsaw, demanded that they be closed down. Perkins initially resisted this, saying that Menzies had to be consulted since 'without doubt, he is very interested in the question of Polish communications in view of the excellent intelligence which is obtained via these channels'.

A compromise agreement allowed the networks to remain open – 'in view of their bulk and the dislocation of intelligence of operational importance that might be caused' – so long as all messages were controlled by SOE rather than the Poles themselves. When the Russians complained that the British were still

supporting 'terrorist activities' in Poland and the Foreign Office in turn
complained to SOE, Perkins simply handed his Polish networks over to SIS

14. PRO HS4/139; HS4/140; Bickham Sweet-Escott, *Baker Street Irregular*
(Methuen, London, 1965); Nicholas Bethell, *The Great Betrayal: The Untold Story
of Kim Philby's Biggest Coup* (Hodder & Stoughton, London, 1984); Bower, op.
cit.

15. Philby, op. cit.; Philip H. J. Davies, 'Organizational Politics and the
Development of Britain's Intelligence Producer/Consumer Interface', *Intelligence
and National Security*, Vol. 10, No. 4 (October 1995); Verrier, op. cit.; Nigel
West, *The Friends: Britain's Post-War Secret Intelligence Operations* (Weidenfeld &
Nicolson, London, 1988); Aldrich, op. cit.; R. V. Jones, *Most Secret War* (Hamish
Hamilton, London, 1978)

16. PRO CAB81/133; CAB81/132

17. 'Mr Churchill Urges Anglo-US Pact: Soviet "Shadow" over Victory', *Daily
Telegraph*, 6 March 1946

18. Jones, op. cit.; PRO CAB81/94; West, op. cit.

19. Benton, op. cit.

20. Information supplied to the author in confidence; interview with Janis
Lukasevics, Latvian Radio, 11 March 1988; Bower, op. cit.; Anthony Cavendish,
*Inside Intelligence* (Collins, London, 1990); Anthony Cavendish, 'Not Very Secret
Service', *Sunday Times*, 24 September 1989; Philby, op. cit. Philby recalled how
in mid-1951 a British aircraft took off from Cyprus and dropped three six-man
groups of NTS members into the Ukraine. 'I do not know what happened to the
parties concerned,' he wrote. 'But I can make an informed guess.'

21. Arnold M. Silver, 'Questions, Questions, Questions: Memories of Oberursel',
*Intelligence and National Security*, Vol. 8, No. 2 (April 1993)

22. PRO FO371/71687; FO371/77623

23. Philby, op. cit.; Diaries of Michael Burke, Boston University Library; Bethell,
op. cit.

24. Information provided to the author in confidence; interview with Simon Preston,
11 October 1995; interview with Michael Giles, 25 October 1995; Cavendish,
*Inside Intelligence*; Anthony Cavendish, 'The Imperfect Spy', *Observer*, 9 July
1989; Tom Bower, *The Perfect English Spy: Sir Dick White and the Secret English
War 1935–1990* (Heinemann, London, 1995); West, op. cit.; John Ranelagh,
*The Agency: The Rise and Decline of the CIA* (Weidenfeld & Nicolson, London,
1986); 'Hunt for Secret US War Gold Grips Austria', *Sunday Times*, 28 January
1996

25. PRO CAB81/124

26. PRO CAB81/93; CAB81/94. British and Russian troops had occupied Iran
during the war to ensure vital communications links

27. C. M. Woodhouse, *Something Ventured* (Granada, London, 1982); Cavendish,
*Inside Intelligence*; Verrier, op. cit.; Kermit Roosevelt, *Countercoup: The Struggle
for the Control of Iran* (McGraw-Hill, New York, 1981)

28. PRO HS4/349; Verrier, op. cit.

29. 'G. M. Frogman Missing After Tests', *Daily Telegraph*, 30 April 1956; 'Frogman
In Hotel Mystery', *Daily Telegraph*, 3 May 1956; 'Frogman Did Secret Work',
*Daily Telegraph*, 4 May 1956; 'Cdr Crabb "On Secret Service": Disciplinary
Steps, Says Premier', *Daily Telegraph*, 10 May 1956; 'Russians Sent Note on
Frogman', *Daily Telegraph*, 12 May 1956; 'Frogman's Suit on Body Standard
Naval Issue', *Daily Telegraph*, 11 June 1957

30. Verrier, op. cit.; Keith Kyle, *Suez* (Weidenfeld & Nicolson, London, 1992);
Richard J. Aldrich, 'Intelligence, Anglo-American Relations and the Suez Crisis,
1956', *Intelligence and National Security*, Vol. 9, No. 3 (July 1994); Anthony
Verrier, 'Why America Wanted Nasser Down But Not Out', *Financial Times*, 12

October 1991; Bower, *The Perfect English Spy*; West, op. cit.; Peter Wright, *Spycatcher: The Candid Autobiography of a Senior Intelligence Officer* (Viking, New York, 1987)

31. Information supplied to the author in confidence; Jim Marchio, 'Resistance Potential and Rollback: US Intelligence and the Eisenhower Administration's Policies Towards Eastern Europe 1953–56', *Intelligence and National Security*, Vol. 10, No. 2 (April 1995); *FRUS 1955–57, Vol. XXV, Eastern Europe* (US Government, Washington, 1990); *The Europa Year Book 1987: A World Survey Vol. 1* (Europa, London, 1987); Christopher Andrew and Oleg Gordievsky, *KGB: The Inside Story of its Foreign Operations from Lenin to Gorbachev* (Hodder & Stoughton, London, 1990); Bob Steers, FSS: Field Security Section (Robin Steers, Heathfield, 1996).

Paul Gorka was one of a group of students recruited in the early 1950s to gather intelligence on Soviet activity inside Hungary. 'In due course, we received coded messages from Vienna asking us for information about Russian troop movements, index numbers of military vehicles, so that a picture could be built up of details of Russian occupation units. We replied with information written in invisible ink in innocuous letters to special addresses.'

But Gorka and his fellow students developed the unfortunate habit of meeting in a popular Budapest espresso bar to discuss their activities and were swiftly rounded up. 'I was interrogated for seven weeks, sometimes in the presence of a Russian major,' Gorka said.

'I was tortured several times. Sometimes I was left in my cell with both feet immersed for hours in icy water, other times I was hung from a beam by my arms handcuffed together. When I was cut down after several hours, my hands were black and so swollen that it was almost impossible to remove the handcuffs. Under torture, I confessed and after a brief trial sent to prison for 15 years.

'Hungarian Ex-spy', *Daily Telegraph*, 28 December 1981; Paul V. Gorka, *Budapest Betrayed* (Oak-Tree Books, London, 1986)

32. PRO CAB81/93; Christopher Mayhew, *Party Games* (Hutchinson, London, 1989); PRO FO371/56886; CAB130/37; W. Scott Lucas and C. J. Morris, 'A Very British Crusade: The Information Research Department and The Beginning of the Cold War', in Aldrich, *British Intelligence Strategy*

33. PRO FO371/56886; FO371/66370; FO1110/16

34. PRO FO930/488; Lucas and Morris, op. cit.

35. Lucas and Morris, op. cit.; 'The British Ministry of Propaganda', *Independent on Sunday*, 26 February 1995; 'Covert in Glory', *New Statesman*, 3 March 1995

36. Information supplied to the author in confidence; Bower, *The Perfect English Spy*; Davies, op. cit.

## Chapter 9

1. Gordon Brook-Shepherd, *The Storm Petrels* (Collins, London, 1977); Phillip Knightley, *Kim Philby: KGB Masterspy* (André Deutsch, London, 1988); Andrew Boyle, *The Climate of Treason*, rev. edn (Coronet, London, 1980); Kim Philby, *My Silent War* (MacGibbon & Kee, London, 1968); Robert Cecil, *A Divided Life: A Biography of Donald Maclean* (Bodley Head, London, 1988)

2. Yuri Modin, *My Five Cambridge Friends* (Headline, London, 1994); BBC Summary of World Broadcasts, 6 January 1988; Soviet Radio Account of Philby's Latvian Television Interview, 30 December 1987

3. Robert Cecil, 'The Cambridge Comintern', in Christopher Andrew and David Dilks (eds.), *The Missing Dimension: Governments and Intelligence Communities in the Twentieth Century* (Macmillan, London, 1983)

4. E. H. Cookridge, *The Third Man* (Arthur Barker, London, 1968)

5. Information made available to the author in confidence; Modin, op. cit.; Christopher Andrew and Oleg Gordievsky, *The KGB: The Story of Its Foreign Operations from Lenin to Gorbachev* (Hodder & Stoughton, London, 1990); Bruce Page, David Leitch and Phillip Knightley, *Philby: The Spy Who Betrayed a Generation* (André Deutsch, London, 1968)

6. Information made available to the author in confidence; Genrikh Borovik, *The Philby Files* (Little Brown, London, 1994); Robert Cecil, 'Donald Maclean', in Lord Blake and C. S. Nicholls (eds.), *Dictionary of National Biography 1981–1985* (OUP, Oxford, 1990)

7. Anne Baker, 'Guy Burgess', in C. S. Nichols (ed.), *Dictionary of National Biography: Missing Persons* (OUP, Oxford, 1993); Goronwy Rees, *A Chapter of Accidents* (Chatto & Windus, London, 1977); Boyle, op. cit.; Jenny Rees, *Looking For Mr Nobody: The Secret Life of Goronwy Rees* (Weidenfeld & Nicolson, London, 1994); Philby, op. cit.

8. Michael Kitson, 'Anthony Blunt', in Blake and Nicholls, op. cit.; Andrew and Gordievsky, op. cit.

9. John Cairncross with Nigel West, *An Agent for the Duration: Memoirs of the Fifth Man* (St Ermin's Press, London, 1996); Knightley, op. cit.; Obituary: 'John Cairncross', *Independent*, 10 October 1995

10. Knightley, op. cit.; Philby, op. cit.; Nigel Clive, 'From War to Peace in SIS', *Intelligence and National Security*, Vol. 10, No. 3 (July 1995)

11. Baker, op. cit.; G. Rees, op. cit.

12. Cecil, *A Divided Life*; Boyle, op. cit.

13. G. Rees, op. cit.; Tom Driberg, *Guy Burgess: Portrait With Background* (Weidenfeld & Nicolson, London, 1956)

14. Andrew and Gordievsky, op. cit.; Knightley, op. cit.; Philby, op. cit.

15. Cecil, 'The Cambridge Comintern'

16. Baker, op. cit.; Andrew and Gordievsky, op. cit.; Modin, op. cit.

17. Barrie Penrose and Simon Freeman, *Conspiracy of Silence: The Secret Life of Anthony Blunt* (Grafton, London, 1986); Cecil, 'The Cambridge Comintern'

18. Cecil, 'The Cambridge Comintern'; PRO CAB81/91; CAB 81/92

19. Cecil, *A Divided Life*; Cecil, 'Donald Maclean'

20. Modin, op. cit.; John Cairncross, *An Agent for the Duration: Memoirs of the Fifth Man* (St Ermin's Press, London, 1996)

21. *Independent*, 10 October 1995; Nigel Clive, 'Paid for by Moscow', *Times Literary Supplement*, 30 December 1994

22. Kenneth Benton, 'The ISOS Years, Madrid 1941–43', *Journal of Contemporary History*, Vol. 30, No. 3 (July 1995); Knightley, op. cit.

23. Philby, op. cit.

24. Borovik, op. cit.; PRO HS4/144; HS4/327; HS4/329; HS4/334; HS4/349; HS4/355; Philby, op. cit.

25. Modin, op. cit.; Cecil, 'The Cambridge Comintern'; PRO CAB81/91; CAB 81/92

26. Cecil, 'The Cambridge Comintern'

27. Modin, op. cit.; Cecil, 'The Cambridge Comintern'; PRO CAB81/133

28. Andrew and Gordievsky, op. cit.; Modin, op. cit.

29. Cecil, 'The Cambridge Comintern'; Philby, op. cit.

30. Philby, op. cit.

31. Cecil, 'The Cambridge Comintern'; Modin, op. cit.

32. Sheila Kerr, 'The Secret Hotline to Moscow: Donald Maclean and the Berlin

Crisis of 1948', in Ann Deighton (ed.), *Britain and the First Cold War* (Macmillan, London, 1990); Cecil, *A Divided Life*

33. Cecil, 'The Cambridge Comintern'; Jozef Garlinski, *Poland, SOE and the Allies* (George Allen & Unwin, London, 1969)

34. Cecil, *A Divided Life*; Baker, op. cit.; Cecil, 'Donald Maclean'; Kitson, op. cit.; Modin, op. cit.

35. Cairncross, op. cit.; Henry Dryden, 'Recollections of Bletchley Park, France, and Cairo', in E. H. Hinsley and Alan Stripp (eds.), *Codebreakers: The Inside Story of Bletchley Park* (OUP, Oxford, 1993)

36. Philby, op. cit.; *Hansard*, House of Commons, 7 November 1955; 'US Spy Agencies Release Decoded KGB Messages From 1940s', Associated Press, 12 July 1995; 'Britain Forced to Reveal Code Breaking that Trapped Spies', *Guardian*, 13 July 1995; Andy Thomas, 'Signals Intelligence after the Second World War', *Intelligence and National Security*, Vol. 3, No. 4 (October 1988)

37. Cecil, *A Divided Life*; *Hansard*, House of Commons, 7 November 1955

38. Cecil, 'The Cambridge Comintern'; 'Donald Maclean's Invaluable Services to Stalin Disclosed', *The Times*, 2 January 1981; Sheila Kerr, 'Familiar Fiction, not the Untold Story', *Intelligence and National Security*, Vol. 9, No. 1 (January 1994)

39. Cecil, 'The Cambridge Comintern'; Kerr, 'Familiar Fiction'

40. Cecil, 'The Cambridge Comintern'; Desmond Bristow, *A Game of Moles* (Warner Books, London, 1994)

41. Philby subsequently said that the speeding fine was all part of a plan to get Burgess back to London to warn Maclean – a claim that features prominently in KGB mythology surrounding the affair (most recently in Modin's own account). But the speeding offence took place in February 1951, and Burgess was told he would have to go home in March. The vital break pointing to Maclean did not occur until mid-April. Andrew and Gordievsky, op. cit.; Knightley, op. cit.; Philby, op. cit.; Modin, op. cit.

42. Philby, op. cit.; Modin, op. cit.

43. Modin, op. cit.; Andrew and Gordievsky, op. cit.

44. Philby, op. cit.

45. Sheila Kerr, 'NATO's First Spies: The Case of the Disappearing Diplomats – Guy Burgess and Donald Maclean', in Beatrice Heuser and Robert O'Neill (eds.), *Securing Peace in Europe, 1945–62: Thoughts for the post-Cold War Era* (Macmillan, London, 1990); *Hansard*, House of Commons, 7 November 1955

46. John Ranelagh, *The Agency: The Rise and Decline of the CIA* (Weidenfeld & Nicolson, London, 1986); Knightley, op. cit.; Sheila Kerr, 'British Cold War Defectors: The Versatile, Durable Tools of Propagandists', in Richard J. Aldrich (ed.), *British Intelligence, Strategy and the Cold War, 1945–51* (Routledge, London, 1993)

47. Information made available to the author in confidence; Flora Solomon and Barnet Litvinoff, *Baku to Baker Street: The Memoirs of Flora Solomon* (Collins, London, 1984); Boyle, op. cit.; Knightley, op. cit.

48. Baker, op. cit.; Knightley, op. cit.; Kerr, 'British Cold War Defectors'

49. Cecil, *A Divided Life*; Cecil, 'Donald Maclean'; Donald Maclean, *British Foreign Policy Since Suez* (Hodder & Stoughton, London, 1970)

50. Kitson, op. cit.; Penrose and Freeman, op. cit.; Boyle, op. cit.

51. Cairncross, op. cit.; Modin, op. cit.; *Independent*, 10 October 1995; 'The Tory and the Traitor', *Observer*, 15 November 1995

52. Knightley, op. cit.; Kerr, 'British Cold War Defectors'; Robert Cecil, 'Philby's Spurious War', *Intelligence and National Security*, Vol. 9, No. 4 (October 1994)

53. Kitson, op. cit.; Penrose and Freeman, op. cit.

54. Cairncross, op. cit.; Modin, op. cit.; Dryden, op. cit.

55. Cecil, *A Divided Life*; Modin, op. cit.; Kerr, 'The Secret Hotline to Moscow'
56. Cecil, 'Donald Maclean'; Kerr, 'British Cold War Defectors'

# Chapter 10

1. John Bruce Lockhart, 'Intelligence: A British View', in Kenneth Robertson (ed.), *British and American Approaches to Intelligence* (Macmillan, London, 1987)
2. Tom Bower, *The Perfect English Spy: Sir Dick White and the Secret English War 1935–1990* (Heinemann, London, 1995); George Blake, *No Other Choice: An Autobiography* (Jonathan Cape, London, 1990)
3. Anthony Verrier, *Through the Looking Glass: British Foreign Policy in the Age of Illusions* (Jonathan Cape, London, 1983); Jerrold Schecter and Peter Deriabin, *The Spy Who Saved The World* (Charles Scribner's Sons, New York, 1992); Gordon Brook-Shepherd, *The Storm Birds: Soviet Post-War Defectors* (Weidenfeld & Nicolson, London, 1988); Bower, op. cit.
4. Verrier, op. cit.; Nigel Clive, 'Sir John Ogilvy Rennie', in Lord Blake and C. S. Nicholls (eds.), *Dictionary of National Biography 1981–1985* (OUP, London, 1990); Bower, op. cit.; *Panorama*, BBC Television, 21 November 1993
5. George Kennedy Young in foreword to Anthony Cavendish, *Inside Intelligence* (Collins, London, 1990)
6. Information supplied to the author in confidence; Nigel Clive, 'Sir Maurice Oldfield' in Blake and Nicholls, op. cit.; Cavendish, op. cit.
7. Brook-Shepherd, op. cit.; Oleg Gordievsky, *Next Stop Execution* (Macmillan, London, 1995); Christopher Andrew and Oleg Gordievsky, *The KGB: The Inside Story of its Foreign Operations from Lenin to Gorbachev* (Hodder & Stoughton, London, 1990); Nigel Clive, 'Paid for By Moscow', *Times Literary Supplement*, 30 December 1994
8. Young, op. cit.; 'Frankly Speaking', *Daily Telegraph*, 29 December 1987; Verrier, op. cit.
9. 'MI6 Spy in Exocet Coup Sues for "Exes"', *Sunday Times*, 27 March 1995; 'Ex-Agent of MI5 Claims £200,000', *The Times*, 28 March 1995; 'Secret Agent Claims MI6 Dumped Him', *Guardian*, 28 March 1995; information from a private source
10. 'MI6 Praises Iraq Export Case Defendant', *Financial Times*, 4 November 1992; 'First for MI6 as former Senior Agent Goes Public', *Guardian*, 20 November 1993; 'Top Committee that Failed to Foresee Kuwait or Falklands', *Guardian*, 2 October 1993
11. Information provided to the author in confidence; James Adams, *The New Spies: Exploring the Frontiers of Espionage* (Hutchinson, London, 1994)
12. C. M. Woodhouse, *Something Ventured* (Granada, London, 1982); Verrier, op. cit.; Laurence Lustgarten and Ian Leigh, *In From the Cold: National Security and Parliamentary Democracy* (OUP, Oxford, 1994); *Intelligence Services Act 1994* (HMSO, London, 1994); 'The Spying Game', *Observer*, 3 April 1994; 'Britain's MI6 Spy Agency Comes in from the Cold War', Reuters, 19 October 1993. In addition to its general CX reports, MI6 provides a daily box of intelligence for the Prime Minister and a weekly digest of the most significant items which is circulated widely within Whitehall (Verrier, op. cit.; The Right Honourable Sir Richard Scott, *Report of the Inquiry into the Export of Defence Equipment and Dual-Use Goods to Iraq and Related Prosecutions* (HMSO, London, 1996))
13. Information supplied to the author in confidence; C. M. Andrew, 'The Growth of the Australian Intelligence Community and the Anglo-Australian Connection', *Intelligence and National Security*, Vol. 4, No. 2 (April 1989); Jeffrey T. Richelson

and Desmond Ball, *The Ties That Bind*, 2nd edn (Unwin Hyman, Boston, 1990); Richard J. Aldrich, 'The Value of Residual Empire: Anglo-American Intelligence Cooperation in Asia after 1945', in Richard J. Aldrich and Michael F. Hopkins (eds.), *Intelligence, Defence and Diplomacy: British Policy in the Post-War World* (Frank Cass, London, 1994); 'Australians told MI6 Runs Their Intelligence Work', *The Times*, 22 February 1994; 'Report Clears Australia's External Spy Agency', Reuters, 24 April 1995

14. Young op. cit.; *Panorama*, 21 November 1993; Adams, op. cit.; *Observer*, 3 April 1994
15. Reuters, 19 October 1993; *Panorama*, 21 November 1993
16. *New Spies for Old*, BBC Radio 4, 20 March 1995; 'Russia Denies Biological Weapon Stockpiling', *Jane's Defence Weekly*, 13 May 1995
17. 'Russian "Spy" and Family in Secret Dash to Britain', *Daily Telegraph*, 14 August 1992; 'Counsellor of Russian Embassy Disappears in Paris', *TASS*, 13 August 1992, 'Russian Spy Ring Smashed', *European*, 29 October 1992; 'Seven Spies Said to Defect in 18 Months', Reuters, 28 October 1992; 'MI5 Blunders Let Smith Slip the Security Net', *Daily Telegraph*, 19 November 1993
18. 'Russian Envoy Ordered out in "Gentlemanly" Row', *Daily Telegraph*, 2 April 1994; 'Accused British Agent Describes his Espionage Activities', Associated Press, 31 March 1994
19. 'Federal Security Service Spokesman Says British Spy Admits His Guilt', BBC Summary of World Broadcasts, 8 May 1996 (NTV Moscow, 6 May 1996); 'Security Service Spokesman Gives Insight Into Character of Arrested Spy', BBC Summary of World Broadcasts, 8 May 1996 (Ekho Moskvy Radio, 7 May 1996); 'Russian Accused of Spying for Britain Said to Be "Up-and-Coming Diplomat"', BBC Summary of World Broadcasts, 13 May 1996 (Interfax, 13 May 1996); 'Russia reopens spy row', Reuters, 18 May 1996; 'Russian diplomat admits he spied for London', *AFP*, 28 July 1996
20. Adams, op. cit.; *Observer*, 3 April 1994; 'The Cocaine Trail Leads to Eastern Europe', *Observer*, 15 November 1992; 'Colombian Sentenced for Drug Trafficking', BBC Summary of World Broadcasts, 31 May 1995 (CTK News Agency, 29 May 1995); Reuters, 'Czech Court Jails Colombian For Cocaine Smuggling', 20 January 1995; 'Former Colombian Official Sentenced to Ten Years for Drug Smuggling', Associated Press, 17 December 1993; 'Former Colombian Official Denies Drug Smuggling', Associated Press, 16 December 1993
21. *Hansard*, House of Commons, 22 February 1994
22. Information made available to the author in confidence; 'Hurd Brings MI6 into the Public Eye', *The Times*, 25 November 1993
23. *Central Intelligence Machinery* (HMSO, London, 1993); Lustgarten and Leigh, op. cit.
24. John Strawson, *The History of the SAS Regiment* (Secker & Warburg, London, 1984); 'We Stole Secret Guns from the Soviet Army', *Daily Star*, 24 May 1990; information made available to the author in confidence
25. *Panorama*, 21 November 1993
26. 'Courteous Spymaster Lifts Lid of Secrecy', Reuters, 24 November 1993; information made available to the author in confidence
27. Information made available to the author in confidence

## Chapter 11

1. PRO HD3/15
2. Ibid.; Richard Deacon, *A History of the British Secret Service* (Muller, London, 1969)
3. PRO HD3/16; HD3/22
4. PRO HD3/35; HD3/17; HD3/14
5. PRO HD3/35; HD3/17; HD3/14; HD3/16
6. PRO HD3/35; HD3/17; HD3/14; HD3/16
7. PRO HD3/14; HD3/15; HD3/16; HD3/17; HD3/35
8. PRO FO800/124; HD3/125; HD3/133; Christopher Andrew, 'Codebreakers and Foreign Offices: The French, British and American Experience', in Christopher Andrew and David Dilks (eds.), *The Missing Dimension: Governments and Intelligence Communities in the Twentieth Century* (Macmillan, London, 1984)
9. PRO WO32/10776; Patrick Beesly, *Room 40: British Naval Intelligence 1914–18* (Hamish Hamilton, London, 1982)
10. Christopher Andrew, *Secret Service: The Making of the British Intelligence Community* (William Heinemann, London, 1985). 'Room 40 OB' was its internal Admiralty address, the OB standing for Old Buildings
11. PRO WO32/10776; R. V. Jones, *Reflections on Intelligence* (Mandarin, London, 1990). During the Second World War, Gill was called back up to take charge of the Radio Security Service, the organization that monitored the radio communications between enemy intelligence and its agents.
It should be noted that the difference between codes and cyphers is often misunderstood. A code substitutes groups of letters or figures for complete words or even concepts. A cypher replaces each individual letter or figure of the original message, either by transposition or by substitution
12. John Ferris, 'British Army and Signals Intelligence in the Field During the First World War', *Intelligence and National Security*, Vol. 3, No. 4 (October 1988)
13. PRO WO32/10776; Jock Haswell, *British Military Intelligence* (Weidenfeld & Nicolson, London, 1973)
14. Hugh Skillen, *Spies of the Airwaves* (Hugh Skillen, Pinner, 1989)
15. Nigel West, *GCHQ: The Secret Wireless War 1900–86* (Weidenfeld & Nicolson, London, 1986)
16. David Kahn, 'Codebreaking in World Wars I and II', in Andrew and Dilks, op. cit.; Beesly, op. cit.
17. Christopher Andrew, *For The President's Eyes Only: Intelligence and the Presidency from Washington to Bush* (HarperCollins, London, 1995)
18. PRO WO32/10776; Keith Jeffery (ed.), 'The Government Code and Cypher School: A Memorandum by Lord Curzon', *Intelligence and National Security*, Vol. 1, No. 3 (October 1986); A. G. Denniston, 'The Government Code & Cypher School between the Wars', *Intelligence and National Security*, Vol. 1, No. 1 (January 1986)
19. Denniston, op. cit.; F. H. Hinsley et al., *British Intelligence in the Second World War Vol. 1* (HMSO, London, 1979); Andrew, 'Codebreakers and Foreign Offices'; Henry Dryden, 'Recollections of Bletchley Park, France and Cairo', in F. H. Hinsley and Alan Stripp (eds.), *Codebreakers: The Inside Story of Bletchley Park* (OUP, Oxford, 1993)
20. Jeffery, op. cit.; Denniston, op. cit.
21. Denniston, op. cit.; Keith Jeffery, 'British Military Intelligence Following World War I', in K. G. Robertson (ed.), *British and American Approaches to Intelligence* (Macmillan, London, 1987); Skillen, op. cit.; Andrew, 'Codebreakers and Foreign Offices'

22. Denniston, op. cit.; Andrew, *Secret Service*
23. Denniston, op. cit.; Anthony Best, *Britain, Japan and Pearl Harbor: Avoiding War in East Asia 1936–41* (Routledge, London, 1995). For examples of the Japanese diplomatic traffic intercepted, see PRO WO208/859 and WO106/5606
24. Denniston, op. cit.; Obituary: 'Leonard Hooper', *Daily Telegraph*, 26 February 1994
25. Conversations and correspondence with Stanley Sedgewick, August 1995
26. Alan Stripp, 'The Enigma Machine: Its Mechanism and Use', in Hinsley and Stripp, op. cit.; Kahn, op. cit.; M. R. D. Foot, 'Enigma', in I. C. B. Dear (ed.), *The Oxford Companion to the Second World War* (OUP, Oxford, 1995)
27. Gordon Welchman, 'From Polish Bomba to British Bombe: The Birth of Ultra', *Intelligence and National Security*, Vol. 1, No. 1 (January 1986); Hinsley and Stripp, op. cit.; Interview with Sir Harry Hinsley, 2 May 1995; Hinsley et al., op. cit., Vols. 1 and 2. At this stage 'Ultra' referred only to the Enigma intercepts; it was not until 4 December 1943 that the JIC decided that 'all special intelligence' should be classified 'Most Secret Ultra' (PRO CAB81/92). Ultra was military, air or naval special intelligence, while the product of diplomatic traffic was Magic (Ralph Bennett, 'Ultra', in Dear, op. cit.)
28. PRO ADM223/297; Hinsley interview; Bennett, op. cit.; Ralph Bennett, *Behind the Battle: Intelligence in the War with Germany, 1939–45* (Sinclair Stevenson, London, 1994); Juergen Rohwer, 'Radio Intelligence and its Role in the Battle of the Atlantic', in Andrew and Dilks, op. cit.
   The Operational Intelligence Centre and Bletchley Park had a number of differences. 'There was a danger of BP's researches being too academic,' one OIC officer wrote in an internal history of the Naval Intelligence Division:

   > Their researches, though brilliantly conducted, were more like a game of chess or the arrangement of the jigsaw puzzle. They set the known against the unknown and proceeded to a dispassionate consideration of deductions. Room 30 (the OIC) saw the problem in a different light, for us the merchantmen and MTBs, the patrol vessels and the Sperrbrecher [blockade runners] lived and moved and had their being in a world vibrant with the noise of battle. It was almost as though with a finger on the enemy pulse we brought a warmth and a sense of reality to our research work which was noticeably lacking from many similar efforts by BP.
   > (PRO ADM223/297)

29. Information supplied to the author in confidence
30. F. H. Hinsley, 'An Introduction to Fish', in Hinsley and Stripp, op. cit.; Hinsley et al., op. cit., Vol. 2
31. Gordon Welchman, *The Hut Six Story* (Allen Lane, London, 1982); Robin Denniston, 'Gordon Welchman', in Lord Blake and C. S. Nicholls (eds.), *Dictionary of National Biography 1981–1985* (OUP, Oxford, 1990); Hinsley et al., op. cit., Vol. 1; A. G. Denniston, op. cit.
32. Ramon Silva, *BBC Monitoring Service: August 1939–August 1979* (BBC, Caversham, 1979); Skillen, op. cit.; PRO ADM223/464
33. PRO ADM223/297; Hinsley and Stripp, op. cit.; Skillen, op. cit.; James Bamford, *The Puzzle Palace* (Sidgwick & Jackson, London, 1982); A. G. Denniston, op. cit.; Bennett, *Behind the Battle*
34. Derek Taunt, 'Hut 6: 1941–1945', in Hinsley and Stripp, op. cit.; Dryden, op. cit.; Bennett, *Behind the Battle*; Skillen, op. cit.
35. Alan Stripp, *Codebreaker in the Far East* (Frank Cass, London, 1989); P. W. Filby, 'Floradora and the Unique Break into One-Time Pad Cyphers', *Intelligence and National Security*, Vol. 10, No. 3 (July 1995). As the title of the second work suggests, the author – one of those involved in breaking the German diplomatic

one-time-pad traffic – believes this to be the only time when a one-time pad has been broken. He wisely adds the rider 'as far as is known'. It is unlikely that having been achieved once, and without the aid of computers, this allegedly impossible feat has not been repeated in the succeeding fifty years. Subsequent National Security Agency (NSA) document releases confirming that the KGB's communications with its agents, known by GCHQ and its American counterparts as Venona, were regularly intercepted and translated during the late 1940s and early 1950s shows that at least one other OTP system has been decyphered. Nor has this been the result of recovered Soviet codebooks. According to NSA, the one-time-pad traffic was decyphered 'purely through sweat-of-the-brow' analysis (see 'Introductory History of VENONA and Guide to Translations', Internet address: hftp://www.nsa.gov/venona)

36. Interview with Sir Harry Hinsley, 2 May 1995

## Chapter 12

1. PRO CAB81/93. Presumably the material released to the historians was that with a disguised source as filtered down to field commanders, since Ultra itself remained secret until the publication of Frederick Winterbotham's book *The Ultra Secret* by Weidenfeld & Nicolson in 1974
2. PRO CAB81/132; CAB81/93; CAB81/94
3. Alan Stripp, 'Japanese Air Force Codes', in F. H. Hinsley and Alan Stripp (eds.), *Codebreakers: The Inside Story of Bletchley Park* (OUP, Oxford, 1993); Alan Stripp, *Codebreaker in the Far East* (Frank Cass, London, 1989); Hugh Skillen, *Spies of the Airwaves* (Hugh Skillen, Pinner, 1989); Desmond Ball, 'Signals Intelligence in India', *Intelligence and National Security*, Vol. 10, No. 3 (July 1995)
4. R. V. Jones, *Reflections on Intelligence* (Mandarin, London, 1990); *Central Intelligence Machinery* (HMSO, London, 1993). The timing of the name change was provided by GCHQ, although it could not determine the precise date. A GCHQ spokesman was adamant that until this time the organization was known officially as GC&CS but said that his research had uncovered a number of titles similar to Government Communications Headquarters – for example, Stanley Sedgewick's job offer refers to the 'Government Communications Centre' – all of which were in use during the Second World War, 'possibly for cover purposes'.
It has previously been suggested that the name change occurred around the time that Denniston and the diplomatic section moved back to London in 1942. But Robin Denniston, Denniston's son, recalls seeing the name GCHQ on a sign outside Bletchley Park in late 1941. Official reports which still refer to the organization as GC&CS as late as 1945 appear to confirm the GCHQ insistence that the name was not officially adopted until 1946. Given that a number of people who worked at Bletchley during the war also recall the use of GCHQ, its use as cover seems the most plausible explanation. If that is correct, then the most logical time for its first use would be when GC&CS moved to Bletchley Park in 1939, as indicated by Nigel West. (Conversations with GCHQ press spokesman on 18 and 27 September 1995; Conversation with Alan Stripp on 18 September 1995. For the document referring to GC&CS in 1945 see *Manpower Requirements for Post-War Intelligence Organizations: Report by the Joint Intelligence Committee*, JIC (45) 293, 13 October 1945, in PRO CAB79/40. Nigel West, *GCHQ: The Secret Wireless War 1900–86* (Weidenfeld & Nicolson, London, 1986, p. 112)

5. The exchange of atomic intelligence between America and Britain was heavily restricted by the 1946 McMahon Act. By late 1947 the JIC was complaining that 'our knowledge about Soviet development of atomic weapons is very scanty'. In a 1948 list of GCHQ priorities, Soviet atomic, chemical and biological weapons capability remained the most important target. PRO CAB81/93; CAB81/132; India Office Library and Records L/WS/1/1196. I am grateful to Richard Aldrich for drawing the last document to my attention. See also Richard Aldrich and Michael Coleman, 'The Cold War, the JIC and British Signals Intelligence', *Intelligence and National Security*, Vol. 4, No. 3 (July 1989)

6. PRO CAB80/39; CAB81/94; CAB81/124; F. H. Hinsley et al., *British Intelligence in the Second World War Vol. 2* (HMSO, London, 1979); Aldrich and Coleman, op. cit.

7. 'US Spy Agencies Release Decoded KGB Messages From 1940s', Associated Press, 12 July 1995; 'Britain Forced to Reveal Code Breaking that Trapped Spies', *Guardian*, 13 July 1995; Andy Thomas, 'Signals Intelligence after the Second World War', *Intelligence and National Security*, Vol. 3, No. 4 (October 1988); West, op. cit. See my Chapter 2 for a description of the UKUSA Accord, the co-operation agreement between Britain and America

8. Thomas, op. cit.; PRO AIR29/1917; AIR29/1918; AIR29/934; *Warning Signal, Newsletter of the GCHQ Trade Unions*, No. 138 (September 1994); West, op. cit.

9. PRO CAB81/131; CAB81/132; Henry Dryden, 'Recollections of Bletchley Park, France and Cairo', in Hinsley and Stripp, op. cit.

10. A. G. Denniston, 'The Government Code & Cypher School Between The Wars', *Intelligence and National Security*, Vol. 1, No. 1 (January 1986); West, op. cit.

11. PRO AIR68/19; Skillen, op. cit.; *Report of the Security Commission, October 1986* (CMD 9923, HMSO, London, 1986); 'Defence Ministry Tries to Recruit Sacked Army Experts at Cut Rate', *The Herald*, 7 January 1995; 'Under US Eyes: The West has a Hidden Advantage over Iraq', *Independent on Sunday*, 30 September 1990

12. Skillen, op. cit.; West, op. cit.; Jeffrey T. Richelson, *Foreign Intelligence Organizations* (Ballinger, Cambridge, Mass, 1988); 'Signals Dutch Leave', *Soldier Magazine*, 8 August 1994; '13 Signal Regiment', *The Rose and the Laurel, Journal of the Intelligence Corps*, December 1994

13. Information supplied to the author in confidence; PRO CAB81/130; Anthony Clayton, *Forearmed: A History of the Intelligence Corps* (Brassey's, London, 1993)

14. PRO AIR20/2669; AIR20/7690; AIR20/7691; ADM167/133; Aldrich and Coleman, op. cit.; Thomas, op. cit.; Richard J. Aldrich, 'Secret Intelligence for a Post-War World: Reshaping the British Intelligence Community, 1944–51', in Richard J. Aldrich (ed.), *British Intelligence, Strategy and the Cold War 1945–51* (Routledge, London, 1992)

15. Thomas, op. cit.

16. Information supplied to the author in confidence; Clayton, op. cit.

17. Richelson, op. cit.; MOD Press Office, 20 September 1995

18. Clayton, op. cit.; Martin Middlebrook, *Operation Corporate: The Story of the Falklands War, 1982* (Viking, London, 1985); 'Headquarters British Forces Falkland Islands', *The Rose and the Laurel, Journal of the Intelligence Corps*, December 1994; 'Belize', *The Rose and the Laurel, Journal of the Intelligence Corps*, December 1994. Communications and Security Group (UK) will be located at the New Defence Intelligence Centre at Chicksands, Bedfordshire, from mid-1997. Chicksands was handed over to the Americans as a communications intelligence base in 1948, but the US facility was closed in 1994 and some of its functions transferred to another US base at Menwith Hill, near Harrogate, North Yorkshire (MOD Press Office; *The Rose and the Laurel, Journal of the*

*Intelligence Corps,* December 1995; 'US to Close British Listening Post in Eavesdropping Transfer', *Guardian,* 16 July 1994)

19. '9 Signal Regiment', *The Rose and the Laurel, Journal of the Intelligence Corps,* December 1991 and December 1994

20. 'Electronic Warfare', in I. C. B. Dear (ed.), *The Oxford Companion to the Second World War* (OUP, Oxford, 1995)

21. Thomas, op. cit.; PRO AIR20/10178; AIR29/1910; PRO AIR29/1911; PRO AIR29/1912; PRO AIR29/1913; 'Spies in the Skies', BBC Television, *Timewatch,* 9 February 1994 – this programme was based on secret US Department of Defense files declassified in March 1993. See also 'Spy Flights Cost US at least 138 Airmen', *Daily Telegraph,* 6 March 1993; 'The Night the RAF "Bombed" Russia: British Pilots Flew Spy Missions for America', *Daily Telegraph,* 7 February 1994, and West, op. cit. The official log of the Lincoln's base at RAF Leconfield records that it was on a 'regular exercise testing reaction to simulated fighter attacks'.

22. West, op. cit.; James Bamford, *The Puzzle Palace* (Sidgwick & Jackson, London, 1982). What appears to have been one of the first fatal missions was a US Navy SIGINT aircraft shot down over Latvian airspace in April 1950 with the loss of ten crew members, including six technical operators. Two of the worst were the shooting down of a USAF EC-130 ELINT aircraft by Soviet MiG fighters over Armenian airspace with the loss of seventeen crew, and the loss of thirty-one men on board a US Navy EC-121 shot down by North Korea in April 1969

23. 'Royal Air Force's Nimrod Electronic Intelligence Aircraft', *Jane's Defence Weekly,* 19 October 1985

24. 'Upgrade Takes Recce Nimrods into 1980s', *Jane's Defence Weekly,* 15 April 1995

25. PRO ADM223/297; Denniston, op. cit.; James Rusbridger and Eric Nave, *Betrayal at Pearl Harbor: How Churchill Lured Roosevelt into War* (Michael O'Mara Books, London, 1991); West, op. cit.; Letter from Composite Signals Organization Committee (elected representative body) to members dated 14 April 1982 and reproduced in Hugh Lanning and Richard Norton-Taylor, *A Conflict of Loyalties: GCHQ 1984–1991* (New Clarion Press, Cheltenham, 1991)

26. Bamford, op. cit.; 'Diplomatic Bag Via Satellite', *The Times,* 2 February 1967

27. Bamford, op. cit.; *Dispatches,* Channel 4 Television, 5 October 1993; 'Rifkind Bans Disclosures on Spy Base', *Guardian,* 13 March 1995

28. Jeffrey T. Richelson, *America's Secret Eyes in Space: The US Keyhole Spy Satellite Program* (Harper & Row, New York, 1990); Jeffrey T. Richelson, 'Spies in the Sky: A Short History of Satellites', *Washington Post,* 25 February 1990

29. Composite Signals Organization Committee letter

30. 'America's Falklands War', *The Economist,* 3 March 1984; 'The Parliamentary Bypass Operation', *New Statesman,* 23 January 1987; 'Zircon Satellite is Abandoned: Thatcher Opts to Rely on US Technology', *The Times,* 6 August 1987

31. Richelson, *Foreign Intelligence Organizations;* 'Spies in the Sky Keep Watch on Iraq', *The Times,* 15 January 1991

32. *Central Intelligence Machinery* (HMSO, London, 1993); *Intelligence Services Act 1994* (HMSO, London, 1994)

33. Richelson, *Foreign Intelligence Organizations;* 'What Our Spies Are Up To Now', *Daily Telegraph,* 22 February 1993; Composite Signals Organisation Committee letter; Conversation with GCHQ Press Office, 26 September 1995; 'Hurd Brings MI6 into the Public Eye', *The Times,* 25 November 1993; *Intelligence and Security Committee, Annual Report 1995* (HMSO, London 1996)

34. *Report of the Security Commission May 1983* (HMSO, London, 1983); Bamford, op. cit.; *Central Intelligence Machinery;* GCHQ Press Office conversation; Richelson, *Foreign Intelligence Organizations;* Thomas, op. cit.; PRO AIR29/1917;

'13 Signal Regiment', *The Rose and the Laurel, Journal of the Intelligence Corps*, December 1994; MOD Press Office, 10 November 1995

35. 'GCHQ Facing Jobs Cuts', *Guardian*, 4 February 1992; 'Other Lives: The Spies Who've Moved Upmarket', *Guardian*, 16 July 1994; 'Spy Rivals Crow as GCHQ Faces Cuts', *Sunday Times*, 26 March 1995; 'GCHQ Facing 40 per cent Job Losses', *Guardian*, 25 September 1995; GCHQ Press Office conversation; 'Counter-Spy to be New Head of MI5', *Daily Telegraph*, 24 November 1995

36. 'GCHQ's Service to US Crucial', *Guardian*, 17 May 1994

## Chapter 13

1. Thomas G. Fergusson, *British Military Intelligence 1870–1914: The Development of a Modern Intelligence Organization* (Arms and Armour Press, London, 1984); Jock Haswell, *British Military Intelligence* (Weidenfeld & Nicolson, London, 1973)
2. Anthony Clayton, *Forearmed: A History of the Intelligence Corps* (Brassey's, London, 1993); Haswell, op. cit.
3. Haswell, op. cit.
4. Major D. S. Hawker, Working Notes for a History of the Intelligence Corps, Intelligence Corps Museum
5. Kirke Papers, Intelligence Corps Museum
6. Fergusson, op. cit.
7. Christopher Andrew, *Secret Service: The Making of the British Intelligence Community* (William Heinemann, London, 1985)
8. Fergusson, op. cit.
9. Walter Lacquer, *A World of Secrets, The Uses and Limits of Intelligence* (Basic, New York, 1985); Fergusson, op. cit.
10. Fergusson, op. cit.
11. WOII G. Downton, Notes and Pictures on the History of Photographic Interpretation, Intelligence Corps Museum; Lacquer, op. cit.
12. Wg Comdr M. T. Thurbon, 'The Origins of Electronic Warfare', *Journal of the Royal United Services Institute*, No. 122 (September 1977); PRO WO32/10776.
The 1918 organization of the Directorate of Military Intelligence was as follows:

| | |
|---|---|
| MIR | Russian section (responsible for intelligence on Russia, Siberia, Central Asia, Persia, Afghanistan, China, Japan and Siam; information emanating from India; and liaison with the General Staff (India) |
| MI1 | Secretariat (responsible for organization; distribution of military policy regarding submarine cables and wireless telegraphy; preparation, distribution and security of War Office cyphers; interior economy of the directorate; interrogation of prisoners of war in the United Kingdom) |
| MI2 | Military information concerning the Americas (except Canada), Spain, Portugal, Italy, Liberia, Tangier, the Balkan States, the Ottoman Empire, Arabia, Sinai, Abyssinia, Egypt, Sudan and West Persia |
| MI3 | Military information concerning France, Belgium, Morocco, Austria, Hungary, Switzerland, Germany, Luxembourg, Holland, Norway, Sweden and Denmark |
| MI4 | Geographical section |
| MI5 | Counter-espionage |
| MI6 | Legal and Economic section |

MI7   Press Control
MI8   Cable Censorship
MI9   Postal Censorship
MI10  Military attachés

13. Clayton, op. cit.; Haswell, op. cit.
14. Haswell, op. cit.
15. Ibid.
16. David Engleheart, 'The ORs' Depot, Winchester', *The Rose and the Laurel, Journal of the Intelligence Corps*, December 1994
17. War Diary, Directorate of Military Intelligence, Organization and Establishments, Intelligence Corps Museum
   The wartime organization of the DMI was as follows:

MI1   Administration and Personnel
MI2   Intelligence on northern and eastern Europe, USSR, Middle East and Asia
MI3   Intelligence on western Europe and the Americas
MI4   Maps (transferred to Directorate of Military Operations in 1940)
MI5   Security Service (Civilian organization)
MI6   Secret Intelligence Service (Civilian Organization)
MI7   Press (transferred to Ministry of Information in 1940)
MI8   Signals Intelligence
MI9   PoW Intelligence
MI10  Technical Intelligence (became part of MI16 at end of war); Road Intelligence (from end of war)
MI11  Field Security
MI12  Postal and Telegraph Censorship (abandoned, reluctantly, at end of war)*
MI14  Intelligence on Germany.
MI15  Photographic Intelligence (transferred to Air Ministry in 1943); Air Defence Intelligence (from 1943)
MI16  Scientific and Technical Intelligence (formed at end of war)
MI17  Co-ordination/JIC
MI19  Interrogation of enemy prisoners/debriefing of refugees

   Sources for above: War Diary, DMI, Organization and Establishments, Intelligence Corps Museum; PRO CAB81/94; CAB81/130; M. R. D. Foot, 'British Intelligence', in I. C. B. Dear (ed.), *The Oxford Companion to the Second World War* (OUP, Oxford, 1995); Clayton, op. cit.; Alan Stripp, *Codebreaker in the Far East* (Frank Cass, London, 1989)
18. Clayton, op. cit.; Richard Deacon, *'C': A Biography of Sir Maurice Oldfield* (Macdonald, London, 1983)
19. PRO CAB81/100
20. PRO ADM223/475; Hinsley et al., *British Intelligence in the Second World War Vol. 1* (HMSO, London, 1979); John Weaver during seminar on 'Photographic Reconnaissance During World War II', RAF Museum Hendon, 10 June 1991
21. PRO CAB81/101
22. 'Joint Air Reconnaissance Intelligence Centre', *The Rose and the Laurel, Journal*

---

* In a report on the *Post-War Organization of Intelligence*, the JIC said of MI12 (Postal and Telegraph Censorship), 'Despite the value of this body in wartime as a source of intelligence and counter-intelligence, it was agreed that its peacetime nucleus should not be brought into the intelligence organization.' (CAB81/130)

*of the Intelligence Corps*, December 1990; PRO CAB81/99; Sebastian Cox, 'Photographic Reconnaissance', in Dear, op. cit.

23. PRO ADM223/297; ADM223/464; ADM223/475; ADM223/619; Wesley K. Wark, 'British Military and Economic Intelligence Assessments of Nazi Germany before the Second World War', in Christopher Andrew and David Dilks (eds.), *The Missing Dimension: Governments and Intelligence Communities in the Twentieth Century* (Macmillan, London, 1984).

The organization of the Naval Intelligence Division in 1941–2 was as follows:

NID 1 Germany and northern Europe
NID 2 Americas
NID 3 Mediterranean; Middle East; north-east and east Africa
NID 4 Far East
NID 5 Geographical Handbooks
NID 6 Topographical
NID 7 Constructional Engineering and Technical Matters
NID 8 Operational Intelligence Centre
NID 9 Y Service
NID 10 Codes and Cyphers
NID 11 PoW Intelligence
NID 12 Special Navy Section, Bletchley Park
NID 14 Secretariat
NID 15 Liaison with other naval departments
NID 16 Soviet Union
NID 17 Liaison with JIC and SIS
NID 18 Naval Intelligence Section, Washington DC
NID 19 Information; press cuttings; liaison with government departments and BBC
NID 20 Vichy France; Iberia; north-west, west and southern Africa
NID 21 Contacts
(PRO ADM223/473)

24. Clayton, op. cit.; Nigel West, *A Matter of Trust, MI5 1945–72* (Coronet, London, 1982)

25. PRO CAB81/92; CAB81/129; Cox, op. cit.; Alex Danchev, 'In the Back Room: Anglo-American Defence Cooperation', 1945–51, in Richard J. Aldrich (ed.), *British Intelligence, Strategy and the Cold War 1945–51* (Routledge, London, 1992). The role of strategic signals intelligence is recorded in my Chapter 12

26. PRO CAB81/93

27. PRO CAB81/134; 'Spies in the Skies', *Timewatch*, BBC Television, 9 February 1994 – this programme was based on secret US Department of Defense files declassified in March 1993. See also 'Spy Flights Cost US at least 138 Airmen', *Daily Telegraph*, 6 March 1993; 'The Night the RAF "Bombed" Russia: British Pilots Flew Spy Missions for America', *Daily Telegraph*, 7 February 1994

28. *The Rose and the Laurel*, December 1990; 'Spies in the Skies'

29. 'Spies in the Skies'

30. Ibid.; *Statement on the Defence Estimates* (Cmd 2800, HMSO, London, 1995); 'Air Forces of the World, United Kingdom', *Flight International*, 5 July 1995

31. *The Rose and the Laurel*, December 1990; R. A. K. Crabtree, 'Battlefield Surveillance by Airborne Stand-Off Radars', in *Defence Systems International: Air Systems* (Sterling Publications International, London, 1991); Jeffrey T. Richelson, *America's Secret Eyes in Space: The US Keyhole Spy Satellite Program* (Harper & Row, New York, 1990); Antony Beevor, *Inside the British Army* (Corgi, London, 1991)

32. 'America's Falklands War', *The Economist*, 3 March 1984; Jeffrey T. Richelson, *Foreign Intelligence Organizations* (Ballinger, Cambridge, Mass., 1988); Jeffrey T. Richelson and Desmond Ball, *The Ties that Bind*, 2nd edn (Unwin Hyman, Boston, 1990); Julian Thompson, *No Picnic* (Leo Cooper, London, 1985); Richelson, *America's Secret Eyes in Space*
33. *The Rose and the Laurel*, December 1990; BBC Summary of World Broadcasts, Part I, *Report on Air Reconnaisance*, 18 February 1994, *Krasnaya Zvezda*, 11 February 1994

# Chapter 14

1. Wesley K. Wark, 'British Military and Economic Intelligence: Assessments of Nazi Germany Before the Second World War', in Christopher Andrew and David Dilks (eds.), *The Missing Dimension: Governments and Intelligence Communities in the Twentieth Century* (Macmillan, London, 1984)
2. PRO CAB81/93; CAB81/94; CAB81/122; CAB81/130; Kenneth Strong, *Men of Intelligence: A Study of the Roles and Decisions of Chiefs of Intelligence from World War II to the Present Day* (Cassell, London, 1970); Richard J. Aldrich, 'Secret Intelligence for a Post-War World: Reshaping the British Intelligence Community, 1944–51', in Richard J. Aldrich (ed.), *British Intelligence, Strategy and the Cold War 1945–51* (Routledge, London, 1993); *Defence Intelligence Staff Induction Briefing Handbook* (Ministry of Defence, London, 1995)
3. Defence Intelligence Staff Briefing, MOD, 15 November 1995; *Defence Intelligence Staff Induction Briefing Handbook*; Lord Justice Scott, *Report of the Inquiry into the Export of Defence Equipment and Dual-Use Goods to Iraq and Related Prosecutions* (HMSO, London, 1996)
4. Alfred Vogts, *The Military Attaché* (Princeton University Press, Princeton, NJ, 1967). PRO WO32/10776. For an example of the current covert activities of military attachés, see 'Military Network Now Handles DoD HUMINT', *Jane's Defence Weekly*, 11 March 1995 and 'Beijing will Expel 2 Americans as Spies', *International Herald Tribune*, 3 August 1995. Although these reports refer to US officers, it should be assumed that similar activities are being undertaken by their British counterparts
5. CAB81/94; Obituary: 'Air Vice-Marshal Gordon Young', *The Times*, 14 December 1993
6. Defence Intelligence Staff Briefing; *Defence Intelligence Staff Induction Briefing Handbook*; 'Intelligence Frontline at Risk in MOD Savings', *The Times*, 7 November 1994; 'Country Briefing: United Kingdom', *Jane's Defence Weekly*, 15 July 1995; Scott, op. cit.
7. Defence Intelligence Staff Briefing; *Defence Intelligence Staff Induction Briefing Handbook*; 'What Our Spies Are Up To Now The Cold War is Over', *Daily Telegraph*, 22 February 1993
8. Defence Intelligence Staff Briefing; *Defence Intelligence Staff Induction Briefing Handbook*; Scott, op. cit.; Antony Beevor, *Inside the British Army* (Corgi, London, 1991); 'Directorate Notes', *The Rose and the Laurel, Journal of the Intelligence Corps*, December 1995
9. Anthony Clayton, *Forearmed: A History of the Intelligence Corps* (Brassey's, London, 1993); Richard J. Aldrich, 'British Strategy and the End of the Empire: South Asia 1945–51', in Aldrich, *British Intelligence*; Keith Jeffrey, 'Intelligence and Counter-Insurgency Operations: Some Reflections on the British Experience',

*Intelligence and National Security*, Vol. 2, No. 1 (January 1987); Anthony M. Perry, 'The Malayan Effect', in *The Rose and the Laurel, Journal of the Intelligence Corps*, December 1990

10. Philip Warner, *The SAS* (Sphere, London, 1983); James Adams, *Secret Armies* (Pan, London, 1988); Clayton, op. cit.

11. Richard Popplewell, "Lacking Intelligence": Some Reflections on Recent Approaches to British Counter-Insurgency, 1900–1960', *Intelligence and National Security*, Vol. 10, No. 2 (April 1995); Jeffrey, op. cit.

12. Michael Russell Rip, 'The Precision Revolution: The Navstar Global Positioning System in the Second Gulf War', *Intelligence and National Security*, Vol. 9, No. 2 (April 1994)

13. Julian Thompson, *No Picnic* (Leo Cooper, London, 1985)

14. Lawrence Freedman, 'Intelligence Operations in the Falklands', *Intelligence and National Security*, Vol. 1, No. 3 (September 1986); Adams, op. cit.; Jeffrey T. Richelson, *Foreign Intelligence Organizations* (Ballinger, Cambridge, Mass., 1988); Jeffrey T. Richelson and Desmond Ball, *The Ties That Bind*, 2nd edn (Unwin Hyman, London, 1990); Clayton, op. cit.; Martin Middlebrook, *Operation Corporate: The Story of the Falklands War, 1982* (Viking, London, 1985); Letter from the Composite Signals Organization Committee (elected representative body) to members dated 14 April 1982 and reproduced in Hugh Lanning and Richard Norton-Taylor, *A Conflict of Loyalties: GCHQ 1984–1991* (New Clarion Press, Cheltenham, 1991); 'British Got Crucial Data in Falklands, Diary Says', *New York Times*, 12 December 1984

15. Clayton, op. cit.; *The British Army in the Falklands* (HMSO, London, 1982); Freedman, op. cit.; Thompson, op. cit.; Scott, op. cit.

16. *Operation Desert Storm Attack Plan* (24th Mechanized Infantry Division, Fort Stewart, Georgia, February 1992); Rip, op. cit.

17. 'Under US Eyes: The West has a Hidden Advantage over Iraq', *Independent on Sunday*, 30 September 1990; Rip, op. cit.; 'Bosnia Underscores Intelligence Gaps', *Aviation Week and Space Technology*, 20 March 1995

18. *Operation Desert Storm Attack Plan*; 'The Gulf War: Spies in Sky Look Over Saddam's Shoulder', *Daily Telegraph*, 29 January 1991; Rip, op. cit.

19. 'Gulf War Failures Cited', *Washington Post*, 11 April 1992; 'Pentagon Report on Persian Gulf War', *New York Times*, 11 April 1992; Sheila Kerr, 'The Debate on US Post-Cold War Intelligence: One More New Botched Beginning', *Defence Analysis*, Vol. 10, No. 3 (1994)

20. 'Operation Gabriel', in *The Rose and the Laurel, Journal of the Intelligence Corps*, December 1995; 'The Former Yugoslavia: Operation Grapple 5', in *The Rose and the Laurel, Journal of the Intelligence Corps*, December 1995; Defence Intelligence Staff Briefing

21. *Aviation Week and Space Technology*, 20 March 1995; Hugh Smith, 'Intelligence and UN Peacekeeping', *Survival*, Vol. 36, No. 3 (Autumn 1994)

22. 'The Former Yugoslavia', *The Rose and the Laurel, Journal of the Intelligence Corps*, December 1994 and December 1995; *Statement on the Defence Estimates 1995* (HMSO, London, 1995)

23. 'The Former Yugoslavia', *The Rose and the Laurel, Journal of the Intelligence Corps*, December 1995; Defence Intelligence Staff Briefing

## Chapter 15

1. 'Ex-Head of Intelligence Says It Helped Arrange Mandela's Release', South African Press Association, 18 February 1992; 'Negotiations: The Long and Winding Road', *Africa Confidential*, 20 March 1992; information supplied to the author in confidence.

   The peaceful transition to black rule in South Africa was set up by the National Intelligence Service, which in 1988 began holding secret talks with Nelson Mandela in Pollsmoor Prison. 'We started to realize that we have to turn our attention to Mr Mandela and other members of the Rivonia group,' said Dr Niel Barnard, the former head of NIS. 'The question was asked whether we could reach a political solution while these persons were incarcerated. We were thus sanctioned by the government to try to establish from Mr Mandela whether he was able to play a role in finding a political solution.'

   Talks with Mandela were followed by secret meetings with the ANC leadership, the first of which took place in Geneva in December 1989. 'For the NIS to meet the ANC in Europe was no easy matter,' Dr Barnard said. 'These were not chaps who could meet openly in some hotel. We knew that when we travelled abroad we were being openly watched, and the same applied to the particular ANC persons. We had to use quite interesting methods to evade observation by other intelligence services.'

   Parallel diplomacy also helped to bring peace to the Middle East. Perhaps surprisingly, Mossad had established an informal channel of communication with the PLO – mainly through the French intelligence services – which the two sides used largely to lay down 'red lines', setting out how far they were prepared to allow the other side to go. This was developed into one-to-one contacts in order to set up the Oslo talks in late 1993 which led to the Middle East peace agreement. (Sources as above)

2. IWM 75/46/12, Papers of Field Marshal Sir John French, Letter to Lord Londonderry dated 3 January 1920

3. PRO CO904/23; IWM 72/82/2, Papers of Lt-Gen. Sir Hugh Jeudwine, *Record of the Rebellion in Ireland in 1920–21 and the Part Played by the Army in Dealing With It, Vol II: Intelligence*

4. PRO CO904/23; IWM 75/46/12, Papers of Field Marshal Sir John French, Report by Basil Thomson on the state of intelligence in Ireland dated September 1916; Tim Pat Coogan, *The IRA* (Fontana, London, 1987)

5. IWM 75/46/12, French Papers, *Report by Basil Thomson*, and *Urgent Inquiry into the Ineffectiveness of the Police to Detect Political Crime, December 1919*

6. PRO CO904/23; IWM 75/46/12, French Papers, *Urgent Inquiry*; IWM 72/82/2, Jeudwine Papers, *Record of the Rebellion*; Kenneth Strong, *Intelligence at the Top: The Recollections of an Intelligence Officer* (Cassell, London, 1968)

7. HLRO F31/1/32; F31/1/33; Richard Thurlow, *The Secret State: British Internal Security in the Twentieth Century* (Blackwell, Oxford, 1994); IWM 76/172/1, Papers of Captain R. D. Jeune.

   Reinforcements for the RIC were found in England. The RIC uniform was a dark-green tunic and black trousers, but since there were insufficient jackets for the new recruits many wore khaki uniform and the dark-green RIC service cap. They were consequently known as the Black and Tans, after the well-known Irish pack of hounds. In fact most of the excesses attributed to the Black and Tans were carried out by the RIC Auxiliary Division, which, although officially enlisted as part of the police, was made up almost entirely of former soldiers. Senior Army officers despised their lack of discipline which led to a number of brutal reprisals – at one point the centre of Cork was razed to the ground in retaliation for an IRA attack. But more junior Army officers appear to have approved. Captain R. D. Jeune, an Army intelligence officer, wrote, 'We often collaborated with them and there was no nonsense with the IRA.'

8. HLRO F31/1/32; F31/1/33; F46/1/27; F27/7/20; Sir John W. Wheeler-Bennett, *John Anderson, Viscount Waverley* (Macmillan, London, 1952); Thomas Jones, *Lloyd George* (OUP, London, 1951); Thurlow, op. cit.
Fisher found that Dublin Castle was 'entirely unconcerned with the exploration or settlement of the problems which the Irish administration exists to solve'. The police required 'drastic overhauling', he added. 'The heads of the Royal Irish Constabulary and the Dublin Metropolitan Police respectively seem to be mediocrities and, while the morale of the former force is getting shaken, the latter force has apparently lost it entirely.'
Cope, who co-wrote the main report, appears to have borrowed Basil Thomson's assessment of the administration's intelligence capability almost word for word:

> There are as many as five separate and distinct systems of intelligence working with the same object, each under different control, viz. the military, naval, two police forces and Scotland Yard. In view of the obvious disadvantages of overlapping in work of this character, we suggest that it would be well worth considering whether these various intelligence systems could not be co-ordinated under a single direction.

9. PRO CO904/188; CAB23/21/29; HLRO F48/6/37; Keith Jeffery, 'British Military Intelligence Following World War I', in K. G. Robertson (ed.), *British and American Approaches to Intelligence* (Macmillan, London, 1987)
10. IWM Misc 175 Item 2658, Joy B. Cave, Unpublished Biography of Major-Gen. Sir H. H. Tudor; Obituary: 'Sir Ormonde Winter', *The Times*, 15 February 1962; Andrew, op. cit.
11. Jeune Papers; Eunan O'Halpin, 'British Intelligence in Ireland, 1914–1921', in Christopher Andrew and David Dilks (eds.), *The Missing Dimension: Governments and Intelligence Communities in the Twentieth Century* (Macmillan, London, 1984); Andrew, op. cit. The amount of money taken from the Secret Service Vote for intelligence work in Ireland rose from £1,412 9s. 5d. in the financial year 1918–19 to £63,602 4s. 9d. in 1920–1
12. Jeune Papers; IWM 72/82/2, Jeudwine Papers; Tim Pat Coogan, *Michael Collins* (Arrow, London, 1991)
13. O'Halpin, op. cit.; IWM 72/82/2, Jeudwine Papers
14. PRO CO904/188, Anderson to Macready, 29 March 1921, and Macready to Anderson, 8 April 1921
15. HLRO F17/1/2; F19/2/13; 'Mr Cope's Great Work for Ireland', *Manchester Guardian*, 3 November 1922; Obituary: 'Sir Alfred Cope', *The Times*, 14 May 1954; Coogan, *Michael Collins*
In his letter to Fisher, Cope added:

> Leaders of SF will not (and cannot) come out openly and stop outrage unless they can go forward with an open and definite undertaking that Dominion Home Rule, or something like it, will be given.
>    The country does not believe the Government and the leaders tell me (those I have met) that the country will believe that a mere promise to them to be given something good, if they and the gunmen are good men, cannot be accepted. The country will think it a ruse to stop outrages.

In a subsequent letter to Sir John Anderson, Cope described a meeting with one of the rebels. 'Saw other man but thought no good opening discussion on first introduction. He had no knowledge of Cork murder (Smyth) and was clearly shocked when we told him. "It's a bad job. But he asked for it." Left open door for further discussion if necessary.' (According to the *Irish Bulletin*, Lt-Col. Bruce Smyth VC, an RIC divisional commissioner, had ordered his men to adopt a shoot-to-kill policy. 'You may make mistakes occasionally, and innocent persons may be shot, but that cannot be helped,' he was quoted as saying. He was subsequently shot dead by a volunteer who told him, 'Your orders were to shoot on sight. You are in sight now, so make ready.'

16. IWM 76/172/1, Jeune Papers. The O'Connor in question may have been Bat O'Connor, a close associate of Michael Collins

17. PRO PRO30/59/1–4, Sturgis Diary; Wheeler-Bennett, op. cit.; M. R. D. Foot, 'Sir Alfred William Cope', in E. T. Williams and Helen M. Palmer (eds.), *Dictionary of National Biography 1951–1960* (OUP, Oxford, 1971); Jones, op. cit.

18. Wheeler-Bennett, op. cit.; Sturgis Diary

19. PRO CO904/100; *Manchester Guardian*, 3 November 1922

20. HLRO F34/1/27; Wheeler-Bennett, op. cit.; Jones, op. cit.; Coogan, *Michael Collins*

21. PRO CO904/23

22. Wheeler-Bennett, op. cit.

23. Robert Kee, *The Green Flag: A History of Irish Nationalism* (Weidenfeld & Nicolson, London, 1972). A paper also prepared in April 1921 by the Irish Office laid out British policy in Ireland. Sinn Fein was divided and there was 'abundant evidence of the existence of a large body who would snatch eagerly at any settlement which gave them something approaching to their ideal of complete control of local affairs', it said:

> Coercive measures, to be effective, must be accompanied continually by plain and unmistakeable evidence of a desire to settle on what a majority of the non-combatants would regard as reasonable terms.
>    In the face of the gunmen, the moderate elements are perforce silent. Herein consists the strong argument for affording at this juncture opportunity for discussion and, if it may be, negotiation. If such an opportunity be afforded, the bitterness resulting from the renewal of the conflict will, it may be hoped, be turned in large measure against the extreme elements which today are the sole obstacle to peace.

(PRO CO904/232, Document prepared by the Irish Office, dated 27 April 1921)

24. Kee, op. cit.; Wheeler-Bennett, op. cit.

25. 'The Last Days of Dublin Castle', *Blackwood's Magazine*, August 1922; Coogan, *Michael Collins*

26. IWM 76/172/1, Jeune Papers; PRO CO904/23; Kee, op. cit.; Wheeler-Bennett, op. cit.
Briefing the Cabinet in London on the possibilities for a truce, Cope argued so strongly for peace that Sir Hamar Greenwood, the Chief Secretary, interrupted him to tell him to 'curb his Sinn Fein tendencies' (Sturgis Diary).

27. PRO CO904/232; HLRO F10/2/50; F10/2/67; F10/2/44; F20/3/20; F10/3/15; F19/5/23; 'Hey Johnny Cope', *Morning Post*, 31 October 1922

28. Brig. G. L. C. Cooper, 'Some Aspects of Conflict in Ulster', *British Army Review*, No. 43 (April 1973)

29. David Charters, 'Intelligence and Psychological Warfare Operations in Northern Ireland', *Journal of the Royal United Services Institute*, September 1977; Anthony Verrier, *Through the Looking Glass: British Foreign Policy in the Age of Illusions* (Jonathan Cape, London, 1983)

30. Charters, op. cit.; Tony Geraghty, *Who Dares Wins* (Arms and Armour Press, London, 1980); Roger Faligot, *Britain's Military Strategy in Ireland: The Kitson Experiment* (Zed Press, London, 1983)

31. Verrier, op. cit.
32. Ibid.; Patrick Bishop and Eamonn Mallie, *The Provisional IRA* (William Heinemann, London, 1987); 'British Spies in Ireland', *Irish Times*, 22 April 1980; The Sunday Times Insight Team, *Ulster* (Penguin, Harmondsworth, 1972); Keith Jeffrey, 'Intelligence and Counter-Insurgency Operations: Some Reflections on the British Experience', *Intelligence and National Security*, Vol. 2, No. 1 (January 1987)
33. Michael Carver, *Out of Step: The Memoirs of Field Marshal Lord Carver* (Hutchinson, London, 1989)
34. Information made available to the author in confidence; Verrier, op. cit.; Merlyn Rees, *Northern Ireland: A Political Perspective* (Methuen, London, 1985)
35. Coogan, *The IRA*; Verrier, op. cit.
36. Rees, op. cit.
37. 'When the IRA Thought They had Britain By The Throat', *Sunday Telegraph*, 26 March 1995; Sean MacStiofain, *Revolutionary in Ireland* (Gordon Cremonesi, Edinburgh, 1975); J. Bowyer Bell, *The Irish Troubles: A Generation of Violence 1967–1992* (Gill and Macmillan, Dublin, 1993)
38. Tim Pat Coogan, *The Troubles: Ireland's Ordeal 1966–1995 and the Search for Peace* (Hutchinson, London, 1995); Barry White, *John Hume* (Blackstaff, Belfast, 1984)
39. Information made available to the author in confidence; Verrier, op. cit.; MacStiofain, op. cit.; White, op. cit.; 'Gerry Adams: The Man We All Love to Hate', *Panorama*, BBC Television, 30 January 1995
40. *Sunday Telegraph*, 26 March 1995; Coogan, *The Troubles*; Bowyer Bell, op. cit.
41. William Whitelaw, *The Whitelaw Memoirs* (Aurum Press, London, 1989); MacStiofain, op. cit.; Verrier, op. cit.; Coogan, *The Troubles*
42. MacStiofain, op. cit.; information supplied to the author in confidence
43. Bishop and Mallie, op. cit.; Charters, op. cit.; Verrier, op. cit.
44. Verrier, op. cit.; *Sunday Telegraph*, 26 March 1995
45. Verrier, op. cit.; Kenneth and Keith Littlejohn robbed a bank in Dublin and then claimed to have done so on behalf of MI6. Even the IRA admitted that much of what they said was 'pure cock and bull', but the fact that subsequent court proceedings were held in camera 'for reasons of national security' seems to confirm that they had some involvement with the British – although not necessarily with MI6, of course. Senior intelligence sources said that even if the Littlejohn's had been MI6 agents – and they were unable to say if they were – their brief would not have extended to robbery. 'The rules of engagement, the terms under which one operates, are pretty clear, pretty tight,' one said:

    They certainly wouldn't stretch to saying: 'It's perfectly all right to say to these guys, "Would you go and rob a bank? Would you become involved in criminal activity of that sort?" You can see the problem. If he comes back and says, "I had a relationship with MI6", which was the case, and then he says, "I robbed a bank and they told me to do it", it's pretty hard to deny it. But I don't know that's what happened.' (Information provided to the author in confidence.)

46. Information provided to the author in confidence; Rees, op. cit.; Coogan, *The IRA*
47. Coogan, *The IRA*; Rees, op. cit.; Bishop and Mallie, op. cit.; Coogan, *The Troubles*
48. 'GOC Attacks Ulster Truce', *Sunday Telegraph*, 13 April 1975; 'Storm Over Ulster GOC's Outburst', *Daily Telegraph*, 14 April 1975
49. Lord Merlyn-Rees, *Hansard*, House of Lords, 9 December 1993; 'Setting Spy Against Spy', *Irish Times*, 24 April 1980. The extent to which the Army indulged

in dirty tricks remains a matter of debate, but the fact that it did is not. Rees told the House of Lords:

> I discovered that the 'dirty tricks' campaign in Northern Ireland – I possess the papers now though I did not have them at the time – included a list of politicians in all parties. They are listed under the headings of sex, politics and finance. It is the most illiterate rubbish that I have ever read, even worse than that found in some of our national newspapers. It was quite extraordinary. A psy-ops operation was run against politicians in the south and politicians in Northern Ireland. The Army was involved in that. I know that it has now stopped – I was told that it was stopped many years ago. But it was out of control.

50. Coogan, *The IRA:* Rees, op. cit.; Bishop and Mallie, op. cit.; Coogan, *The Troubles*
51. 'RUC Anti-terrorism Officers Attack MI5 Tactics in Northern Ireland', *The Times*, 26 October 1993; 'Army Spy Games Infuriate RUC', *Sunday Times*, 3 July 1994; Jeffrey, op. cit.; 'Ulster Intelligence Tactics Reviewed', *The Times*, 9 March 1992; 'Ceasefire Costs MI5 its Biggest Contract', *Guardian*, 28 August 1995
52. Charters, op. cit.; Verrier, op. cit.; Mark Urban, *Big Boys' Rules: The SAS and the Secret Struggle against the IRA* (Faber and Faber, London, 1992); MacStiofain, op. cit.
53. Information provided to the author in confidence; Andy McNab, *Immediate Action* (Bantam Press, London, 1995); James Adams, *The New Spies: Exploring the Frontiers of Espionage* (Hutchinson, London, 1994)
54. Information provided to the author in confidence; Urban, op. cit.
55. Harry McCallion, *Killing Zone* (Bloomsbury, London, 1995); Urban, op. cit.; Peter Taylor, *Stalker: The Search For The Truth* (Faber, London, 1987); 'Peace Dividend Likely to Carry High Price Tag', *The Times*, 2 September 1994
56. Information supplied to the author in confidence; McCallion, op. cit.; McNab, op. cit.; Urban, op. cit.; Craig Kitson and Alex Taylor, *Inside the SAS* (Bloomsbury, London, 1992)
57. Force Intelligence Unit was formerly 12 Intelligence and Security Company. The Information Database Management Company was formerly 125 Intelligence Section. The Incident Investigation Company was previously known as Weapons Intelligence.
    'Force Intelligence Unit', *The Rose and the Laurel, Journal of the Intelligence Corps*, December 1994 and December 1995; Faligot, op. cit.
58. Stella Rimington, 'National Security and International Understanding', Lecture to the English-Speaking Union, Skinners' Hall, City of London, 4 October 1995; 'Military Backing for MI5 to take Ulster Lead Role', *Daily Telegraph*, 9 May 1992; 'MI5 to Lead Fight against IRA Terror,' *Daily Telegraph*, 9 May 1992
59. 'Kintyre and Internment: What the IRA Knew', *Sunday Business Post*, 5 June 1994; 'Leading MI5 Officer was One of Kintyre Crash Victims', *Irish Times*, 4 June 1994; 'Northern Ireland: Death of Senior Intelligence Officers in Helicopter Crash', *Keesing's Record of World Events*, article ref. 40068, 30 June 1994
60. 'Threat of Terror is Still There', *Belfast Telegraph*, 16 March 1995
61. David Beresford, *Ten Dead Men* (Grafton, London, 1987); 'Revealed: Man Who Met the IRA: Secret Go-between was MI6 Agent', *Sunday Telegraph*, 12 December 1993; 'Major Masterstroke Retains Ulster's Peace Momentum', *Guardian*, 22 October 1994; 'MI6 in Contact with IRA since 1970s', *Sunday Times*, 12 December 1993; 'Former MI6 Man in Talks', *Guardian*, 13 December 1993; *On The Record*, BBC Television, 28 November 1993; 'SF Talks Date Back to Thatcher Era', *Irish*

*Times*, 29 November 1993; Gerry Adams, *Free Ireland: Towards a Lasting Peace* (Brandon, Dingle, Co. Kerry, 1995)

62. *Guardian*, 22 October 1994; G. Adams, op. cit.

63. *Irish Times*, 29 November 1993; 'Ministers Covered up Sinn Fein Dialogue', *Observer*, 28 November 1993; *Sunday Telegraph*, 12 December 1993; *Hansard*, House of Commons, 22 February 1994

64. 'The Ulster Dialogue', *Daily Telegraph*, 30 November 1993; 'Talks and The Troubles', *Observer*, 5 December 1993; *Guardian*, 22 October 1994; 'DUP Rejects Mayhew Denial of Panorama Claim', *Irish Times*, 22 February 1994; George Drower, *John Hume: Peacemaker* (Victor Gollancz, London, 1995)

65. 'Talking to Mr Adams', *Panorama*, BBC Television, 29 November 1993

# Chapter 16

1. 'Interpol Gears up for Euro-Crime Wave', *Sunday Telegraph*, 2 June 1996

2. PRO HO144/93424; Bernard Porter, 'A Historiography of the Early Special Branch', *Intelligence and National Security*, Vol. 1, No. 3 (September 1986); Bernard Porter, *Plots and Paranoia: A History of Political Espionage in Britain 1790–1988* (Unwin Hyman, London, 1989); Bernard Porter, *The Origins of the Vigilant State: The London Metropolitan Police Special Branch before the First World War* (London, Weidenfeld & Nicolson, 1987); Richard Thurlow, *The Secret State: British Internal Security in the Twentieth Century* (Blackwell, Oxford, 1994); Keith Jeffery, 'British Military Intelligence Following World War I', in K. G. Robertson (ed.), *British and American Approaches to Intelligence* (Macmillan, London, 1987)

3. Peter Gill, *Policing Politics: Security Intelligence and the Liberal Democratic State* (Frank Cass, London, 1994)

4. Home Office, *Guidelines on Special Branch Work in Great Britain* (HMSO, London, 1994)

5. Home Office, op. cit.; 'Branch Roots', *Police Review*, 9 December 1994; 'Terror Squad Targets Animal Rights Extremists', *Daily Telegraph*, 6 March 1995

6. 'Why The Branch Faces a Cut', *Daily Telegraph*, 6 March 1995

7. Robert Fleming with Hugh Miller, *Scotland Yard* (Michael Joseph, London, 1994); *Fourth Report from the Home Affairs Committee of the House of Commons, Session 1984–85, on the Special Branch* (HMSO, London, 1985); *The Work of a Special Branch* (HMSO, London, 1984); Home Office, op. cit.; *Police Review*, 9 December 1994

8. Home Office, op. cit.; 'Brixton Escape Police Cleared', *Daily Telegraph*, 19 May 1992

9. Home Office, op. cit.

10. Interview with Cmdr John Grieve, Director of Intelligence at Scotland Yard, 25 April 1995; Gill, op. cit.

11. Information provided to the author in confidence; 'Drug War Speculation over MI5 Head's Trip to Moscow', *Daily Telegraph*, 7 September 1992, 'New KGB Chief Meets Hurd', TASS, 1 September 1991; *The Intelligence Services Act 1994* (HMSO, London, 1994); Albert Pacey, Director of the National Criminal Intelligence Service, in a speech to the 2nd NCIS International Conference on Organized Crime, Bramshill, Hants, 22 May 1995; Commons Select Committee on Home Affairs, *Organized Crime: Minutes of Evidence and Memoranda* (HMSO, London, 1994)

12. 'The Next Threat', *Foreign Report*, 14 September 1995; Hoffman, op. cit.; Dick Thornburgh, 'The Internationalization of Business Crime', *Transnational Organized Crime*, Vol. 1, No. 1 (Spring 1995)

13. Grieve interview; Commons Select Committee on Home Affairs, op. cit.; 'The Next Threat', *Foreign Report*, 14 September 1995
14. Mark Galeotti, 'The Drug Threat From Eastern Europe', *Jane's Intelligence Review*, November 1995; information provided to the author in confidence; Commons Select Committee on Home Affairs, op. cit.; 'Where The Best Gun-Runners Go Clubbing', *Observer*, 2 July 1995; 'Russia: World's Drugs Capital?', *Foreign Report*, 27 April 1995
15. Galeotti, op. cit.
16. Grieve interview; Pacey speech; 'Russian *Mafia* targets Britain', *Sunday Times*, 17 April 1994
17. Commons Select Committee on Home Affairs, op. cit.; 'Baby Seat Used to Smuggle *Mafia* Drug Money', *Daily Telegraph*, 24 November 1995; Ko-Lin Chin, 'Triad Societies in Hong Kong', *Transnational Organized Crime*, Vol. 1, No. 1 (Spring 1995); 'Big Trouble Looms in Little China', *Observer*, 24 September 1995; 'Police Fear Japanese *Mafia* is Moving into Britain, *Guardian*, 28 September 1992
18. *National Criminal Intelligence Service Annual Report 1994/95* (Central Office of Information, London, 1995)
19. Grieve interview
20. 'Police Demand Their "FBI" to Fend off MI5', *Observer*, 13 November 1994
21. Commons Select Committee on Home Affairs, op. cit.
22. 'Police Want to Take Lead in MI5 Link-up', *Daily Telegraph*, 14 October 1995; 'No FBI-Style Policing Here, Says Howard', Press Association, 16 October 1995
23. Detective Superintendent Larry Covington, NCIS, Lecture on Organized Crime, *Proceedings of the Security and Intelligence Studies Group Workshop on Intelligence Policy 1995, Reading, 23 September 1995*; Andy McNab, *Immediate Action* (Bantam Press, London, 1994); Michael Portillo, British Defence Secretary, Speech to Conference on British Security 2010, 16 November 1995
24. Grieve interview
25. 'Studies in Power: A Fair Cop?', *Independent on Sunday*, 12 November 1995; 'Yard Apology for Letting in Gangster', *Daily Telegraph*, 15 September 1995
26. Commons Select Committee on Home Affairs, op. cit.; *National Criminal Intelligence Service Annual Report 1994/95*
27. Commons Select Committee on Home Affairs, op. cit.; K. G. Robertson, 'Police Intelligence Co-operation in Europe: Rhetoric or Reality', *Journal of Economic and Social Intelligence*, Vol. 3, No. 1 (1993); John Benyon, 'Policing the European Union: The Changing Basis of Co-operation on Law Enforcement', *International Affairs*, Vol. 70, No. 3 (1994)
28. Kenneth G. Robertson, 'Practical Police Co-operation in Europe: The Intelligence Dimension', in Malcolm Anderson and Monica den Boer (eds.), *Policing Across National Boundaries* (Pinter, London, 1994); Stella Rimington, 'National Security and International Understanding', Lecture to the English-Speaking Union, Skinners Hall, City of London, 4 October 1995
29. Grieve interview
30. Commons Select Committee on Home Affairs, op. cit.; 'Police Scrutinise Futures Markets', *Financial Times*, 9 February 1994; 'Bank Aims to Clean Out Laundrymen', *Independent*, 16 November 1992
31. 'Colombia Drug Chiefs Enlist US Firms', *International Herald Tribune*, 1 November 1995; 'When Crime and Foreign Policy Meet', *Wall Street Journal*, 25 October 1995
32. Pacey speech; Commons Select Committee on Home Affairs, op. cit.
33. 'Police Abandon 70 Major Trials', *Daily Telegraph*, 23 March 1994
34. 'Save This Threatened Species: Police Informers Make a Vital Contribution to Crime Detection, *Daily Telegraph*, 20 September 1993

35. *Daily Telegraph*, 14 October 1995; Bruce Hoffman, ' "Holy Terror": The Implications of Terrorism Motivated by A Religious Imperative', June 1995 (Updated version of report originally published as RAND Paper P-7834, The RAND Corporation, July 1993); *New Spies For Old*, BBC Radio 4, 21 March 1995

36. Grieve interview.

One of the most graphic examples of a criminal case involving intelligence being aborted to protect sources of information began in the early hours of 3 February 1993 when two police officers on patrol in the Thames Valley became suspicious of a Maestro van. When they stopped and searched it they discovered a radio scanner, balaclava helmets, rope ladders and home-made Molotov cocktails. The three men inside the van were members of the Animal Liberation Front who were planning to release animals being delivered to a slaughterhouse and to set fire to the transporter. They exercised their right to silence during questioning by police and were subsequently charged with conspiracy to cause criminal damage.

During the trial at Reading Crown Court, defence lawyers asked that files on the three accused held in the Animal Rights National Index be disclosed and, to the dismay of officers working on the case, the judge agreed. 'The information they were requesting would have had the effect of dismantling our intelligence database, exposing our techniques and putting informants at risk,' said Det. Chief Supt Brian Ridley, of the Metropolitan Police. 'Frankly, if we have to disclose that sort of detail even when it is of little or no relevance to the case, we might as well pack up and go home.'

The prosecution was forced to withdraw its case and the three men walked free, stopping on the steps of the court to make a full admission to a waiting television crew. (Commons Select Committee on Home Affairs, op. cit.; *Daily Telegraph*, 23 March 1994)

37. Stella Rimington, James Smart Lecture, City of London Police Headquarters, 3 November 1994

38. Grieve interview

## Chapter 17

1. Numbers 13

2. Edward Luttwak, *Disarming the World's Economies* (Center for Strategic and International Studies, Washington DC, 1990); Vincent Cable, 'What is International Economic Security?', *International Affairs*, Vol. 71, No. 2 (1995); 'A New Order for the Spies', *Daily Telegraph*, 24 January 1992; 'CIA Fighting to Survive without KGB', *Guardian*, 6 September 1991; Admiral Stansfield Turner, 'Intelligence for a New World Order', *Foreign Affairs*, Vol. 70, No. 4 (Fall 1991)

3. Information on intelligence priorities made available to the author in confidence

4. Information made available to the author in confidence

5. Information made available to the author in confidence

6. PRO BT61/60/8

7. PRO HD3/91; HD3/125

8. PRO BT61/60/8; WO32/10776

9. PRO BT61/60/9; CAB24/247; A. G. Denniston, 'The Government Code & Cypher School Between The Wars', *Intelligence and National Security*, Vol. 1, No. 1 (January 1986); F. H. Hinsley et al., *British Intelligence in the Second World War Vol. 1* (HMSO, London, 1979); Edward Thomas, 'The Evolution of the JIC System up to and during World War II', in Christopher Andrew and Jeremy Noakes, *Intelligence and International Relations 1909–1945* (University of Exeter,

1987); Christopher Andrew, *Secret Service: The Making of the British Intelligence Community* (William Heinemann, London, 1985); Wesley K. Wark, 'British Military and Economic Intelligence: Assessments of Nazi Germany Before the Second World War', in Christopher Andrew and David Dilks (eds.), *The Missing Dimension: Governments and Intelligence Communities in the Twentieth Century* (Macmillan, London, 1984); Philip H. J. Davies, 'Organizational Politics and the Development of Britain's Intelligence Producer/Consumer Interface', *Intelligence and National Security*, Vol. 10, No. 4 (October 1995)

10. PRO: CAB81/92; CAB81/93; CAB81/94; CAB81/122; Davies, op. cit.

11. *The Security Service Act 1989* (HMSO, London, 1989); *Intelligence Services Act 1994* (HMSO, London, 1994); *Interim Report of the Intelligence and Security Committee* (Cmd 2873, HMSO, London, May 1995); *New Spies For Old*, BBC Radio 4, 28 March 95; *Central Intelligence Machinery* (HMSO, London, 1993); 'Picking the Lock of Britain's Security', *Guardian*, 6 April 1988; *Daily Telegraph*, 24 January 1992; Laurence Lustgarten and Ian Leigh, *In From the Cold: National Security and Parliamentary Democracy* (OUP, Oxford, 1994)

12. 'On Her Majesty's Secret Service', *Panorama*, BBC Television, 22 November 1993

13. *Call Nick Ross*, BBC Radio 4, 16 June 1992; 'Former GCHQ Official Confirms Monitoring', *Guardian*, 17 June 1992; Denniston, op. cit.; Hinsley et al., op. cit.; 'Still All to Play for in the Spying Game', *Guardian*, 23 November 1994; 'Cabinet Chief Insists Evidence to Scott Inquiry Remains Secret', *Guardian*, 13 February 1995; 'Early Intelligence Files Implicated Robert Maxwell', *Financial Times*, 15 June 1992; Lustgarten and Leigh, op. cit.; *Daily Telegraph*, 24 January 1992; Hugh Lanning and Richard Norton-Taylor, *A Conflict of Loyalties: GCHQ 1984–1991* (New Clarion Press, Cheltenham, 1991); GCHQ advertisement for linguists (entitled 'The Language of Intelligence'), *Guardian*, 20 November 1995

14. *Guardian*, 23 November 1994

15. 'Cloak and Dagger as R&D; The French Do It. The Brits Do It But Corporate Spying May Not Be for Us', *Washington Post*, 27 June 1993; 'CIA Targets Overseas Firms, But Draws a Line', *Washington Post*, 5 March 1995; Letters to the Editor: 'Spy vs. Spy, Economically Speaking', *Washington Post*, 19 March 1995

16. James Woolsey, Hearing of the Select Committee on Intelligence, 2 February 1993; *Washington Post*, 27 June 1993; 'Administration to Consider Giving Spy Data to Business; CIA Designee Says Topic is "Hottest" in Field', *Washington Post*, 3 February 1993

17. Peter Schweizer, *Friendly Spies* (Atlantic Monthly Press, New York, 1993); 'Economic Intelligence is Spy's New Target', *Financial Times*, 24 February 1995; Count Alexandre de Marenches, *The Evil Empire* (Sidgwick and Jackson, London, 1986)

18. Jeffrey T. Richelson, *Foreign Intelligence Organizations* (Ballinger, Cambridge, Mass, 1988); 'Goodbye to M', *The Economist*, 20 November 1982; 'On His Socialists' Secret Service', *The Economist*, 27 November 1982; *New Spies For Old*; *Exposé*, NBC Television, 12 September 1991; 'French Government Spied against US Business, TV Report Says', Associated Press, 13 September 1991

19. 'US Demands for Economic Intelligence up Sharply, Gates Says', *Washington Post*, 14 April 1992; 'America Attacks French Claims of Embassy Spying', *The Times*, 23 February 1995; *Exposé*, Associated Press, 13 September 1991; 'FBI Confirms French Security Agents Targeted Hi-Tech Firms', *The Times*, 20 November 1990; *Daily Telegraph*, 24 January 1992; *Washington Post*, 27 June 1993

20. *Daily Telegraph*, 24 January 1992; *Washington Post*, 27 June 1993; *New Spies For Old*

21. *Washington Post*, 27 June 1993; *New Spies For Old*; *Financial Times*, 24 February 1995; *Exposé*, September 1991; Associated Press, 13 September 1991; 'Industrial Spying Comes in From the Cold', Reuters, 3 August 1992

22. 'US to Protest Industrial Spying by Allies', *Washington Post*, 30 April 1993; 'Defense Firms Irked by US Decision on Paris Air Show', Reuters, 29 April 1993; 'France Said to Recall Spies Found in US Industry', Reuters, 30 April 1993; 'France Appoints New Spy Chief after Scandals', Reuters, 3 June 1993; 'Canada Spy-catcher says High-tech Firms Targeted', Reuters, 13 April 1994

23. *The Times*, 23 February 1995; 'Spies Who Just Can't Come in from the Cold', *Toronto Star*, 26 February 1995; *New Spies For Old*; Reuters, 30 April 1993

24. 'France Sets up Trade Intelligence Body', Reuters, 22 March 1995

25. Schweitzer, op. cit.; *Washington Post*, 3 February 1993; *New Spies For Old*; *Washington Post*, 27 June 1993

26. Nicholas Eftiamiades, *Chinese Intelligence Operations* (Naval Institute Press, Annapolis, Md, 1994); 'China Seen Using Close US Ties for Espionage', *LA Times*, 20 November 1988

27. Eftiamiades, op. cit.; 'President Tells China to Sell Seattle Firm', *Washington Post*, 3 February 1990

28. Amy W. Knight, *The KGB, Police and Politics in the Soviet Union* (Unwin Hyman, Boston, 1990); *Daily Telegraph*, 24 January 1992; Christopher Andrew and Oleg Gordievsky, *KGB: The Inside Story* (Hodder & Stoughton, London, 1990); Associated Press, 3 April 1985

29. 'KGB Figure Called a Spy for France', *New York Times*, 8 January 1986; 'France Expels Four Soviet Officials for Espionage', *Washington Post*, 4 February 1986; Linda Melvern, Nick Anning and David Hebditch, *Techno-Bandits* (Houghton Mifflin, Boston, 1984); John E. Carlson, 'The KGB', in James Cracraft (ed.), *The Soviet Union Today: An Interpretive Guide* (University of Chicago Press, 1988); Andrew and Gordievsky, op. cit.; 'Report in French Newspaper Le Monde Claims Industrial Espionage Saved Soviets 256 Million Dollars in Advanced Technology Research between 1976 and 1980', Associated Press, 3 April 1985

30. Philip Hanson, 'Soviet Industrial Espionage', *Bulletin of the Atomic Scientists*, No. 43 (April 1987); Andrew and Gordievsky, op. cit.

31. *Soviet Acquisition of Militarily Significant Western Technology: An Update* (US Government Printing Office, Washington DC, 1985); Gordon Brook-Shepherd, *The Storm Birds: Soviet Post-War Defectors* (Weidenfeld & Nicolson, London, 1988); *New York Times*, 8 January 1986; *Washington Post*, 4 February 1986; Andrew and Gordievsky, op. cit.; Knight, op. cit.; Carlson, op. cit.

32. Andrew and Gordievsky, op. cit.; 'Expert Says Soviets are Still Spying in US; Warsaw Pact isn't', *Washington Post*, 30 October 1991

33. *Daily Telegraph*, 24 January 1992; James Adams, *The New Spies: Exploring the Frontiers of Espionage* (Hutchinson, London, 1994)

34. *Daily Telegraph*, 24 January 1992; *The Times*, 20 November 1990

35. Jay T. Young, 'US Intelligence Assessment in a Changing World', *Intelligence and National Security*, Vol. 8, No. 2 (April 1993); 'FBI Confirms French Security Agents Targeted Hi-Tech Firms', *The Times*, 20 November 1990

36. 'After The Wars: Can "Real Men" Make Policy?', *Washington Post*, 28 June 1992; 'Spies Come in from the Cold', *Independent*, 20 August 1990

37. *Washington Post*, 27 June 1993; 'CIA, FBI Chiefs Warn Panel Over Economic Espionage', *Washington Post*, 30 April 1992; Samuel D. Porteous, 'Economic Intelligence: Issues Arising from Increased Government Involvement with the Private Sector', *Intelligence and National Security*, Vol. 9, No. 4 (October 1994); Schweizer, op. cit.; Reuters, 30 April 1993; Reuters, 3 August 1992

38. Walter Lacquer, *A World of Secrets: The Uses and Limits of Intelligence* (Basic, New York, 1985); John Ranelagh, *The Agency: The Rise and Decline of the CIA* (Weidenfeld & Nicolson, London, 1986); James Bamford, *The Puzzle Palace* (Sidgwick & Jackson, London, 1982)

39. 'Security Agency Debates New Role: Economic Spying', *New York Times*, 28

June 1990; Lacquer, op. cit.; US Senate, *Final Report of the Select Committee to Study Governmental Operations with Respect to Intelligence Activities* (US Government Printing Office, Washington DC, 1976); Sheila Kerr, 'The Debate on US Post-Cold War Intelligence: One More New Botched Beginning', *Defence Analysis*, Vol. 10, No. 3 (1994)

40. *Washington Post*, 5 March 1995
41. *Dispatches*, Channel 4 Television, 5 October 1993; 'US Spied on British Defence Projects', Reuters, 5 October 1993
42. *The Times*, 20 November 1990; Reuters, 3 August 1992; Woolsey, op. cit.; *Washington Post*, 30 April 1993; 'US Spy Chief Targets Foreign Industrial Espionage', Reuters, 10 March 1993; 'Woolsey: Why the CIA is Still in Need of Human Touch', *Jane's Defence Weekly*, 6 August 1994; *Washington Post*, 5 March 1995
43. 'French Resent US Coups in New Espionage', *Washington Post*, 26 February 1995; 'US Spies Beat French at Their Own Double Game', *Guardian*, 27 February 1995; 'The Trade Spy: US Government Officials Say French Also Seek Economic Secrets', *Washington Post*, 23 February 1995; 'In From the Cold and Down to Business', *The Herald*, 11 January 1994; *Financial Times*, 24 February 1995; *Washington Post*, 5 March 1995; *The Times*, 23 February 1995; 'As the Ads Say, CIA is Looking for a Few Good Economists', *Washington Post*, 27 December 1990
44. *Washington Post*, 14 April 1992; 'New CIA Chief's First Week Wins Kudos From Congress', Associated Press, 19 May 1995; 'US President Clinton Sets out Spy Target Priorities for CIA', Associated Press, 10 March 1995; *A National Security Strategy of Engagement and Enlargement* (The White House, Washington DC, February 1995)
45. 'The CIA vs. Soviet Reality', *Washington Post*, 19 May 1988; Robert Gates, Speech to the Foreign Policy Association, New York, 20 May 1992
46. 'Panel Says US Intelligence Agencies Shouldn't Spy for Industry', Associated Press, 5 August 1993
47. Young, op. cit.
48. Admiral Stansfield Turner, 'Intelligence for a New World Order', *Foreign Affairs*, Vol. 70, No. 4 (Fall 1991); *Washington Post*, 3 February 1993
49. Porteous, op. cit.; Stanley Kober, 'The CIA as Economic Spy: The Misuse of US Intelligence After The Cold War', *Policy Analysis* (The CATO Institute), No. 185 (8 December 1992); Associated Press, 5 August 1993

## Chapter 18

1. 'Russian Link to Nuclear Racket', *Guardian*, 15 August 1994; 'Atomic Racket Chills the West', *Sunday Times*, 21 August 1994
2. Christoph Bluth, 'Nuclear Proliferation', *Proceedings of the Security and Intelligence Studies Group Workshop on Intelligence Policy 1995, Reading, 23 September 1995*; International Institute for Strategic Studies, *Strategic Survey 1994/95* (OUP, Oxford, 1995); 'US Defence Secretary Perry Warns Against Curbs on Dismantling Soviet Nuclear Complex', Associated Press, 6 January 1995; 'US Spending Too Little to Help Russian Nuclear Security, Scientists Say', Associated Press, 30 August 1995
3. Guy Standing and Daniel Vaughan-Whitehead, *Minimum Wages in Central Europe: From Protection to Destitution* (Central European University Press, Budapest, 1995); '75 Per Cent of Russian Officers Went Unpaid in September', Agence France Press, 14 October 1995; 'Russian Soldiers Help Restore Power at

Naval Bases', Reuters, 22 September 1995; 'Power Supply Restored to Nuclear Sub Base at Gun Point', TASS, 22 September 1995; Bluth, op. cit.; 'Poverty Puts Nuclear Materials on the Market', *Guardian*, 15 August 1994; 'The Worst May Be Yet To Come', *Intersec*, Vol. 5, Issue 5 (May 1995)

4. 'Russian Mafia Has Nuclear Technology – Germany', Reuters, 11 June 1994; 'German Court Sentences Nuclear Smugglers Despite Plea of Entrapment', Associated Press, 17 July 1995; 'Minister Defends German Plutonium Sting', Reuters, 28 September 1995

5. 'Nuclear Smuggler Confesses in German Court', Associated Press, 21 June 1995; 'Radioactive Material Seized by Slovak Police Identified as Uranium-238', BBC Summary of World Broadcasts, 26 April 1995 (Czech Radio-Radiozurnal, 24 April 1995); 'Nuclear Materials For Sale: On Alert Against "Greatest Long-Term Threat"', Associated Press, 24 March 1995; 'Czech Republic: Police confirm Unprecedented Seizure of Uranium', BBC Summary of World Broadcasts, 22 December 1994 (CTK News Agency, 20 December 1994); 'Czech Republic: Police Seize Significant Quantity of Enriched Uranium in Prague', BBC Summary of World Broadcasts, 21 December 1994 (CTK News Agency, 19 December 1994); 'Czech Police Seize Three Kilograms of Top Grade Uranium', Associated Press, 19 December 1994

6. 'No Black Market For Nuclear Material – Report', Reuters, 13 May 1995

7. Bruce Hoffman, 'Responding to Terrorism Across the Technological Spectrum', in *Terrorism and Political Violence*, Vol. 6, No. 3 (Autumn 1994); Bruce Hoffman, 'The Threat From Politically Motivated Violence', *Proceedings of the Security and Intelligence Studies Group Workshop on Intelligence Policy 1995, Reading, 23 September 1995*; Bluth, op. cit.; International Institute for Strategic Studies, op. cit.

8. 'CIA Says Nuclear Smuggling Reports Usually Involve Small Quantity or Scams', Associated Press, 29 August 1995; 'Loss of Nuclear Weapons Still Primary Concern', *Jane's Defence Weekly*, 2 September 1995

9. 'Indian Prime Minister Warns Pakistan', TASS, 11 April 1990; *New Spies for Old*, BBC Radio 4, 28 March 1995; 'US Wants to Help Defuse Hostility between India and Pakistan over Kashmir', Associated Press, 20 May 1990; 'Pakistan "Nuclear War Threat"', *Sunday Times*, 27 May 1990; 'Pakistan Bomb Reports Set Delhi Alarm Bells Ringing', TASS, 28 May 1990; 'Indian Expert on Pakistani Military Preparations', TASS, 31 May 1990; 'India and Pakistan Agree on Non-attack of Nuclear Facilities', BBC Summary of World Broadcasts, 28 January 1991 (All-India Radio, Delhi Home Service, in English, 27 January 1991); Bruce Vaughn, 'The Use and Abuse of the Intelligence Services in India', *Intelligence and National Security*, Vol. 8, No. 1 (January 1993); information given to the author in confidence

10. 'Nightmare in the Making', *Jane's Defence Weekly*, 3 June 1995

11. Stella Rimington, 'National Security and International Understanding', Lecture to the English-Speaking Union, Skinners Hall, City of London, 4 October 1995

12. Bruce Hoffman, ' "Holy Terror": The Implications of Terrorism Motivated by a Religious Imperative', June 1995. Updated version of report originally published as RAND Paper P-7834, The RAND Corporation (July 1993)

13. Hoffman, 'Responding to Terrorism Across the Technological Spectrum'; Hoffman, ' "Holy Terror": The Implications of Terrorism Motivated by A Religious Imperative'; 'The Price of Fanaticism', *Time*, 3 April 1995; *New Spies For Old*, BBC Radio 4, 21 March 1995; 'Religious Fanaticism Fuels Terrorism', *International Herald Tribune*, 31 October 1995; 'Oklahoma City – The Aftermath', *Intersec*, Vol. 5 Issue 5 (May 1995)

14. 'The Worst May Be Yet To Come', *Intersec*, Vol. 5, Issue 5 (May 1995); 'Terrorism Fight Changes Tack: Police Investigations Move from the IRA to

"Apocalyptic" Groups', *Guardian*, 21 August 1995; 'Terrorist Police Study Threat of Doomsday Cults', *The Times*, 21 August 1995

15. Rimington, op. cit.

16. Mark Urban, *Big Boys' Rules: The SAS and the Secret Struggle Against the IRA* (Faber, London, 1992); 'To Kill, or Watch and Wait', *Daily Telegraph*, 28 January 1992; ' "Dirty Fight" Could Take Out Terrorists', *Scotland on Sunday*, 7 November 1993; 'Ulster Killings Expose Crisis In Spy Network', *Daily Telegraph*, 2 November 1993; 'Security Chiefs Must Stand by Their Men', *Sunday Telegraph*, 9 February 1992

17. Bruce Hoffman, 'The Role of Foreign Policy, Intelligence, and Law Enforcement in the Prevention of Transnational Terrorism', *Low Intensity Conflict and Law Enforcement*, Vol. 4, No. 1 (Summer 1995); 'Thatcher Angered by Hostage Deal', *Guardian*, 1 December 1987; 'Britain's Refusal to Talk "Shameful" ', *Guardian*, 6 May 1988; 'Britain Wants Ban on Terrorist Deals', *The Times*, 12 November 1986; 'Security Agencies Link up to Tackle International Threat, *The Times*, 30 January 1991

18. Rimington, op. cit.

19. 'Police Want to Take Lead in MI5 Link-up', *Daily Telegraph*, 13 October 1995

20. See the discussion of the Fatman trial in Chapter 6; 'Howard Crackdown On Courtroom Ambushes Attacked By Lawyers', Press Association, 16 May 1995; New Law to Stop Court Ambushes by Defence Lawyers, *The Times*, 17 May 1995; 'Howard Moves to Abolish "Ambush" Defence Tactic', *Daily Telegraph*, 17 May 1995; Laurence Lustgarten and Ian Leigh, *In From the Cold: National Security and Parliamentary Democracy* (OUP, Oxford, 1994)

21. *Intelligence Services Act 1994* (HMSO, London, 1994)
There is a danger that the reforms of the disclosure rules have already swung the balance, between allowing the police and the Security Service to protect their sources and ensuring a fair trial too far in favour of the prosecution. Despite the strong argument in favour of reform, the disclosure rules were introduced only following a number of prominent cases in which the Court of Appeal ruled that crucial evidence which might have led to a acquittal had been withheld by the prosecution or the police.
The Home Affairs Committee has expressed concern that the new proposals may not sufficiently safeguard the defence – in particular if defence witnesses, having been disclosed, are themselves subject to potentially intimidatory inquiries by the police. In its report on organized crime, the committee said, 'We consider there is some danger that this proposal goes too far towards the prosecution side to the detriment of the defence.' (House of Commons Home Affairs Committee, *Organized Crime* (HMSO, London, 1995); Press Association, 16 May 1995; *The Times*, 17 May 1995; *Daily Telegraph*, 17 May 1995; *Intelligence Services Act 1994*; Lustgarten and Leigh, op. cit.

22. 'Inside Story: Truth and the Big Guns', *Guardian*, 18 February 1995; Richard Norton-Taylor with Mark Lloyd, *Truth is a Difficult Concept: Inside the Scott Inquiry* (Fourth Estate, London, 1995)

23. Lawrence Freedman, 'Intelligence Operations in the Falklands', *Intelligence and National Security*, Vol. 1, No. 3 (September 1986); 'Gulf War Failures Cited', *Washington Post*, 11 April 1992; 'Pentagon Report on Persian Gulf War', *New York Times*, 11 April 1992; Ralph Bennett, 'Ultra', in I. C. B. Dear (ed.), *The Oxford Companion to the Second World War* (OUP, Oxford, 1995); 'Deutch: CIA Trying to Provide Military with Better Intelligence', Associated Press, 6 July 1995; 'CIA to Alter its Priorities in Information Gathering; Deutch to Focus on Military, Criminals, Terrorists', *Washington Post*, 13 July 1995

24. Defence Intelligence Staff Briefing, 15 November 1995

25. Information supplied to the author in confidence; 'GCHQ's Service to US

Crucial', *Guardian*, 17 May 1994; Michael Portillo, British Defence Secretary, Speech to Conference on British Security 2010, 16 November 1995

26. *Intelligence Services Act 1994*; *Interim Report of the Intelligence and Security Committee* (Cmd 2873, HMSO, London, 1995); 'Security MPs in "Ring of Secrecy": Whitehall "Cell" for New Committee on Intelligence Service', *Guardian*, 16 January 1994; Intelligence and Security Committee, *Annual Report 1995* (HMSO, London, 1996)
27. 'Clinton Urges CIA to Recover from Spy Scandal', Reuters, 14 July 1995
28. Michael Portillo, British Defence Secretary, Speech at the Navy Board's Briefing Day for Retired Admirals, 20 November 1995

# Select Bibliography

Adams, James, *The New Spies: Exploring the Frontiers of Espionage* (Hutchinson, London, 1994)

Aldrich, Richard J. (ed.), *British Intelligence, Strategy and the Cold War, 1945–51* (Routledge, London, 1992)

Aldrich, Richard J., and Hopkins, Michael F. (eds.), *Intelligence, Defence and Diplomacy, British Policy in the Post-War World* (Frank Cass, London, 1994)

Andrew, Christopher, *Secret Service: The Making of the British Intelligence Community* (William Heinemann, London, 1985)

Andrew, Christopher, and Dilks, David (eds.), *The Missing Dimension: Governments and Intelligence Communities in the Twentieth Century* (Macmillan, London, 1984)

Andrew, Christopher, and Noakes, Jeremy, *Intelligence and International Relations 1909–1945* (University of Exeter, 1987)

Bamford, James, *The Puzzle Palace* (Sidgwick & Jackson, London, 1982)

Blake, George, *No Other Choice: An Autobiography* (Jonathan Cape, London, 1990)

Borovik, Genrikh, *The Philby Files* (Little, Brown, London, 1994)

Bower, Tom, *The Perfect English Spy: Sir Dick White and the Secret War 1935–90* (William Heinemann, London, 1995)

Bower, Tom, *The Red Webb: MI6 and the KGB Master Coup* (Aurum Press, London, 1989)

Boyle, Andrew, *The Climate of Treason* (Coronet, London, rev. edn, 1980)

Brook-Shepherd, Gordon, *The Storm Birds: Soviet Post-War Defectors* (Weidenfeld & Nicolson, London, 1988)

Brook-Shepherd, Gordon, *The Storm Petrels* (Collins, London, 1977)

Cairncross, John, *An Agent for the Duration: Memoirs of the Fifth Man* (St Ermin's Press, London, 1996)

Cavendish, Anthony, *Inside Intelligence* (Collins, London, 1990)

Cecil, Robert, *A Divided Life: A Biography of Donald Maclean* (Bodley Head, London, 1988)

Clayton, Anthony, *Forearmed: A History of the Intelligence Corps* (Brasseys, London, 1993)

Deacon, Richard, *A History of the British Secret Service* (Muller, London, 1969)

Dear, I. C. B. (ed.), *The Oxford Companion to the Second World War* (OUP, Oxford, 1995)

Fergusson, Thomas G., *British Military Intelligence 1870–1914: The Development of a Modern Intelligence Organization* (Arms and Armour Press, London, 1984)

Gill, Peter, *Policing Politics: Security Intelligence and the Liberal Democratic State* (Frank Cass, London, 1994)

Haswell, Jock, *British Military Intelligence* (Weidenfeld & Nicolson, London, 1973)

Hinsley, F. H., et al., *British Intelligence in the Second World War* (HMSO, London, 1979–1990)

Hinsley, F. H., and Stripp, Alan (eds.), *Codebreakers: The Inside Story of Bletchley Park* (OUP, Oxford, 1993)

Jones, R. V., *Most Secret War* (Hamish Hamilton, London, 1978)

Jones, R. V., *Reflections on Intelligence* (Mandarin, London, 1990)

Knightley, Phillip, *Kim Philby: KGB Masterspy* (André Deutsch, London, 1988)

Knightley, Phillip, *The Second Oldest Profession: The Spy as Bureaucrat, Patriot, Fantasist and Whore* (André Deutsch, London, 1986)

Lacquer, Walter, *A World of Secrets: The Uses and Limits of Intelligence* (Basic, New York, 1985)

Lanning, Hugh, and Norton-Taylor, Richard, *A Conflict of Loyalties: GCHQ 1984–1991* (New Clarion Press, Cheltenham, 1991)

Lustgarten, Laurence, and Leigh, Ian, *In From the Cold: National Security and Parliamentary Democracy* (OUP, Oxford, 1994)

McNab, Andy, *Immediate Action* (Bantam Press, London, 1995)

Masterman, J. C., *The Double-Cross System of the War of 1939–45* (Yale University Press, London and New Haven, 1972)

Modin, Yuri, *My Five Cambridge Friends* (Headline, London, 1994)

Parritt, Lt-Col B. A. H., *The Intelligencers: The Story of British Military Intelligence up to 1914* (Templer Press, Ashford, 1971)

Philby, Kim, *My Silent War* (MacGibbon & Kee, London, 1968)

Porter, Bernard, *The Origins of the Vigilant State: The London Metropolitan Police Special Branch before the First World War* (Weidenfeld & Nicolson, London, 1987)

Porter, Bernard, *Plots and Paranoia: A History of Political Espionage in Britain 1790–1988* (Unwin Hyman, London, 1989)

Richelson, Jeffrey T., *A Century of Spies* (OUP, Oxford, 1995)

Richelson, Jeffrey T., *Foreign Intelligence Organizations* (Ballinger, Cambridge, Mass, 1988)

Richelson, Jeffrey T., and Ball, Desmond, *The Ties That Bind* (Unwin Hyman, Boston, 2nd edn, 1990)

Robertson, K. G. (ed.), *British and American Approaches to Intelligence* (Macmillan, London, 1987)

Stripp, Alan, *Codebreaker in the Far East* (Frank Cass, London, 1989)

Thurlow, Richard, *The Secret State: British Internal Security in the Twentieth Century* (Blackwell, Oxford, 1994)

Verrier, Anthony, *Through the Looking Glass: British Foreign Policy in the Age of Illusions* (Jonathan Cape, London, 1983)

Welchman, Gordon, *The Hut Six Story* (Allen Lane, London, 1982)

West, Nigel, *The Friends: Britain's Post-War Secret Intelligence Operations* (Weidenfeld & Nicolson, London, 1988)

West, Nigel, *GCHQ: The Secret Wireless War 1900–86* (Weidenfeld & Nicolson, 1986)

West, Nigel, *A Matter of Trust, MI5 1945–72* (Coronet, London, 1982)

West, Nigel, *MI5: British Security Service Operations 1909–45* (Bodley Head, London, 1981)

West, Nigel, *MI6: British Secret Intelligence Service Operations 1909–1945* (Weidenfeld & Nicolson, London, 1983)

Wright, Peter, *Spycatcher: The Candid Autobiography of a Senior Intelligence Officer* (Viking, New York, 1987)

# Index